WHAT IS AN EMOTION?

What Is an Emotion?

CLASSIC READINGS IN
PHILOSOPHICAL PSYCHOLOGY

CHESHIRE CALHOUN
ROBERT C. SOLOMON

New York   Oxford
OXFORD UNIVERSITY PRESS
1984

Oxford University Press

Oxford   New York
Athens   Auckland   Bangkok   Bogotá   Buenos Aires   Calcutta
Cape Town   Chennai   Dar es Salaam   Delhi   Florence   Hong Kong   Istanbul
Karachi   Kuala Lumpur   Madrid   Melbourne   Mexico City   Mumbai
Nairobi   Paris   São Paulo   Singapore   Taipei   Tokyo   Toronto   Warsaw

and associated companies in
Berlin   Ibadan

Published by Oxford University Press, Inc.,
198 Madison Avenue, New York, New York 10016
http://www.oup-usa.org

Oxford is a registered trademark of Oxford University Press

Library of Congress Cataloging-in-Publication Data

Main entry under title:
What is an emotion?
Bibliography: p.
1. Emotions—Addresses, essays, lectures.
I. Calhoun, Cheshire.   II. Solomon, Robert C.
BF531.W48 1984   152.4   82-24597
ISBN 0-19-503355-8
ISBN 0-19-503304-3 (pbk.)

Printing (last digit): 9

Printed in the United States of America
on acid-free paper

Preface

The nature of emotion is a subject common to a number of disciplines, including philosophical psychology and the philosophy of mind, the psychology of motivation, learning theory and educational psychology, psychiatry, metapsychology, and theology. It also presents us with a particularly illuminating, but often neglected aspect of the history of ideas.

We can learn a great deal about the history and continuing paradigms of philosophy and psychology by looking at what the great thinkers, otherwise employed in building "the great chain of being" and sharpening the faculties of human "reason," had to say about the "affective" side of our psychology. Many neglected it altogether. Some treated the emotions with disdain, as the "lower" part of the soul. It was in reaction to such attitudes and the exclusive celebration of reason that David Hume sounded the rebellion that still motivates much of the current controversies: "reason is, and ought to be, the slave of the passions."

This book is an attempt to capture this rich history of theories and debates about emotion in a single text, appropriate for any course or study in which this history and the nature of emotion can play an important role. We have tried to present selections from many sources, from philosophy, psychology, and biology; from distant history and contemporary debates; from a variety of philosophical and psychological orientations.

We begin, in Part I, with four classic readings, from Aristotle, Descartes, Spinoza, and Hume. In Part II, we then offer some representation of the classic theories from psychology and biology, where these fields were once a part of philosophy. (William James was both a philosopher and a psychologist; Charles Darwin quite rightly called himself a "natural philosopher.") In Part III, we have included a sampling of the extensive work on emotion that has been developed in Europe over the past century, much of it unknown to theorists in America and England at the time. In some cases, we encountered a problem in the difficulty and accessibility of the key writings. For example, Martin Heidegger's insightful but—to the novice—incomprehensible discussion of moods and emotions has been further closed off to the general public by his literary executors. To compensate for both the extreme difficulty of his text and the impossibility of obtaining reprint permissions, we solicited the aid of Heidegger scholar Charles Guignon, who has admirably summarized both Heidegger's theory and the difficult philosophy in which it is embedded. Finally, in Part IV, we have included a small sampling of the now extensive discussion of emotions among British and American philosophers.

We have summarized the considerations bearing on the question, "What is an emotion?" in our introduction, and provided brief introductions to each selection as well. At the end of the book, there is an extensive annotated bibliography. Our hope is that this text will serve not only as a collection of important historical documents but also as a source book for the continuing debate on the nature of emotion.

Charleston, South Carolina   C. C.
Austin, Texas   R. C. S.
January, 1983

Contents

WHAT IS AN EMOTION?

Introduction

Cheshire Calhoun and Robert C. Solomon

"WHAT IS AN EMOTION?"

One hundred years ago, the American philosopher and psychologist William James asked that question in the title of an essay in the British journal *Mind*. Both philosophers and psychologists have been debating, refuting, and revising his answer ever since.

The question was not original with James, of course. Twenty-five hundred years ago, Plato and Aristotle debated the nature of emotions, and Aristotle, in his *Rhetoric*, developed a strikingly modern theory of emotion that stands up to the most contemporary criticism and provides an important alternative to the still dominant Jamesian theory.

The Jamesian theory, simply stated, is that an emotion is a physiological reaction, essentially, its familar sensory accompaniment—a "feeling." The Aristotelean view, by way of contrast, involves a conception of emotion as a more or less intelligent way of conceiving of a certain situation, dominated by a desire (for example, in anger, the desire for revenge). Between these two theories, so far apart in both time and temperament, much of the modern debate continues. On the one side, there is the obvious involvement of physiological reactions and sensations in the experience of an emotion. On the other side, there is the fact that our emotions are often intelligent, indeed, sometimes more appropriate and insightful than the calm deliberations we call "reason." In the so-called "heat of the moment" (although not all emotions generate "heat," as we shall see), the intelligence of our emotions may not be so obvious as their brute physicality. Nevertheless, these two sets of considerations, the physical and the conceptual, are both essential to any adequate answer to the question "What is an emotion?"

Accordingly, many of the more modern theories involve what some have called a "two components" view of emotion, one physiological, the other "cognitive" (that is, involving concepts and beliefs). In psychology, Columbia University psychologists Stanley Schachter and Jerome E. Singer have stated this neo-Jamesian "two components" view rather bluntly: an emotion is a physiological reaction, as James insisted, but it is also the cognitive activity of "labeling," that is, identifying the emotion as an emotion of a certain sort, which involves "appropriate" knowledge of circumstances.

In philosophy, predictably, much more attention has been paid to the "cognitive" side of the analysis: What is the connection between an emotion and certain beliefs? If a person is embarrassed, he or she must believe that the situation is awkward, for example; if a person is in love, he or she must believe that the loved one has at least some virtues or attractions. But is the emotion just the set of beliefs? Or perhaps it is the set of beliefs plus some identifiable physiological reaction? Recent work in philosophy has concentrated on the role of belief in emotion and the precise connection between a belief or beliefs and the emotion. For example, it has been suggested that certain beliefs are antecedent conditions for particular emotions; it has also been suggested that beliefs are a logically essential component of emotion, that certain beliefs are identical to emotion and that emotions simply tend to cause certain kinds of beliefs (for instance, jealousy causes a person to be suspicious or love causes a person to think the best of the person loved). Determining the precise connection between emotion and belief has become one of the focal points of current controversies.

Although we often speak of emotions as being "inside" us, it is clear that the analysis of emotion cannot be limited to the "inner" aspects of physiology and psychology, to visceral disturbances, sensations, desires, and beliefs. Emotions almost always have an "outward" aspect as well, most obviously, their "expression" in behavior. How important is behavior in this analysis? Obviously, we typically identify other peoples' emotions by watching what they do, but is this part of the emotion itself or only a symptom of it? Many philosophers and psychologists have come to identify, even to define, emotions as distinctive patterns of behavior. What part do the circumstances play in the emotion, apart from (sometimes) causing it? Does the culture have any part in the analysis? Could one fall in love, for instance, if one had been raised in a culture where romantic love was virtually unheard of? ("How many people," wrote the French aphorist La Rochefoucauld, "would never have loved if they had not heard the word?")

In this book, we have tried to include a representative sample of the classic and contemporary answers to these questions. The selections range from Aristotle to the present, and represent authors from various disciplines as well as various philosophical orientations. In this introduction, we provide the reader with an outline of the various approaches to the philosophy of emotions and a taste of the various questions that have come to define the literature on the subject. The leading theories of emotion are discussed first; then the problems encountered in the analysis of emotions are introduced.

FIVE MODELS OF EMOTION

The topic of emotion is not the privileged province of any one discipline, but the task of advancing a clearly defined theory of emotion has traditionally fallen on philosophers and psychologists. Aristotle and the Stoics produced two of the earliest accounts of emotion, and subsequently, other philosophers and psychologists produced many others. But in spite of its long history, emotion was not regarded as a significant philosophical subject in its own right. Theories of emotion were advanced within the context of broader issues, such as the analysis and classification of mental phenomena in general and the origin of moral knowledge (we will see this especially in discussing evaluative theories of emotion). But within the past decade or two, the intellectual climate has altered radically. Emotion, as an independent field of study, is attracting substantial and increasing philosophical interest. This focus on emotion may mirror the general introversion (some would say "narcissism") of recent years, which has been most apparent at the popular level. But it also shows that there is a need for a comprehensive account of emotion to replace the piecemeal accounts that have inevitably resulted from emotion's being given a backseat to other philosophical and psychological issues.

In approaching emotion theory, we might begin by surveying those problem areas that have bothered both philosophers and psychologists. One of the most basic problems has to do with distinguishing between emotions and other mental phenomena. How, for instance, do emotions differ from sensory perceptions, from purely physical states of agitation or excitement, and from the more "cognitive" activities of judging and believing? Or do they? René Descartes and David Hume draw an analogy between emotions and sensory perceptions, stressing the passivity of both phenomena and their difference from such mental *acts* as willing and judging. Francis Hutcheson and William James go even farther, arguing, in different ways, that emotions *are* a special kind of perception. Although the notion that emotions are both passive and irrational (meaning noncognitive as well as unreasonable) has long held sway, some contemporary philosophers, such as Errol Bedford and Jean-Paul Sartre, have challenged this idea by arguing that emotions resemble judgments (especially value judgments) or even that emotions are a sort of judgment or belief. Others, like Franz Brentano, insist that emotions are distinct mental phenomena that cannot be explained by analogy with or as constituted out of other sorts of mental phenomena.

Second to the classification of emotions among mental phenomena stands the task of classifying particular emotions into generic types. One way of doing this would be to group together emotions that bear a family resemblance to each other—sympathy, pity, and compassion, for example, as compared to anger, resentment, and indignation. In a more general way, one might distinguish the so-called "objectless" moods, for example, euphoria and anxiety, from such feelings as jealousy and envy, which always have an object. Any classification depends, in large measure, on how an emotion is analyzed. Analyses that emphasize the "feel" of an emotion usually also classify emotions into those, like aesthetic delight and enjoyment, that are typically "mild" or "calm" and those, like rage, that are essentially "violent" or turbulent. (Hume makes this distinction between "calm" and "violent" emotions.) Analyses that emphasize the evaluative nature of emotions typically distinguish between evaluative emotions and mere passionate emotional reactions. (This distinction is characteristic of most evaluative theories, including Brentano's and Scheler's.)

A third problem area—the physiological basis of emotion—has been and continues to be controversial. Physiological changes, for example, being under the influence of drugs or being physically exhausted, may alter our emotions; and some emotions are typically accompanied by physiological changes (think, for example, of the flush of embarrassment). As we shall see, a significant group of emotion theories make physiological disturbances or the perception of these disturbances central to an account of what an emotion is or at least to an account of a particular kind of emotion (see especially Descartes's, James's, and Darwin's theories). But today, many philosophers and psychologists deny that these disturbances are an important or even a necessary component of emotion. (See, for example, the selection from Ryle.)

Although not integral to a theory of emotion (in the way the other three issues are), the concern about the role emotions play or should play in our moral and practical lives has often led to interest in theories of emotion. Central to Aristotle's concept of moral virtue, for instance, is the notion that our emotions should be appropriate to the situation—felt toward the right individual, under the right circumstances, and in the right amount, being neither too violent nor too calm. Among seventeenth- and eighteenth-century moral philosophers, benevolence, sympathy, and respect figure as important motives for moral action. Indeed, Hutcheson, Hume, and Kant all developed theories of emotion largely in response to questions about moral motivation and knowledge. And, as we shall see in discussing the evaluative theories of emotion, many philosophers have argued that emotions play a critical role in our awareness and knowledge of moral and aesthetic and other values.

In emotion theory, the basic issue is the analysis of emotion into its components or aspects. Given the long history and interdisciplinary sources of thought about emotion, it would be surprising indeed if theories of emotion could be tidily classified. Nevertheless, to organize our own thoughts on what an emotion is, we might indulge in a bit of oversimplification, by surveying the general types of analyses, keeping in mind that this constitutes an overview of the primary emphases of different theories of emotion. With this precautionary note, let us look at five important approaches to the analysis of emotion, which we might call the sensation, physiological, behavioral, evaluative, and cognitive. Each emphasizes a different component of emotion. Sensation theories (Hume) and physiological theories (Descartes, James) both stress the actual "feel" of an emotion, although they disagree over whether it is primarily a psychological feeling (e.g., of being overwhelmed) or a feeling of actual physiological changes (e.g., the feeling of one's stomach churning, in disgust). Causal explanations of emotions figure prominently in the analysis in both theories. In behavioral theories, as the name suggests, special attention is paid to the distinctive behaviors associated with different emotions. Emotions are analyzed either as the cause of such behaviors (Darwin) or as actually consisting solely or primarily of patterns of behavior (Dewey, Ryle). Evaluative theories (Brentano, Scheler) compare pro- and con-emotional attitudes (liking, disliking, loving, hating, etc.) and positive and negative value judgments. In this sort of analysis, the "object" of the emotion is important. Finally, cognitive theories, which cover a wide spectrum of particular theories, focus on the connection between emotions and our beliefs about the world, ourselves, and others. For instance, emotions seem to depend on certain beliefs (envy depends on the belief that someone else has a better lot than we do, for example) and may alter our perception of and beliefs about the world.

Sensation and Physiological Theories

Among theories of emotion, the ones that agree with popular conceptions of emotion, as well as certain obvious features of at least some emotions, are those that fall under the head of sensation and physiological. Prior to any theoretical reflection on emotion, it may seem obvious that emotions are something we *feel* inside us (the pangs of remorse, the thrills of love, the cold sinking of fear), which subsequently find expression in action. It may also seem obvious that emotions overcome us. They are uninvited, troublesome intruders, distracting us from carrying out our best intentions, thwarting an "objective" view of things, and compelling us to behave in regrettable, or at least irrational, ways. To a large extent, sensation and physiological theories of emotion describe this familiar feeling.

Both sensation and physiological theories begin from the observation that mental and physical agitation, excitement, and arousal frequently, if not always, accompany emotional experiences. Thus, emotion is considered primarily or exclusively a "feeling"—a discernible and sometimes violent sensation—which occurs to us, lasting over a determinate time period, and which may have a definite location in the body (the queasy stomach of disgust, the pounding heart of fear, etc.). Being essentially simple "feels" or sensations, emotions offer little substance for analysis. The theorist of emotion must content himself with detailing the causal origins of different emotions and with the effects of emotions on our behavior and cognition.

However much sensation and physiological theories may share certain themes, they differ on one central point. Sensation theorists are only interested in the psychology of emotion—with how people *experience* their emotions. By contrast, physiological theorists, though secondarily interested in the psychology of emotion, pursue the *physiological basis* of emotional experience—what we feel when angry are various physiological changes and disturbances.

David Hume's theory of emotion (Part I) clearly illustrates a pure sensation theory. Unlike physiological theorists, Hume ignores the physiological attendants of emotion. Indeed, in his view, emotions differ from physical pains and pleasures precisely because emotions need not be accompanied by definite, localizable physical sensations. Emotions, nevertheless, have a characteristic feel. They are sensations, if not specifically physical sensations, and we may distinguish one emotion from another in part by determining how it feels. Such attention to the psychological or mental feel, as opposed to feelings of physical disturbance, allows sensation theorists to distinguish between mild emotions such as aesthetic enjoyment and violent emotions such as rage. The distinction between calm emotions, which generally have only a mental feel, and violent ones, which generally involve physiological disturbances, is central to Hume's classification of emotions. By contrast, in physiological theories, in which sensations of physical disturbance are all-important, aesthetic enjoyment and kindred mild emotions do not appear to be emotions at all. They can only be counted emotions by stretching the theory to its limit, for example, by postulating very mild, almost indiscernible physiological disturbances. (James, a physiological theorist, comes very close to doing this. He remarks that the so-called "intellectual feelings" are almost invariably accompanied by physiological disturbances: "The bodily sounding-board is at work, as careful introspection will show, far more than we usually suppose.")

The most notable physiological theory is William James's theory of emotion. Armed with some rudimentary knowledge of the brain, the nervous system, and viscera, James works through an account (advanced for his time) of the physiological disturbances underlying emotions. (It is interesting to compare James's account with Descartes's antiquated physiological theory.) James argues that the feel of emotion—which, for him, equals the emotion itself—is, in fact, nothing but the perception of these physiological disturbances. To defend this claim—that the perception of physiological disturbances *is* the emotion—James asks us to imagine what an emotion would be like if we remove from it all feelings of agitation, clamminess, trembling, flushing, etc. We will be left, he says, with only an intellectual perception, for example, the perception of danger without the actual feeling of fear.

However convincing James's argument may be, one should be wary of it on two counts. First, it shows, at most, that physiological disturbances are *necessary* to emotion (we cannot have the emotion without the bodily change), not that the emotion is nothing but the perception of bodily change. Try similarly imagining fear without the perception of danger. In the absence of any awareness of danger, clamminess and rapid breathing might be interpreted as a sign of illness. Second, even if flushes, chills, and the like are necessary features of emotion, they seem to be necessary only to what philosophers call "occurrent" emotions, that is, emotional experiences that happen at specific times and have determinate durations. (Consider, for example, such statements as "I'm so embarrassed, I could cry" or "I was so mad, I saw red.") Physiological disturbances do not seem to be necessary to what philosophers call "dispositional" emotions. That is, we sometimes ascribe emotions to ourselves without implying that at each moment we are actually *feeling* or experiencing the emotion. Thus, we say, "I've loved her for years" or "For a long time, I've been afraid he would do that" without meaning that at each moment we are experiencing a detectable feeling of love or fear.

In reading sensation and physiological theories of emotion, it is important to mark the extensive use of causal analyses. Sensation and physiological theories *necessitate* causal analyses; since, as basically simple, unanalyzable "feels," emotions cannot be made up of desires, behaviors, the awareness of objects, and so on. Anger, for example, is simply the feeling of reddening, trembling, etc. Shouting, desiring revenge, and being aware of an insulting person are not additional components of anger. They are the causes and effects of anger. An insult may cause us to become angry; anger causes us to shout and desire revenge. Although Hume employs causal analyses in his description of "direct" and "indirect" emotions, the use of causal analyses is nowhere more overwhelmingly evident than in Descartes's ruthlessly mechanistic description of emotion. Fear, for instance, is analyzed as follows: A frightening beast approaches. Via the eyes and nerve fibers, an image of the beast is cast on the brain. This sets in motion the "animal spirits," which flow to the back and dispose the legs for flight. The same motion of "animal spirits" rarefies the blood, sending "animal spirits" back to the brain to fortify and maintain the passion of fear (Article XXXVI). The whole process appears to occur without the intervention of consciousness. And indeed, Descartes claims that the physiological disturbances in fear may cause flight independent of any voluntary action (Article XXXVIII). What is particularly significant (and, as we shall see, particularly questionable) about not only Descartes's causal analysis, but also about any equally extensive causal analysis is that it means that emotions have only a contingent, empirical tie with their associated features—with a certain object or situation, with emotional behavior, and with desire. As a result, it is thus possible for a person to be embarrassed about being late while doubting that she is. (See Thalberg's discussion of this point.)

We will look at further criticisms of sensation and physiological theories shortly.

Behavioral Theories

Although philosophers who advocate sensation and physiological theories of emotion make the "feel" or subjective experience of emotion central to their analyses of emotion, proponents of behavioral theories concentrate on another prominent feature of emotion—emotional behavior. For them, observable behavior, not private experience, is the basis for analyzing emotion. Some behavioral theorists even deny that the "feel" of emotion plays *any* part in the analysis of emotion. This turn from the "feel" of emotion to emotional behavior in part reflects a difference in the way behavioral theorists look at emotions. As long as we try to "get at" what an emotion is by thinking about our own experiences of anger, love, and the like, it seems natural to think of emotion as being primarily something we feel inside us. But not only do we experience our own emotions, we *observe* emotions in others. We see guilt "written all over" someone's face; we see the glare of hostility or the flush of excitement; and we may hear the tremor of sorrow in another's voice or the anger in verbal abuse. Moreover, we sometimes discover our own true feelings by observing our actions. We may find ourselves talking constantly about a certain person and only then realize that we have fallen in love. There are also good philosophical reasons for observing behavior rather than concentrating exclusively on the subjective "feel," in an analysis of emotion. As we shall see, claiming that emotions are private, inner experiences leads to the paradoxical conclusion that we can never be mistaken about our own emotions and that we can never have reliable knowledge of the emotions of others.

"Emotional behavior" is actually an umbrella term covering not only deliberate or voluntary verbal and physical actions, such as shouting joyously or embracing a friend affectionately, but also innate or reflexive "behaviors," such as weeping in grief or starting at a surprising sound, as well as (for some theorists) unspoken thoughts and obvious physiological changes like the blush of embarrassment. Some emotional behaviors may be learned and culture-dependent (e.g., kneeling in reverence), whereas others (e.g., blushing), are innate. Some may be voluntary expressions of emotion, others involuntary. Moreover, most contemporary writers who advocate behavioral theories talk not only about the actual manifestation or performance of emotional behaviors, but also about a *disposition* to exhibit them. (Gilbert Ryle, for example, argues that anger is a tendency or disposition to shout, redden, and engage in verbal abuse in the sort of way that brittleness is the tendency to shatter when hit. A disposition is not a desire. To say that someone is disposed to blush when embarrassed is simply to say that she is likely to blush.)

Charles Darwin made the first extensive study of emotional behavior and attempted to explain its origin by its utility for survival. In his major work on emotional behavior, *The Expression of the Emotions in Man and Animals,* Darwin formulated three principles to explain the origin of emotional behaviors. First, some emotional behaviors, he argued, clearly originated in deliberate attempts to relieve sensations or gratify desires; thus, he postulated that writhing may help lessen physical pain and that a dog lays back his ears in fear or anger to prevent them from being torn in a fight. Such serviceable behaviors become habitual in an animal and, argued Darwin, eventually innate. (Darwin accepted Lamark's now discredited view that habits can be genetically transmitted.) This is the principle of serviceable associated habits. Second, other emotional behaviors, such as a dog's wagging his tail, apparently serve no useful purpose; but they arise, Darwin thought, as the antithesis of serviceable behaviors associated with opposite emotions (in this case, as the antithesis of the dog's erect tail in anger). This is the principle of antithesis. Finally, although some physiological changes, such as the forceful inspiration of air, may serve to prepare one for action, other physiological changes, such as blushing and blanching, apparently serve no useful purpose, but rather are the result of the person's excited bodily state during an emotional experience. Darwin called this the principle of the direct action on the body of the excited nervous system.

Strictly speaking, Darwin's work on emotional behavior is not a theory of *emotion*. For him, emotional behavior is neither wholly nor primarily constitutive of emotion, but rather *expresses* or is a *sign* of emotion. The emotion itself is a distinct phenomenon, which *causes* emotional behavior. About emotion, Darwin says very little. He apparently agreed with sensation and physiological theorists that emotions are private, inner experiences (and hence the sort of experience for which one can have only an outward sign).

Darwin's theory of emotional behavior revealed the need for an adequate account of the connection between emotion and behavior. In his "The Theory of Emotion" (Part II), John Dewey argued that Darwin's notion of expression fails to explain why certain behaviors characterize certain emotions. Saying that trembling and rapid breathing express fear does not explain why just these behaviors typically accompany fear. Applying Darwin's own concept—that emotional behaviors derive from useful responses to emotional situations—Dewey argues that emotional behavior is not caused by a preexistent emotion. The behavior is determined by the situation and can be explained by referring to movements that were originally, or still are, useful in meeting such a situation. Trembling and rapid breathing, for instance, characterize fear because they are preparatory to flight from a dangerous situation. Emotional behaviors, thus, are elicited directly by external stimuli, and not by some internal "feel" called the emotion.

Dewey also criticized Darwin's concept of expression, arguing that only to the observer do behaviors appear to express emotions. To the experiencer, all behavior associated with emotion is partially constitutive of the emotion itself. Emotions, according to Dewey, have three components: (1) an intellectual component, or the idea of the object of emotion; (2) a "feel," or in Dewey's terms, a *quale;* and (3) a disposition to behave, or a way of behaving. For Dewey, "the mode of behavior is the primary thing, and . . . the ideal and the emotional excitation [the "feel"] are constituted at one and the same time." In other words, the idea of the object of emotion as well as the peculiar "feel" of an emotion are both products of emotional behavior. In suddenly coming upon a bear, for instance, one instinctively prepares for flight. There is a moment of tension, of rapid breathing, when the whole body readies itself for action. As a result, the bear is first perceived as a bear-to-be-run-away-from; and the feeling of fear is (as James argued) the feeling of these physical changes.

There are other, more serious problems with the view that behavior expresses some inner, private emotional phenomenon. (Indeed, the more general thesis that *all* mental events and states are inner private phenomena poses philosophical difficulties.) First, if an emotion *is* only a private inner experience, a "feel," each person necessarily has privileged access to and knowledge of his or her own emotions. For the same reason, we apparently could never be mistaken about what we feel; or at least, there would be no way of detecting our mistakes, since we could label emotions only by their "feel." That we are always in the best position to know our own emotions and that we cannot mistakenly label them is questionable. Freudian and other psychoanalysts work on the assumption that a person *can* make mistakes about or even be unaware of what he or she feels and that the psychoanalyst may be in a much better position than the patient to determine the patient's true feelings. And we do seem to make mistakes about our own emotions (think of the boy who avowedly hates the girl down the street, but later discovers he loves her), whereas others correctly recognized them (his parents knew all along). Many philosophers argue that we appeal to behavior, not to the "feel" of an emotion, in correcting ourselves and in recognizing others' emotions. It will not do to reply that in cases of mistakes we correct ourselves by "refeeling" the emotion; this raises a second problem, namely, how does one know that one is refeeling the *same* emotion rather than simply feeling a different one? Nor will it do to reply that even if others may disagree with the way we label our own emotions, we are still in the best position to determine what emotions we feel; for even were this so, it may only be because we are in a better position to know the full range of our behaviors and not because we have privileged access to some private inner experience.

Second, although we can be certain of our own emotions, we can know other people's emotions only inferentially (from what they say and do), and thus only tentatively. Because we blush when we are embarrassed, we reason that, by analogy, when another person blushes, he must be embarrassed. But without the possibility of confirming this inference by direct access to the experience of others, the analogy does not prove that when others blush they feel any emotion or the same one we do. Yet our ascriptions of emotions to others rarely take this tentative form. We do not have to infer that our boss is mad at us. We know. The emotion, and not merely its expression, seems to be a public phenomenon.

In view of considerations like these, both psychological behaviorists like John Watson (the father of behaviorism) and B. F. Skinner, as well as philosophical behaviorists like Gilbert Ryle, eschew the idea that behavior merely expresses or signals some inner private emotional phenomenon. They argue instead that behavior and the disposition to behave actually constitute the emotion itself. In *The Concept of Mind* (Part IV), Ryle argues that all mental terms (e.g., "feels angry," "believes," "suspects") can be defined solely in terms of behavior and that all ascriptions of mental states or events to ourselves and others can be fully justified by appeal to a person's behavior or disposition to behave in characteristic ways. This means, in effect, that because mental terms refer to behavior and dispositions to behave, mental states and events, including emotions, are no more private than physical states.

Evaluative Theories

As a rule, what we feel about other people, events, and things in our lives generally indicates how we value them. What we love, admire, envy, and feel proud of we also value; what we hate, fear, and find shameful or revolting we think ill of. Thus, many contemporary philosophers argue that there is a logical connection between emotions and evaluative beliefs. It is part of the logic of shame, for instance, that anyone who feels ashamed must also hold some belief to the effect that she has acted wrongly. Such theories (which we will say more about in the following section) make emotions logically dependent on evaluations. But there is another important group of theories that hold more straightforwardly that emotions *are* (at least in part) evaluations. These theories we call evaluative theories of emotion.

In just what sense emotions *are* evaluations depends on the particular evaluative theory. According to some theorists (e.g., Sartre and Solomon), emotions are or resemble unspoken value judgments or beliefs. Gloom is a belief that nothing is worthwhile. According to others (e.g., Hutcheson and Scheler), emotions are "perceptions" of value analogous to sensory perceptions of colors and sounds. In enjoying a painting, we "see" that it is beautiful. Still other theorists (e.g., Hume and Brentano) hold that emotions are simply pleasant or unpleasant sensations or pro- or con-attitudes on which we formulate our value beliefs. Because we admire a person's character, we deem it good. [The differences here obviously stem partially from a disagreement over the kind of mental phenomena emotions are (see the discussion on p.6).]

In addition to stressing the evaluative function of emotion, many of these theorists develop complex analyses of emotion. Central to the theories of Brentano, Scheler, Sartre, and Solomon, for example, is the idea that emotions are "intentionally" directed toward objects in the world. That is, insofar as emotions are felt of, about, or toward things in the world, they are not just brute "feels," like a twinge or pang; they are a way of being conscious or aware of the world. Being proud of an achievement is one way of being aware of it. (There are, of course, other ways of being conscious of an achievement that do not necessarily involve pride—remembering it, imagining it, or acknowledging it, for example.) These theorists also isolate other components of emotion. Scheler, for example, argues that emotions have a distinctive "feel," whereas Sartre stresses the importance of physical agitation in at least some emotions. Brentano argues that emotions are extremely complex phenomena, suggesting that anger contains, in addition to a con-attitude, a desire for revenge, a state of physical agitation, and various bodily gestures, such as clenching one's fist and gritting one's teeth.

Regardless of the differences among evaluative theories, all paint a uniquely rational picture of emotion. Far from being "blind," irrational reactions that may prevent our viewing the world "objectively," emotions are epistemologically important mental phenomena that complement reason's insight by leading to the world of moral, aesthetic, and religious values. Sometimes, of course, our emotions do lead us astray. What we hate may be quite laudable. But an evaluative theory of emotion tries to show what went wrong in these cases rather than assuming that emotions necessarily obscure or distort our vision of the world.

The best-known evaluative theories are probably the moral sense and moral sentiment theories developed in the eighteenth century by a group of British moral philosophers, including Lord Shaftesbury (*Characteristics of Men, Manners, Opinions, Times*), Francis Hutcheson (see especially *Illustrations on the Moral Sense* and *A System of Moral Philosophy*), and David Hume (see "Of the Passions" in Part I). None of these, though, are evaluative theories of emotion in general. That is, in moral sense and sentiment theories, only certain "intellectual" pleasures and pains (e.g., aesthetic enjoyment and moral approval) have an evaluative function. The ordinary gamut of emotions—resentment, fear, hope, etc.—are more or less "blind" or irrational emotional responses. In fact, most evaluative theories, and not simply moral sentiment ones, are limited in just this way because they must take into account the fact that our emotions frequently seem to be out of step with the real values of things (we fall in love with a scoundrel and dislike a virtuous person). This suggests that emotions are *not* evaluative or at least that they are not reliably evaluative. One way out of this difficulty is simply to dichotomize the emotional sphere into evaluative emotions and "blind" emotions. Unfortunately, this precludes any theory of emotion in general and has the serious drawback of casting doubt on whether the few evaluative "emotions" are emotions. (If moral approval, for example, differs so from the common run of emotions, why consider it an emotion?)

Whereas Lord Shaftesbury introduced the idea of special moral feelings, Francis Hutcheson formulated the first detailed evaluative theory of emotion. Hutcheson postulated the existence of "inner senses" (e.g., a moral sense and a sense of beauty) analogous to the five external senses. These inner senses enable us to experience such pleasant feelings as moral approval and aesthetic enjoyment. Hutcheson's suggestion was that, being analogous to seeing and hearing, pleasant and painful feelings (each with its own distinctive "feel") "perceive" moral and aesthetic values.

Both Hutcheson's contemporaries and later philosophers questioned the existence of inner senses comparable to the external senses. David Hume subsequently abandoned this analogy between emotion and perception, though he still defended special evaluative sentiments. As we saw earlier, for Hume, emotions are simple "feels" (unlike sensory perceptions). As a result, Hume argued that moral and aesthetic sentiments do not perceive values. Nevertheless, we may appeal to feelings of moral approval or aesthetic enjoyment in making value judgments because, he argued, a "value" is simply the power of a person or thing to evoke these sentiments.

After the eighteenth century, British moralists lost interest in moral sense and sentiment theories. But interest in an evaluative theory of emotion was rekindled among continental moralists in the nineteenth and the twentieth century. Among those who constructed new evaluative theories were Alexius Meinong (*On Emotional Presentation*), Franz Brentano, and Max Scheler (Part II).

In *The Origin of Our Knowledge of Right and Wrong*, Brentano sketches an evaluative theory of emotion *in general*. All emotions contain an evaluative pro- or con-attitude. Thus, resentment, hope, joy, and despair function equally to assess our situation. But our assessments may be wrong. Our hatred for and consequent condemnation of another person may be unwarranted. In handling such cases of seemingly irrational emotions (emotions that conflict with actual values), Brentano draws an analogy between emotion and judging. If we look at the sorts of judgments we make, we find that some are what Brentano calls "blind" judgments, whereas others are "evident" or "insightful." Many of our judgments arise from instinct, habit, or prejudice (think, for example, of the stereotyped beliefs many have about intellectuals, women drivers, and gay men). Although we may be strongly convinced of their truth, we can find no rational grounds to support them. "What is affirmed in this way may be true," argues Brentano, "but it is just as likely to be false. For these judgments involve nothing that manifests correctness." In contrast, other judgments *are* manifestly correct—claims, for instance, about what we are now thinking, as well as mathematical and logical judgments. These judgments appear "evident," certain, and infallible. Emotions, too, Brentano thinks, may have or may lack "evidence." At times, we love or hate things out of instinct, habit, or prejudice. The miserly love of money is love of this sort, and, according to Brentano, we do not experience the "correctness" of our love or its being evidently a love of what is worthy of love. (Would the miser have to agree?) At other times, say, in loving wisdom, we experience the "correctness" of our love. We are certain we love what is good and worthy of being loved. In likening "correct" emotions to evident judgments, Brentano solved a major problem of the moral sentiment theorists, namely, "What guarantees that what we admire, enjoy, or love is in fact good (especially since not everyone admires, enjoys, or loves the same things)?" For Brentano, it is the experience of correctness.

Following Brentano, Max Scheler, like the earlier moral sentiment theorists, once again distinguishes between evaluative emotions (what he calls "feeling-functions") and nonevaluative emotions ("feeling-states"). Evaluative emotions are intentional mental acts—ways of being aware of the world. Through such emotions we become aware of values in much the way that in seeing we perceive colors and shapes. In enjoying Van Gogh's "Starry Night," for instance, we "see" that it is beautiful. Nonevaluative emotions, by contrast, are emotional reactions to what we have already deemed good or bad. They are not a form of awareness. Although Scheler was not entirely consistent on this point, he apparently thought that most emotions (joy, fear, anger, etc.) are "feeling-states" and do not contain an evaluative component.

From the moral sentiment theorists through Scheler, evaluative theories emerged, not so much from a desire to understand emotion as from an effort to come to grips with the source of value-knowledge. On the other hand, Sartre and Solomon tackled emotion head-on, developing a very different sort of evaluative theory in which emotions color or embue the world with value. Unlike the preceding theorists, Sartre presupposes the possibility of making evaluations independently of emotion. Emotion itself, which is always brought forth by some problematic situation, "magically transforms" the situation by re-evaluating it in the sense of projecting a new value-structure. In the gloom that besets us after a loss, we emotionally re-evaluate the world into an evaluatively neutral one (everything is grey, nothing is interesting), attempting to minimize our sense of loss by denying that anything is worthwhile. This is effected through emotional behavior—avoiding bright and busy places, sitting quietly alone, etc. The evaluative transformation effected by emotion occurs entirely at the prereflective level. We do not deliberately alter the world's value-structure nor are we aware of having done so. "If emotion is a joke, it is a joke we believe in." In emotion, we find ourselves in a reality we ourselves have projected. And according to Sartre, the state of physical agitation and disturbance characteristic of many emotions represents the seriousness with which we believe in this world-view. In his theory, the rationality of emotion derives not from its reflecting the true values of things, but in its subjectively transforming problematic and undesirable situations.

Cognitive Theories

In the physiological theories of Descartes and James, consciousness plays practically no part, either as partially constituting emotion or in generating and maintaining it. Emotions are immediate reflex responses to situations without the intermediary of conscious interpretation or cognition of the emotional context. Here emotion truly stands opposed to reason, when "reason" broadly means any kind of cognitive or interpretive activity. At their far extreme, such accounts are what might be called "cognitive" theories of emotion—ones in which emotions are regarded as being either wholly or partially cognitions or as being logically or causally dependent on cognitions. "Cognition" here does not necessarily mean an act of knowing (although, as in Brentano's theory of correct emotion, it may). Cognition, in this context, may be simply a belief about or an interpretation of a thing or state of affairs. Many of the theories already discussed under different heads could also be labeled cognitive theo-ries. For Hume, certain beliefs are causally required to produce "direct" and "indirect" passions (although not for the calm moral and aesthetic sentiments). Almost all the evaluative theories are sim-ilarly cognitive (moral sentiment theories pose a special problem, since it is not clear whether moral sentiments are themselves a sort of cognition or whether they are simply pleasures that provide the basis for evaluative beliefs). For both Brentano and Scheler, at least some emotions are themselves cognitions of value; for Sartre and Solomon, emotions are evaluative interpretations. Schacter and Singer's psychological theory also emphasizes the role of cognition in emotional experiences. On the basis of experimental studies, they argue that a state of physiological arousal *and* an awareness and interpretation of one's situation are both crucial to emotion. Meet-ing a man with a gun in a dark alley may induce physiological exci-tation (as in the James-Lange theory), but the experience of fear depends on a cognitive interpretation of the situation's implications. (One must call upon a whole system of knowledge and past experi-ence concerning the use of guns and the probable intent of anyone lurking in dark alleys with a gun.) In the absence of such cognitions, no amount of physiological disturbance will ever be experienced as and labeled an emotion.

Although Hume and Schacter and Singer argue that beliefs cause emotions, and many evaluative theorists argue that emotions are in part beliefs, in another set of more contemporary cognitive theories, a logical connection between emotion and cognition is postulated. For the most part, these latter theories derive from a general philo-sophical movement called "ordinary language philosophy," or "lin-guistic philosophy," the main thesis of which is that if we wish to understand a given phenomenon, we should examine the way we talk about it and especially the logical restrictions governing the use of terms referring to this phenomenon. So, in the case of emotion, we should examine the criteria for the correct use of emotion terms. Under what conditions, for example, does it make sense to say "I am angry"? (Can you be angry at an inanimate object or at someone who you doubt has harmed you in any way? Here it is not a question of what you, in fact, *feel,* but what you can, logically, say about your emotions.)

Errol Bedford takes this approach ("Emotions," Part IV), arguing that emotions logically presuppose both evaluative and factual beliefs and that each type of emotion has a typical set of beliefs. Thus, he argues that "emotion words form part of the vocabulary of appraisal and criticism." The claim, "I am angry at my sister," says something not only about my own emotional state, but also indicates some negative evaluation of my sister. It is, so to speak, an indirect value-judgment. Because emotion statements function in this way, they logically presuppose some evaluative belief. In this view, it is a linguistic error, a misuse of language, to say, "I am angry at my sister, but I don't believe she can be criticized in any way." Emotions also presuppose factual beliefs about the emotional context. Hope and joy, for example, depend on different assessments of the probability of an event. One can be joyous about an event that actually has happened or is very likely to happen, but not about one that one sincerely doubts will happen. (Contrast this with hope. We cannot hope for what has already transpired, and perhaps not even for what is very likely to occur, although we can hope for what is unlikely, e.g., winning a lottery.) Beliefs about responsibility and about personal and social relationships may also enter into emotions. Embarrassment and shame differ in their ascriptions of responsibility (one can be embarrassed about an unintentional Freudian slip, but not ashamed of it). Similarly, jealousy and envy presuppose different social relationships. Without further explanation, it would be incorrect to say that one is jealous of the love affair two strangers are conducting (although one might well be envious).

One advantage of any cognitive theory is that a clear analysis of the *rationality* of emotions is possible. For, although our emotions may be irrational or inappropriate to the actual situation, they are so only because we hold mistaken or unjustifiable beliefs about the situation. (I may be furious at my sister for having gossiped about me, when in fact she hasn't.) The tables are thus turned; it is "reason," not emotion, that should be charged with irrationality.

Granting that emotions in some way involve cognition, it is an open question and a topic of considerable debate just how cognition is related to emotion. Is cognition causally necessary? Is it logically necessary? Or is an emotion itself a cognition? Irving Thalberg weighs the merits of the causal versus the logical account, and opts for an alternative that combines both views.

TEN PROBLEMS IN THE ANALYSIS OF EMOTION

What Counts as an Emotion?

It would be a mistake to pretend that there is agreement as to what are to be considered emotions. Certain passions seem to be included in every list of emotions, notably, anger, fear, jealousy, and especially intense forms of love. Some have been the subject of protracted philosophical debate. Is respect, for example, an emotion? According to some moral philosophers, Immanuel Kant's entire ethics, in which respect for the moral law is considered to be a motive quite different from other desires and emotions, turns on this point. Is love an emotion? Certainly the adolescent variety of romantic love must be said to be so, with its typical physiological disturbances and its uncompromising obsessiveness. But what about the "conjugal" love of a long-married couple, in which such physiological disturbances are rarely (if ever) in evidence? What about the love of country or, Hume's example, the love of justice? Should these long-term, relatively calm emotions be called "emotions"? Or are we to call emotions only those rather violent passions, which so often present themselves explosively, momentarily, and "irrationally"? Hume insisted that we should so designate both the "calm" and the "violent" passions and that the former were often much more important in our understanding of human nature than the latter. In particular, that general sentiment that the eighteenth-century philosophers (not only Hume, but also Jean-Jacques Rousseau and Adam Smith, to name but three) called "sympathy" seemed to be essential to morality and to our good conception of ourselves. Before we can answer the question, "What is an emotion?" we would first need to agree about what are classified as emotions.

Are moods emotions? What about joy, gloom, dread, or anxiety? Does it matter that moods may be protracted over a period of days or weeks, whereas most of the violent emotions last minutes or hours? Does it matter that most moods seem to be far less distinct about their objects—what they are "about"—than are most emotions? What about such passions as "the love of life," the fear of the unknown, or being "angry with the world"? What about those moods that do seem to be "about" something in particular, for instance, being depressed about that letter or being anxious about being rejected? Are moods emotions? Are emotions short-term, specific moods? Or should moods and emotions be sharply distinguished, as two quite distinct types of passion?

Some philosophers have attempted to distinguish between emotions and moods and between the short-term violent emotions and the longer-term calm emotions, with the distinction between an "episode" and a "disposition." An episode is an ongoing event, usually short term and distinctly bound in time. ("I got angry when he walked in the door and I didn't calm down until I heard him leave.") A disposition is a tendency to be subject to certain kinds of episodes. ("Whenever I see her, I get goosebumps all over.") The distinction was made central to the philosophy of mind by Gilbert Ryle in his epoch-making *Concept of Mind* (1949). Ryle analyzed most mental events in terms of dispositions to behave in certain ways, but the distinction is now often used in a more general way. It has been suggested (for instance, by William Alston in the article on "Feeling and Emotion" in the *Encyclopedia of Philosophy*) that emotions as such are episodic, consisting of an immediate feeling and a physiological reaction, but many emotion-terms signify not emotions as such, but rather dispositions to an emotion. Long-term anger, on this account, should not properly be thought of as anger as such, but rather as the disposition to get angry under certain circumstances. "Conjugal" love, too, is often taken not to be the emotion of love (exemplified by our adolescent in love), although it might well be taken to be a disposition to have a wide variety of episodic emotions, not all of which are loving (jealousy and resentment, for example.)

Distinctions between the "calm" and the "violent" emotions and between episodic and dispositional emotion-terms show us that we must be extremely cautious in asking "What is an emotion?" as if emotions were a set of homogeneous phenomena. Some emotions seem to be more physical than others; some seem wholly tied to a person's beliefs so that physical expression and physiology seem all but irrelevant. Some emotions seem bound to the immediate circumstances, others seem to be possible under almost any circumstances. Some emotions are clearly connected with pleasure and pain; others, such as scientific curiosity or the love of justice, would seem to be largely "selfless." Some emotions can be easily changed through rational discussion; others cannot be. Some emotions seem to be completely beyond our control, whereas others seem to be largely willful and voluntary. Amelie Rorty has shown that lists of "emotions" have not always been the same, even over the past few years.[1] As the analyses and the questions change, so do lists, and so the two questions, "What is an emotion?" and "What counts as an emotion?" turn out to be related. One cannot answer one without providing some sort of answer to the other.

Which Emotions Are Basic?

Since ancient times, theorists of emotion have attempted to list the "basic" emotions, emotions found in virtually everyone, presumably from birth, that combine to form the more specialized and sophisticated emotions. Descartes, for instance, listed six such basic emotions: wonder, love, hatred, desire, joy, and sadness (Article LXIX). All other emotions, Descartes suggested, are "composed of these." The American behaviorist John Watson, more frugal in his emotional metaphysics, listed only three "basic" emotions: anger, fear, and love (in the primitive sense of "dependency"). The molecules of our emotional life are composed of these elemental atoms, according to his view. Spinoza suggests that jealousy is a combination of hatred and envy. Freud, taking jealousy to be a far more complex emotion, breaks it down into grief, sadness, enmity, self-hate, and "the narcissistic wound."

What are the basic emotions? Before making yet another attempt to answer that question, it is essential to be clear about what it is that is being asked. Must a "basic" emotion be universal to all human beings? Or might there be different "basic" emotions in different cultures? Must a "basic" emotion be manifest from infancy or is it possible that these emotions are learned or developed? Must a "basic" emotion be an atomistic component in our emotional chemistry, which itself cannot be broken down? Or might a "basic" emotion itself be a complex structure, a *gestalt* that gives rise to other emotions not through combination, but rather through dissolution or transformation? Indeed, are there "basic" emotions at all or might there be only an enormously complex matrix of various emotions, interwoven as different parts of a broad tapestry, so complex that few of us ever experience more than a part of it? Or, conversely, might there be one or a few basic emotions, with the difference between

1. Amelie Rorty, *Explaining Emotions* (Los Angeles: University of California Press, 1980).

our many expressions of emotion being the difference in the way we think of or "label" the emotion as expressed, perhaps a difference in circumstance rather than structure?

What Are Emotions About? (Intentionality)

As we suggested earlier, one of the most controversial issues to emerge in contemporary analyses of emotion is "intentionality," or what an emotion is "about." The phenomenon is simple to describe. An emotion is not simply an "inner" feeling, like a headache; it also has an "outer" reference, to some situation, person, object, or state of affairs. A person in love loves someone. (Even a person "in love with love" loves someone or other as the "object" of his or her love.) One is angry about something, even if one seems to be angry about everything else as well. Some emotions refer back to oneself—shame and pride, for instance—but they still have a reference over and above whatever feelings, physiology, and behavior characterize the emotion.

These are simple observations, but the philosophical ramifications are numerous. The Scholastic philosophers of the late Middle Ages pointed out a curious feature of intentionality, which they called "intentional inexistence." (This terminology was reintroduced into modern philosophy by Franz Brentano in the nineteenth century.) The object of an emotion (or any "mental act"), as an intentional object, need not exist. One could fall in love, for example, with a fictional character, perhaps a character in a movie or a novel, who does not exist. We often become angry about supposed events, which turn out not to have occurred, and we grieve over supposed losses, which we later find out to have been falsely reported. Such examples raise ominous ontological problems, which have been the subject of philosophical debates for centuries. The "object" of such emotions—what they are "about"—is not an actual object, and so the connection between the emotion and its object cannot be the ordinary relationship between subject and object as in "Joe watched Harry" or "Fred kicked George." If Joe is angry because he believes that Harry stole his car (which he, in fact, did not), the object of Joe's emotion is the curious object THAT HARRY STOLE HIS CAR. But if there is no such fact or state of affairs, how then are we to describe the status of the "object" Joe's emotion is "about?" We cannot properly say that Joe is angry "about nothing," but neither can we literally say that he is angry about Harry's theft of his car. The problems of intentionality arise from the simple observation that our emotions are "about something." What is the relationship that this misleadingly simple word "about" represents? David Hume introduced the phenomenon of intentionality into modern discussions (without using that word) and pointed out the awkward relationship between an emotion and its intentional object—what it is "about"—and the difference between the object and the psychological cause of the emotion (that set of circumstances that brought it about). Pride, for instance, is analyzed by Hume as an emotion caused by the idea of our own accomplishment, which, in turn, produces in us another idea, of SELF, which is pride's object. This clumsy relation between cause, emotion, and object, which he describes as "an impression betwixt two ideas," involves an idea of one's self both as cause and as object. What is the connection between the two? Is the intentional object nothing other than the cause of an emotion? But the cause must be an actual event or a state of affairs (e.g., a perception or a thought, as well as an incident or a situation); the object, however, must have that curious property of "intentional inexistence." In cases in which a person's emotion is mistaken, then the cause is clearly different from the object. Some philosophers have concluded, therefore, that the object is *always* something other than the cause of the emotion. (See Kenny, Part IV.)

Current controversies over the intentionality of emotions is further confused by the unclear relationships between the intentionality of emotion and the forms of language used to describe intentionality (often called "intensionality" with an "s"). Intentionality requires that particular emotions have particular sorts of objects; intensionality requires that certain descriptions of an emotion entail certain descriptions of its object. For example, calling an emotion "pride" seems to require that what one is proud of be described as one's own accomplishment or achievement. This general question was raised obliquely by Hume, who called the connection between an emotion and the idea that was its object a "natural" connection, an ambiguous term that helped obscure the question whether the connection was simply a causal connection between ideas, as Hume's theory generally advocated, or a logical connection of some sort, such that an emotion without a certain (kind of) object could not (logically) be said to be that certain kind of emotion. To be afraid, for instance, requires an object that is believed to be fearsome; otherwise, there is no fear. Contemporary American and British authors have elevated this problem to the very center of the debates concerning emotions; we shall see several treatments (e.g., by Kenny in Part IV).

The problematic connection between an emotion and its "object" is further complicated by the fact that different emotions are "about" different aspects of an object. This has lead several authors, following the German phenomenologist Edmund Husserl, to distinguish between different "levels" of intentionality and also between the intentional object and the intentional "act" of an emotion. For example, a person might love Sarah's hair without loving Sarah, or vice versa. One might be angry about a single bad performance without being angry about the play itself. One might feel ashamed of one's behavior without hating oneself altogether. Amelie Rorty, for instance, distinguishes between the "object" and the "target" of an emotion, the former referring to the overall object, the latter referring only to that particular aspect relevant to the emotion. The same object or aspect might be the reference of very different emotional "acts," and a particular emotional act, for example, resentment, might well refer to a number of different aspects of the person resented.

Explaining Emotions

Emotions can be explained in at least two distinctive ways, both of which can be initiated by such a query as "Why did he get so angry?" The first kind of explanation might be simply exemplified by the answer, "He didn't sleep at all last night." The second can be illustrated by "He thought she was trying to kill him." The first refers to the cause of the emotion, the second to the intentional object of the emotion.

Causal explanations of emotion may have the law-like form, "whenever X happens, then E (an emotion) occurs," but more often such law-like generalizations are merely implied. To say, for example, that "She got angry because she saw the orange wall" leaves the extent of the causal generalization open. (Not everyone gets angry when they see an orange wall, nor is it clear that what is implied is that she gets angry whenever she sees an orange wall.) A causal explanation of an emotion may be as simple as the designation of the incident that "triggered it," or it may be as complex and as detailed as the whole causal history of a certain emotion in a certain person. But what is critical to every causal explanation is that it cites antecedent conditions or events without which the particular emotion would not have come about (leaving aside the complex question of alternative causes).

An intentional explanation, on the other hand, explains an emotion in terms of the viewpoint of the subject, whether or not the "object" he or she describes can also play a part in a causal explanation. One might say that causal explanations are "objective" and are (at least sometimes) independent of the viewpoint of the subject, whereas intentional explanations always depend on the viewpoint of the subject. A more technical way of making this point, in the language of "intensionality," would be to say that the causal explanation of an emotion involves descriptions that are "transparent" and can be rendered in a number of ways that are independent of the subject, whereas intentional explanations involve descriptions that are "opaque" and presuppose descriptions that accurately characterize the subject's point of view. For example, a causal explanation of "Joe got angry when he saw the snake" might just as well be given as "Joe got angry when he saw the garden hose, which he mistook for a snake." But this is not a possible description of the object of his emotion for Joe at the time; the causal explanation can describe the garden hose in any number of ways; the intentional explanation is limited to some description of a snake, since that was the object of Joe's anger.

Physiological explanations are an important form of causal explanation. We often explain a person's irritability by citing the fact that he or she had too little sleep or too much to drink. Physiological explanations are explanations that quite obviously apply whether or not the subject is aware of them. Every emotion, for instance, has its proximate causes in the brain, but only a neurophysiologist could possibly know this, and even then, it would be an odd explanation for a person to offer as an account of his or her own behavior.

More problematic are explanations citing psychological causes. For example, we can explain the fact that a person gets angry whenever he sees a poster advertising the Spanish bullfighter "El Cordobes" by pointing out that such posters remind him of his old Spanish girlfriend, who left him in Pamplona. But the poster—or more accurately, his seeing of the poster—is not, then, the object, but rather the cause of the emotion, and the explanation is essentially a causal one. The anger is about being left by his girlfriend, but the causal chain leading up to thinking about his girlfriend need not be part of the anger or its object at all. (Indeed, it is possible that the person never consciously notices the poster or the sequence of associations that lead up to his being angry; he notices only that he is suddenly thinking about his old girlfriend and is angry.)

Sometimes, the causal explanation and the intentional explanation appear to be identical. This was the awkwardness of Hume's analysis of pride, in which "self" occurred both as the cause and as the object of the emotion. Nevertheless, the two explanations may play very different roles in our account of emotion. The causal history of an emotion and the intentional explanation of the way the subject sees the world through a certain emotion will most certainly overlap and interact at many points, but nevertheless, it is important to distinguish between them. Psychologists, one might argue, are essentially interested in the causal explanations of emotion; phenomenologists are essentially interested in the intentional accounts of emotion. Philosophers, in general, embrace aspects of both psychology and phenomenology and are often torn between the two types of account; not surprisingly, they have long tried to integrate them into a unified form of explanation.

A third type of explanation is usually given less attention than the other two. Sometimes, the answer to the question, "Why is he so angry?" may be neither a reference to a cause nor a reference to the object of the emotion, but rather an answer in terms of a person's motivation in having a certain emotion. "Because he finds that he always gets his way when he gets angry" is an explanation in terms of the anticipated "payoff" of an emotion. By getting angry, for instance, a person may find that he or she feels extremely self-righteous, and that this is a pleasant or enjoyable feeling. A person who is "in love with love" may fall in love in order to enjoy the psychological benefits of that emotion, and this may be a better answer to the question "Why?" than any description of the cause or the person (currently) loved.

The Rationality of Emotions

It is too often suggested that emotions are essentially "irrational," without attempting to explain what this means. First of all, if emotions involve beliefs, it is clear that they are not *non*-rational, like a simple headache or painful hangnail. Because they are, in part, "cognitive" and "evaluative" phenomena, emotions presuppose rationality in the psychological sense—the ability to use concepts and have *reasons* for what one does or feels. Whether these reasons are *good* reasons, however, is another matter.

To say that emotions are *ir*rational, in one sense, is to admit that they are rational (in the above psychological sense), but also to deny that they have good reasons behind them. For instance, it might be suggested that emotions involve evaluations, but that these evaluations are almost always mistaken and short-sighted, and occasionally correct only by accident. But this view has little plausibility, given the perceptiveness of many emotions. Indeed, one could argue much more strongly, as does Hume, that we would have no values if it were not for our emotions (although Hume confused the issue by further insisting on a rigid distinction between reason and passions, such that emotions were by their very nature "irrational"). Perhaps emotions are, by their very nature, "subjective" phenomena; and yet, as Pascal stated metaphorically, "the heart has its reasons" too. Our emotions are sometimes more insightful than the more detached and impersonal deliberations of reason. A spontaneous burst of anger or affection may be far more significant and faithful to our needs and principles than too-protracted internal debates and "rationalizations," which give too much credence to other people's advice and to principles we do not really believe in. Indeed, it is sometimes irrational to be detached and impersonal, and it is here that the rationality of emotions is most in evidence.

Emotions as such are neither rational nor irrational. Some emotions are incredibly stupid, others insightful. The German philosopher Nietzsche suggests that "all passions have a phase when they are merely disastrous, when they drag down their victim with the weight of stupidity," but he then goes on to argue that this is no reason to reject the passions; it is rather a reason to educate them. Becoming angry at one's boss over a trifling comment may be stupid in the extreme, but getting angry at a certain point in a political

meeting may be a stroke of genius. Falling in love may be the smart-
est, or the dumbest, thing a particular person ever does, and fear in
the proper context, Aristotle argued in his *Ethics*, may be far more
rational and essential to courage than mere foolhardiness, the
absence of appropriate fear.

Emotions and Ethics

Because emotions can be rational or irrational, intelligent or stupid,
foolish or insightful, their role in ethics becomes far more complex
and more central than a great many philosophers and moralists have
suggested. On the one side, there is a long tradition of moral philosophers, Hume most famously, who juxtaposed reason and emotion and insisted that emotion, not reason, was the heart of ethics
("reason is, and ought to be, the slave of the passions"). On the other
side, the philosopher Immanuel Kant, for instance, argued that
morality was a strictly rational endeavor and that the emotions (or
what he more generally called "the inclinations") were not essential
to morality. What both philosophers have tended to neglect are those
aspects of emotions (or at least, of some emotions) that are themselves rational and have thus undermined the premise of the entire
dispute.

   This age-old set of ethical theories has again come into prominence in recent philosophy. In England and America, a broad set of
"meta-ethical" (literally, "about ethics") views have been defended
under the general title "non-cognitivism," on the basis that ethical
judgments could not be *known* and could not be said to be either
true or false. A powerful subset of such theories are the so-called
"emotivist" theories of ethics, which, as the very name indicates,
held that ethics are claims of emotion rather than claims of belief.
One well-known defender of the "emotivist" theory, A. J. Ayer of
Oxford University, insisted that claims such as "this is good" really
mean no more than "Hooray!" In America, Charles Stevenson similarly challenged 25 centuries of moral philosophy by distinguishing
between "attitude" and "belief," insisting that ethical views are
strictly a matter of the former, not the latter, thus updating Hume,
but without invoking Hume's sophisticated theory of emotions.

   The connection between emotions and ethics, despite these artificial and sometimes destructive distinctions, has always been close.
Aristotle, in his *Ethics*, insists that the "good man" should feel the

right emotions at the right times, and not feel the wrong ones. Several prominent moral philosophers in Britain in the eighteenth century, who were sometimes called "moral sentiment theorists," insisted that moral motivation could only be understood in terms of certain crucial emotions, in particular such empathetic emotions as "sympathy" and "compassion." In their theories, we come to appreciate another dimension of emotion, which goes beyond the question "What is an emotion?" and also beyond the various attempts to understand and explain emotions. This new question is the *value* of emotion, and the comparative values of various emotions. "Nothing great has been done without passion" is an aphorism that has been quoted by dozens of thinkers, not only Hegel and Nietzsche, from whom we would expect such a statement, but also Immanuel Kant (in his lectures on history). And as for the value of the various emotions, the Bible is filled with injunctions for and against the emotions on an ethical basis. Pride, envy, and anger are "deadly" sins; faith, hope, and charity are cardinal virtues. We have long been told to avoid such "negative" emotions as hatred in favor of such "positive" emotions as love. But what does this distinction between "positive" and "negative" emotions mean? Does it refer only to the fact that some emotions are hostile and others benign? Or is it the health of the person who has them that is in question (as Spinoza argued)? How do we evaluate our emotions? and How do our emotions determine our ethical evaluations? These questions are closely related, and the entire history of ethics shows that we cannot provide a satisfactory answer to one without the other.

Emotions and Culture

Emotions are often treated as matters of "instinct," as vestiges of a more primitive past, as aspects of our biology as much as of our psychology, unlearned and uneducatable. But insofar as emotions involve concepts and beliefs, they may also be learned in a particular culture and, perhaps, learned somewhat differently in different cultures. It has often been assumed, for example, by some major anthropologists (Lindzey, 1954; Leach, 1981),[2] that emotions are essentially

2. See, e.g., *Culture Theory: Essays on the Social Origins of Mind, Self and Emotion*, R. Schweder, ed. (Cambridge: Cambridge University Press, 1984).

the same in all people, the world over. But, whether or not this is true, it would seem that it is a matter to be intensively investigated. There is some evidence that suggests that emotions may be different in different cultures. Anthropologist Jean L. Briggs, for instance, published a book some years ago entitled *Never in Anger,* in which she argued that certain Eskimo tribes do not get angry. It is not just that they do not express anger; they do not feel angry, either. Indeed, they do not even have a word for anger in their vocabulary (the closest word to it, significantly, means "childish"). It has been noted that a great many cultures do not share our obsession with romantic love and that such emotions as envy, jealousy, and grief obviously have very different fates in different cultures. How much these are matters of emphasis or differences in expression, how much they are matters, rather, of the circumstances in which people feel this or that emotion—should be investigated and debated. But at least it is clear that, as we learn more about emotions and those aspects of emotion that are more than physiological, such cross-cultural questions will become increasingly important, both for our understanding of emotions and "human nature" and our answering of the more pressing ethical questions of our age.

Emotions and Expression

Earlier in this introduction, we saw that the expression of emotion in behavior has often been considered a part of the essence of emotion. Indeed, the more radical behaviorists have argued that an emotion ultimately is nothing more than a pattern of behavior. This, however, leaves the exact connection between an emotion and its expression a matter of some confusion. If, for example, an emotion is nothing other than a certain disposition to behave in certain characteristic ways, as Gilbert Ryle argued, then the connection between an emotion and its expression is more one of definition than of cause and effect. Indeed, the suggestion that one might have a certain emotion without the appropriate dispositions to behave becomes non-sensical. On the other hand, it has always been a popular ploy of science fiction writers, and travel writers, too, to suggest that other people, under other circumstances, might express their emotions very differently. Edgar Rice Burroughs, the creator of Tarzan, suggested a people who cry when they are happy and laugh when they are angry. (There are, in fact, very good examples of both of these in real life.) But if we can so easily imagine emotions without their usual expression, then the logical link between emotion and expression seems weakened considerably. Perhaps we could say that every emotion demands *some* expression, and that the disposition to "vigorous action," as William James called it, is an intrinsic part of every emotion. But this weakens the behavioral thesis and certainly tells us very little about the differences between emotions. Moreover, however attractive the idea of "vigorous action" may be when the more violent emotions are concerned, it is hard to see how it is relevant, much less essential, to the calmer emotions, such as devout faith or long-lasting love. Our primary example of emotional expression must not be the tendency to kick the cat in a fit of rage. The most meaningful expression of an emotion may well be nothing more than a telling glance or a certain spring in one's stride. But then again, it may be that the whole of one's behavior, and nothing less, is the context in which emotions are expressed, rather than the action or gesture.

One might catalog the more typical expressions of emotion, and, working backward, surmise, along with Darwin, what purpose such emotions and their expression served in the days before they were subjected to such rigorous scrutiny and societal control. (Darwin suggests that our inclination to gnash our teeth when angry represents an earlier tendency to bite our enemies.) But the more philosophical question concerns the nature of expression itself. In what sense does an action or a gesture "express" (literally, "force out") an emotion? Sometimes, the connection between the desires built into the emotion and the expression in action could not be clearer. For example, if Aristotle is right about anger being the desire for vengeance, then it would be hard to question the appropriateness of punitive action, for instance, raising a fist or a sword, as an expression of that emotion. But when the natural expression is supressed— when we are angry with a superior or someone stronger than ourselves—that is when the nature of expression becomes particularly difficult to understand. Why bother to kick a tree or bite one's lip? What do muttered curses under the breath do for us, and, taking direct action as our paradigm, why should such pointless gestures count as expression at all? Not all expression serves a purpose, but neither is the expression of emotion to be classified simply as "non-purposive behavior." The understanding of emotional expression thus is complicated in just the same way as the understanding of emotion itself, and we should probably conclude that, to a certain extent, they are one and the same.

Emotions and Responsibility

Insofar as our emotions are physiological reactions, or the movement of what Descartes called "animal spirits," our passions do indeed render us "passive." They happen to us; we "suffer" them (the meaning of the word passion in the "Passion of Christ"). But if our emotions have other components, such as beliefs and ways of behaving, it is not so clear that we are—as the saying goes—the "victims" of our emotions. We are, to a certain extent, responsible for our beliefs, and we can control our behavior, even our engrained habits, if only with some effort.

A large part of our literature is filled with tales about people who are "captive" of their emotions, and some of our most popular metaphors make emotions sound as if they do indeed "happen" to us. We are "struck" by jealousy, "paralyzed" by guilt, and "surprised" by love. We use our emotions as excuses, as in "I couldn't help it; I was so angry at the time" or "Don't blame him, he's in love." But there are considerations that point to a very different view of our ability to control our emotions. First, of course, there are any number of ways of controlling the expression or the circumstances of our emotions, the first by refusing to allow ourselves certain actions, the second by staying away from those situations in which we know that certain emotional reactions are likely to occur. But although control of the expression is not yet control of the emotion, William James pointed out that acting *as if* one has (or does not have) a certain emotion may well be instrumental in altering the emotion itself. By refusing to cry, he suggests, a woman may also keep herself from becoming sad. In such circumstances, we are not so much the victims of our emotions as we are the authors of them.

Sometimes, we find ourselves actively creating an emotion for ourselves, "working ourselves up" into a rage or setting ourselves up for disappointment. A person who "falls in love" may well have been preparing for the alleged "fall" for years, and, even in the throes of infatuation, it is an open question how much a person is the "captive" of his or her emotion and how much the obsession is willfully maintained, and even protected against distraction or interference by any number of voluntary means.

Insofar as our emotions involve beliefs, and insofar as we are in some sense responsible for what we believe, we are also responsible for our emotions. A student with false beliefs, in a subject in which he or she is expected to be thoroughly prepared, is not excused by ignorance. A bigot is not unaccountable for his or her beliefs, even if he or she has been brought up in an environment in which such beliefs were common. Insofar as anger involves a sense of injustice, that sense of injustice is subject to all the rational constraints and responsibilities of any more reflective moral claim. Insofar as jealousy involves some claim about "rights" to another person, jealousy is subject to the reasons relevant to such beliefs. And insofar as love is a judgment of the "beauty" of another person, as Plato claimed so dramatically in his *Symposium,* that, too, is a view for which a person must be held responsible, although, in this case, we are usually willing to concede the point without much argument.

Being responsible for our emotions to some extent is not the same as being able to control them, but it is clear that the two sets of considerations belong together and that at least some degree of control is presumed in assigning responsibility. This does not mean that a person must be able to change his or her emotions "at will" (although it is possible to do this to a greater extent than we think). It does mean that the extent to which our emotions are voluntary and corrigible, and the extents to which the various emotions are voluntary and corrigible, should be seriously investigated and analyzed and that emotion should not be dismissed as mere passivity, which provides us with so many convenient excuses.

Emotions and Knowledge

Among the various ways we have of controlling or eliciting our emotions (taking drugs, avoiding or looking for certain situations), by far the most philosophical, and sometimes the most effective, is self-understanding. A further knowledge of ourselves and our emotions may be the first step to changing our emotions, and gaining a new fact or two may be a sure way of getting rid of, or adding, an emotion. In the simplest possible case, finding out that the belief upon which one's emotion is based is false immediately changes the emotion. For instance, Joe is angry at Harry for stealing his car; then he finds that Harry did not, in fact, steal the car so he is no longer angry, since there is no longer anything to be angry "about." If beliefs are essential components of emotion, then a change in the belief will typically (although not always) alter the emotion, and knowledge must be considered as contributing to, not opposing, our emotions. Of course, there are irrational emotions, based upon demonstrably false beliefs. And it is also true that, even with a radical change in knowledge, the emotion may still remain. (For example, Joe may find out that Harry did not steal his car, but he is still furious with Harry for making him think that he had stolen the car.) But even if changing beliefs does not always change an emotion, knowledge is nevertheless a critical determinant of emotion, and often the test of its rationality as well.

The beliefs that are essential to our emotions, however, are not always so readily apparent or so easily changed. Emotion and self-understanding are often more complexly related than our simple example above would suggest; in clinical psychology, they are even more complex. What one thinks is the object of an emotion (Joe's anger at Harry for stealing the car, for example) is not always the real object of emotion, which one might not want to admit to oneself (in our example, the fact that Harry had just made a fool of Joe). Moreover, sometimes the set of beliefs, and thus the nature of emotion, is not recognized. Thus, resentment, a particularly degrading emotion, often gets interpreted as hatred or anger; romantic love, a notoriously dangerous emotion, frequently appears in life as well as in fiction under the guise of any number of other, even opposed emotions (notably, hatred). In either case, whether it is the object of the emotion or the emotion itself that is not known, we might say, following Freud, that the emotion is "unconscious." Nothing particularly mysterious is thus asserted about the nature of the mind; it is only to say that, because of the complexity of the beliefs that constitute our emotions, and because of our own not infrequent interest in believing what we would like to believe about ourselves instead of what is true or more plausible, we do not always recognize our emotions for what they are, and we are not always willing (nor is it always reasonable) to consider the beliefs that make them up in the detached and impersonal way that usually passes for "rationality."

Nevertheless, self-knowledge makes changing our emotions possible. "Where there is id, let ego be," said Freud; the more we know about ourselves, the more we can control our emotions. This is, of course, the most practical reason for studying emotions, whether on an individual and personal basis in ourselves or on a more abstract level, such as the attempts to answer the question "What is an emotion?" collected in this volume. Indeed, coming to recognize the true nature of emotions may help us change our emotions. Suppose that I come to realize that I am angry not because I have been wronged, but rather because I am desperately trying to defend myself in a peculiarly embarrassing position. Or suppose that I come to recognize that I am jealous not because I actually love so-and-so, but rather because I am resentful that anyone should take away something that "belongs" to me. With such a simple self-understanding, my jealousy disappears. Indeed, so powerful is this ability of self-understanding to change our emotions that Freud, early in his career, came to believe in "the talking cure," in which simply coming to understand our emotions, "bringing them to consciousness," would be sufficient to "defuse" them and to give us control over them.

Freud's rationalist optimism was in error; many emotions proved to be far too intractable to be easily susceptible to "the talking cure." Furthermore, Freud, in his emphasis on eliminating harmful irrational emotions, failed to pay as much attention to the emotions that are positive and rational. In a case of righteous anger, for instance, the more self-understanding one gains—including an understanding of how deeply one has been offended—the *more* angry one becomes. Similarly, the more a lover dwells on and comes to understand the virtues of his or her loved one, the more love grows (a process the French novelist Stendhal creatively identified as "crystallization," the multiplication of a lover's virtues the more one comes to see).

Knowledge and self-understanding help to control or to elicit our emotions, but we also gain knowledge and self-understanding through our emotions. Although it is often said that emotions are "blind," the fact is that, through our emotions, we often perceive certain details and situations (pertaining to the emotion) far more sharply and insightfully than we would otherwise. We can often learn far more about our values and morals by paying attention to our emotions than by listening to the more abstract deliberations of "practical reason," and moral theorists, of whom Hume is perhaps the most representative, are right, at least in part, when they insist that we "know" what is right and wrong from our "sentiments" rather than from arguments. Without emotion, there would be no values, rather only rules and methods without inspiration. It is emotion, not reflection, that most endows the world with meaning.

Emotion and knowledge are far more personal than the traditional emphasis on reason and understanding—as opposed to the passions—would suggest. Indeed, some emotions, for example, scientific curiosity and a love of the truth, are essential to the advancement of knowledge. For too long we have emphasized the impersonal demands of knowledge instead of the passion to know, and both knowledge and passion have suffered. So, too, much of the impetus behind the new wave of interest in emotions is the desire to learn how to elicit those much valued emotions that have too long been left to the random contingencies of childhood—not only curiosity and the passion for truth, but also the passion for justice and *com*-passion, life-long love, and even, at the right times and to a degree, righteous indignation. These are not momentary intrusions in our lives, but their very core, and the source of our ideals. Once we begin thinking of emotions in this way, as well as through the more traditional concern for those emotions that seem to be a form of madness or an irrational obsession, the importance of studying the emotions should become all the more apparent, not just as an intellectual curiosity, but also as a practical and personal necessity. "The unexamined life is not worth living," said Socrates. That is the spirit of this collection of essays, as we recognize that emotions, though often neglected in philosophy, have always been essential to life.

Part One
THE HISTORICAL BACKGROUND

Interest in human emotions goes back as far as philosophy itself, although this interest is often subsidiary to interests in ethics or "human nature." Plato and Aristotle argued about the nature of emotions and their expression in their debates on the efficacy of rhetoric and the place of the theater in the emotional life of society, and Aristotle dealt at length with some emotions (e.g., pride) in his *Ethics*. Two thousand years later, the French philosopher René Descartes advanced a theory of the "passions" as part of his overall theory of mind and body, with the emotions occupying an awkward middle position. Descartes's Dutch contemporary, Benedict Spinoza, defended a theory of emotions as part of his overall ethical theory and, in the next century in Britain, the Scottish philosopher David Hume gave a particularly sophisticated account of the emotions in his theory of human nature. Here, we present selections from Aristotle, Descartes, Spinoza, and Hume.

Aristotle

(384 – 322 B.C.)

INTRODUCTION

As one of the indisputably two or three great philosophers in the history of Western thought, Aristotle has always been seriously considered on almost every philosophical topic—logic, metaphysics, ethics, aesthetics, politics, and even (during their early development) the natural sciences. It is therefore odd that Aristotle's insightful theory of emotion, which in many ways anticipates contemporary theories, has been virtually ignored. Little has been written about it, and even those philosophers who write on historical theories of emotion rarely mention Aristotle. Some of the problem has to do with the fact that Aristotle's theory is mostly contained in his treatise on *Rhetoric*, which is no longer a standard subject for philosophers and other academics. But the emotions were an important topic for Aristotle, who was just as much a psychologist as a philosopher and just as interested in motivating people (especially to do the morally right thing) as in analyzing them. Aristotle discusses emotions in the *Rhetoric*, in *de Anima*, and in his *Nicomachean Ethics*, in which correct emotion is a large part of virtue.

In *de Anima*, Aristotle characterizes the human "soul" or "psyché," which is best translated as "life principle." (Thus, plants have souls too insofar as they grow and reproduce, and animals have souls insofar as they can feel, move, and desire). Following his predecessor, Plato, Aristotle divides the human soul into a rational and an irrational part. But unlike Plato, Aristotle does not make a sharp division between the two parts. He argues that they necessarily form a unity, and this is particularly true of emotions that involve a cognitive element, including beliefs and expectations about one's situation, as well as physical sensations.

Aristotle's analysis of emotion is remarkable both for its insights and for the fact that it avoids most of the problems that have plagued all theories of emotion. He avoids mind-body dualism by arguing in *de Anima* that beliefs, bodily motions, and physiological changes are inseparable elements of emotion. Thus, he avoids distinguishing too sharply between the rational (or cognitive) and the irrational (or physical) elements of emotion, recognizing that emotions can be both in varying degrees of complexity. Similarly, he avoids treating emotions as irrational, uncontrolled responses to situations. Our emotions may, at times, be unwarranted, but just as often they may be warranted. Aristotle especially develops this point in the *Nicomachean Ethics*, in which he argues that virtue (e.g., courage and generosity) is largely a matter of feeling the right thing; thus, the courageous individual is neither fearless nor overwhelmed by fear in a dangerous situation. He also argues that we can mold our emotions through education and habit. And, in the *Rhetoric*, Aristotle sees that what characterizes many emotions is a strong moral belief about how others should behave. This is nowhere more evident than in his analysis of anger.

What Aristotle has to say about anger illustrates the complexity of his view of emotion. Among the necessary elements of and conditions for anger, for example, we find moral beliefs about the wrongness of contempt, spite, and insolence; beliefs about our social status and how individuals should be treated; a desire for revenge, and pleasure in the contemplation of revenge; and frequently, a special circumstance (e.g., being insulted in front of rivals or admirers provokes greater anger than being insulted in front of people whose opinions we do not care about). Only recently have philosophers begun to give similarly complex accounts of emotions.

From Rhetoric (1378ᵃ20 –1380ᵃ4)[1]

We shall define an emotion as that which leads one's condition to become so transformed that his judgment is affected, and which is accompanied by pleasure and pain. Examples of emotions include anger, pity, fear, and the like, as well as the opposites of these. We will need with each of these emotions to investigate three particulars; in investigating anger, for instance, we will ask what the temperament is of angry people, with whom they most often become angry, and at what sort of things. To grasp one or two but not all three of these conditions would make it impossible to induce anger in one's audience. The same is true with the other emotions. So, just as we listed propositions in what we said earlier, let us do this again in analyzing these emotions in the same way.

Let anger be defined as a distressed desire for conspicuous vengeance in return for a conspicuous and unjustifiable contempt of one's person or friends. If this indeed defines anger, then the anger of the angry person is necessarily always directed towards someone in particular, e.g., Cleon, but not towards all of humanity; also of necessity is that this individual has done or intended to do something to him or one of his friends, and that accompanying every outburst of anger is a certain pleasure derived from the hope for revenge. I say "pleasure" because it is pleasant to contemplate achieving one's goals; and no one attempts to achieve what seems to be impossible for himself, so the angry man attempts to achieve what is possible for himself. The poet spoke correctly when he said that anger,

> Much sweeter than dripping honey,
> Swells in men's hearts.

Pleasure follows upon anger for this reason and because the mind is consumed with thoughts of vengeance; like dreams, the visions then conjured up create pleasure.

Slighting is the implementing of an opinion about what one considers to be worthless; for we think both the good and the bad to be

---

1. Translated by Jon D. Solomon, Assistant Professor of Classics at the University of Arizona, especially for this volume.

worthy of attention (as well as what is potentially good or bad), but we do not consider whatever is of little or no account to be worthy of attention.

There are three forms of slighting—scorn, spite, and insolence. One slights what he scorns, for whatever one thinks to be worthy of nothing he scorns, and he slights what is worthy of nothing. Then one who is spiteful is also scornful, for spite involves the interference in another's wishes, not to achieve anything for oneself, but only to make sure that the other achieves nothing. Since he achieves nothing for himself, he slights the other. It is evident that the other does not intend to harm him; if he did, it would then be a matter of fear, not of slighting. It is evident also that he does not intend to help him to any appreciable degree, for there would then be an attempt at creating a friendship.

To act insolently constitutes a form of slighting, for insolence involves doing and saying things that produce shame for the person to whom these things are done or said—so that something else might happen to him (other than what has already happened), but for the other's pleasure. If it were done in retaliation, then this would not be insolence, but sheer vengeance. The insolent person derives pleasure from this because he sees others suffer and thus considers himself quite superior. The young and the rich often derive pleasure from such insolence, for they consider themselves superior when acting insolently. Dishonor is an act of insolence, and the one who dishonors is one who slights, since that which is worthy of nothing—of neither good or bad—has no honor. For this reason the angered Achilles says,

He has dishonored me; he has himself taken and keeps my prize.

and,

I am without honor, as if some foreigner.

and shows that he is angered for this very reason. Some think it fitting that they be esteemed by those of lesser birth, ability, nobility, or whatever quality in which one is generally superior to another; for example, the rich man considers himself worthy of esteem from a poor man where wealth is concerned, as does the rhetorician from one who is inarticulate, the ruler from the governed, and even the hopeful ruler from those he hopes to rule. So it is said,

> The anger of divine kings is mighty,

and,

> But he holds his anger for another day;

the cause of their vexation is their superior station, and still others feel anger at those from whom they expect the proper care, for example, from those for whom he—either acting by himself or *via* his agents or friends—has done or is doing willful or willed service.

It is now evident from these analyses what the temperament is of angered people, at whom they become angered, and for what reasons. They become angry when they are in distress, for one in distress desires something. If someone should in any manner stand in one's way, for instance, if one should directly prevent a thirsty man from drinking (or even if it is done indirectly, he will appear to be doing the same thing), or if someone opposes, fails to assist, or in some other way annoys a distressed person, he will become angry at any of those individuals. For this reason the sick, the poor, those at war, the lover, and anyone with an unsatisfied desire, are prone to anger and irascibility, particularly against those who make light of their present distress. Examples include the ill person angry at those making light of his illness, the poor man angry at those making light of his poverty, the warrior angry at those making light of his struggle, the lover at those making light of his love, and so forth, for each person is predisposed towards his own kind of anger caused by his own sort of distress. He will also anger if he should happen to receive the opposite of what he expected, for the unexpected creates a greater bitterness just as it can create the greater joy if one attains his desires contrary to his expectations. From these observations the hours, periods, moods, and ages most conducive to anger become apparent, as do the places and occasions; and the more intense or numerous these conditions are, the more conducive to anger they become.

We have now seen what sort of temperament belongs to people predisposed to anger. They become angry at those who laugh, scoff, and jeer at them—all acts of insolence—and at those doing them harm in manners which represent an attitude of insolence. This harm cannot be either retaliatory or beneficial to the doers, for then it would not seem to be an act of insolence. They also become angry at those who malign them or scorn matters they take greatly to heart; zealous philosophers and those concerned with their appearance, to cite just two of many examples, anger at those who scorn philosophy and those who scorn their appearance, respectively. Such anger becomes increasingly severe if the angered individuals suspect that this ability or quality does not belong or appear to belong to them, for they do not mind the ridicule when they feel thoroughly superior in those abilities or qualities at which others scoff. Anger is also directed at their friends more often than at others, since better treatment is expected from them, and also at those who normally give honor to or take thought of them, but then cease to act in this way; the angry individuals here assume they are being scorned, for otherwise they would be treated in the same way as usual. They also become angry at those who fail to repay or inadequately repay acts of kindness and at inferiors who work against them, for any such people appear to have a scornful attitude; in the latter example the angered individuals are opposed by those who consider them inferior, and in the former they have offered kindness to those who consider them inferior.

They especially anger at those of no account who slight them, since we suggested that an anger resulting from a slight was directed towards those who have no right to slight another, and it is one's inferiors who have no right to do so. They also become angry at their friends who fail to speak well of them or who fail to treat them well, or especially when they do the opposite, or when they do not understand their needs (just as Antiphon's Plexippus failed to understand Meleager's needs). It is a sign of contempt to fail to perceive the needs of a friend, since we do not forget those who are on our mind. One also angers at those who celebrate or act quite cheerfully in his misfortunes; either action is a sign of enmity or slight. One also feels anger against those who show no concern for the pains they have given him, which explains why one becomes angry with messengers who bring bad news. One also feels anger at those who listen to talk about him or ogle at his weaknesses, for it is as if they are slighters or enemies; friends would sympathize, since everyone is pained to focus on his own weaknesses. In addition, one angers at those who slight him in the presence of five classes of people—those who envy him, those he admires, those by whom he wishes to be admired, those whom he respects, and those who respect him. When people slight him in the presence of these, they incite him to an even greater anger. One also feels anger at those who slight those whom it would be a disgrace not to defend—parents, children, wives, subordinates—or to those who do not return a favor (since such a slight is an impropriety), or to those who pretend not to know about a matter he feels to be of importance, since this is an act of scorn. And one feels anger toward those beneficent to others, but not to him as well, for it is again an act of scorn to deem everyone else worthy of treatment he is not deemed worthy to receive. Forgetfulness, even of something so insignificant as a name, also produces anger, since forgetfulness as well seems to be a sign of slight and since forgetfulness derives from neglect, which is a slight.

We have now established simultaneously at whom one becomes angry, the temperament of the angry person, and the causes for his anger. It is clear that in his speech the orator must create in his audience a temperament suitable for anger and establish his adversaries as those to be held liable for what makes his audience anger and as the sort of men at whom they should be angry.

From On the Soul (403ᵃ2 – 403ᵇ19)[1]

Do the conditions of the soul belong as well to the body or is there one that belongs only to the soul itself? We encounter this difficulty here, and it is a difficulty neither avoidable nor easily treated. It seems that most of the soul's conditions—anger, courage, desire, and any sensation—neither act nor are activated without the body. The act of thinking probably belongs to the soul alone, but if even this thinking happens to be some sort of imagination or connected with imagination then it, too, can belong to the body as well as the soul.

1. Translated by Jon D. Solomon, Assistant Professor of Classics at the University of Arizona, especially for this volume.

If any aspect of what the soul does or of what is done to the soul belongs to the soul alone, then the soul can be individually identified; but if these do not belong to the soul alone, it cannot be individually identified. It would be similar to straightness in that there is much occurring where there is straightness, such as the touching of a bronze sphere at a point, even though straightness as a separate entity will not be able to touch a sphere in this way.

One cannot separate it if it needs be in connection with the body. Apparently then all the conditions of the soul are connected with the body, including anger, gentleness, fear, pity, courage, not to mention joy, loving, and hating, for the body is affected by each of these. Evidence for this is found in our not being provoked to anger or fear after encountering a blatantly powerful stimulus, even though at other times we are provoked by small, slight stimuli—when the body is in a physical state resembling that occurring when there is actual anger. Here is still another example: we sometimes feel the conditions of fear even when there is nothing fearful present.

If this is so, it is clear that the soul's conditions are material considerations, in which case when one defies something such as anger, he looks for some movement of some sort of body or part of a body or function of a body from some origin and for some reason.

Because of this, the investigation of the soul or its representations must be the science of nature—"physics," for the physicist and the dialectician would define each of the soul's conditions differently. What is anger? One might define it as the desire for vengeance or some such feeling, the other as the boiling of the heart's blood and warmth. One applies the form and the concept, the other the substance. This "concept" is an actuality, and if this actuality exists then it must consist of some substance. This applies, for example, to the concept of the house—a shelter that protects against destruction by wind, rain, or heat. The one describes the form and the purpose; the other describes a house as stones, brick, and wood.

Which of these is the physicist? The one concerned with the substance and who ignores the concept? The one concerned with the concept alone? Or the one concerned with both? What of the other? Is he not the one concerned with the inseparable and unified conditions of the substance? But the physicist concerns himself with all acts and conditions of a body and its substance. Part of what does not apply to these concerns are for another investigator, a craftsman such as a carpenter or physician; another part, an inseparable part yet one that is by extraction not a condition of some body, is for the mathematician; and the part utterly separable is for the First Philosopher. But enough of this investigation. We were saying that the conditions of the soul are somehow not separable from the physical substance of life to which anger and fear belong, not at all substances like a line or plane.

From Nicomachean Ethics (1125ᵇ26 –1126ᵇ9)[1]

In analyzing states connected with anger, mildness is a mean between the extremes. The middle emotion has actually no name, as is almost true for the extremes. We place mildness in the middle more to the side of lacking in anger, which also has no name. The other extreme, the excess of angry emotion, one might label as "irascibility." The condition itself is anger, which is caused by many different things. If one becomes angry at what and at whom he should, not to mention in the way and when and for as long as he should, he is praised. Thus we might call him mild mannered, since mildness is what is praised. After all, the mild-mannered man is not bothered or influenced by his emotional condition, but is provoked only in that way and at those matters and for that much time as the situation dictates. His fault lies more in leaning towards the side of the lacking in anger since the mild-mannered man is more forgiving than vengeful.

To be lacking in anger, as if it involved some sort of "unanger," is to merit criticism; they are thought to be fools who fail to become angry at those matters they ought, or in the way or when or at whom they ought. Such a person will appear to be without feeling or invulnerable, and in not turning to anger he will not protect himself and will slavishly have to suffer insult to himself and those around him.

1. Translated by Jon D. Solomon, Assistant Professor of Classics at the University of Arizona, especially for this volume.

The excess of angry emotion can be applied to the same parameters—becoming angry at those matters and at whom one should not, and becoming more angry than one should and more swiftly and for too long a time. Yet not all of these manifestations of excess are present in the same instance. They could not be, for evil destroys even itself, and consummate anger becomes unbearable.

This sort of anger rises swiftly and is aimed at those matters and at those people it ought not, and more vehemently than it ought, and yet it ceases just as swiftly—the best aspect of this condition. They who lose their anger swiftly do so because they do not persevere in their anger, but in characteristic brevity unload their anger freely and then become calm.

Hot-tempered people, because of this excess, anger swiftly and at everything and at everyone, whence their name. Bitter people have an anger difficult to be reconciled and one that lasts a long time; they persevere in their anger. Only vengeance produces a cessation, since retaliation puts an end to anger by exchanging pleasure for pain. Before or without retaliation, those people carry their emotional burden. No one can see their hidden anger to talk them out of it, and it will gnaw away at them as time passes. Such a person becomes an annoyance to his friends as well as to himself.

We describe as "unbearable" those who bear anger in those matters not deserving of anger, and who bear more and longer lasting anger than they should, and who are not reconciled shy of vengeance and punishment.

We place the excess of anger in contrast to mildness. It occurs more frequently—not to forgive is more human—and "unbearable" people are worse to encounter.

What was said earlier is demonstrated also in this argument, and that is that it is not an easy task to delincate how, at whom, at what, and for how long one should anger, nor at what point justifiable anger turns to unjustifiable. He who swerves a bit towards excess of or to the lacking in anger is not to be blamed; at times we praise those who are lacking in anger and call them mild mannered, and at other times we praise the unbearably angry as being manly and equipped for leadership. How far and how much one has to swerve before he becomes no longer praiseworthy is not easy to specify. The criteria belong within the circumstances and one's perception of them. On the other hand, this much is in fact evident: The middle

tendency is praiseworthy, that in which one angers with those people and at those matters he should, in the way he should, for as
much time as he should, and so on; and the excessive tendency and
the tendency to be lacking in anger are blameworthy proportionately
to their amount. Surely, we should grasp onto the middle tendency.

René Descartes

(1596 – 1650)

INTRODUCTION

Descartes was a physically weak, but mentally energetic child, who spent much of his time, then and for the rest of his life, reading, thinking, and writing. He was raised in the scholastic tradition, in which all questions were appealed to authority; but Descartes rebelled against this, even as a student, and insisted on "the natural light of reason" and the ability of the individual to resolve questions for himself. With this attitude, the methods of mathematics quite naturally appealed to him, and he soon developed the idea that these methods could be applied to other fields as well, notably physics and philosophy. The foundation of his philosophy, accordingly, is a deductive method, the goal being absolute certainty. This required at least one indubitable premise; and Descartes found it in his realization that he could not doubt his own existence, summarized in the familiar formula, "I think, therefore I am." He quickly argued from this premise that his belief in God could be equally certain and, therefore, so could his confidence in his own sense perceptions, since the accuracy of these was guaranteed by God's goodness. It was in these deliberations that he also developed his dualistic distinction between mind (whose existence, thoughts, beliefs, etc., I know immediately) and body (whose existence and features I know only through sense perceptions), particularly in his *Meditations* of 1641. Descartes spent the last years of his life in somewhat heated controversy over his doctrines and almost one-half of his life in exile from France. He died in Sweden.

The key to Descartes's theory of emotion and to his theory of mind, in general, is his metaphysical distinction between two kinds of substance—mental and physical. The mind, according to Descartes, is "unextended substance," defined by its properties of thought and free will. Bodies, on the other hand, are extended in space and subject to the mechanical laws of physics. A general task of Descartes's philosophy, therefore, is to explain how such different substances (which, by definition, are wholly self-contained and independent of one another) might interact. His answer is crude and not entirely consistent. He sometimes argues (e.g., in the work the following selection is drawn from) that mind and body come together in a small gland at the base of the brain, the pineal gland, the function of which was then entirely unknown. Other times he argues that the mind can interact with any part of the body by means of what he calls "animal spirits" (minute particles of blood), which carry messages to various parts of the body.

This dualistic view of mind and body raises special problems when the topic is emotion. Emotions, which are a subset of that general group of psychic phenomena Descartes refers to as "the passions," seem to be split between the mind and the body; and this accounts for some of the problems Descartes had with his own theory. On the one hand, Descartes thinks of emotions as feelings of physical agitation and excitement; and he endeavors to describe, in terms appropriate to the level of scientific knowledge at his time, what happens in the body when we experience an emotion. So, for instance, he points out how the blood rushes out of the heart in fear and the animal spirits move from the brain to the limbs, disposing us for flight. To the extent that Descartes thinks of emotions as sensations, his theory of emotion sets the stage for many later theories, such as Hume's (Part I) and James's (Part II), which treat emotions as nothing but sensations of agitation. But Descartes does not confine himself to this physiological analysis of emotion. He also describes emotions in straightforward mentalistic language, speaking of the perceptions, desires, and beliefs associated with different emotions. And so, for example, he says that wonder depends on our perceiving a thing's novelty and believing it worthy of much consideration and that hatred arises from the perception of a thing's hurtfulness and involves a desire to avoid it. In recognizing the conceptual dimension of emotions, Descartes appears to be struggling toward a more cognitive picture of emotions, a picture characteristic of many contemporary theories of emotion.

From The Passions of the Soul

OF THE PASSIONS IN GENERAL, AND INCIDENTALLY OF THE WHOLE NATURE OF MAN.

ARTICLE I

That What in Respect of a Subject Is Passion, Is in Some Other Regard Always Action

There is nothing in which the defective nature of the sciences which we have received from the ancients appears more clearly than in what they have written on the passions; for, although this is a matter which has at all times been the object of much investigation, and though it would not appear to be one of the most difficult, inasmuch as since every one has experience of the passions within himself, there is no necessity to borrow one's observations from elsewhere in order to discover their nature; yet that which the ancients have taught regarding them is both so slight, and for the most part so far from credible, that I am unable to entertain any hope of approximating to the truth excepting by shunning the paths which they have followed. This is why I shall be here obliged to write just as though I were treating of a matter which no one had ever touched on before me; and, to begin with, I consider that all that which occurs or that happens anew, is by the philosophers, generally speaking, termed a passion, in as far as the subject to which it occurs is concerned, and an action in respect of him who causes it to occur. Thus although the agent and the recipient are frequently very different, the action and the passion are always one and the same thing, although having different names, because of the two-diverse subjects to which it may be related.

ARTICLE XVII

What the Functions of the Soul Are

After having thus considered all the functions which pertain to the body alone, it is easy to recognise that there is nothing in us which we ought to attribute to our soul excepting our thoughts, which are mainly of two sorts, the one being the actions of the soul, and the other its passions. Those which I call its actions are all our desires, because we find by experience that they proceed directly from our soul, and appear to depend on it alone: while, on the other hand, we may usually term one's passions all those kinds of perception or forms of knowledge which are found in us, because it is often not our soul which makes them what they are, and because it always receives them from the things which are represented by them.

ARTICLE XVIII

Of the Will

Our desires, again, are of two sorts, of which the one consists of the actions of the soul which terminate in the soul itself, as when we desire to love God, or generally speaking, apply our thoughts to some object which is not material; and the other of the actions which terminate in our body, as when from the simple fact that we have the desire to take a walk, it follows that our legs move and that we walk.

ARTICLE XIX

Of the Perceptions

Our perceptions are also of two sorts, and the one have the soul as a cause and the other the body. Those which have the soul as a cause are the perceptions of our desires, and of all the imaginations or other thoughts which depend on them. For it is certain that we cannot desire anything without perceiving by the same means that we desire it; and, although in regard to our soul it is an action to desire something, we may say that it is also one of its passions to perceive that it desires. Yet because this perception and this will are really one and the same thing, the more noble always supplies the denomination, and thus we are not in the habit of calling it a passion, but only an action.

ARTICLE XXII

Of the Difference Which Exists Among the Other Perceptions

All the perceptions which I have not yet explained come to the soul by the intermission of the nerves, and there is between them this difference, that we relate them in the one case to objects outside which strike our senses, in the other to our soul.

ARTICLE XXIII

Of the Perceptions Which We Relate to Objects Which Are Without Us

Those which we relate to the things which are without us, to wit to the objects of our senses, are caused, at least when our opinion is not false, by these objects which, exciting certain movements in the organs of the external senses, excite them also in the brain by the intermission of the nerves, which cause the soul to perceive them. Thus when we see the light of a torch, and hear the sound of a bell, this sound and this light are two different actions which, simply by the fact that they excite two different movements in certain of our nerves, and by these means in the brain, give two different sensations to the soul, which sensations we relate to the subjects which we suppose to be their causes in such a way that we think we see the torch itself and hear the bell, and do not perceive just the movements which proceed from them.

ARTICLE XXIV

Of the Perceptions Which We Relate to Our Body

The perceptions which we relate to our body, or to some of its parts, are those which we have of hunger, thirst, and other natural appetites, to which we may unite pain, heat, and the other affections which we perceive as though they were in our members, and not as in objects which are outside us; we may thus perceive at the same time and by the intermission of the same nerves, the cold of our hand and the heat of the flame to which it approaches; or, on the other hand, the heat of the hand and the cold of the air to which it is exposed, without there being any difference between the actions which cause us to feel the heat or the cold which is in our hand, and those which make us perceive that which is without us, excepting that from the one of these actions following upon the other, we judge that the first is already in us, and what supervenes is not so yet, but is in the object which causes it.

ARTICLE XXV

Of the Perceptions Which We Relate to Our Soul

The perceptions which we relate solely to the soul are those whose effects we feel as though they were in the soul itself, and as to which we do not usually know any proximate cause to which we may relate them: such are the feelings of joy, anger, and other such sensations, which are sometimes excited in us by the objects which move our nerves and sometimes also by other causes. But, although all our perceptions, both those which we relate to objects which are outside us, and those which we relate to the diverse affections of our body, are truly passions in respect of our soul, when we use this word in its most general significance, yet we are in the habit of restricting it to the signification of those alone which are related to soul itself; and it is only these last which I have here undertaken to explain under the name of the passions of the soul.

ARTICLE XXVI

That the Imaginations Which only Depend on the Fortuitous Movements of the Spirits, May Be Passions Just as Truly as the Perceptions Which Depend on the Nerves

It remains for us to notice here that all the same things which the soul perceives by the intermission of the nerves, may also be represented by the fortuitous course of the animal spirits, without there being any other difference excepting that the impressions which come into the brain by the nerves are usually more lively or definite than those excited there by the spirits, which caused me to say in Article XXI that the former resemble the shadow or picture of the latter. We must also notice that it sometimes happens that this picture is so similar to the thing which it represents that we may be mistaken therein regarding the perceptions which relate to objects which are outside us, or at least those which relate to certain parts of our body, but that we cannot be so deceived regarding the passions, inasmuch as they are so close to, and so entirely within our soul, that it is impossible for it to feel them without their being actually such as it feels them to be. Thus often when we sleep, and sometimes even when we are awake, we imagine certain things so forcibly, that we think we see them before us, or feel them in our body, although they do not exist at all; but although we may be asleep, or dream, we cannot feel sad or moved by any other passion without its being very true that the soul actually has this passion within it.

ARTICLE **XXVII**

The Definition of the Passions of the Soul

After having considered in what the passions of the soul differ from all its other thoughts, it seems to me that we may define them generally as the perceptions, feelings, or emotions of the soul which we relate specially to it, and which are caused, maintained, and fortified by some movement of the spirits.

ARTICLE **XXVIII**

Explanation of the First Part of This Definition

We may call them perceptions when we make use of this word generally to signify all the thoughts which are not actions of the soul, or desires, but not when the term is used only to signify clear cognition; for experience shows us that those who are the most agitated by their passions, are not those who know them best; and that they are of the number of perceptions which the close alliance which exists between the soul and the body, renders confused and obscure. We may also call them feelings because they are received into the soul in the same way as are the objects of our outside senses, and are not otherwise known by it; but we can yet more accurately call them emotions of the soul, not only because the name may be attributed to all the changes which occur in it—that is, in all the diverse thoughts which come to it, but more especially because of all the kinds of thought which it may have, there are no others which so powerfully agitate and disturb it as do these passions.

ARTICLE XXIX

Explanation of the Second Part

I add that they particularly relate to the soul, in order to distinguish them from the other feelings which are related, the one to outside objects such as scents, sounds, and colours; the others to our body such as hunger, thirst, and pain. I also add that they are caused, maintained, and fortified by some movement of the spirits, in order to distinguish them from our desires, which we may call emotions of the soul which relate to it, but which are caused by itself; and also in order to explain their ultimate and most proximate cause, which plainly distinguishes them from the other feelings.

ARTICLE XXXIV

How the Soul and the Body Act on One Another

Let us then conceive here that the soul has its principal seat in the little gland which exists in the middle of the brain, from whence it radiates forth through all the remainder of the body by means of the animal spirits, nerves, and even the blood, which, participating in the impressions of the spirits, can carry them by the arteries into all the members. And recollecting what has been said above about the machine of our body, i.e. that the little filaments of our nerves are so distributed in all its parts, that on the occasion of the diverse movements which are there excited by sensible objects, they open in diverse ways the pores of the brain, which causes the animal spirits contained in these cavities to enter in diverse ways into the muscles, by which means they can move the members in all the different ways in which they are capable of being moved; and also that all the other causes which are capable of moving the spirits in diverse ways suf-fice to conduct them into diverse muscles; let us here add that the small gland which is the main seat of the soul is so suspended between the cavities which contain the spirits that it can be moved by them in as many different ways as there are sensible diversities in the object, but that it may also be moved in diverse ways by the soul, whose nature is such that it receives in itself as many diverse impressions, that is to say, that it possesses as many diverse perceptions as there are diverse movements in this gland. Reciprocally, likewise, the machine of the body is so formed that from the simple fact that this gland is diversely moved by the soul, or by such other cause, whatever it is, it thrusts the spirits which surround it towards the pores of the brain, which conduct them by the nerves into the muscles, by which means it causes them to move the limbs.

ARTICLE XXXV

Example of the Mode in Which the Impressions of the Objects Unite in the Gland Which Is in the Middle of the Brain

Thus, for example, if we see some animal approach us, the light reflected from its body depicts two images of it, one in each of our eyes, and these two images form two others, by means of the optic nerves, in the interior surface of the brain which faces its cavities; then from there, by means of the animal spirits with which its cavities are filled, these images so radiate towards the little gland which is surrounded by these spirits, that the movement which forms each point of one of the images tends towards the same point of the gland towards which tends the movement which forms the point of the other image, which represents the same part of this animal. By this means the two images which are in the brain form but one upon the gland, which, acting immediately upon the soul, causes it to see the form of this animal.

ARTICLE XXXVI

Example of the Way in Which the Passions Are Excited in the Soul

And, besides that, if this figure is very strange and frightful—that is, if it has a close relationship with the things which have been formerly hurtful to the body, that excites the passion of apprehension in the soul and then that of courage, or else that of fear and consternation according to the particular temperament of the body or the strength of the soul, and according as we have to begin with been secured by defence or by flight against the hurtful things to which the present impression is related. For in certain persons that disposes the brain in such a way that the spirits reflected from the image thus formed on the gland, proceed thence to take their places partly in the nerves which serve to turn the back and dispose the legs for flight, and partly in those which so increase or diminish the orifices of the heart, or at least which so agitate the other parts from whence the blood is sent to it, that this blood being there rarefied in a different manner from usual, sends to the brain the spirits which are adapted for the maintenance and strengthening of the passion of fear, i.e. which are adapted to the holding open, or at least reopening, of the pores of the brain which conduct them into the same nerves. For from the fact alone that these spirits enter into these pores, they excite a particular movement in this gland which is instituted by nature in order to cause the soul to be sensible of this passion; and because these pores are principally in relation with the little nerves which serve to contract or enlarge the orifices of the heart, that causes the soul to be sensible of it for the most part as in the heart.

ARTICLE XXXVII

How It Seems as Though They Are all Caused by Some Movement of the Spirits

And because the same occurs in all the other passions, to wit, that they are principally caused by the spirits which are contained in the cavities of the brain, inasmuch as they take their course towards the nerves which serve to enlarge or contract the orifices of the heart, or to drive in various ways to it the blood which is in the other parts, or, in whatever other fashion it may be, to carry on the same passion, we may from this clearly understand why I have placed in my definition of them above, that they are caused by some particular movement of the animal spirits.

ARTICLE XXXVIII

Example of the Movements of the Body Which Accompany the Passions and Do Not Depend on the Soul

For the rest, in the same way as the course which these spirits take towards the nerves of the heart suffices to give the movement to the gland by which fear is placed in the soul, so, too, by the simple fact that certain spirits at the same time proceed towards the nerves which serve to move the legs in order to take flight, they cause another movement in the same gland, by means of which the soul is sensible of and perceives this flight, which in this way may be excited in the body by the disposition of the organs alone, and without the soul's contributing thereto.

ARTICLE XXXIX

How One and the Same Cause May Excite Different Passions in Different Men

The same impression which a terrifying object makes on the gland, and which causes fear in certain men, may excite in others courage and confidence; the reason of this is that all brains are not constituted in the same way, and that the same movement of the gland which in some excites fear, in others causes the spirits to enter into the pores of the brain which conduct them partly into the nerves which serve to move the hands for purposes of self-defence, and partly into those which agitate and drive the blood towards the heart in the manner requisite to produce the spirits proper for the continuance of this defence, and to retain the desire of it.

ARTICLE XL

The Principal Effect of the Passions

For it is requisite to notice that the principal effect of all the passions in men is that they incite and dispose their soul to desire those things for which they prepare their body, so that the feeling of fear incites it to desire to fly, that of courage to desire to fight, and so on.

ARTICLE XLV

What Is the Power of the Soul in Reference to its Passions

Our passions cannot likewise be directly excited or removed by the action of our will, but they can be so indirectly by the representation of things which are usually united to the passions which we desire to have, and which are contrary to those which we desire to set aside. Thus, in order to excite courage in oneself and remove fear, it is not sufficient to have the will to do so, but we must also apply ourselves to consider the reasons, the objects or examples which persuade us that the peril is not great; that there is always more security in

defence than in flight; that we should have the glory and joy of having vanquished, while we could expect nothing but regret and
shame for having fled, and so on.

ARTICLE XLVI

*The Reason Which Prevents the Soul From Being Able Wholly to
Control Its Passion*

And there is a special reason which prevents the soul from being
able at once to change or arrest its passions, which has caused me to
say in defining them that they are not only caused, but are also maintained and strengthened by some particular movement of the spirits.
This reason is that they are nearly all accompanied by some commotion which takes place in the heart, and in consequence also in
the whole of the blood and the animal spirits, so that until this commotion has subsided, they remain present to our thought in the same
manner as sensible objects are present there while they act upon the
organs of our senses. And as the soul, in rendering itself very atten-
tive to some other thing, may prevent itself from hearing a slight
noise or feeling a slight pain, but cannot prevent itself in the same
way from hearing thunder or feeling the fire which burns the hand,
it may similarly easily get the better of the lesser passions, but not
the most violent and strongest, excepting after the commotion of the
blood and spirits is appeased. The most that the will can do while
this commotion is in its full strength is not to yield to its effects and
to restrain many of the movements to which it disposes the body.
For example, if anger causes us to lift our hand to strike, the will
can usually hold it back; if fear incites our legs to flee, the will can
arrest them, and so on in other similar cases.

ARTICLE XLVIII

*How We Recognise the Strength or Infirmity of Souls, and What Is
Lacking in Those That Are Most Feeble*

And it is by success in these combats that each individual can discover the strength or the weakness of his soul; for those in whom by
nature the will can most easily conquer the passions and arrest the
movements of the body which accompany them, without doubt possess the strongest souls. But there are those people who cannot bring

their strength to the test, because they never cause their will to do battle with its proper arms, but only with those with which certain passions furnish it in order to resist certain others. That which I call its proper arms consists of the firm and determinate judgments respecting the knowledge of good and evil, in pursuance of which it has resolved to conduct the actions of its life; and the most feeble souls of all are those whose will does not thus determine itself to follow certain judgments, but allows itself continually to be carried away by present passions, which, being frequently contrary to one another, draw the will first to one side, then to the other, and, by employing it in striving against itself, place the soul in the most deplorable possible condition. Thus when fear represents death as an extreme evil, and one which can only be avoided by flight, ambition on the other hand sets forth the infamy of this flight as an evil worse than death. These two passions agitate the will in diverse ways; and in first obeying one and then the other, it is in continual opposition to itself, and thus renders the soul enslaved and unhappy.

OF THE NUMBER AND ORDER OF THE PASSIONS AND AN EXPOSITION OF THE SIX PRIMITIVE PASSIONS

ARTICLE LI

What Are the First Causes of the Passions

We know from what has been said above that the ultimate and most proximate cause of the passions of the soul is none other than the agitation with which the spirits move the little gland which is in the middle of the brain. But that does not suffice to distinguish one from another; it is necessary to investigate their sources, and to examine their first causes: and, although they may sometimes be caused by the action of the soul which determines itself to conceive of this or that object, and also simply by the temperament of the body or by the impressions which are fortuitously met with in the brain, as happens when we feel sad or joyous without being able to give a reason, it yet appears by what has been said, that in all cases the same passions can also be excited by the objects which move the senses, and that these objects are their most ordinary and principal causes; from which it follows that in order to find them all, it is sufficient to consider all the effects of these objects.

ARTICLE LII

What Is Their Mode of Operation and How They May Be Enumerated

I notice besides, that the objects which move the senses do not excite diverse passions in us because of all the diversities which are in them, but only because of the diverse ways in which they may harm or help us, or in general be of some importance to us; and that the customary mode of action of all the passions is simply this, that they dispose the soul to desire those things which nature tells us are of use, and to persist in this desire, and also bring about that same agitation of spirits which customarily causes them to dispose the body to the movement which serves for the carrying into effect of these things; that is why, in order to enumerate them, we must merely examine in their order in how many diverse ways which are significant for us, our senses can be moved by their objects; and I shall here make an enumeration of all the principal passions according to the order in which they may thus be found.

ARTICLE LXIX

That There Are Only Six Primitive Passions

But the number of those which are simple and primitive is not very large. For, in making a review of all those which I have enumerated, we may easily notice that there are but six which are such, i.e. wonder, love, hatred, desire, joy and sadness; and that all the others are composed of some of these six or are species of them. That is why, in order that their multitude may not embarrass my readers, I shall here treat the six primitive passions separately; and afterwards I shall show in what way all the others derive from them their origin.

ARTICLE LXX

Of Wonder; Its Definition and Cause

Wonder is a sudden surprise of the soul which causes it to apply itself to consider with attention the objects which seem to it rare and extraordinary. It is thus primarily caused by the impression we have in the brain which represents the object as rare, and as consequently worthy of much consideration; then afterwards by the movement of the spirits, which are disposed by this impression to tend with great force towards the part of the brain where it is, in order to fortify and conserve it there; as they are also disposed by it to pass thence into the muscles which serve to retain the organs of the senses in the same situation in which they are, so that it is still maintained by them, if it is by them that it has been formed.

ARTICLE LXXIV

The End Which the Passions Serve, and to What They Are Detrimental

And it is easy to understand from what has been said above, that the utility of all the passions consists alone in their fortifying and perpetuating in the soul thoughts which it is good it should preserve, and which without that might easily be effaced from it. And again, all the harm which they can cause consists in the fact that they fortify and conserve these thoughts more than necessary, or that they fortify and conserve others on which it is not good to dwell.

ARTICLE LXXIX

The Definition of Love and Hate

Love is an emotion of the soul caused by the movement of the spirits which incites it to join itself willingly to objects which appear to it to be agreeable. And hatred is an emotion caused by the spirits which incite the soul to desire to be separated from the objects which present themselves to it as hurtful. I say that these emotions are caused by the spirits in order to distinguish love and hate, which are passions and depend on the body, both from the judgments which also induce the soul by its free will to unite itself with the things which it esteems to be good, and to separate itself from those it holds to be evil, and from the emotions which these judgments excite of themselves in the soul.

ARTICLE LXXX

What It Is to Join or Separate Oneself by One's Free Will

For the rest, by the word will I do not here intend to talk of desire, which is a passion apart, and one which relates to the future, but of the consent by which we consider ourselves from this time forward as united with what we love, so that we imagine a whole of which we conceive ourselves as only constituting one part, while the thing loved constitutes another part. In the case of hatred, on the other hand, we consider ourselves only and as a whole, entirely separated from the matter for which we possess an aversion.

ARTICLE LXXXII

How Very Different Passions Agree, Inasmuch as They Participate in Love

There is also no need to distinguish as many kinds of love as there are diverse objects which we may love; for, to take an example, although the passions which an ambitious man has for glory, a miser for money, a drunkard for wine, a brutal man for a woman whom he desires to violate, a man of honour for his friend or mistress, and a good father for his children, may be very different, still, inasmuch as they participate in love, they are similar. But the four first only have love for the possession of the objects to which their passion relates, and do not have any for the objects theselves, for which they only have desire mingled with other particular passions. But the love which a good father has for his children is so pure that he desires to have nothing from them, and does not wish to possess them otherwise than he does, nor to be united with them more closely than he already is. For, considering them as replicas of himself, he seeks their good as his own, or even with greater care, because, in setting before himself that he or they form a whole of which he is not the best part, he often prefers their interests to his, and does not fear losing himself in order to save them. The affection which honourable men have for their friends is of this nature even though it is rarely so perfect; and that which they have for their mistress participates largely in it, but it also participates a little in the others.

ARTICLE LXXXVI

The Definition of Desire

The passion of desire is an agitation of the soul caused by the spirits which dispose it to wish for the future the things which it represents to itself as agreeable. Thus we do not only desire the presence of the absent good, but also the conservation of the present, and further, the absence of evil, both of that which we already have, and of that which we believe we might experience in time to come.

ARTICLE LXXXVIII

Its Different Species

There would be more reason in distinguishing desire into as many different species as there are different objects sought after; since, for example, curiosity, which is none other than a desire for knowledge, differs much from desire for glory, and this again from desire for vengeance, and so on in the case of other objects. But it is here sufficient to know that there are as many species of the passions as there are of love and hatred, and that the most important and strongest are those which take their rise from the emotions of delight and revulsion.

ARTICLE XCI

The Definition of Joy

Joy is an agreeable emotion of the soul in which consists the enjoyment that the soul possesses in the good which the impressions of the brain represent to it as its own. I say that it is in this emotion that the enjoyment of the good consists; for as a matter of fact the soul receives no other fruits from all the good things that it possesses; and while it has no joy in these, it may be said that it does not enjoy them more than if it did not possess them at all. I add also that it is of the good which the impressions of the brain represent to it as its own, in order not to confound this joy, which is a passion, with the joy that is purely intellectual, and which comes into the soul by the action of the soul alone, and which we may call an agreeable emotion excited in it, in which the enjoyment consists which it has in the good which its understanding represents to it as its own. It is true that while the soul is united to the body this intellectual joy can hardly fail to be accompanied by that which is a passion; for as soon as our understanding perceives that we possess some good thing, even although this good may be so different from all that pertains to body that it is not in the least capable of being imagined, imagination does not fail immediately to make some impression in the brain from which proceeds the movement or the spirits which excites the passion of joy.

ARTICLE XCII

The Definition of Sadness

Sadness is a disagreeable languor in which consists the discomfort and unrest which the soul receives from evil, or from the defect which the impressions of the brain set before it as pertaining to it. And there also is an intellectual sadness which is not passion, but which hardly ever fails to be accompanied by it.

ARTICLE XCIII

The Causes of These Two Passions

But when intellectual joy or sadness thus excites that which is a passion their cause is evident enough; and we see from their definitions that joy proceeds from the belief that we have of possessing some good, and sadness from the belief that we have of possessing some evil or defect. It often, however, happens that we feel sad or joyful without being thus able distinctly to observe the good or evil which are the causes of it; e.g. when this good or this evil form their impressions in the brain without the intermission of the soul, sometimes because they only pertain to the body, and sometimes, too, although they pertain to the soul, because it does not consider them as good and evil, but under some other form the impression of which is joined to that of good and of evil in the brain.

Benedict Spinoza

(1632-1677)

INTRODUCTION

Spinoza developed his theory of emotion in reaction to Descartes's treatise; but his theory, in fact, echoed that of the Stoics, particularly Chrysippus and Seneca, a thousand years earlier. The Stoics saw emotions as erred judgments about the world, false and destructive ways of seeing life and its misfortunes. In emotions, we rebel against life's tragedies and rejoice in its fortunes; but, wordly events are totally outside human control. And so we should replace emotions with reason and what they called "psychic indifference" (*apatheia*, or apathy). Spinoza, too, saw the world as wholly determined, wholly outside our control; and so his conception of wisdom is, ultimately, self-control, a refusal to be "moved" by emotion, an attempt to "see through" emotions with reason. Also, like the Stoics, he viewed emotions as a species of thoughts, albeit misguided thoughts.

The central work of Spinoza's career is his *Ethics,* which is, at first glance, primarily a work in metaphysics; but it actually is, as the title tells us, a systematic view of the world, aimed primarily at answering such questions as "What am I to do?" "What can I hope for?" and "What is the meaning of life?" In style, the *Ethics* (from which the following selection is taken) is a formidable, quasi-mathematical deductive sequence modeled after Euclid's geometry, in which every argument begins with another already demonstrated one, and the whole is based on a series of definitions and first principles. Spinoza first argues that the entire universe consists of a single "substance," which he tells us is "God." (This identification of

God with the universe is usually called "pantheism.") Among God's many attributes are thought and physical matter. By making thought and matter attributes in this way, rather than independent substances, Spinoza avoids the problem of interaction that plagued Descartes, since mind and body are but two such attributes of the one substance.

In this cosmic identification of God with the universe, we as individuals have little significance, and, in any case, we are simply tiny particles in the grand scheme of things. Spinoza then goes on to argue that everything that happens in the universe is determined by God and therefore necessary. We cannot change anything, and there is no point whatsoever in our bemoaning our misfortunes or cursing tragedy; we can only understand them. According to Spinoza, there is no free will; and he argues that our every idea and intention is but a modification in the great mind of God and thus determined: "In the mind there is no free will; but the mind is determined to wish this or that by a cause, which has been determined by another cause, and so on to infinity."

In his Part III, reprinted here, Spinoza introduces his theory of emotion. Like the Stoics before him, he sees the emotions as flawed thoughts about the world, misunderstandings. He defines emotions as "modifications of the body, which increase or decrease our active powers," for example, anger, which spurs us on, and sadness, which hinders us. He adds that all emotions are ultimately defined by reference to pleasure and pain; and he distinguishes the passive emotions, which originate from outside of us, from the active emotions, which are the outcome of our own natures and a pleasurable sense of heightened activity. The ills of life, Spinoza tells us, are due to the passive emotions, which cause us pain and lower our vitality.

Spinoza was brought up an orthodox Jew in Amsterdam, where his parents had fled the Spanish Inquisition. His early studies were in Hebrew—the Bible and the Talmud; later he read medieval philosophy. At the age of twenty-four, he was excommunicated from the Jewish community because of his pantheistic philosophy; at age thirty, he began his *Ethics,* which he was to finish in 1675. He lived a lonely life wandering around Holland, earning a frugal living as a lensgrinder, and died of tuberculosis at the age of forty-five.

From Ethics

(PART III) ON THE ORIGIN AND NATURE OF THE EMOTIONS

Most writers on the emotions and on human conduct seem to be treating rather of matters outside nature than of natural phenomena following nature's general laws. They appear to conceive man to be situated in nature as a kingdom within a kingdom: for they believe that he disturbs rather than follows nature's order, that he has absolute control over his actions, and that he is determined solely by himself. They attribute human infirmities and fickleness, not to the power of nature in general, but to some mysterious flaw in the nature of man, which accordingly they bemoan, deride, despise, or, as usually happens, abuse: he, who succeeds in hitting off the weakness of the human mind more eloquently or more acutely than his fellows, is looked upon as a seer. Still there has been no lack of very excellent men (to whose toil and industry I confess myself much indebted), who have written many noteworthy things concerning the right way of life, and have given much sage advice to mankind. But no one, so far as I know, has defined the nature and strength of the emotions, and the power of the mind against them for their restraint.

I do not forget, that the illustrious Descartes, though he believed that the mind has absolute power over its actions, strove to explain human emotions by their primary causes, and, at the same time, to point out a way, by which the mind might attain to absolute dominion over them. However, in my opinion, he accomplishes nothing beyond a display of the acuteness of his own great intellect, as I will show in the proper place. For the present I wish to revert to those, who would rather abuse or deride human emotions than understand them. Such persons will doubtless think it strange that I should attempt to treat of human vice and folly geometrically, and should wish to set forth with rigid reasoning those matters which they cry out against as repugnant to reason, frivolous, absurd, and dreadful. However, such is my plan. Nothing comes to pass in nature, which can be set down to a flaw therein; for nature is always the same, and everywhere one and the same in her efficacy and power of action; that is, nature's laws and ordinances, whereby all things come to pass

73

and change from one form to another, are everywhere and always the same; so that there should be one and the same method of understanding the nature of all things whatsoever, namely, through nature's universal laws and rules. Thus the passions of hatred, anger, envy, and so on, considered in themselves, follow from this same necessity and efficacy of nature; they answer to certain definite causes, through which they are understood, and possess certain properties as worthy of being known as the properties of anything else, whereof the contemplation in itself affords us delight. I shall, therefore, treat of the nature and strength of the emotions according to the same method, as I employed heretofore in my investigations concerning God and the mind. I shall consider human actions and desires in exactly the same manner, as though I were concerned with lines, planes, and solids.

Definitions

I. By an *adequate* cause, I mean a cause through which its effect can be clearly and distinctly perceived. By an *inadequate* or partial cause, I mean a cause through which, by itself, its effect cannot be understood.

II. I say that we *act* when anything takes place, either within us or externally to us, whereof we are the adequate cause; that is (by the foregoing definition) when through our nature something takes place within us or externally to us, which can through our nature alone be clearly and distinctly understood. On the other hand, I say that we are passive as regards something when that something takes place within us, or follows from our nature externally, we being only the partial cause.

III. By *emotion* I mean the modifications of the body, whereby the active power of the said body is increased or diminished, aided or constrained, and also the ideas of such modifications.

N.B. If we can be the adequate cause of any of these modifications, I then call the emotion an activity, otherwise I call it a passion, or state wherein the mind is passive.

Postulates

I. The human body can be affected in many ways, whereby its power of activity is increased or diminished, and also in other ways which do not render its power of activity either greater or less.

II. The human body can undergo many changes, and, nevertheless, retain the impressions or traces of objects, and, consequently, the same images of things.

PROP. I. *Our mind is in certain cases active, and in certain cases passive. In so far as it has adequate ideas, it is necessarily active, and in so far as it has inadequate ideas, it is necessarily passive.*

PROP. XIII. *When the mind conceives things which diminish or hinder the body's power of activity, it endeavours, as far as possible, to remember things which exclude the existence of the first-named things.*

Proof.—So long as the mind conceives anything of the kind alluded to, the power of the mind and body is diminished or constrained (cf. III. xii. Proof); nevertheless it will continue to conceive it, until the mind conceives something else, which excludes the present existence thereof (II. xvii.); that is (as I have just shown), the power of the mind and of the body is diminished, or constrained, until the mind conceives something else, which excludes the existence of the former thing conceived: therefore the mind (III. ix.), as far as it can, will endeavour to conceive or remember the latter. *Q.E.D.*

Corollary.—Hence it follows, that the mind shrinks from conceiving those things, which diminish or constrain the power of itself and of the body.

Note.—From what has been said we may clearly understand the nature of Love and Hate. *Love* is nothing else but *pleasure accompanied by the idea of an external cause: Hate* is nothing else but *pain accompanied by the idea of an external cause.* We further see, that he who loves necessarily endeavours to have, and to keep present to him, the object of his love; while he who hates endeavours to remove and destroy the object of his hatred. But I will treat these matters at more length hereafter.

PROP. XIV. *If the mind has once been affected by two emotions at the same time, it will, whenever it is afterwards affected by one of the two, be also affected by the other.*

Proof.—If the human body has once been affected by two bodies at once, whenever afterwards the mind conceives one of them, it will straightway remember the other also (II. xvii.). But the mind's conceptions indicate rather the emotions of our body than the nature of external bodies (II. xvi. Coroll. ii.); therefore, if the body, and consequently the mind (III. Def. iii.) has been once affected by two emotions at the same time, it will, whenever it is afterwards affected by one of the two, be also affected by the other.

PROP. XV. *Anything can, accidentally, be the cause of pleasure, pain, or desire.*

Proof.—Let it be granted that the mind is simultaneously affected by two emotions, of which one neither increases nor diminishes its power of activity, and the other does either increase or diminish the said power (III. Post. i.). From the foregoing proposition it is evident that, whenever the mind is afterwards affected by the former, through its true cause, which (by hypothesis) neither increases nor diminishes its power of action, it will be at the same time affected by the latter, which does increase or diminish its power of activity, that is (III. xi. note) it will be affected with pleasure or pain. Thus the former of the two emotions will, not through itself, but accidentally, be the cause of pleasure or pain. In the same way also it can be easily shown, that a thing may be accidentally the cause of desire. *Q.E.D.*

[In Prop. IX, Spinoza tells us, "the term desire is generally applied to men, in so far as they are conscious of their appetite, and may accordingly be thus defined: *Desire is appetite with consciousness thereof.* It is thus plain from what has been said, that in no case do we strive for, wish for, long for, or desire anything, because we deem it to be good, but on the other hand, we deem a thing to be good, because we strive for it, wish for it, long for it, or desire it."]

Corollary.—Simply from the fact that we have regarded a thing with the emotion of pleasure or pain, though that thing be not the efficient cause of the emotion, we can either love or hate it.

Proof.—For from this fact alone it arises (III. xiv.), that the mind afterwards conceiving the said thing is affected with the emotion of pleasure or pain, that is (III. xi. note), according as the power of the mind and body may be increased or diminished, &c.; and consequently (III. xii.), according as the mind may desire or shrink from the conception of it.

PROP. LIII. *When the mind regards itself and its own power of activity, it feels pleasure; and that pleasure is greater in proportion to the distinctness wherewith it conceives itself and its own power of activity.*

Proof.—A man does not know himself except through the modifications of his body, and the ideas thereof (II. xix. and xxiii.). When, therefore, the mind is able to contemplate itself, it is thereby assumed to pass to a greater perfection, or (III. xi. note) to feel pleasure; and the pleasure will be greater in proportion to the distinctness, wherewith it is able to conceive itself and its own power of activity. *Q.E.D.*

Corollary.—This pleasure is fostered more and more, in proportion as a man conceives himself to be praised by others. For the more he conceives himself as praised by others, the more will he imagine them to be affected with pleasure, accompanied by the idea of himself (III. xxix. note); thus he is (III. xxvii.) himself affected with greater pleasure, accompanied by the idea of himself. *Q.E.D.*

PROP. LIV. *The mind endeavours to conceive only such things as assert its power of activity.*

Proof.—The endeavour or power of the mind is the actual essence thereof (III. vii.); but the essence of the mind obviously only affirms that which the mind is and can do; not that which it neither is nor can do; therefore the mind endeavours to conceive only such things as assert or affirm its power of activity. *Q.E.D.*

PROP. LV. *When the mind contemplates its own weakness, it feels pain thereat.*

Proof.—The essence of the mind only affirms that which the mind is, or can do; in other words, it is the mind's nature to conceive only such things as assert its power of activity (last Prop.). Thus, when we say that the mind contemplates its own weakness, we are merely saying that while the mind is attempting to conceive something which asserts its power of activity, it is checked in its endeavour—in other words (III. xi. note), it feels pain. *Q.E.D.*

Corollary.—This pain is more and more fostered, if a man conceives that he is blamed by others; this may be proved in the same way as the corollary to III. liii.

Note.—This pain, accompanied by the idea of our own weakness, is called *humility;* the pleasure, which springs from the contemplation of ourselves, is called *self-love* or *self-complacency.* And inasmuch as this feeling is renewed as often as a man contemplates his own virtues, or his own power of activity, it follows that everyone is fond of narrating his own exploits, and displaying the force both of his body and mind, and also that, for this reason, men are troublesome one to another. Again, it follows that men are naturally envious (III. xxiv. note, and III. xxxii. note), rejoicing in the shortcomings of their equals, and feeling pain at their virtues. For whenever a man conceives his own actions, he is affected with pleasure (III. liii.), in proportion as his actions display more perfection, and he conceives them more distinctly—that is (II. xl. note), in proportion as he can distinguish them from others, and regard them as something special.

Definitions of the Emotions

I. *Desire* is the actual essence of man, in so far as it is conceived, as determined to a particular activity by some given modification of itself.

Explanation.—We have said above, in the note to Prop. ix. of this part, that desire is appetite, with consciousness thereof; further, that appetite is the essence of man, in so far as it is determined to act in a way tending to promote its own persistence. But, in the same note, I also remarked that, strictly speaking, I recognize no distinction between appetite and desire. For whether a man be conscious of his appetite or not, it remains one and the same appetite. Thus, in order to avoid the appearance of tautology, I have refrained from explaining desire by appetite; but I have taken care to define it in such a manner, as to comprehend, under one head, all those endeavours of human nature, which we distinguish by the terms appetite, will, desire, or impulse. I might, indeed, have said, that desire is the essence of man, in so far as it is conceived as determined to a particular activity; but from such a definition (cf. II. xxiii.) it would not follow that the mind can be conscious of its desire or appetite. Therefore, in order to imply the cause of such consciousness, it was necessary to add, *in so far as it is determined by some given modification, &c.* For, by a modification of man's essence, we understand every disposition of the said essence, whether such disposition be innate, or whether it be conceived solely under the attribute of thought, or solely under the attribute of extension, or whether, lastly, it be referred simultaneously to both these attributes. By the term desire, then, I here mean all man's endeavours, impulses, appetites, and volitions, which vary according to each man's disposition, and are, therefore, not seldom opposed one to another, according as a man is drawn in different directions, and knows not where to turn.

II. *Pleasure* is the transition of a man from a less to a greater perfection.

III. *Pain* is the transition of a man from a greater to a less perfection.

I, therefore, recognize only three primitive or primary emotions (as I said in the note to III. xi.), namely, pleasure, pain, and desire.

VI. *Love* is pleasure, accompanied by the idea of an external cause.

Explanation.—This definition explains sufficiently clearly the essence of love; the definition given by those authors who say that love is *the lover's wish to unite himself to the loved object* expresses a property, but not the essence of love; and, as such authors have not sufficiently discerned love's essence, they have been unable to acquire a true conception of its properties, accordingly their definition is on all hands admitted to be very obscure. It must, however, be noted, that when I say that it is a property of love, that the lover should wish to unite himself to the beloved object, I do not here mean by *wish* consent, or conclusion, or a free decision of the mind (for I have shown such, in II. xlviii., to be fictitious); neither do I mean a desire of being united to the loved object when it is absent, or of continuing in its presence when it is at hand; for love can be conceived without either of these desires; but by *wish* I mean the contentment, which is in the lover, on account of the presence of the beloved object, whereby the pleasure of the lover is strengthened, or at least maintained.

VII. *Hatred* is pain, accompanied by the idea of an external cause.

IX. *Aversion* is pain, accompanied by the idea of something which is accidentally the cause of pain (cf. III. xv. note).

X. *Devotion* is love towards one whom we admire.

XI. *Derision* is pleasure arising from our conceiving the presence of a quality, which we despise, in an object which we hate.

Explanation.—In so far as we despise a thing which we hate, we deny existence thereof (III. lii. note), and to that extent rejoice (III. xx.). But since we assume that man hates that which he derides, it follows that the pleasure in question is not without alloy (cf. III. xlvii. note).

XII. *Hope* is an inconstant pleasure, arising from the idea of something past or future, whereof we to a certain extent doubt the issue.

XIII. *Fear* is an inconstant pain arising from the idea of something past or future, whereof we to a certain extent doubt the issue (cf. III. xviii. note).

Explanation. —From these definitions it follows, that there is no hope unmingled with fear, and no fear unmingled with hope. For he, who depends on hope and doubts concerning the issue of anything, is assumed to conceive something, which excludes the existence of the said thing in the future; therefore he, to this extent, feels pain (cf. III. xix.); consequently, while dependent on hope, he fears for the issue. Contrariwise he, who fears, in other words doubts, concerning the issue of something which he hates, also conceives something which excludes the existence of the thing in question; to this extent he feels pleasure, and consequently to this extent he hopes that it will turn out as he desires (III. xx.).

XIV. *Confidence* is pleasure arising from the idea of something past or future, wherefrom all cause of doubt has been removed.

XV. *Despair* is pain arising from the idea of something past or future, wherefrom all cause of doubt has been removed.

Explanation. —Thus confidence springs from hope, and despair from fear, when all cause for doubt as to the issue of an event has been removed: this comes to pass, because man conceives something past or future as present and regards it as such, or else because he conceives other things, which exclude the existence of the causes of his doubt. For, although we can never be absolutely certain of the issue of any particular event (II. xxxi. Coroll.), it may nevertheless happen that we feel no doubt concerning it. For we have shown, that to feel no doubt concerning a thing is not the same as to be quite certain of it (II. xlix. note). Thus it may happen that we are affected by the same emotion of pleasure or pain concerning a thing past or future, as concerning the conception of a thing present; this I have already shown in III. xviii., to which, with its note, I refer the reader.

XVI. *Joy* is pleasure accompanied by the idea of something past, which has had an issue beyond our hope.

XVII. *Disappointment* is pain accompanied by the idea of something past, which has had an issue contrary to our hope.

XVIII. *Pity* is pain accompanied by the idea of evil, which has befallen someone else whom we conceive to be like ourselves (cf. III. xxii. note, and III. xxvii. note).

Explanation. —Between pity and sympathy (*misericordia*) there seems to be no difference, unless perhaps that the former term is used in reference to a particular action, and the latter in reference to a disposition.

XIX. *Approval* is love towards one who has done good to another.

XX. *Indignation* is hatred towards one who has done evil to another.

Explanation. —I am aware that these terms are employed in senses somewhat different from those usually assigned. But my purpose is to explain, not the meaning of words, but the nature of things. I therefore make use of such terms, as may convey my meaning without any violent departure from their ordinary signification. One statement of my method will suffice. As for the cause of the abovemed emotions see III. xxvii. Coroll. i., and III xxii. note.

XXIII. *Envy* is hatred, in so far as it induces a man to be pained by another's good fortune, and to rejoice in another's evil fortune.

Explanation. —Envy is generally opposed to sympathy, which, by doing some violence to the meaning of the word, may therefore be thus defined:

XXIV. *Sympathy* (*misericordia*) is love, in so far as it induces a man to feel pleasure at another's good fortune, and pain at another's evil fortune.

XXVI. *Humility* is pain arising from a man's contemplation of his own weakness of body or mind.

Explanation. —Self-complacency is opposed to humility, in so far as we thereby mean pleasure arising from a contemplation of our own power of action; but, in so far as we mean thereby pleasure accompanied by the idea of any action which we believe we have performed by the free decision of our mind, it is opposed to repentance, which we may thus define:

XXVII. *Repentance* is pain accompanied by the idea of some

action, which we believe we have performed by the free decision of our mind.

XXVIII. *Pride* is thinking too highly of one's self from self-love.

Explanation. —Thus pride is different from partiality, for the latter term is used in reference to an external object, but pride is used of a man thinking too highly of himself. However, as partiality is the effect of love, so is pride the effect or property of *self-love,* which may therefore be thus defined, *love of self or self-approval, in so far as it leads a man to think too highly of himself.* To this emotion there is no contrary. For no one thinks too meanly of himself because of self-hatred; I say that no one thinks too meanly of himself, in so far as he conceives that he is incapable of doing this or that. For whatsoever a man imagines that he is incapable of doing, he imagines this of necessity, and by that notion he is so disposed, that he really cannot do that which he conceives that he cannot do. For, so long as he conceives that he cannot do it, so long is he not determined to do it, and consequently so long is it impossible for him to do it. However, if we consider such matters as only depend on opinion, we shall find it conceivable that a man may think too meanly of himself; for it may happen, that a man, sorrowfully regarding his own weakness, should imagine that he is despised by all men, while the rest of the world are thinking of nothing less than of despising him. Again, a man may think too meanly of himself, if he deny of himself in the present something in relation to a future time of which he is uncertain. As, for instance, if he should say that he is unable to form any clear conceptions, or that he can desire and do nothing but what is wicked and base, &c. We may also say, that a man thinks too meanly of himself, when we see him from excessive fear of shame refusing to do things which others, his equals, venture. We can, therefore, set down as a contrary to pride an emotion which I will call self-abasement, for as from self-complacency springs pride, so from humility springs self-abasement, which I will accordingly thus define:

XXIX. *Self-abasement* is thinking too meanly of one's self by reason of pain.

Explanation. —We are nevertheless generally accustomed to oppose pride to humility, but in that case we pay more attention to the effect of either emotion than to its nature. We are wont to call *proud* the man who boasts too much (III. xxx. note), who talks of nothing but his own virtues and other people's faults, who wishes to be first; and lastly who goes through life with a style and pomp suitable to those far above him in station. On the other hand, we call *humble* the man who too often blushes, who confesses his faults, who sets forth other men's virtues, and who, lastly, walks with bent head and is negligent of his attire. However, these emotions, humility and self-abasement, are extremely rare. For human nature, considered in itself, strives against them as much as it can (see III. xiii. liv.); hence those, who are believed to be most self-abased and humble, are generally in reality the most ambitious and envious.

XXX. *Honour* is pleasure accompanied by the idea of some action of our own, which we believe to be praised by others.

XXXI. *Shame* is pain accompanied by the idea of some action of our own, which we believe to be blamed by others.

Explanation.—On this subject see the note to III. xxx. But we should here remark the difference which exists between shame and modesty. Shame is the pain following the deed whereof we are ashamed. Modesty is the fear or dread of shame, which restrains a man from committing a base action. Modesty is usually opposed to shamelessness, but the latter is not an emotion, as I will duly show; however, the names of the emotions (as I have remarked already) have regard rather to their exercise than to their nature.

I have now fulfilled my task of explaining the emotions arising from pleasure and pain. I therefore proceed to treat of those which I refer to desire.

XXXII. *Regret* is the desire or appetite to possess something, kept alive by the remembrance of the said thing, and at the same time constrained by the remembrance of other things which exclude the existence of it.

Explanation.—When we remember a thing, we are by that very fact, as I have already said more than once, disposed to contemplate it with the same emotion as if it were something present; but this disposition or endeavour, while we are awake, is generally checked by the images of things which exclude the existence of that which we remember. Thus when we remember something which affected us with a certain pleasure, we by that very fact endeavour to regard it with the same emotion of pleasure as though it were present, but this endeavour is at once checked by the remembrance of things which exclude the existence of the thing in question. Wherefore regret is, strictly speaking, a pain opposed to that pleasure, which arises from the absence of something we hate (cf. III. xlvii, note). But, as the name regret seems to refer to desire, I set this emotion down, among the emotions springing from desire.

XXXIII. *Emulation* is the desire of something, engendered in us by our conception that others have the same desire.

Explanation. —He who runs away, because he sees others running away, or he who fears, because he sees others in fear; or again, he who, on seeing that another man has burnt his hand, draws towards him his own hand, and moves his body as though his own hand were burnt; such an one can be said to imitate another's emotion, but not to emulate him; not because the causes of emulation and imitation are different, but because it has become customary to speak of emulation only in him, who imitates that which we deem to be honourable, useful, or pleasant. As to the cause of emulation, cf. III. xxvii. and note. The reason why this emotion is generally coupled with envy may be seen from III. xxxii. and note.

XXXIV. *Thankfulness* or *Gratitude* is the desire or zeal springing from love, whereby we endeavour to benefit him, who with similar feelings of love has conferred a benefit on us. Cf. III. xxxix. note and xl.

XXXV. *Benevolence* is the desire of benefiting one whom we pity. Cf. III. xxvii. note.

XXXVI. *Anger* is the desire, whereby through hatred we are induced to injure one whom we hate, III. xxxix.

XXXVII. *Revenge* is the desire whereby we are induced, through mutual hatred, to injure one who, with similar feelings, has injured us. (See III. xl. Coroll. ii. and note.)

XXXVIII. *Cruelty* or *savageness* is the desire, whereby a man is impelled to injure one whom we love or pity.

Explanation. —To cruelty is opposed clemency, which is not a passive state of the mind, but a power whereby man restrains his anger and revenge.

XXXIX. *Timidity* is the desire to avoid a greater evil, which we dread, by undergoing a lesser evil. Cf. III. xxxix. note.

XL. *Daring* is the desire, whereby a man is set on to do something dangerous which his equals fear to attempt.

XLI. *Cowardice* is attributed to one, whose desire is checked by the fear of some danger which his equals dare to encounter.

Explanation.—Cowardice is, therefore, nothing else but the fear of some evil, which most men are wont not to fear; hence I do not reckon it among the emotions springing from desire. Nevertheless, I have chosen to explain it here, because, in so far as we look to the desire, it is truly opposed to the emotion of daring.

The definitions of jealousy and other waverings of the mind I pass over in silence, first, because they arise from the compounding of the emotions already described; secondly, because many of them have no distinctive names, which shows that it is sufficient for practical purposes to have merely a general knowledge of them. However, it is established from the definitions of the emotions, which we have set forth, that they all spring from desire, pleasure, or pain, or, rather, that there is nothing besides these three; wherefore each is wont to be called by a variety of names in accordance with its various relations and extrinsic tokens. If we now direct our attention to these primitive emotions, and to what has been said concerning the nature of the mind, we shall be able thus to define the emotions, in so far as they are referred to the mind only.

General Definition of the Emotions

Emotion, which is called a passivity of the soul, is a confused idea, whereby the mind affirms concerning its body, or any part thereof, a force for existence *(existendi vis)* greater or less than before, and by the presence of which the mind is determined to think of one thing rather than another.

Explanation.—I say, first, that emotion or passion of the soul is *a confused idea.* For we have shown that the mind is only passive, in so far as it has inadequate or confused ideas. (III. iii.) I say, further, *whereby the mind affirms concerning its body or any part thereof a force for existence greater than before.* For all the ideas of bodies, which we possess, denote rather the actual disposition of our own body (II. xvi. Coroll. ii.) than the nature of an external body. But the idea which constitutes the reality of an emotion must denote or express the disposition of the body, or of some part thereof, which is possessed by the body, or some part thereof, because its power of action or force for existence is increased or diminished, helped or hindered. But it must be noted that, when I say *a greater or less force for existence* than before, I do not mean that the mind compares the present with the past disposition of the body, but that the idea which constitutes the reality of an emotion affirms something of the body, which, in fact, involves more or less of reality than before.

And inasmuch as the essence of mind consists in the fact (II. xi. xiii.), that it affirms the actual existence of its own body, and inasmuch as we understand by perfection the very essence of a thing, it follows that the mind passes to greater or less perfection, when it happens to affirm concerning its own body, or any part thereof, something involving more or less reality than before.

When, therefore, I said above that the power of the mind is increased or diminished, I merely meant that the mind had formed of its own body, or of some part hereof, an idea involving more or less of reality, than it had already affirmed concerning its own body. For the excellence of ideas, and the actual power of thinking are measured by the excellence of the object. Lastly, I have added *by the presence of which the mind is determined to think of one thing rather than another,* so that, besides the nature of pleasure and pain, which the first part of the definition explains, I might also express the nature of desire.

(PART V) OF THE POWER OF THE UNDERSTANDING, OR OF HUMAN FREEDOM

Preface

At length I pass to the remaining portion of my Ethics, which is concerned with the way leading to freedom. I shall therefore treat therein of the power of the reason, showing how far the reason can control the emotions, and what is the nature of Mental Freedom or Blessedness; we shall then be able to see, how much more powerful the wise man is than the ignorant. It is no part of my design to point out the method and means whereby the understanding may be perfected, nor to show the skill whereby the body may be so tended, as to be capable of the due performance of its functions. The latter question lies in the province of Medicine, the former in the province of Logic. Here, therefore, I repeat, I shall treat only of the power of the mind, or of reason; and I shall mainly show the extent and nature of its dominion over the emotions, for their control and moderation. That we do not possess absolute dominion over them, I have already shown. Yet the Stoics have thought, that the emotions depended absolutely on our will, and that we could absolutely govern them. But these philosophers were compelled, by the protest of experience, not from their own principles, to confess, that no slight practice and zeal is needed to control and moderate them: and this someone endeavoured to illustrate by the example (if I remember rightly) of two dogs, the one a house-dog and the other a hunting-dog. For by long training it could be brought about, that the house-dog should become accustomed to hunt, and the hunting-dog to cease from running after hares. To this opinion Descartes not a little inclines. For he maintained, that the soul or mind is specially united to a particular part of the brain, namely, to that part called the pineal gland, by the aid of which the mind is enabled to feel all the movements which are set going in the body, and also external objects, and which the mind by a simple act of volition can put in motion in various ways. He asserted, that this gland is so suspended in the midst of the brain, that it could be moved by the slightest motion of the animal spirits: further, that this gland is suspended in the midst of the brain in as many different manners, as the animal spirits can impinge thereon; and, again, that as many different marks are impressed on the said gland, as there are different external objects which impel the animals spirits towards it; whence it follows, that if the will of the soul suspends the gland in a position, wherein it has already been suspended once before by the animal spirits driven in one way or another, the gland in its turn reacts on the said spirits, driving and determining them to the condition wherein they were, when repulsed before by a similar position of the gland. He further asserted, that every act of mental volition is united in nature to a certain given motion of the gland. For instance, whenever anyone desires to look at a remote object, the act of volition causes the pupil of the eye to dilate, whereas, if the person in question had only thought of the dilatation of the pupil, the mere wish to dilate it would not have brought about the result, inasmuch as the motion of the gland, which serves to impel the animal spirits towards the optic nerve in a way which would dilate or contract the pupil, is not associated in nature with the wish to dilate or contract the pupil, but with the wish to look at remote or very near objects. Lastly, he maintained that, although every motion of the aforesaid gland seems to have been united by nature to one particular thought out of the whole number of our thoughts, from the very beginning of our life, yet it can nevertheless become through habituation associated with other thoughts; this he endeavours to prove in the *Passions de l'âme*, I. 50. He thence concludes, that there is no soul so weak, that it cannot, under proper direction, acquire absolute power over its passions. For passions as defined by him are "perceptions, or feelings, or disturbances of the soul, which are referred to the soul as species, and which (mark the expression) are produced, preserved, and strengthened through some movement of the spirits." (*Passions de l'âme*, I. 27.) But, seeing that we can join any motion of the gland, or consequently of the spirits, to any volition, the determination of the will depends entirely on our own powers; if, therefore, we determine our will with sure and firm decisions in the direction to which we wish our actions to tend, and associate the motions of the passions which we wish to acquire with the said decisions, we shall acquire an absolute dominion over our passions. Such is the doctrine of this illustrious philosopher (in so far as I gather it from his own words); it is one which, had it been less ingenious, I could hardly believe to have proceeded from so great a man. Indeed, I am lost in wonder, that a philosopher, who had stoutly asserted, that he would draw no conclusions which do not follow from self-evident premisses, and would affirm nothing which he did not clearly and distinctly perceive, and who had so often taken to task the scholastics for wishing to explain obscurities through occult qualities, could maintain a hypothesis, beside which occult qualities are commonplace. What does he understand, I ask, by the union of the mind and the body? What clear and distinct conception has he got of thought in most intimate union with a certain particle of extended matter? Truly I should like him to explain this union through its proximate cause. But he had so distinct a conception of mind being distinct from body, that he could not assign any particular cause of the union between the two, or of the mind itself, but was obliged to have recourse to the cause of the whole universe, that is to God. Further, I should much like to know, what degree of motion the mind can impart to this pineal gland, and with what force can it hold it suspended? For I am in ignorance, whether this gland can be agitated more slowly or more quickly by the mind than by the animal spirits, and whether the motions of the passions, which we have closely united with firm decisions, cannot be again disjoined therefrom by physical causes; in which case it would follow that, although the mind firmly intended to face a given danger, and had united to this decision the motions of boldness, yet at the sight of the danger the gland might become suspended in a way, which would preclude the mind thinking of anything except running away. In truth, as there is no common standard of volition and motion, so is there no comparison possible between the powers of the mind and power or strength of the body; consequently the strength of one cannot in any wise be determined by the strength of the other. We may also add, that there is no gland discoverable in the midst of the brain, so placed that it can thus easily be set in motion in so many ways, and also that all the nerves are not prolonged so far as the cavities of the brain. Lastly, I omit all the assertions which he makes concerning the will and its freedom, inasmuch as I have abundantly proved that his premises are false. Therefore, since the power of the mind, as I have shown above, is defined by the understanding only, we shall determine solely by the knowledge of the mind the remedies against the emotions, which I believe all have had experience of, but do not accurately observe or distinctly see, and from the same basis we shall deduce all those conclusions, which have regard to the mind's blessedness.

PROP. I. *Even as thoughts and the ideas of things are arranged and associated in the mind, so are the modifications of body or the images of things precisely in the same way arranged and associated in the body.*

PROP. II *If we remove a disturbance of the spirit, or emotion, from the thought of an external cause, and unite it to other thoughts, then will the love or hatred towards that external cause, and also the vacillations of spirit which arise from these emotions, be destroyed.*

PROP. III. *An emotion, which is a passion, ceases to be a passion, as soon as we form a clear and distinct idea thereof.*

Corollary.—An emotion therefore becomes more under our control, and the mind is less passive in respect to it, in proportion as it is more known to us.

PROP. IV. *There is no modification of the body, whereof we cannot form some clear and distinct conception.*

Corollary.—Hence it follows that there is no emotion, whereof we cannot form some clear and distinct conception. For an emotion is the idea of a modification of the body (by the general Def. of the Emotions), and must therefore (by the preceding Prop.) involve some clear and distinct conception.

PROP. VI. *The mind has greater power over the emotions and is less subject thereto, in so far as it undertands all things as necessary.*

Proof.—The mind understands all things to be necessary (I xxix.) and to be determined to existence and operation by an infinite chain of causes; therefore (by the foregoing Proposition), it thus far brings it about, that it is less subject to the emotions arising therefrom, and (III. xlviii.) feels less emotion towards the things themselves. *Q.E.D.*

PROP. VII. *Emotions which are aroused or spring from reason, if we take account of time, are stronger than those which are attributable to particular objects that we regard as absent.*

PROP. VIII. *An emotion is stronger in proportion to the number of simultaneous concurrent causes whereby it is aroused.*

Proof.—Many simultaneous causes are more powerful than a few (III. vii.): therefore (IV. v.), in proportion to the increased number of simultaneous causes whereby it is aroused, emotion becomes stronger. *Q.E.D.*

PROP. IX. *An emotion which is attributable to many and diverse causes which the mind regards as simultaneous with the emotion itself is less hurtful, and we are less subject thereto and less affected towards each of its causes, than if it were a different and equally powerful emotion attributable to fewer causes or to a single cause.*

Proof.—An emotion is only bad or hurtful, in so far as it hinders the mind from being able to think (IV. xxvi. xxvii.); therefore, an emotion, whereby the mind is determined to the contemplation of several things at once, is less hurtful than another equally powerful emotion, which so engrosses the mind in the single contemplation of a few objects or of one, that it is unable to think of anything else; this was our first point. Again, as the mind's essence, in other words, its power (III. vii.), consists solely in thought (II. xi.), the mind is less passive in respect to an emotion, which causes it to think of several things at once, than in regard to an equally strong emotion, which keeps it engrossed in the contemplation of a few or of a single object: this was our second point. Lastly, this emotion (III. xlviii.), in so far as it is attributable to several causes, is less powerful in regard to each of them. *Q.E.D.*

PROP X. *So long as we are not assailed by emotions contrary to our nature, we have the power of arranging and associating the modifications of our body according to the intellectual order.*

Proof.—The emotions, which are contrary to our nature, that is (IV. xxx.), which are bad, are bad in so far as they impede the mind from understanding (IV. xxvii.). So long, therefore, as we are not assailed by emotions contrary to our nature, the mind's power, whereby it endeavours to understand things (IV. xxvi.), is not impeded, and therefore it is able to form clear and distinct ideas and to deduce them one from another (II. xl. note ii. and xlvii. note); consequently we have in such cases the power of arranging and associating the modifications of the body according to the intellectual order. *Q.E.D.*

Note.—Such are the doctrines which I had purposed to set forth concerning the mind, in so far as it is regarded without relation to the body; whence, as also from I. xxi. and other places, it is plain that our mind, in so far as it understands, is an eternal mode of thinking, which is determined by another eternal mode of thinking, and this other by a third, and so on to infinity; so that all taken together at once constitute the eternal and infinite intellect of God.

PROP. XLI. *Even if we did not know that our mind is eternal, we should still consider as of primary importance piety and religion, and generally all things which, in Part IV., we showed to be attributable to courage and high-mindedness.*

Proof.—The first and only foundation of virtue, or the rule of right living is (IV. xxii. Coroll. and xxiv.) seeking one's own true interest. Now, while we determined what reason prescribes as useful, we took no account of the mind's eternity, which has only become known to us in this Fifth Part. Although we were ignorant at that time that the mind is eternal, we nevertheless stated that the qualities attributable to courage and high-mindedness are of primary importance. Therefore, even if we were were still ignorant of this doctrine, we should yet put the aforesaid precepts of reason in the first place. *Q.E.D.*

Note.—The general belief of the multitide seems to be different. Most people seem to believe that they are free, in so far as they may obey their lusts, and that they cede their rights, in so far as they are bound to live according to the commandments of the divine law. They therefore believe that piety, religion, and, generally, all things attributable to firmness of mind, are burdens, which, after death, they hope to lay aside, and to receive the reward for their bondage, that is, for their piety and religion; it is not only by this hope, but also, and chiefly, by the fear of being horribly punished after death, that they are induced to live according to the divine commandments, so far as their feeble and infirm spirit will carry them. . . .

PROP. XLII. *Blessedness is not the reward of virtue, but virtue itself; neither do we rejoice therein, because we control our lusts, but, contrariwise, because we rejoice therein, we are able to control our lusts.*

Proof. — Blessedness consists in love towards God (V. xxxvi. and note), which love springs from the third kind of knowledge (V. xxxii. Coroll.); therefore this love (III. iii. lix.) must be referred to the mind, in so far as the latter is active; therefore (IV. Def. viii.) it is virtue itself. This was our first point. Again, in proportion as the mind rejoices more in this divine love or blessedness, so does it the more understand (V. xxxii.); that is (V. iii. Coroll.), so much the more power has it over the emotions, and (V. xxxviii.) so much the less is it subject to those emotions which are evil; therefore, in proportion as the mind rejoices in this divine love or blessedness, so has it the power of controlling lusts. And, since human power in controlling the emotions consists solely in the understanding, it follows that no one rejoices in blessedness, because he has controlled his lusts but, contrariwise, his power of controlling his lusts arises from his blessedness itself. *Q.E.D.*

David Hume

(1711-1776)

INTRODUCTION

Although now considered a major figure in the history of philosophy, David Hume was more esteemed in his day as a historian than as a philosopher. In 1739, while still in his twenties, he published *A Treatise of Human Nature,* which, in his words, "fell stillborn from the press." Though it received little recognition during Hume's lifetime, the *Treatise* is now considered a landmark work in both epistemology and ethics. In the *Treatise,* Hume defended a radically skeptical view of human knowledge. He argued, for example, that since our ordinary beliefs in general causal laws, in the endurance of objects, and in the existence of God cannot be proven true through experience, they do not count as genuine knowledge; these beliefs are simply a matter of custom or habit. This skeptical view of human knowledge in large part motivated Hume's successor, Kant, to write his famous *Critique of Pure Reason.* In the *Treatise,* Hume also joined in the battle then raging between those moral philosophers who believed moral knowledge is based on reason and those who believed it is based on feeling. Hume argued there, as well as in *An Enquiry Concerning the Principles of Morals,* published in 1751, that we are guided in our judgments of what is morally right and wrong by certain feelings of approval and disapproval, which he called moral sentiments. In defense of this, Hume argued that if feeling did not play an important part in moral knowledge, we would never be motivated to do the right thing and to avoid the wrong.

Hume is perhaps best known for his work on moral sentiments, a topic pioneered by his predecessor, Francis Hutcheson, but his theory of moral sentiments fits within a general theory and classification of emotions. Reprinted here is an excerpt from Book II of the *Treatise*, "Of the Passions," which is devoted to his theory of emotion. Hume also published a dissertation, "Of the Passions," in 1757. He was the first philosopher to give serious attention to the role ideas and beliefs play in generating emotions as well as the first to hint at the idea that emotions are always felt "about" or "toward" objects. [See Brentano (Part III) for a fuller explanation of this idea, which is called "intentionality."]

Following in Descartes's footsteps, Hume defines emotion as varying degrees of physical and possibly mental agitation. There are, in his view, both "calm" emotions, like the moral sentiments that involve little agitation, as well as "violent" emotions, such as anger and love. Since these sensations are simple and unanalyzable, Hume argues that a theory of emotion cannot be about the component "parts" of emotion. Rather, the task of such a theory should be the enumeration of the causes of emotion and any other conditions associated with emotions. With this in mind, Hume classifies emotions into two general categories—"direct" and "indirect"—each category having a distinct type of causal history. Joy, grief, and hope are direct emotions; they are caused simply by feelings of pleasure or pain. Receiving an unexpected gift, for example, gives us pleasure and this, in turn, causes joy. In contrast, indirect emotions, such as love, hatred, and pride, are caused by pleasures or pains plus certain beliefs about the object and its association with some person. It is in his analysis of these indirect emotions that Hume contributes most to the theory of emotion. He sees, for example, that taking pride in a house causally depends on our believing we own the house; and pride is always accompanied by the idea of self. (That is, even though we talk about being proud of the house, we think of it as reflecting well on ourselves, e.g., by indicating our social status; and so, in a sense, we are always also proud of ourselves.)

Hume's theory of emotion, like any of the theories within the Cartesian tradition (e.g., Jame's), can be criticized for being overly simplistic. Are emotions really nothing but simple sensations of agitation, or do they not also include behavioral and other features? Although Hume's view of emotions as simple unanalyzable sensations prevents him from seeing that emotions are always felt about or toward things (i.e., that they are intentional), his claim that indirect emotions and the idea of some person always go together is at least a step in this direction. Contemporary philosophers still share Hume's interest in the causes of emotion (though many reject his account); and Hume's theory of emotion, especially as it relates to his moral theory, is still a topic of concern.

From A Treatise of Human Nature

Of The Passions

Division of the Subject

As all the perceptions of the mind may be divided into *impressions* and *ideas,* so the impressions admit of another division into *original* and *secondary.* This division of the impressions is the same with that which I formerly made use of when I distinguish'd them into impressions of *sensation* and *reflexion.* Original impressions or impressions of sensation are such as without any antecedent perception arise in the soul, from the constitution of the body, from the animal spirits, or from the application of objects to the external organs. Secondary, or reflective impressions are such as proceed from some of these original ones, either immediately or by the interposition of its idea. Of the first kind are all the impressions of the senses, and all bodily pains and pleasures: Of the second are the passions, and other emotions resembling them.

'Tis certain, that the mind, in its perceptions, must begin somewhere; and that since the impressions precede their correspondent ideas, there must be some impressions, which without any introduction make their appearance in the soul. As these depend upon natural and physical causes, the examination of them wou'd lead me too far from my present subject, into the sciences of anatomy and natural philosophy. For this reason I shall here confine myself to those other impressions, which I have call'd secondary and reflective, as arising either from the original impressions, or from their ideas. Bodily pains and pleasures are the source of many passions, both when felt and consider'd by the mind; but arise originally in the soul, or in the body, whichever you please to call it, without any preceding thought or perception. A fit of the gout produces a long train of passions, as grief, hope, fear; but is not deriv'd immediately from any affection or idea.

The reflective impressions may be divided into two kinds, *viz.* the *calm* and the *violent.* Of the first kind is the sense of beauty and deformity in action, composition, and external objects. Of the second are the passions of love and hatred, grief and joy, pride and humility. This division is far from being exact. The raptures of poetry and music frequently rise to the greatest height; while those other impressions, properly called *passions,* may decay into so soft an emotion, as to become, in a manner, imperceptible. But as in general the passions are more violent than the emotions arising from beauty and deformity, these impressions have been commonly distinguish'd from each other. The subject of the human mind being so copious and various, I shall here take advantage of this vulgar and specious division, that I may proceed with the greater order; and having said all I thought necessary concerning our ideas, shall now explain these violent emotions or passions, their nature, origin, causes, and effects.

When we take a survey of the passions, there occurs a division of them into *direct* and *indirect.* By direct passions I understand such as arise immediately from good or evil, from pain or pleasure. By indirect such as proceed from the same principles, but by the conjunction of other qualities. This distinction I cannot at present justify or explain any farther. I can only observe in general, that under the indirect passions I comprehend pride, humility, ambition, vanity, love, hatred, envy, pity, malice, generosity, with their dependants. And under the direct passions, desire, aversion, grief, joy, hope, fear, despair and security. I shall begin with the former.

SECTION II

Of Pride and Humility; Their Objects and Causes

The passions of PRIDE and HUMILITY being simple and uniform impressions, 'tis impossible we can ever, by a multitude of words, give a just definition of them, or indeed of any of the passions. The utmost we can pretend to is a description of them, by an enumeration of such circumstances, as attend them: But as these words, *pride* and *humility,* are of general use, and the impressions they represent the most common of any, every one, of himself, will be able to form a just idea of them, without any danger of mistake. For which reason, not to lose time upon preliminaries, I shall immediately enter upon the examination of these passions.

'Tis evident, that pride and humility, tho' directly contrary, have yet the same OBJECT. This object is self, or that succession of related ideas and impressions, of which we have an intimate memory and consciousness. Here the view always fixes when we are actuated by either of these passions. According as our idea of ourself is more or less advantageous, we feel either of those opposite affections, and are elated by pride, or dejected with humility. Whatever other objects may be comprehended by the mind, they are always consider'd with a view to ourselves; otherwise they wou'd never be able either to excite these passions, or produce the smallest encrease or diminution of them. When self enters not into the consideration, there is no room either for pride or humility.

But tho' that connected succession of perceptions, which we call *self,* be always the object of these two passions, 'tis impossible it can be their CAUSE, or be sufficient alone to excite them. For as these passions are directly contrary, and have the same object in common; were their object also their cause; it cou'd never produce any degree of the one passion, but at the same time it must excite an equal degree of the other; which opposition and contrariety must destroy both. 'Tis impossible a man can at the same time be both proud and humble; and where he has different reasons for these passions, as frequently happens, the passions either take place alternately; or if they encounter, the one annihilates the other, as far as its strength goes, and the remainder only of that, which is superior, continues to operate upon the mind. But in the present case neither of the passions cou'd ever become superior; because supposing it to be the view only of ourself, which excited them, that being perfectly indifferent to either, must produce both in the very same proportion; or in other words, can produce neither. To excite any passion, and at the same time raise an equal share of its antagonist, is immediately to undo what was done, and must leave the mind at last perfectly calm and indifferent.

We must, therefore, make a distinction betwixt the cause and the object of these passions; betwixt that idea, which excites them, and that to which they direct their view, when excited. Pride and humility, being once rais'd, immediately turn our attention to ourself, and regard that as their ultimate and final object; but there is something farther requisite in order to raise them: Something, which is peculiar to one of the passions, and produces not both in the very same degree. The first idea, that is presented to the mind, is that of the cause or productive principle. This excites the passion, connected with it; and that passion, when excited, turns our view to another idea, which is that of self. Here then is a passion plac'd betwixt two ideas, of which the one produces it, and the other is produc'd by it. The first idea, therefore, represents the *cause*, the second the *object* of the passion.

To begin with the causes of pride and humility; we may observe, that their most obvious and remarkable property is the vast variety of *subjects*, on which they may be plac'd. Every valuable quality of the mind, whether of the imagination, judgment, memory or disposition; wit, good-sense, learning, courage, justice, integrity; all these are the causes of pride; and their opposites of humility. Nor are these passions confin'd to the mind, but extend their view to the body likewise. A man may be proud of his beauty, strength, agility, good mien, address in dancing, riding, fencing, and of his dexterity in any manual business or manufacture. But this is not all. The passion looking farther, comprehends whatever objects are in the least ally'd or related to us. Our country, family, children, relations, riches, houses, gardens, horses, dogs, cloaths; any of these may become a cause either of pride or of humility.

From the consideration of these causes, it appears necessary we shou'd make a new distinction in the causes of the passion, betwixt that *quality*, which operates, and the *subject*, on which it is plac'd. A man, for instance, is vain of a beautiful house, which belongs to him, or which he has himself built and contriv'd. Here the object of the passion is himself, and the cause is the beautiful house: Which cause again is sub-divided into two parts, *viz.* the quality, which operates upon the passion, and the subject, in which the quality inheres. The quality is the beauty, and the subject is the house, consider'd as his property or contrivance. Both these parts are essential, nor is the distinction vain and chimerical. Beauty, consider'd merely as such, unless plac'd upon something related to us, never produces any pride or vanity; and the strongest relation alone, without beauty, or something else in its place, has as little influence on that passion.

Since, therefore, these two particulars are easily separated, and there is a necessity for their conjunction, in order to produce the passion, we ought to consider them as component parts of the cause; and infix in our minds an exact idea of this distinction.

Of the Influence of These Relations on Pride and Humility

These principles being establish'd on unquestionable experience, I begin to consider how we shall apply them, by revolving over all the causes of pride and humility, whether these causes be regarded, as the qualities, that operate, or as the subjects, on which the qualities are plac'd. In examining these *qualities* I immediately find many of them to concur in producing the sensation of pain and pleasure, independent of those affections, which I here endeavour to explain. Thus the beauty of our person, of itself, and by its very appearance, gives pleasure, as well as pride; and its deformity, pain as well as humility. A magnificent feast delights us, and a sordid one displeases. What I discover to be true in some instances, I *suppose* to be so in all; and take it for granted at present, without any farther proof, that every cause of pride, by its peculiar qualities, produces a separate pleasure, and of humility a separate uneasiness.

Again, in considering the *subjects,* to which these qualities adhere, I make a new *supposition,* which also appears probable from many obvious instances, *viz.* that these subjects are either parts of ourselves, or something nearly related to us. Thus the good and bad qualities of our actions and manners constitute virtue and vice, and determine our personal character, than which nothing operates more strongly on these passions. In like manner, 'tis the beauty or deformity of our person, houses, equipage, or furniture, by which we are render'd either vain or humble. The same qualities, when transfer'd to subjects, which bear us no relation, influence not in the smallest degree either of these affections.

Having thus in a manner suppos'd two properties of the causes of these affections, *viz.* that the *qualities* produce a separate pain or pleasure, and that the *subjects,* on which the qualities are plac'd, are related to self; I proceed to examine the passions themselves, in order to find something in them, correspondent to the suppos'd properties of their causes. *First,* I find, that the peculiar object of pride and humility is determin'd by an original and natural instinct, and that 'tis absolutely impossible, from the primary constitution of the mind, that these passions shou'd ever look beyond self, or that individual person, of whose actions and sentiments each of us is intimately conscious. Here at last the view always rests, when we are actuated by either of these passions; nor can we, in that situation of mind, ever lose sight of this object. For this I pretend not to give any reason; but consider such a peculiar direction of the thought as an original quality.

The *second* quality, which I discover in these passions, and which I likewise consider as an original quality, is their sensations, or the peculiar emotions they excite in the soul, and which constitute their very being and essence. Thus pride is a pleasant sensation, and humility a painful; and upon the removal of the pleasure and pain, there is in reality no pride nor humility. Of this our very feeling convinces us; and beyond our feeling, 'tis here in vain to reason or dispute.

If I compare, therefore, these two *establish'd* properties of the passions, *viz.* their object, which is self, and their sensation, which is either pleasant or painful, to the two *suppos'd* properties of the causes, *viz.* their relation to self, and their tendency to produce a pain or pleasure, independent of the passion; I immediately find, that taking these suppositions to be just, the true system breaks in upon me with an irresistible evidence. That cause, which excites the passion, is related to the object, which nature has attributed to the passion; the sensation, which the cause separately produces, is related to the sensation of the passion: From this double relation of ideas and impressions, the passion is deriv'd. The one idea is easily converted into its cor-relative; and the one impression into that, which resembles and corresponds to it: With how much greater facility must this transition be made, where these movements mutually assist each other, and the mind receives a double impulse from the relations both of its impressions and ideas?

That we may comprehend this the better, we must suppose, that nature has given to the organs of the human mind, a certain disposition fitted to produce a peculiar impression or emotion, which we call *pride:* To this emotion she has assign'd a certain idea, *viz.* that of *self,* which it never fails to produce. This contrivance of nature is easily conceiv'd. We have many instances of such a situation of affairs. The nerves of the nose and palate are so dispos'd, as in certain circumstances to convey such peculiar sensations to the mind:

The sensations of lust and hunger always produce in us the idea of those peculiar objects, which are suitable to each appetite. These two circumstances are united in pride. The organs are so dispos'd as to produce the passion; and the passion, after its production, naturally produces a certain idea. All this needs no proof. 'Tis evident we never shou'd be possest of that passion, were there not a disposition of mind proper for it; and 'tis as evident, that the passion always turns our view to ourselves, and makes us think of our own qualities and circumstances. . . .

The difficulty, then, is only to discover this cause, and find what it is that gives the first motion to pride, and sets those organs in action, which are naturally fitted to produce that emotion. Upon my consulting experience, in order to resolve this difficulty, I immediately find a hundred different causes, that produce pride; and upon examining these causes, I suppose, what at first I perceive to be probable, that all of them concur in two circumstances; which are, that of themselves they produce an impression, ally'd to the passion, and are plac'd on a subject, ally'd to the object of the passion. When I consider after this the nature of *relation,* and its effects both on the passions and ideas, I can no longer doubt, upon these suppositions, that 'tis the very principle, which gives rise to pride, and bestows motion on those organs, which being naturally dispos'd to produce that affection, require only a first impulse or beginning to their action. Any thing, that gives a pleasant sensation, and is related to self, excites the passion of pride, which is also agreeable, and has self for its object.

What I have said of pride is equally true of humility. The sensation of humility is uneasy, as that of pride is agreeable; for which reason the separate sensation, arising from the causes, must be revers'd, while the relation to self continues the same. Tho' pride and humility are directly contrary in their effects, and in their sensations, they have notwithstanding the same object; so that 'tis requisite only to change the relation of impressions, without making any change upon that of ideas. Accordingly we find, that a beautiful house, belonging to ourselves, produces pride; and that the same house, still belonging to ourselves, produces humility, when by any accident its beauty is chang'd into deformity, and thereby the sensation of pleasure, which corresponded to pride, is transform'd into pain, which is related to humility. The double relation between the ideas and impressions subsists in both cases, and produces an easy transition from the one emotion to the other.

Of Love and Hatred

Of the Objects and Causes of Love and Hatred

'Tis altogether impossible to give any definition of the passions of *love* and *hatred;* and that because they produce merely a simple impression, without any mixture or composition. 'Twou'd be as unnecessary to attempt any description of them, drawn from their nature, origin, causes and objects; and that both because these are the subjects of our present enquiry, and because these passions of themselves are sufficiently known from our common feeling and experience. This we have already observ'd concerning pride and humility, and here repeat it concerning love and hatred; and indeed there is so great a resemblance betwixt these two sets of passions, that we shall be oblig'd to begin with a kind of abridgment of our reasonings concerning the former, in order to explain the latter.

As the immediate *object* of pride and humility is self or that identical person, of whose thoughts, actions, and sensations we are intimately conscious; so the *object* of love and hatred is some other person, of whose thoughts, actions, and sensations we are not conscious. This is sufficiently evident from experience. Our love and hatred are always directed to some sensible being external to us; and when we talk of *self-love,* 'tis not in a proper sense, nor has the sensation it produces any thing in common with that tender emotion, which is excited by a friend or mistress. 'Tis the same case with hatred. We may be mortified by our own faults and follies; but never feel any anger or hatred, except from the injuries of others.

But tho' the object of love and hatred be always some other person, 'tis plain that the object is not, properly speaking, the *cause* of these passions, or alone sufficient to excite them. For since love and hatred are directly contrary in their sensation, and have the same object in common, if that object were also their cause, it wou'd produce these opposite passions in an equal degree; and as they must, from the very first moment, destroy each other, none of them wou'd ever be able to make its appearance. There must, therefore, be some cause different from the object.

If we consider the causes of love and hatred, we shall find they are very much diversify'd, and have not many things in common. The virtue, knowledge, wit, good sense, good humour of any person, produce love and esteem; as the opposite qualities, hatred and contempt. The same passions arise from bodily accomplishments, such as beauty, force, swiftness, dexterity; and from their contraries; as likewise from the external advantages and disadvantages of family, possessions, cloaths, nation and climate. There is not one of these objects, but what by its different qualities may produce love and esteem, or hatred and contempt.

From the view of these causes we may derive a new distinction betwixt the *quality* that operates, and the *subject* on which it is plac'd. A prince, that is possess'd of a stately palace, commands the esteem of the people upon that account; and that *first,* by the beauty of the palace, and *secondly,* by the relation of property, which connects it with him. The removal of either of these destroys the passion; which evidently proves that the cause is a compounded one.

'Twou'd be tedious to trace the passions of love and hatred, thro' all the observations which we have form'd concerning pride and humility, and which are equally applicable to both sets of passions. 'Twill be sufficient to *remark* in general, that the object of love and hatred is evidently some thinking person; and that the sensation of the former passion is always agreeable, and of the latter uneasy. We may also *suppose* with some shew of probability, *that the cause of both these passions is always related to a thinking being,* and *that the cause of the former produce a separate pleasure, and of the latter a separate uneasiness.*

One of these suppositions, *viz.* that the cause of love and hatred must be related to a person or thinking being, in order to produce these passions, is not only probable, but too evident to be contested. Virtue and vice, when consider'd in the abstract; beauty and deformity, when plac'd on inanimate objects; poverty and riches, when belonging to a third person, excite no degree of love or hatred, esteem or contempt towards those, who have no relation to them. A person looking out at a window, sees me in the street, and beyond me a beautiful palace, with which I have no concern: I believe none will pretend, that this person will pay me the same respect, as if I were owner of the palace.

'Tis not so evident at first sight, that a relation of impressions is requisite to these passions, and that because in the transition the one impression is so much confounded with the other, that they become in a manner undistinguishable. But as in pride and humility, we have easily been able to make the separation, and to prove, that every cause of these passions produces a separate pain or pleasure, I might here observe the same method with the same success, in examining particularly the several causes of love and hatred. But as I hasten to a full and decisive proof of these systems, I delay this examination for a moment: And in the mean time shall endeavour to convert to my present purpose all my reasonings concerning pride and humility, by an argument that is founded on unquestionable experience.

There are few persons, that are satisfy'd with their own character, or genius, or fortune, who are not desirous of shewing themselves to the world, and of acquiring the love and approbation of mankind. Now 'tis evident, that the very same qualities and circumstances, which are the causes of pride or self-esteem, are also the causes of vanity or the desire of reputation; and that we always put to view those particulars with which in ourselves we are best satisfy'd. But if love and esteem were not produc'd by the same qualities as pride, according as these qualities are related to ourselves or others, this method of proceeding wou'd be very absurd, nor cou'd men expect a correspondence in the sentiments of every other person, with those themselves have entertain'd. 'Tis true, few can form exact systems of the passions, or make reflexions on their general nature and resemblances. But without such a progress in philosophy, we are not subject to many mistakes in this particular, but are sufficiently guided by common experience, as well as by a kind of *presensation;* which tells us what will operate on others, by what we feel immediately in ourselves. Since then the same qualities that produce pride or humility, cause love or hatred; all the arguments that have been employ'd to prove, that the causes of the former passions excite a pain or pleasure independent of the passion, will be applicable with equal evidence to the causes of the latter. . . .

Regard now with attention the nature of these passions, and their situation with respect to each other. 'Tis evident here are four affections, plac'd, as it were, in a square or regular connexion with, and distance from each other. The passions of pride and humility, as well as those of love and hatred, are connected together by the identity of their object, which to the first set of passions is self, to the second some other person. These two lines of communication or connexion form two opposite sides of the square. Again, pride and love are agreeable passions; hatred and humility uneasy. This similitude of sensation betwixt pride and love, and that betwixt humility and hatred form a new connexion, and may be consider'd as the other two sides of the square. Upon the whole, pride is connected with humility, love with hatred, by their objects or ideas: Pride with love, humility with hatred, by their sensations or impressions.

Of the Will and Direct Passions

A passion is an original existence, or, if you will, modification of existence, and contains not any representative quality, which renders it a copy of any other existence or modification. When I am angry, I am actually possest with the passion, and in that emotion have no more a reference to any other object, than when I am thirsty, or sick, or more than five foot high. 'Tis impossible, therefore, that this passion can be oppos'd by, or be contradictory to truth and reason; since this contradiction consists in the disagreement of ideas, consider'd as copies, with those objects, which they represent.

What may at first occur on this head, is, that as nothing can be contrary to truth or reason, except what has a reference to it, and as the judgments of our understanding only have this reference, it must follow, that passions can be contrary to reason only so far as they are *accompany'd* with some judgment or opinion. According to this principle, which is so obvious and natural, 'tis only in two senses, that any affection can be call'd unreasonable. First, When a passion, such as hope or fear, grief or joy, despair or security, is founded on the supposition of the existence of objects, which really do not exist. Secondly, When in exerting any passion in action, we chuse means insufficient for the design'd end, and deceive ourselves in our judgment of causes and effects. Where a passion is neither founded on false suppositions, nor chuses means insufficient for the end, the understanding can neither justify nor condemn it. 'Tis not contrary to reason to prefer the destruction of the whole world to the scratching of my finger. 'Tis not contrary to reason for me to chuse my total ruin, to prevent the least uneasiness of an *Indian* or person wholly unknown to me. 'Tis as little contrary to reason to prefer even my own acknowledg'd lesser good to my greater, and have a more ardent affection for the former than the latter. A trivial good may, from certain circumstances, produce a desire superior to what arises from the greatest and most valuable enjoyment; nor is there any thing more extraordinary in this, than in mechanics to see one pound weight raise up a hundred by the advantage of its situation. In short, a passion must be accompany'd with some false judgment, in order to its being unreasonable; and even then 'tis not the passion, properly speaking, which is unreasonable, but the judgment.

The consequences are evident. Since a passion can never, in any sense, be call'd unreasonable, but when founded on a false supposition, or when it chuses means insufficient for the design'd end, 'tis impossible, that reason and passion can ever oppose each other, or dispute for the government of the will and actions. The moment we perceive the falshood of any supposition, or the insufficiency of any means our passions yield to our reason without any opposition. I may desire any fruit as of an excellent relish; but whenever you convince me of my mistake, my longing ceases. I may will the performance of certain actions as means of obtaining any desir'd good; but as my willing of these actions is only secondary, and founded on the supposition, that they are causes of the propos'd effect; as soon as I discover the falshood of that supposition, they must become indifferent to me.

'Tis natural for one, that does not examine objects with a strict philosophic eye, to imagine, that those actions of the mind are entirely the same, which produce not a different sensation, and are not immediately distinguishable to the feeling and perception. Reason, for instance, exerts itself without producing any sensible emotion; and except in the more sublime disquisitions of philosophy, or in the frivolous subtilties of the schools, scarce ever conveys any pleasure or uneasiness. Hence it proceeds, that every action of the mind, which operates with the same calmness and tranquillity, is confounded with reason by all those, who judge of things from the first view and appearance. Now 'tis certain, there are certain calm desires and tendencies, which, tho' they be real passions, produce little emotion in the mind, and are more known by their effects than by the immediate feeling or sensation. These desires are of two kinds; either certain instincts originally implanted in our natures, such as benevolence and resentment, the love of life, and kindness to children; or the general appetite to good, and aversion to evil, consider'd merely as such. When any of these passions are calm, and cause no disorder in the soul, they are very readily taken for the determinations of reason, and are suppos'd to proceed from the same faculty, with that, which judges of truth and falshood. Their nature and principles have been suppos'd the same, because their sensations are not evidently different.

Beside these calm passions, which often determine the will, there are certain violent emotions of the same kind, which have likewise a great influence on that faculty. When I receive any injury from another, I often feel a violent passion of resentment, which makes me desire his evil and punishment, independent of all considerations of pleasure and advantage to myself. When I am immediately threaten'd with any grievous ill, my fears, apprehensions, and aversions rise to a great height, and produce a sensible emotion.

The common error of metaphysicians has lain in ascribing the direction of the will entirely to one of these principles, and supposing the other to have no influence. Men often act knowingly against their interest: For which reason the view of the greatest possible good does not always influence them. Men often counter-act a violent passion in prosecution of their interests and designs: 'Tis not therefore the present uneasiness alone, which determines them. In general we may observe, that both these principles operate on the will; and where they are contrary, that either of them prevails, according to the *general* character or *present* disposition of the person. What we call strength of mind, implies the prevalence of the calm passions above the violent; tho' we may easily observe, there is no man so constantly possess'd of this virtue, as never on any occasion to yield to the sollicitations of passion and desire. From these variations of temper proceeds the great difficulty of deciding concerning the actions and resolutions of men, where there is any contrariety of motives and passions.

Of the Causes of the Violent Passions

There is not in philosophy a subject of more nice speculation than this of the different *causes* and *effects* of the calm and violent passions. 'Tis evident passions influence not the will in proportion to their violence, or the disorder they occasion in the temper; but on the contrary, that when a passion has once become a settled principle of action, and is the predominant inclination of the soul, it commonly produces no longer any sensible agitation. As repeated custom and its own force have made every thing yield to it, it directs the actions and conduct without that opposition and emotion, which so naturally attend every momentary gust of passion. We must, therefore, distinguish betwixt a calm and a weak passion; betwixt a violent and a strong one. But notwithstanding this, 'tis certain, that when we wou'd govern a man, and push him to any action, 'twill commonly be better policy to work upon the violent than the calm passions, and rather take him by his inclination, than what is vulgarly call'd his *reason*. We ought to place the object in such particular situations as are proper to encrease the violence of the passion. For we may observe, that all depends upon the situation of the object, and that a variation in this particular will be able to change the calm and the violent passions into each other. Both these kinds of passions pursue good, and avoid evil; and both of them are encreas'd or diminish'd by the encrease or diminution of the good or evil. But herein lies the difference betwixt them: The same good, when near, will cause a violent passion, which, when remote, produces only a calm one. As this subject belongs very properly to the present question concerning the will, we shall here examine it to the bottom, and shall consider some of those circumstances and situations of objects, which render a passion either calm or violent.

'Tis a remarkable property of human nature, that any emotion, which attends a passion, is easily converted into it, tho' in their natures they be originally different from, and even contrary to each other. 'Tis true; in order to make a perfect union among passions, there is always requir'd a double relation of impressions and ideas; nor is one relation sufficient for that purpose. But tho' this be confirm'd by undoubted experience, we must understand it with its proper limitations, and must regard the double relation, as requisite only to make one passion produce another. When two passions are already produc'd by their separate causes, and are both present in the mind, they readily mingle and unite, tho' they have but one relation, and sometimes without any. The predominant passion swallows up the inferior, and converts it into itself. The spirits, when once excited, easily receive a change in their direction; and 'tis natural to imagine this change will come from the prevailing affection. The connexion is in many respects closer betwixt any two passions, than betwixt any passion and indifference.

It may not be improper, before we leave this subject of the will, to resume, in a few words, all that has been said concerning it, in order to set the whole more distinctly before the eyes of the reader. What we commonly understand by *passion* is a violent and sensible emotion of mind, when any good or evil is presented, or any object, which, by the original formation of our faculties, is fitted to excite an appetite. By *reason* we mean affections of the very same kind with the former; but such as operate more calmly, and cause no disorder in the temper: Which tranquillity leads us into a mistake concerning them, and causes us to regard them as conclusions only of our intellectual faculties. Both the *causes* and *effects* of these violent and calm passions are pretty variable, and depend, in a great measure, on the peculiar temper and disposition of every individual. Generally speaking, the violent passions have a more powerful influence on the will; tho' 'tis often found, that the calm ones, when corroborated by reflection, and seconded by resolution, are able to controul them in their most furious movements. What makes this whole affair more uncertain, is, that a calm passion may easily be chang'd into a violent one, either by a change of temper, or of the circumstances and situation of the object, as by the borrowing of force from any attendant passion, by custom, or by exciting the imagination. Upon the whole, this struggle of passion and of reason, as it is call'd, diversifies human life, and makes men so different not only from each other, but also from themselves in different times. Philosophy can only account for a few of the greater and more sensible events of this war; but must leave all the smaller and more delicate revolutions, as dependent on principles too fine and minute for her comprehension.

Of the Direct Passions

'Tis easy to observe, that the passions, both direct and indirect, are founded on pain and pleasure, and that in order to produce an affection of any kind, 'tis only requisite to present some good or evil. Upon the removal of pain and pleasure there immediately follows a removal of love and hatred, pride and humility, desire and aversion, and of most of our reflective or secondary impressions.

The impressions, which arise from good and evil most naturally, and with the least preparation are the *direct* passions of desire and aversion, grief and joy, hope and fear, along with volition. The mind by an *original* instinct tends to unite itself with the good, and to avoid the evil, tho' they be conceiv'd merely in idea, and be consider'd as to exist in any future period of time.

But supposing that there is an immediate impression of pain or pleasure, and *that* arising from an object related to ourselves or others, this does not prevent the propensity or aversion, with the consequent emotions, but by concurring with certain dormant principles of the human mind, excites the new impressions of pride or humility, love or hatred. That propensity, which unites us to the object, or separates us from it, still continues to operate, but in conjunction with the *indirect* passions, which arise from a double relation of impressions and ideas.

These indirect passions, being always agreeable or uneasy, give in their turn additional force to the direct passions, and encrease our desire and aversion to the object. Thus a suit of fine cloaths produces pleasure from their beauty; and this pleasure produces the direct passions, or the impressions of volition and desire. Again, when these cloaths are consider'd as belonging to ourself, the double relation conveys to us the sentiment of pride, which is an indirect passion; and the pleasure, which attends that passion, returns back to the direct affections, and gives new force to our desire or volition, joy or hope.

When good is certain or probable, it produces JOY. When evil is in the same situation there arises GRIEF or SORROW.

When either good or evil is uncertain, it gives rise to FEAR or HOPE, according to the degrees of uncertainty on the one side or the other.

DESIRE arises from good consider'd simply, and AVERSION is deriv'd from evil. The WILL exerts itself, when either the good or the absence of the evil may be attain'd by any action of the mind or body.

Beside good and evil, or in other words, pain and pleasure, the direct passions frequently arise from a natural impulse or instinct, which is perfectly unaccountable. Of this kind is the desire of punishment to our enemies, and of happiness to our friends; hunger, lust, and a few other bodily appetites. These passions, properly speaking, produce good and evil, and proceed not from them, like the other affections.

Part Two
THE MEETING OF PHILOSOPHY AND PSYCHOLOGY

It is only recently that the various disciplines concerned with emotions were separated from each other and scattered into separate university departments with self-consciously different methodologies. William James, for example, would not have understood the separation of philosophy and psychology (they were one and the same department at Harvard in his days), and he himself was trained as a physician, which is evident, especially, in his works in psychology. Almost all the authors in the following section integrate philosophy, psychology, and biology into their views. Charles Darwin was primarily a biologist, of course, but his writings are filled with philosophical speculations and psychological observations. James's 1884 essay—"What is an Emotion?"—is one of the classic starting points from which almost all studies of emotion begin today, either in agreement or in reaction. Walter Cannon, the most prominent of a number of early pragmatist critics of James's theory, was a physiologist. John Dewey, a fellow "pragmatist," nevertheless found serious inadequacies in James's too-physical theory. Schachter and Singer are contemporary psychologists who revised James as a partially "cognitive" theory. Freud, a contemporary and admirer of James, amends the study of emotions to account for "unconscious" emotions and to provide for that "free-floating" emotion, anxiety.

Charles Robert Darwin

(1809-1882)

INTRODUCTION

Charles Darwin's greatest contribution, the theory of species evolution through natural selection, not only revolutionized scientific thought, but sent reverberations throughout other fields as well; we now have, for example, evolutionary theories of ethics, epistemology, and society. And by challenging the doctrine of the fixity of the species, as well as suggesting an alternative explanation of the apparent design in nature, Darwin's theory of evolution raised serious theological questions and doubts. Darwin presented his theory in two major works, *Origin of the Species* (1859) and *The Descent of Man* (1871).

Darwin's original training was not in the biological sciences, but rather in medicine. Unsuccessful at pursuing his father's medical profession, Darwin began studying theology at Cambridge, intending to become a country clergyman; but before he could assume his clerical duties, he signed on as naturalist for a scientific expedition on the H.M.S. *Beagle*. On this expedition (1831–1836), he noticed differences in species that suggested to him that they had not arisen in their present form, but rather had evolved over time. Darwin found an explanation for how this evolution would occur in Malthus's work which compared the arithmetical increase in food supplies to the geometrical increase in animal populations—during the inevitable competition for food, only the fittest would survive. And the possibility of chance variations, already known to horticulturalists and breeders, would explain how new characteristics might arise.

After publishing *Origin,* Darwin applied his general theory of evolution and natural selection to specific cases. As one might expect, Darwin's interest in the emotions was part of this endeavor. As early as *Origin,* Darwin argues that emotions and emotional expression in man and animals are similar; and his belief that man evolved from lower lifeforms, furthered this comparison. This argument is codified in his *The Expression of Emotion in Man and Animals,* published in 1872. In the following excerpt from that work, Darwin outlines the three main principles explaining the origin of emotional expression. Some emotional expressions originally arise because they are useful in dealing with the emotion-arousing situation; they thus have survival value. Others are simply the opposite of those useful emotional behaviors associated with an opposite emotion. And yet others, such as trembling, are simply a result of the physiological changes that occur during emotional experiences.

Darwin's theory of the origin of emotional expression, like his theory of evolution, in general, can be criticized because there is no direct evidence to support it. And to the extent that Darwin's account of emotional expression depends heavily on the Lamarkean thesis that acquired habits can be passed on genetically, it is now discredited. Darwin does, however, ask some interesting and troublesome questions. What is the relation between expressing our emotions and the intensity of the emotion? (Does suppressing an emotion make it more or less intense?) To what extent is human expression of emotion innate and to what extent is it learned or determined by one's culture? Moreover, Darwin's emphasis on the purposefulness of emotional behavior finds echoes in later theories, such as those of James and Dewey.

From the Expression of Emotion in Man and Animals

GENERAL PRINCIPLES OF EXPRESSION

I will begin by giving the three Principles, which appear to me to account for most of the expressions and gestures involuntarily used by man and the lower animals, under the influence of various emotions and sensations.

I. *The principle of serviceable associated Habits.* —Certain complex actions are of direct or indirect service under certain states of the mind, in order to relieve or gratify certain sensations, desires, &c.; and whenever the same state of mind is induced, however feebly, there is a tendency through the force of habit and association for the same movements to be performed, though they may not then be of the least use. Some actions ordinarily associated through habit with certain states of the mind may be partially repressed through the will, and in such cases the muscles which are least under the separate control of the will are the most liable still to act, causing movements which we recognize as expressive. In certain other cases the checking of one habitual movement requires other slight movements; and these are likewise expressive.

II. *The principle of Antithesis.* —Certain states of the mind lead to certain habitual actions, which are of service, as under our first principle. Now when a directly opposite state of mind is induced, there is a strong and involuntary tendency to the performance of movements of a directly opposite nature, though these are of no use; and such movements are in some cases highly expressive.

III. *The principle of actions due to the constitution of the Nervous System, independently from the first of the Will, and independently to a certain extent of Habit.* —When the sensorium is strongly excited, nerve-force is generated in excess, and is transmitted in certain definite directions, depending on the connection of the nerve-cells, and partly on habit: or the supply of nerve-force may, as it appears, be interrupted. Effects are thus produced which we recognize as expressive. This third principle may, for the sake of brevity, be called that of the direct action of the nervous system.

With respect to our *first Principle,* it is notorious how powerful is the force of habit. The most complex and difficult movements can in time be performed without the least effort or consciousness. It is not positively known how it comes that habit is so efficient in facilitating complex movements; but physiologists admit "that the conducting power of the nervous fibres increases with the frequency of their excitement." This applies to the nerves of motion and sensation, as well as to those connected with the act of thinking. That some physical change is produced in the nerve-cells or nerves which are habitually used can hardly be doubted, for otherwise it is impossible to understand how the tendency to certain acquired movements is inherited.

From the foregoing remarks it seems probable that some actions, which were at first performed consciously, have become through habit and association converted into reflex actions, and are now so firmly fixed and inherited, that they are performed, even when not of the least use, as often as the same causes arise, which originally excited them in us through the volition. In such cases the sensory nerve-cells excite the motor cells, without first communicating with those cells on which our consciousness and volition depend. It is probable that sneezing and coughing were originally acquired by the habit of expelling, as violently as possible, any irritating particle from the sensitive air-passages. As far as time is concerned, there has been more than enough for these habits to have become innate or converted into reflex actions; for they are common to most or all of the higher quadrupeds, and must therefore have been first acquired at a very remote period. Why the act of clearing the throat is not a reflex action, and has to be learnt by our children, I cannot pretend to say; but we can see why blowing the nose on a handkerchief has to be learnt.

So again it appears probable that starting was originally acquired by the habit of jumping away as quickly as possible from danger, whenever any of our senses gave us warning. Starting, as we have seen, is accompanied by the blinking of the eyelids so as to protect the eyes, the most tender and sensitive organs of the body; and it is, I believe, always accompanied by a sudden and forcible inspiration, which is the natural preparation for any violent effort.

It further deserves notice that reflex actions are in all probability liable to slight variations, as are all corporeal structures and instincts; and any variations which were beneficial and of sufficient importance, would tend to be preserved and inherited. Thus reflex actions, when once gained for one purpose, might afterwards be modified independently of the will or habit, so as to serve for some distinct purpose. Such cases would be parallel with those which, as we have every reason to highly complex ones have been developed through the preservation of variations of pre-existing instincts—that is, through natural selection.

I have discussed at some little length, though as I am well aware, in a very imperfect manner, the acquirement of reflex actions, because they are often brought into play in connection with movements expressive of our emotions; and it was necessary to show that at least some of them might have been first acquired through the will in order to satisfy a desire, or to relieve a disagreeable sensation.

We will now consider our second Principle, that of Antithesis. Certain states of the mind lead ... to certain habitual movements which were primarily, or may still be, of service; and we shall find that when a directly opposite state of mind is induced, there is a strong and involuntary tendency to the performance of movements of a directly opposite nature, though these have never been of any service. . . .

When a dog approaches a strange dog or man in a savage or hostile frame of mind he walks upright and very stiffly; his head is slightly raised, or not much lowered; the tail is held erect and quite rigid; the hairs bristle, especially along the neck and back; the pricked ears are directed forwards, and the eyes have a fixed stare. These actions, as will hereafter be explained, follow from the dog's intention to attack his enemy, and are thus to a large extent intelligible. As he prepares to spring with a savage growl on his enemy, the canine teeth are uncovered, and the ears are pressed close backwards on the head; but with these latter actions, we are not here concerned. Let us now suppose that the dog suddenly discovers that the man he is approaching, is not a stranger, but his master; and let it be observed how completely and instantaneously his whole bearing is reversed. Instead of walking upright, the body sinks downwards or even crouches, and is thrown into flexuous movements; his tail, instead of being held stiff and upright, is lowered and wagged from side to side; his hair instantly becomes smooth; his ears are depressed and drawn backwards, but not closely to the head; and his lips hang loosely. From the drawing back of the ears, the eyelids become elongated, and the eyes no longer appear round and staring. It should be added that the animal is at such times in an excited condition from joy; and nerve-force will be generated in excess, which naturally leads to action of some kind. Not one of the above movements, so clearly expressive of affection, are of the least direct service to the animal. They are explicable, as far as I can see, solely from being in complete opposition or antithesis to the attitude and movements which, from intelligible causes, are assumed when a dog intends to fight, and which consequently are expressive of anger.

If we now turn to the gestures which are innate or common to all the individuals of the same species, and which come under the present head of antithesis, it is extremely doubtful, whether any of them were at first deliberately invented and consciously performed. With mankind the best instance of a gesture standing in direct opposition to other movements, naturally assumed under an opposite frame of mind, is that of shrugging the shoulders. This expresses impotence or an apology,—something which cannot be done, or cannot be avoided. The gesture is sometimes used consciously and voluntarily, but it is extremely improbable that it was at first deliberately invented, and afterwards fixed by habit; for not only do young children sometimes shrug their shoulders under the above states of mind, but the movement is accompanied, as will be shown in a future chapter, by various subordinate movements, which not one man in a thousand is aware of, unless he has specially attended to the subject.

Hence for the development of the movements which come under the present head, some other principle, distinct from the will and consciousness, must have intervened. This principle appears to be that every movement which we have voluntarily performed throughout our lives has required the action of certain muscles; and when we have performed a directly opposite movement, an opposite set of muscles has been habitually brought into play—as in turning to the right or to the left, in pushing away or pulling an object towards us, and in lifting or lowering a weight. So strongly are our intentions and movements associated together, that if we eagerly wish an object to move in any direction, we can hardly avoid moving our bodies in the same direction, although we may be perfectly aware that this can have no influence. . . . A man or child in a passion, if he tells any one in a loud voice to begone, generally moves his arm as if to push him away, although the offender may not be standing near, and although there may be not the least need to explain by a gesture what is meant. On the other hand, if we eagerly desire some one to approach us closely, we act as if pulling him towards us; and so in innumerable other instances.

As the performance of ordinary movements of an opposite kind, under opposite impulses of the will, has become habitual in us and in the lower animals, so when actions of one kind have become firmly associated with any sensation or emotion, it appears natural that actions of a directly opposite kind, though of no use, should be unconsciously performed through habit and association, under the influence of a directly opposite sensation or emotion. On this principle alone can I understand how the gestures and expressions which come under the present head of antithesis have originated. If indeed they are serviceable to man or to any other animal, in aid of inarticulate cries or language, they will likewise be voluntarily employed, and the habit will thus be strengthened. But whether or not of service as a means of communication, the tendency to perform opposite movements under opposite sensations or emotions would, if we may judge by analogy, become hereditary through long practice; and there cannot be a doubt that several expressive movements due to the principle of antithesis are inherited.

We now come to our third Principle, namely, that certain actions which we recognize as expressive of certain states of the mind, are the direct result of the constitution of the nervous system, and have been from the first independent of the will, and, to a large extent, of habit. When the sensorium is strongly excited nerve-force is generated in excess, and is transmitted in certain directions, dependent on the connection of the nerve-cells, and, as far as the muscular system is concerned, on the nature of the movements which have been habitually practised. Or the supply of nerve-force may, as it appears, be interrupted. Of course every movement which we make is determined by the constitution of the nervous system; but actions performed in obedience to the will, or through habit, or through the principle of antithesis, are here as far as possible excluded. Our present subject is very obscure, but, from its importance, must be discussed at some little length; and it is always advisable to perceive clearly our ignorance.

The most striking case, though a rare and abnormal one, which can be adduced of the direct influence of the nervous system, when strongly affected, on the body, is the loss of colour in the hair, which has occasionally been observed after extreme terror or grief. One authentic instance has been recorded, in the case of a man brought out for execution in India, in which the change of colour was so rapid that it was perceptible to the eye.

Another good case is that of the trembling of the muscles, which is common to man and to many, or most, of the lower animals. Trembling is of no service, often of much disservice, and cannot have been at first acquired through the will, and then rendered habitual in association with any emotion. I am assured by an eminent authority that young children do not tremble, but go into convulsions under the circumstances which would induce excessive trembling in adults. Trembling is excited in different individuals in very different degrees, and by the most diversified causes,—by cold to the surface, before fever-fits, although the temperature of the body is then above the normal standard; in blood-poisoning, delirium tremens, and other diseases; by general failure of power in old age; by exhaustion after excessive fatigue; locally from severe injuries, such as burns; and, in an especial manner, by the passage of a catheter. Of all emotions, fear notoriously is the most apt to induce trembling; but so do occasionally great anger and joy. I remember once seeing a boy who had just shot his first snipe on the wing, and his hands trembled to such a degree from delight, that he could not for some time reload his gun; and I have heard of an exactly similar case with an Australian savage, to whom a gun had been lent. Fine music, from the vague emotions thus excited, causes a shiver to run down the backs of some persons. There seems to be very little in common in the above several physical causes and emotions to account for trembling; and Sir J. Paget, to whom I am indebted for several of the above statements, informs me that the subject is a very obscure one. As trembling is sometimes caused by rage, long before exhaustion can have set in, and as it sometimes accompanies great joy, it would appear that any strong excitement of the nervous system interrupts the steady flow of nerve-force to the muscles.

Finally, so many expressive movements can be explained, as I trust will be seen in the course of this volume, through the three principles which have now been discussed, that we may hope here-after to see all thus explained, or by closely analogous principles. It is, however, often impossible to decide how much weight ought to be attributed, in each particular case, to one of our principles, and how much to another; and very many points in the theory of Expression remain inexplicable.

We will now consider how far the will and consciousness have come into play in the development of the various movements of expression. As far as we can judge, only a few expressive movements ... are learnt by each individual; that is, were consciously and voluntarily performed during the early years of life for some definite object, or in imitation of others, and then became habitual. The far greater number of the movements of expression, and all the more important ones, are, as we have seen, innate or inherited; and such cannot be said to depend on the will of the individual. Nevertheless, all those included under our first principle were at first voluntarily performed for a definite object,—namely, to escape some danger, to relieve some distress, or to gratify some desire. For instance, there can hardly be a doubt that the animals which fight with their teeth, have acquired the habit of drawing back their ears closely to their heads, when feeling savage, from their progenitors having voluntarily acted in this manner in order to protect their ears from being torn by their antagonists; for those animals which do not fight with their teeth do not thus express a savage state of mind. We may infer as highly probable that we ourselves have acquired the habit of contracting the muscles round the eyes, whilst crying gently, that is, without the utterance of any loud sound, from our progenitors, especially during infancy, having experienced, during the act of screaming, an uncomfortable sensation in their eyeballs. Again, some highly expressive movements result from the endeavour to check or prevent other expressive movements; thus the obliquity of the eyebrows and the drawing down of the corners of the mouth follow from the endeavour to prevent a screaming-fit from coming on, or to check it after it has come on. Here it is obvious that the consciousness and will must at first have come into play; not that we are conscious in these or in other such cases what muscles are brought into action, any more than when we perform the most ordinary voluntary movements.

With respect to the expressive movements due to the principle of antithesis, it is clear that the will has intervened, though in a remote and indirect manner. So again with the movements coming under our third principle; these, in as far as they are influenced by nerve-force readily passing along habitual channels, have been determined by former and repeated exertions of the will. The effects indirectly due to this latter agency are often combined in a complex manner, through the force of habit and association, with those directly resulting from the excitement of the cerebro-spinal system. This seems to be the case with the increased action of the heart under the influence of any strong emotion. When an animal erects its hair, assumes a threatening attitude, and utters fierce sounds, in order to terrify an enemy, we see a curious combination of movements which were originally voluntary with those that are involuntary. It is, however, possible that even strictly involuntary actions, such as the erection of the hair, may have been affected by the mysterious power of the will.

In the course of the foregoing remarks and throughout this volume, I have often felt much difficulty about the proper application of the terms, will, consciousness, and intention. Actions, which were at first voluntary, soon became habitual, and at last hereditary, and may then be performed even in opposition to the will. Although they often reveal the state of the mind, this result was not at first either intended or expected. Even such words as that "certain movements serve as a means of expression" are apt to mislead, as they imply that this was their primary purpose or object. This, however, seems rarely or never to have been the case; the movements having been at first either of some direct use, or the indirect effect of the excited state of the sensorium. An infant may scream either intentionally or instinctively to show that it wants food; but it has no wish or intention to draw its features into the peculiar form which so plainly indicates misery; yet some of the most characteristic expressions exhibited by man are derived from the act of screaming, as has been explained.

The movements of expression in the face and body, whatever their origin may have been, are in themselves of much importance for our welfare. They serve as the first means of communication between the mother and her infant; she smiles approval, and thus encourages her child on the right path, or frowns disapproval. We readily perceive sympathy in others by their expression; our sufferings are thus mitigated and our pleasures increased; and mutual good feeling is thus strengthened. The movements of expression give vividness and energy to our spoken words. They reveal the thoughts and intentions of others more truly than do words, which may be falsified.... The free expression by outward signs of an emotion intensifies it. On the other hand, the repression, as far as this is possible, of all outward signs softens our emotions. He who gives way to violent gestures will increase his rage; he who does not control the signs of fear will experience fear in a greater degree; and he who remains passive when overwhelmed with grief loses his best chance of recovering elasticity of mind. These results follow partly from the intimate relation which exists between almost all the emotions and their outward manifestations; and partly from the direct influence of exertion on the heart, and consequently on the brain. Even the simulation of an emotion tends to arouse it in our minds. Shakespeare, who from his wonderful knowledge of the human mind ought to be an excellent judge, says:—

> Is it not monstrous that this player here,
> But in a fiction, in a dream of passion,
> Could force his soul so to his own conceit,
> That, from her working, all his visage wann'd;
> Tears in his eyes, distraction in 's aspect,
> A broken voice, and his whole function suiting
> With forms to his conceit? And all for nothing!
>
> *Hamlet,* Act II. sc. 2.

William James

(1842-1910)

INTRODUCTION

Although William James received his training in medicine and began his career teaching anatomy and physiology at Harvard in 1873, he became increasingly interested in psychology and philosophy. By 1890, when he published his famous *Principles of Psychology*, he was a professor of philosophy at Harvard. James's wide-ranging philosophical interests included ethics, religion, and epistemology; he was one of the central figures in the American philosophical movement known as pragmatism.

James applied both his psychological knowledge and philosophical acumen in developing his theory of emotion. His essay—"What Is an Emotion?"—which is reprinted here, was published in *Mind* in 1884. About the time that James was developing his theory, a Danish psychologist, C. G. Lange, was working on a similar one. The theory, accordingly, is often called the James-Lange theory; and the two authors collaborated on a defense of their theory in *The Emotions*, published in 1885.

The James-Lange theory begins with a definition of emotion as the perception of physiological disturbances caused by our awareness of events and objects in our environment. When we stumble suddenly upon a snake, for example, our muscles involuntarily contract and our respiration increases in an instinctive preparation for flight; and fear of the snake is nothing, but the perception of these involuntary, instinctive, physiological changes. In defense of this definition, James points out that if we abstract from our experience of emotion all the characteristic bodily symptoms, we find we have left only a "cold and neutral state of intellectual perception." Because it defines emotion in terms of physical sensations the James-Lange theory falls squarely within the Cartesian tradition. But it is a more sophisticated theory, relying heavily on then-current scientific knowledge of physiology, neurology, and animal behavior, including Darwin's investigations of emotional expression in man and animals.

Viewing emotions as perceptions of physiological disturbances leads to a curious reversal of what we ordinarily consider to be the causal order of events. James says we do not cry because we feel sad, but we feel sad because we cry, angry because we strike, afraid because we tremble. Thus, the physiological reaction is central to emotion; and "feeling sad" is not the cause of this reaction, but instead our experience of that reaction. James leaves largely unspecified how events and objects in our environment come to produce these physiological disturbances, though he says in certain instances that our instincts are called upon. (Thus, he suggests that we instinctively fear a snake and are instinctively revolted by the sight of blood.) And James is singularly vague in explaining how we can identify and distinguish among many different emotions simply on the basis of the physiological changes associated with them; this has led to the most devastating criticism of his entire theory. (See Cannon and Dewey, for example.)

The James-Lange theory has influenced both psychology and philosophy and is perhaps the only theory of emotion to have an equal impact in both fields. But many theorists—including those who continue to accept its basic physiological emphasis—find it inadequate as it stands. The complaint is that the theory neglects the cognitive, behavioral, and other, more sophisticated aspects of emotion and fails to account for the many subtle distinctions between similar emotions (e.g., shame and embarrassment, fear and anxiety, love and infatuation). Nevertheless, it continues to be the starting-point for most contemporary theories of emotion, however they may disagree on its initial formulation.

From What Is an Emotion?

The physiologists who, during the past few years, have been so industriously exploring the functions of the brain, have limited their attempts at explanation to its cognitive and volitional performances. Dividing the brain into sensorial and motor centres, they have found their division to be exactly paralleled by the analysis made by empirical psychology, of the perceptive and volitional parts of the mind into their simplest elements. But the *æsthetic* sphere of the mind, its longings, its pleasures and pains, and its emotions, have been so ignored in all these researches that one is tempted to suppose that if either Dr. Ferrier or Dr. Munk were asked for a theory in brain-terms of the latter mental facts, they might both reply, either that they had as yet bestowed no thought upon the subject, or that they had found it so difficult to make distinct hypotheses, that the matter lay for them among the problems of the future, only to be taken up after the simpler ones of the present should have been definitively solved.

And yet it is even now certain that of two things concerning the emotions, one must be true. Either separate and special centres, affected to them alone, are their brain-seat, or else they correspond to processes occurring in the motor and sensory centres, already assigned, or in others like them, not yet mapped out. If the former be the case we must deny the current view, and hold the cortex to be something more than the surface of "projection" for every sensitive spot and every muscle in the body. If the latter be the case, we must ask whether the emotional "process" in the sensory or motor centre be an altogether peculiar one, or whether it resembles the ordinary perceptive processes of which those centres are already recognized to be the seat. The purpose of the following pages is to show that the last alternative comes nearest to the truth, and that the emotional brain-processes not only resemble the ordinary sensorial brain-processes, but in very truth *are* nothing but such processes variously combined. . . .

I should say first of all that the only emotions I propose expressly to consider here are those that have a distinct bodily expression. That there are feelings of pleasure and displeasure, of interest and excitement, bound up with mental operations, but having no obvious bodily expression for their consequence, would, I suppose, be held true by most readers. Certain arrangements of sounds, of lines, of colours, are agreeable, and others the reverse, without the degree of the feeling being sufficient to quicken the pulse or breathing, or to prompt to movements of either the body or the face. Certain sequences of ideas charm us as much as others tire us. It is a real intellectual delight to get a problem solved, and a real intellectual torment to have to leave it unfinished. The first set of examples, the sounds, lines, and colours, are either bodily sensations, or the images of such. The second set seem to depend on processes in the ideational centres exclusively. Taken together, they appear to prove that there are pleasures and pains inherent in certain forms of nerve-action as such, wherever that action occur. The case of these feelings we will at present leave entirely aside, and confine our attention to the more complicated cases in which a wave of bodily disturbance of some kind accompanies the perception of the interesting sights or sounds, or the passage of the exciting train of ideas. Surprise, curiosity, rapture, fear, anger, lust, greed, and the like, become then the names of the mental states with which the person is possessed. The bodily disturbances are said to be the "manifestation" of these several emotions, their "expression" or "natural language"; and these emotions themselves, being so strongly characterised both from within and without, may be called the *standard* emotions.

Our natural way of thinking about these standard emotions is that the mental perception of some fact excites the mental affection called the emotion, and that this latter state of mind gives rise to the bodily expression. My thesis on the contrary is that *the bodily changes follow directly the* PERCEPTION *of the exciting fact, and that our feeling of the same changes as they occur IS the emotion.* Common sense says, we lose our fortune, are sorry and weep; we meet a bear, are frightened and run; we are insulted by a rival, are angry and strike. The hypothesis here to be defended says that this order of sequence is incorrect, that the one mental state is not immediately induced by the other, that the bodily manifestations must first be interposed between, and that the more rational statement is that we feel sorry because we cry, angry because we strike, afraid because we tremble, and not that we cry, strike, or tremble, because we are sorry, angry, or fearful, as the case may be. Without the bodily states following on the perception, the latter would be purely cognitive in form, pale, colourless, destitute of emotional warmth. We might then see the bear, and judge it best to run, receive the insult and deem it right to strike, but we could not actually *feel* afraid or angry.

Stated in this crude way, the hypothesis is pretty sure to meet with immediate disbelief. And yet neither many nor far-fetched considerations are required to mitigate its paradoxical character, and possibly to produce conviction of its truth.

To begin with, readers ... do not need to be reminded that the nervous system of every living thing is but a bundle of predispositions to react in particular ways upon the contact of particular features of the environment. As surely as the hermit-crab's abdomen presupposes the existence of empty whelk-shells somewhere to be found, so surely do the hound's olfactories imply the existence, on the one hand, of deer's or foxes' feet, and on the other, the tendency to follow up their tracks. The neural machinery is but a hyphen between determinate arrangements of matter outside the body and determinate impulses to inhibition or discharge within its organs. When the hen sees a white oval object on the ground, she cannot leave it; she must keep upon it and return to it, until at last its transformation into a little mass of moving chirping down elicits from her machinery an entirely new set of performances. The love of man for woman, or of the human mother for her babe, our wrath at snakes and our fear of precipices, may all be described similarly, as instances of the way in which peculiarly conformed pieces of the world's furniture will fatally call forth most particular mental and bodily reactions, in advance of, and often in direct opposition to, the verdict of our deliberate reason concerning them. The labours of Darwin and his successors are only just beginning to reveal the universal parasitism of each special creature upon other special things, and the way in which each creature brings the signature of its special relations stamped on its nervous system with it upon the scene.

Every living creature is in fact a sort of lock, whose wards and springs presuppose special forms of key,—which keys however are not born attached to the locks, but are sure to be found in the world near by as life goes on. And the locks are indifferent to any but their own keys. The egg fails to fascinate the hound, the bird does not fear the precipice, the snake waxes not wroth at his kind, the deer cares nothing for the woman or the human babe....

Now among these nervous anticipations are of course to be reckoned the emotions, so far as these may be called forth directly by the perception of certain facts. In advance of all experience of elephants no child can but be frightened if he suddenly find one trumpeting and charging upon him. No woman can see a handsome little naked baby without delight, no man in the wilderness see a human form in the distance without excitement and curiosity. I said I should consider these emotions only so far as they have bodily movements of some sort for their accompaniments. But my first point is to show that their bodily accompaniments are much more far-reaching and complicated than we ordinarily suppose.

In the earlier books on Expression, written mostly from the artistic point of view, the signs of emotion visible from without were the only ones taken account of. Sir Charles Bell's celebrated *Anatomy of Expression* noticed the respiratory changes; and Bain's and Darwin's treatises went more thoroughly still into the study of the visceral factors involved,—changes in the functioning of glands and muscles, and in that of the circulatory apparatus. But not even a Darwin has exhaustively enumerated *all* the bodily affections characteristic of any one of the standard emotions. More and more, as physiology advances, we begin to discern how almost infinitely numerous and subtle they must be. The researches of Mosso with the plethysmograph have shown that not only the heart, but the entire circulatory system, forms a sort of sounding-board, which every change of our consciousness, however slight, may make reverberate. Hardly a sensation comes to us without sending waves of alternate constriction and dilatation down the arteries of our arms. The blood-vessels of the abdomen act reciprocally with those of the more outward parts. The bladder and bowels, the glands of the mouth, throat, and skin, and the liver, are known to be affected gravely in certain severe emotions, and are unquestionably affected transiently when the emotions are of a lighter sort. That the heart-beats and the rhythm of breathing play a leading part in all emotions whatsoever, is a matter too notorious for proof. And what is really equally prominent, but less likely to be admitted until special attention is drawn to the fact, is the continuous co-operation of the voluntary muscles in our emotional states. Even when no change of outward attitude is produced, their inward tension alters to suit each varying mood, and is felt as a difference of tone or of strain. In depression the flexors tend to prevail; in elation or belligerent excitement the extensors take the lead. And the various permutations and combinations of which these organic activities are susceptible, make it abstractly possible that no shade of emotion, however slight, should be without a bodily reverberation as unique, when taken in its totality, as is the mental mood itself.

The immense number of parts modified in each emotion is what makes it so difficult for us to reproduce in cold blood the total and integral expression of any one of them. We may catch the trick with the voluntary muscles, but fail with the skin, glands, heart, and other viscera. Just as an artificially imitated sneeze lacks something of the reality, so the attempt to imitate an emotion in the absence of its normal instigating cause is apt to be rather "hollow."

The next thing to be noticed is this, that every one of the bodily changes, whatsoever it be, is *felt,* acutely or obscurely, the moment it occurs. If the reader has never paid attention to this matter, he will be both interested and astonished to learn how many different local bodily feelings he can detect in himself as characteristic of his various emotional moods. It would be perhaps too much to expect him to arrest the tide of any strong gust of passion for the sake of any such curious analysis as this; but he can observe more tranquil states, and that may be assumed here to be true of the greater which is shown to be true of the less. Our whole cubic capacity is sensibly alive; and each morsel of it contributes its pulsations of feeling, dim or sharp, pleasant, painful, or dubious, to that sense of personality that every one of us unfailingly carries with him. It is surprising what little items give accent to these complexes of sensibility. When worried by any slight trouble, one may find that the focus of one's bodily consciousness is the contraction, often quite inconsiderable, of the eyes and brows. When momentarily embarrassed, it is something in the pharynx that compels either a swallow, a clearing of the throat, or a slight cough; and so on for as many more instances as might be named. Our concern here being with the general view rather than with the details, I will not linger to discuss these but, assuming the point admitted that every change that occurs must be felt, I will pass on.

I now proceed to urge the vital point of my whole theory, which is this. If we fancy some strong emotion, and then try to abstract from our consciousness of it all the feelings of its characteristic bodily symptoms, we find we have nothing left behind, no "mind-stuff" out of which the emotion can be constituted, and that a cold and neutral state of intellectual perception is all that remains. It is true, that although most people, when asked, say that their introspection verifies this statement, some persist in saying theirs does not. Many cannot be made to understand the question. When you beg them to imagine away every feeling of laughter and of tendency to laugh from their consciousness of the ludicrousness of an object, and then to tell you what the feeling of its ludicrousness would be like, whether it be anything more than the perception that the object belongs to the class "funny," they persist in replying that the thing proposed is a physical impossibility, and that they always *must* laugh, if they see a funny object. Of course the task proposed is not the practical one of seeing a ludicrous object and annihilating one's tendency to laugh. It is the purely speculative one of subtracting certain elements of feeling from an emotional state supposed to exist in its fulness, and saying what the residual elements are. I cannot help thinking that all who rightly apprehend this problem will agree with the proposition above laid down. What kind of an emotion of fear would be left, if the feelings neither of quickened heart-beats nor of shallow breathing, neither of trembling lips nor of weakened limbs, neither of goose-flesh nor of visceral stirrings, were present, it is quite impossible to think. Can one fancy the state of rage and picture no ebullition of it in the chest, no flushing of the face, no dilatation of the nostrils, no clenching of the teeth, no impulse to vigorous action, but in their stead limp muscles, calm breathing, and a placid face? The present writer, for one, certainly cannot. The rage is as completely evaporated as the sensation of its so-called manifestations, and the only thing that can possibly be supposed to take its place is some cold-blooded and dispassionate judicial sentence, confined entirely to the intellectual realm, to the effect that a certain person or persons merit chastisement for their sins. In like manner of grief: what would it be without its tears, its sobs, its suffocation of the heart, its pang in the breast-bone? A feelingless cognition that certain circumstances are deplorable, and nothing more. Every passion in turn tells the same story. A purely disembodied human emotion is a nonentity. I do not say that it is a contradiction in the nature of things, or that pure spirits are necessarily condemned to cold intellectual lives; but I say that for *us,* emotion dissociated from all bodily feeling is inconceivable. The more closely I scrutinise my states, the more persuaded I become, that whatever moods, affections, and passions I have, are in very truth constituted by, and made up of, those bodily changes we ordinarily call their expression or consequence; and the more it seems to me that if I were to become corporeally anæsthetic, I should be excluded from the life of the affections, harsh and tender alike, and drag out an existence of merely cognitive or intellectual form. Such an existence, although it seems to have been the ideal of ancient sages, is too apathetic to be keenly sought after by those born after the revival of the worship of sensibility, a few generations ago.

But if the emotion is nothing but the feeling of the reflex bodily effects of what we call its "object," effects due to the connate adaptation of the nervous system to that object, we seem immediately faced by this objection: most of the objects of civilised men's emotions are things to which it would be preposterous to suppose their nervous systems connately adapted. Most occasions of shame and many insults are purely conventional, and vary with the social environment. The same is true of many matters of dread and of desire, and of many occasions of melancholy and regret. In these cases, at least, it would seem that the ideas of shame, desire, regret, &c., must first have been attached by education and association to these conventional objects before the bodily changes could possibly be awakened. And if in *these* cases the bodily changes follow the ideas, instead of giving rise to them, why not then in all cases?

To discuss thoroughly this objection would carry us deep into the study of purely intellectual Æsthetics. A few words must here suffice. We will say nothing of the argument's failure to distinguish between the idea of an emotion and the emotion itself. We will only recall the well-known evolutionary principle that when a certain power has once been fixed in an animal by virtue of its utility in presence of certain features of the environment, it may turn out to be useful in presence of other features of the environment that had originally nothing to do with either producing or preserving it. A nervous tendency to discharge being once there, all sorts of unforeseen things may pull the trigger and let loose the effects. That among these things should be conventionalities of man's contriving is a matter of no psychological consequence whatever. The most important part of my environment is my fellow-man. The consciousness of his attitude towards me is the perception that normally unlocks most of my shames and indignations and fears. The extraordinary sensitiveness of this consciousness is shown by the bodily modifications wrought in us by the awareness that our fellow-man is noticing us *at all*. No one can walk across the platform at a public meeting with just the same muscular innervation he uses to walk across his room at home. No one can give a message to such a meeting without organic excitement. "Stage-fright" is only the extreme degree of that wholly irrational personal self-consciousness which every one gets in some measure, as soon as he feels the eyes of a number of strangers fixed upon him, even though he be inwardly convinced that their feeling towards him is of no practical account. This being so, it is not surprising that the additional persuasion that my fellow-man's attitude means either well or ill for me, should awaken stronger emotions still. In primitive societies "Well" may mean handing me a piece of beef, and "Ill" may mean aiming a blow at my skull. In our "cultured age," "Ill" may mean cutting me in the street, and "Well," giving me an honorary degree. What the action itself may be is quite insignificant, so long as I can perceive in it intent or *animus*. *That* is the emotion-arousing perception; and may give rise to as strong bodily convulsions in me, a civilised man experiencing the treatment of an artificial society, as in any savage prisoner of war, learning whether his captors are about to eat him or to make him a member of their tribe.

But now, this objection disposed of, there arises a more general doubt. Is there any evidence, it may be asked, for the assumption that particular perceptions *do* produce wide-spread bodily effects by a sort of immediate physical influence, antecedent to the arousal of an emotion or emotional idea?

The only possible reply is, that there is most assuredly such evidence. In listening to poetry, drama, or heroic narrative, we are often surprised at the cutaneous shiver which like a sudden wave flows over us, and at the heartswelling and the lachrymal effusion that unexpectedly catch us at intervals. In listening to music, the same is even more strikingly true. If we abruptly see a dark moving form in the woods, our heart stops beating, and we catch our breath instantly and before any articulate idea of danger can arise. If our friend goes near to the edge of a precipice, we get the well-known feeling of "all-overishness," and we shrink back, although we positively *know* him to be safe, and have no distinct imagination of his fall. The writer well remembers his astonishment, when a boy of seven or eight, at fainting when he saw a horse bled. The blood was in a bucket, with a stick in it, and, if memory does not deceive him, he stirred it round and saw it drip from the stick with no feeling save that of childish curiosity. Suddenly the world grew black before his eyes, his ears began to buzz, and he knew no more. He had never heard of the sight of blood producing faintness or sickness, and he had so little repugnance to it, and so little apprehension of any other sort of danger from it, that even at that tender age, as he well remembers, he could not help wondering how the mere physical presence of a pailful of crimson fluid could occasion in him such formidable bodily effects.

Imagine two steel knife-blades with their keen edges crossing each other at right angles, and moving too and fro. Our whole nervous organisation is "on-edge" at the thought; and yet what emotion can be there except the unpleasant nervous feeling itself, or the dread that more of it may come? The entire fund and capital of the emotion here is the senseless bodily effect the blades immediately arouse. This case is typical of a class: where an ideal emotion seems to precede the bodily symptoms, it is often nothing but a representation of the symptoms themselves. One who has already fainted at the sight of blood may witness the preparations for a surgical operation with uncontrollable heart-sinking and anxiety. He anticipates certain feelings, and the anticipation precipitates their arrival. I am told of a case of morbid terror, of which the subject confessed that what possessed her seemed, more than anything, to be the fear of fear itself. In the various forms of what Professor Bain calls "tender emotion," although the appropriate object must usually be directly contemplated before the emotion can be aroused, yet sometimes thinking of the symptoms of the emotion itself may have the same effect. In sentimental natures, the thought of "yearning" will produce real "yearning." And, not to speak of coarser examples, a mother's imagination of the caresses she bestows on her child may arouse a spasm of parental longing.

In such cases as these, we see plainly how the emotion both begins and ends with what we call its effects or manifestations. It has no mental *status* except as either the presented feeling, or the idea, of the manifestations; which latter thus constitute its entire material, its sum and substance, and its stock-in-trade. And these cases ought to make us see how in all cases the feeling of the manifestations may play a much deeper part in the constitution of the emotion than we are wont to suppose.

If our theory be true, a necessary corollary of it ought to be that any voluntary arousal of the so-called manifestations of a special emotion ought to give us the emotion itself. Of course in the majority of emotions, this test is inapplicable; for many of the manifestations are in organs over which we have no volitional control. Still, within the limits in which it can be verified, experience fully corroborates this test. Everyone knows how panic is increased by flight, and how the giving way to the symptoms of grief or anger increases those passions themselves. Each fit of sobbing makes the sorrow more acute, and calls forth another fit stronger still, until at last repose only ensues with lassitude and with the apparent exhaustion of the machinery. In rage, it is notorious how we "work ourselves up" to a climax by repeated outbreaks of expression. Refuse to express a passion, and it dies. Count ten before venting your anger, and its occasion seems ridiculous. Whistling to keep up courage is no mere figure of speech. On the other hand, sit all day in a moping posture, sigh, and reply to everything with a dismal voice, and your melancholy lingers. There is no more valuable precept in moral education than this, as all who have experience know: if we wish to conquer undesirable emotional tendencies in ourselves, we must assiduously, and in the first instance cold-bloodedly, go through the *outward motions* of those contrary dispositions we prefer to cultivate. The reward of persistency will infallibly come, in the fading out of the sullenness or depression, and the advent of real cheerfulness and kindliness in their stead. Smooth the brow, brighten the eye, contract the dorsal rather than the ventral aspect of the frame, and speak in a major key, pass the genial compliment, and your heart must be frigid indeed if it do not gradually thaw!

The only exceptions to this are apparent, not real. The great emotional expressiveness and mobility of certain persons often lead us to say "They would feel more if they talked less." And in another class of persons, the explosive energy with which passion manifests itself on critical occasions, seems correlated with the way in which they bottle it up during the intervals. But these are only eccentric types of character, and within each type the law of the last paragraph prevails. The sentimentalist is so constructed that "gushing" is his or her normal mode of expression. Putting a stopper on the "gush" will only to a limited extent cause more "real" activities to take its place; in the main it will simply produce listlessness. On the other hand the ponderous and bilious "slumbering volcano," let him repress the expression of his passions as he will, will find them expire if they get no vent at all; whilst if the rare occasions multiply which he deems worthy of their outbreak, he will find them grow in intensity as life proceeds.

I feel persuaded there is no real exception to the law. The formidable effects of suppressed tears might be mentioned, and the calming results of speaking out your mind when angry and having done with it. But these are also but specious wanderings from the rule. Every perception must lead to *some* nervous result. If this be the normal emotional expression, it soon expends itself, and in the natural course of things a calm succeeds. But if the normal issue be blocked from any cause, the currents may under certain circumstances invade other tracts, and there work different and worse effects. Thus vengeful brooding may replace a burst of indignation; a dry heat may consume the frame of one who fain would weep, or he may, as Dante says, turn to stone within; and then tears or a storming-fit may bring a grateful relief. When we teach children to repress their emotions, it is not that they may *feel* more, quite the reverse. It is that they may *think* more; for to a certain extent whatever nerve-currents are diverted from the regions below, must swell the activity of the thought-tracts of the brain.

The last great argument in favour of the priority of the bodily symptoms to the felt emotion, is the ease with which we formulate by its means pathological cases and normal cases under a common scheme. In every asylum we find examples of absolutely unmotived fear, anger, melancholy, or conceit; and others of an equally unmotived apathy which persists in spite of the best of outward reasons why it should give way. In the former cases we must suppose the nervous machinery to be so "labile" in some one emotional direction, that almost every stimulus, however inappropriate, will cause it to upset in that way, and as a consequence to engender the particular complex of feelings of which the psychic body of the emotion consists. Thus, to take one special instance, if inability to draw deep breath, fluttering of the heart, and that peculiar epigastric change felt as "precordial anxiety," with an irresistible tendency to take a somewhat crouching attitude and to sit still, and with perhaps other visceral processes not now known, all spontaneously occur together in a certain person; his feeling of their combination *is* the emotion of dread, and he is the victim of what is known as morbid fear. A friend who has had occasional attacks of this most distressing of all maladies, tells me that in his case the whole drama seems to centre about the region of the heart and respiratory apparatus, that his main effort during the attacks is to get control of his inspirations and to slow his heart, and that the moment he attains to breathing deeply and to holding himself erect, the dread, *ipso facto,* seems to depart.

If our hypothesis be true, it makes us realise more deeply than ever how much our mental life is knit up with our corporeal frame, in the strictest sense of the term. Rapture, love, ambition, indignation, and pride, considered as feelings, are fruits of the same soil with the grossest bodily sensations of pleasure and of pain. But it was said at the outset that this would be affirmed only of what we then agreed to call the "standard" emotions; and that those inward sensibilities that appeared devoid at first sight of bodily results should be left out of our account. We had better, before closing, say a word or two about these latter feelings.

They are, the reader will remember, the moral, intellectual, and æsthetic feelings. Concords of sounds, of colours, of lines, logical consistencies, teleological fitnesses, affect us with a pleasure that seems ingrained in the very form of the representation itself, and to borrow nothing from any reverberation surging up from the parts below the brain. The Herbartian psychologists have tried to distinguish feelings due to the *form* in which ideas may be arranged. A geometrical demonstration may be as "pretty," and an act of justice as "neat" as a drawing or a tune, although the prettiness and neatness seem here to be a pure matter of sensation, and there to have nothing to do with sensation. We have then, or some of us seem to have, genuinely *cerebral* forms of pleasure and displeasure, apparently not agreeing in their mode of production with the so-called "standard" emotions we have been analysing. And it is certain that readers whom our reasons have hitherto failed to convince, will now start up at this admission, and consider that by it we give up our whole case. Since musical perceptions, since logical ideas, can immediately arouse a form of emotional feeling, they will say, is it not more natural to suppose that in the case of the so-called "standard" emotions, prompted by the presence of objects or the experience of events, the emotional feeling is equally immediate, and the bodily expression something that comes later and is added on?

But a sober scrutiny of the cases of pure cerebral emotion gives little force to this assimilation. Unless in them there actually be coupled with the intellectual feeling a bodily reverberation of some kind, unless we actually laugh at the neatness of the mechanical device, thrill at the justice of the act, or tingle at the perfection of the musical form, our mental condition is more allied to a judgment of right than to anything else. And such a judgment is rather to be classed among awarenesses of truth: it is a *cognitive* act. But as a matter of fact the intellectual feeling hardly ever does exist thus unaccompanied. The bodily sounding-board is at work, as careful introspection will show far more than we usually suppose. Still, where long familiarity with a certain class of effects has blunted emotional sensibility thereto as much as it has sharpened the taste and judgment, we do get the intellectual emotion, if such it can be called, pure and undefiled. And the dryness of it, the paleness, the absence of all glow, as it may exist in a thoroughly expert critic's mind, not only shows us what an altogether different thing it is from the "standard" emotions we considered first, but makes us suspect that almost the entire difference lies in the fact that the bodily sounding-board, vibrating in the one case, is in the other mute. "Not so very bad" is, in a person of consummate taste, apt to be the highest limit of approving expression. "*Rien ne me choque*" is said to have been Chopin's superlative of praise of new music. A sentimental layman would feel, and ought to feel, horrified, on being admitted into such a critic's mind, to see how cold, how thin, how void of human significance, are the motives for favour or disfavour that there prevail. The capacity to make a nice spot on the wall will outweigh a picture's whole content; a foolish trick of words will preserve a poem; an utterly meaningless fitness of sequence in one musical composition set at naught any amount of "expressiveness" in another.

I remember seeing an English couple sit for more than an hour on a piercing February day in the Academy at Venice before the celebrated "Assumption" by Titian; and when I, after being chased from room to room by the cold, concluded to get into the sunshine as fast as possible and let the pictures go, but before leaving drew reverently near to them to learn with what superior forms of susceptibility they might be endowed, all I overheard was the woman's voice murmuring: "What a *deprecatory* expression her face wears! What self-abneg*ation!* How *unworthy* she feels of the honour she is receiving!" Their honest hearts had been kept warm all the time by a glow of spurious sentiment that would have fairly made old Titian sick. Mr. Ruskin somewhere makes the (for him) terrible admission that religious people as a rule care little for pictures, and that when they do care for them they generally prefer the worst ones to the best. Yes! in every art, in every science, there is the keen perception of certain relations being *right* or not, and there is the emotional flush and thrill consequent thereupon. And these are two things, not one. In the former of them it is that experts and masters are at home. The latter accompaniments are bodily commotions that they may hardly feel, but that may be experienced in their fulness by *Crétins* and Philistines in whom the critical judgment is at its lowest ebb. The "marvels" of Science, about which so much edifying popular literature is written, are apt to be "caviare" to the men in the laboratories. Cognition and emotion are parted even in this last retreat,— who shall say that their antagonism may not just be one phase of the world-old struggle known as that between the spirit and the flesh?— a struggle in which it seems pretty certain that neither party will definitively drive the other off the field.

To return now to our starting-point, the physiology of the brain. If we suppose its cortex to contain centres for the perception of changes in each special sense-organ, in each portion of the skin, in each muscle, each joint, and each viscus, and to contain absolutely nothing else, we still have a scheme perfectly capable of representing the process of the emotions. An object falls on a sense-organ and is apperceived by the appropriate cortical centre; or else the latter, excited in some other way, gives rise to an idea of the same object. Quick as a flash, the reflex currents pass down through their preordained channels, alter the condition of muscle, skin and viscus; and these alterations, apperceived like the original object, in as many specific portions of the cortex, combine with it in consciousness and transform it from an object-simply-apprehended into an object-emotionally-felt. No new principles have to be invoked, nothing is postulated beyond the ordinary reflex circuit, and the topical centres admitted in one shape or another by all to exist.

It must be confessed that a crucial test of the truth of the hypothesis is quite as hard to obtain as its decisive refutation. A case of complete internal and external corporeal anæsthesia, without motor alteration or alteration of intelligence except emotional apathy, would afford, if not a crucial test, at least a strong presumption, in favour of the truth of the view we have set forth; whilst the persistence of strong emotional feeling in such a case would completely overthrow our case. Hysterical anæsthesias seem never to be complete enough to cover the ground. Complete anæsthesias from organic disease, on the other hand, are excessively rare. In the famous case of Remigius Leims, no mention is made by the reporters of his emotional condition, a circumstance which by itself affords no presumption that it was normal, since as a rule nothing ever *is* noticed without a pre-existing question in the mind. Dr. Georg Winter has recently described a case somewhat similar, and in reply to a question, kindly writes to me as follows:—"The case has been for a year and a half entirely removed from my observation. But so far as I am able to state, the man was characterised by a certain mental inertia and indolence. He was tranquil, and had on the whole the temperament of a phlegmatic. He was not irritable, not quarrelsome, went quietly about his farm-work, and left the care of his business and housekeeping to other people. In short, he gave one the impression of a placid countryman, who has no interests beyond his work." Dr. Winter adds that in studying the case he paid no particular attention to the man's psychic condition, as this seemed *"nebensächlich"* to his main purpose. I should add that the form of my question to Dr. Winter could give him no clue as to the kind of answer I expected.

Of course, this case proves nothing, but it is to be hoped that asylum-physicians and nervous specialists may begin methodically to study the relation between anæsthesia and emotional apathy. If the hypothesis here suggested is ever to be definitively confirmed or disproved it seems as if it must be by them, for they alone have the data in their hands.

Walter B. Cannon

(1871-1945)

INTRODUCTION

Walter Cannon, a leading American physiologist, received his medical degree from Harvard University in 1900, and held the position of Higginson professor of physiology at Harvard from 1906 until he retired in 1942. His studies of shock during World War I and his later research on the endocrine system led to his developing the theory of homeostasis, that is, that ongoing physiological processes serve to maintain the stability of bodily systems.

Cannon's work on the physiology of the gastrointestinal tract (summarized in his 1911 paper, "The Mechanical Factors of Digestion") led quite naturally to a more general interest in the bodily changes associated not only with hunger, but also with pain, fear, rage, and other intense emotions. A four-year study at the Harvard Physiological Laboratory culminated in his major work, *Bodily Changes in Pain, Hunger, Fear and Rage,* in which he demonstrates how the physiological changes associated with these states contribute to the individual's welfare and self-preservation. Following publication of this work, Cannon realized how his results could be used to critique the James-Lange theory of emotion. Although in formulating their theory James and Lange described the physiological changes that occur during emotional states, neither conducted experiments to confirm the truth of their thesis that emotions are nothing but the perception of these physiological changes. James, for instance, merely argued that in imagining an emotion without its attendant physiological changes, one inevitably loses sight of the emotion itself. Walter Cannon, however, tested this claim experimentally, reporting his results in the second edition of *Bodily Changes in Pain, Hunger, Fear and Rage*. He confirmed the correlation between emotion and visceral disturbances; but, on the basis of experiments specifically designed to test the James-Lange theory, concluded that emotions cannot be simply the perception of these visceral disturbances. Excerpted below is Cannon's forceful attack on the James-Lange theory.

From Bodily Changes in Pain, Hunger, Fear and Rage

A Critical Examination of the James-Lange Theory of Emotions

The famous theory of emotions associated with the names of James and Lange was propounded by them independently. James first presented his view in 1884, Lange's monograph appeared in Danish in 1885. The cardinal points in their respective ideas of the nature of emotions are so well known that for purposes of comment only brief references need be made to them. James' theory may be summarized, in nearly his own terms, as follows. An object stimulates one or more sense organs; afferent impulses pass to the cortex and the object is perceived; thereupon currents run down to muscles and viscera and alter them in complex ways; afferent impulses from these disturbed organs course back to the cortex and when there perceived transform the "object-simply-apprehended" to the "object-emotion-ally-felt." In other words, "the feeling of the bodily changes as they occur is the emotion—the common sensational, associational and motor elements explain all." The main evidence cited for the theory is that we are aware of the tensions, throbs, flushes, pangs, suffocations—we feel them, indeed, the moment they occur—and that if we should take away from the picture of a fancied emotion these bodily symptoms, nothing would be left.

According to Lange stimulation of the vasomotor center is "the root of the causes of the affections, however else they may be con-

[handwritten margin annotations: "James's theory that Cannon tries to disprove"]

stituted." We owe all the emotional side of our mental life," he wrote, "our joys and sorrows, our happy and unhappy hours, to our vasomotor system. If the impressions which fall upon our senses did not possess the power of stimulating it, we would wander through life unsympathetic and passionless, all impressions of the outer world would only enrich our experience, increase our knowledge, but would arouse neither joy nor anger, would give us neither care nor fear." Since we are unable to differentiate subjectively between feelings of a central and peripheral origin, subjective evidence is unreliable. But because wine, certain mushrooms, hashish, opium, a cold shower, and other agencies cause physiological effects which are accompanied by altered states of feeling, and because abstraction of the bodily manifestations from a frightened individual leaves nothing of his fear, the emotion is only a perception of changes in the body. It is clear that Lange had the same conception as James, but elaborated it on a much narrower basis—on changes in the circulatory system alone.

The backflow of impulses from the periphery, on which James relied to account for the richness and variety of emotional feeling, was assumed to arise from all parts of the organism, from the muscles and skin as well as the viscera. To the latter, however, he inclined to attribute the major rôle—on "the visceral and organic part of the expression," he wrote, "it is probable that the chief part of the felt emotion depends." We may distinguish, therefore, his two sources of the afferent stream. We shall now consider critically the visceral source. In connection therewith we shall comment on Lange's idea that the vasomotor center holds the explanation of emotional experience.

TOTAL SEPARATION OF THE VISCERA FROM THE CENTRAL NERVOUS SYSTEM DOES NOT ALTER EMOTIONAL BEHAVIOR

Sherrington transected the spinal cord and the vagus nerves of dogs so as to destroy any connection of the brain with the heart, the lungs, the stomach and the bowels, the spleen, the liver and other abdominal organs—indeed, to isolate all the structures in which formerly feelings were supposed to reside. Recently Lewis and Britton and I have succeeded in keeping cats in a healthy state for many months after removal of the entire sympathetic division of the autonomic system, the division which operates in great excitement. Thus all vascular reactions controlled by the vasomotor center were abolished; secretion from the adrenal medulla could no longer be evoked; the action of the stomach and intestines could not be inhibited, the hairs could not be erected, and the liver could not be called upon to liberate sugar into the blood stream. These extensively disturbing operations had little if any effect on the emotional responses of the animals. In one of Sherrington's dogs, having a "markedly emotional temperament," the surgical reduction of the sensory field caused no obvious change in her emotional behavior; "her anger, her joy, her disgust, and when provocation arose, her fear, remained as evident as ever." And in the sympathectomized cats all superficial signs of rage were manifested in the presence of a barking dog—hissing, growling, retraction of the ears, showing of the teeth, lifting of the paw to strike—*except* erection of the hairs. Both sets of animals behaved with full emotional expression in all the organs still connected with the brain; the only failure was in organs disconnected. The absence of reverberation from the viscera did not alter in any respect the appropriate emotional display; its only abbreviation was surgical.

As Sherrington has remarked, with reference to his head-and-shoulder dogs, it is difficult to think that the perception initiating the wrathful expression should bring in sequel angry conduct and yet have been impotent to produce "angry feeling."

At this point interpretations differ. Angell has argued that Sherrington's experiments afford no evidence that visceral sensation plays no part in the emotional psychosis, and further that they do not prove that the psychic state, "emotion," precedes its "expression." And Perry has declared that whether, in the absence of sensations from the organs surgically isolated, the emotion is *felt* remains quite undecided.

It must be admitted, of course, that we have no real basis for either affirming or denying the presence of "felt emotion" in these reduced animals. We have a basis, however, for judging their relation to the James-Lange theory. James attributed the chief part of the felt emotion to sensations from the viscera, Lange attributed it wholly to sensations from the circulatory system. Both affirmed that if these organic sensations are removed *imaginatively* from an emotional experience nothing is left. Sherrington and the Harvard group varied this procedure by removing the sensations *surgically*. In their animals all visceral disturbances through sympathetic channels—the channels for nervous discharge in great excitement—were abolished. The possibility of return impulses by these channels, and in Sherrington's animals by vagus channels as well, were likewise abolished. According to James's statement of the theory the felt emotion should have very largely disappeared, and according to Lange's statement it should have wholly disappeared (without stimulation of our vasomotor system, it will be recalled, impressions of the outer world "would arouse neither joy nor anger, would give us neither care nor fear"). The animals *acted*, however, insofar as nervous connections permitted, with no lessening of the intensity of emotional display. In other words, operations which, in terms of the theory, largely or completely destroy emotional feeling, nevertheless leave the animals behaving as angrily, as joyfully, as fearfully as ever.

THE SAME VISCERAL CHANGES OCCUR IN VERY DIFFERENT EMOTIONAL STATES AND IN NON-EMOTIONAL STATES

The preganglionic fibers of the sympathetic division of the autonomic system are so related to the outlying neurones, as we have seen, that the resulting innervation of smooth muscles and glands throughout the body is not particular but diffuse. At the same time with the diffuse emission of sympathetic impulses adrenin is poured into the blood. Since it is thereby generally distributed to all parts and has the same effects as the sympathetic impulses wherever it acts, the humoral and the neural agents coöperate in producing diffuse effects. In consequence of these arrangements the sympathetic system goes into action as a unit—there may be minor variations as, for example, the presence or absence of sweating, but in the main features integration is characteristic.

The visceral changes wrought by sympathetic stimulation may be listed as follows: acceleration of the heart, contraction of arterioles, dilation of bronchioles, increase of blood sugar, inhibition of activity of the digestive glands, inhibition of gastro-intestinal peristalsis, sweating, discharge of adrenin, widening of the pupils and erection of hairs. These changes are seen in great excitement under any circumstances. They occur in such readily distinguishable emotional states as fear and rage. Fever and also exposure to cold are known to induce most of the changes—certainly a faster heart rate, vasocon-striction, increased blood sugar, discharge of adrenin and erection of the hairs. Asphyxia at the stimulating stage evokes all the changes enumerated above, with the possible exception of sweating. A too great reduction of blood sugar by insulin provokes the "hypoglyce-mic reaction"—characterized by pallor, rapid heart, dilated pupils, discharge of adrenin, increase of blood sugar and profuse sweating.

In this group of conditions which bring about in the viscera changes which are typical of sympathetic discharge are such intense and distinct emotions as fear and rage, such relatively mild affective states as those attending chilliness, hypoglycemia and difficult res-piration, and such a markedly different experience as that attending the onset of fever. The responses in the viscera seem too uniform to offer a satisfactory means of distinguishing emotions which are very different in subjective quality. Furthermore, if the emotions were due to afferent impulses from the viscera, we should expect not only that fear and rage would feel alike but that chilliness, hypoglycemia, asphyxia, and fever should feel like them. Such is not the case.

In commenting on this criticism of the James-Lange theory Angell admits that there may be a considerable matrix of substan-tially identical visceral excitement for some emotions, but urges that the differential features may be found in the extra-visceral distur-bances, particularly in the differences of tone in skeletal muscles. Perry likewise falls back on the conformation of the proprioceptive patterns, on the "motor set" of the expression, to provide the dis-tinctive elements of the various affective states. The possible contri-bution of skeletal muscles to the genesis of the felt emotion will be considered later. At present the fact may be emphasized that Lange derived no part of the emotional psychosis from that source; and James attributed to it a minor rôle—the chief part of the felt emotion depended on the visceral and organic part of the expression.

THE VISCERA ARE RELATIVELY INSENSITIVE STRUCTURES

There is a common belief that the more deeply the body is pene-trated the more sensitive does it become. Such is not the fact. Whereas in a spinal nerve trunk the sensory nerve fibers are probably always more numerous than the motor, in the nerves distributed to the viscera the afferent (sensory) fibers may be only one-tenth as numerous as the efferent. We are unaware of the contractions and relaxations of the stomach and intestines during digestion, of the rubbing of the stomach against the diaphragm, of the squeezing motions of the spleen, of the processes in the liver—only after long search have we learned what is occurring in these organs. Surgeons have found that the alimentary tract can be cut, torn, crushed or burned in operations on the unanesthetized human subject without evoking any feeling of discomfort. We can feel the thumping of the heart because it presses against the chest wall, we can also feel the throbbing of blood vessels because they pass through tissues well supplied with sensory nerves, and we may have abdominal pains but apparently because there are pulls on the parietal peritoneum. Normally the visceral processes are extraordinarily undemonstrative. And even when the most marked changes are induced in them, as when adrenalin acts, the results, as we shall see, are sensations mainly attributable to effects on the cardiovascular system.

VISCERAL CHANGES ARE TOO SLOW TO BE A SOURCE OF EMOTIONAL FEELING

The viscera are composed of smooth muscle and glands—except the heart, which is modified striate muscle. The motions of the body with which we are familiar result from quick-acting striate muscle, having a true latent period of less than 0.001 second. Notions of the speed of bodily processes acquired by observing the action of skeletal muscle we should not apply to other structures. Smooth muscle and glands respond with relative sluggishness. Although Stewart found that the latent period of smooth muscle of the cat was about 0.25 second, Sertoli observed that it lasted for 0.85 second in the dog and 0.8 second in the horse. Langley reported a latent period of 2 to 4 seconds on stimulating the *chorda tympani* nerve supply to the submaxillary salivary gland; and Pavlov a latent period of about 6 *minutes* on stimulating the vagus, the secretory nerve of the gastric glands. Again, Wells and Forbes noted that the latent period of the psychogalvanic reflex (in man), which appears to be a phenomenon due to sweat glands, was about 3 seconds.

In contrast to these long delays before peripheral action in visceral structures barely starts are the observations of Wells; he found that the latent period of affective reactions to pictures of men and women ended not uncommonly within 0.8 second. More recent studies with odors as stimuli have yielded a similar figure (personal communication). According to the James-Lange theory, however, these affective reactions result from reverberations from the viscera. But how is that possible? To the long latent periods of smooth muscles and glands, cited above, there must be added the time required for the nerve impulses to pass from the brain to the periphery and thence back to the brain again. It is clear that the organic changes could not occur soon enough to be the occasion for the appearance of affective states, certainly not the affective states studied by Wells.

ARTIFICIAL INDUCTION OF THE VISCERAL CHANGES TYPICAL OF STRONG EMOTIONS DOES NOT PRODUCE THEM

That adrenin acts in the body so as to mimic the action of sympathetic nerve impulses has repeatedly been mentioned. When injected directly into the blood stream or under the skin it induces dilation of the bronchioles, constriction of blood vessels, liberation of sugar from the liver, stoppage of gastro-intestinal functions, and other changes such as are characteristic of intense emotions. If the emotions are the consequence of the visceral changes we should reasonably expect them, in accordance with the postulates of the James-Lange theory, to follow these changes in all cases. Incidental observations on students who received injections of adrenalin sufficiently large to produce general bodily effects have brought out the fact that no specific emotion was experienced by them—a few who had been in athletic competitions testified to feeling "on edge," "keyed up," just as before a race. In a careful study of the effects of adrenin on a large number of normal and abnormal persons Marañon has reported that the subjective experiences included sensations of precardial or epigastric palpitation, of diffuse arterial throbbing, of oppression in the chest and tightness in the throat, of trembling, of chilliness, of dryness of the mouth, of nervousness, malaise and weakness. Associated with these sensations there was *in certain cases* an indefinite affective state coldly appreciated, and without real emotion. The subjects remarked, "I feel as if afraid," "as if awaiting a great joy," "as if moved," "as if I were going to weep without knowing why," "as if I had a great fright yet am calm," "as if they are about to do something to me." In other words, as Marañon remarks, a clear distinction is drawn "between the perception of the peripheral phenomena of vegetative emotion (i.e., the bodily changes) and the psychical emotion proper, which does not exist and which permits the subjects to report on the vegetative syndrome with serenity, without true feeling." In a smaller number of the affected cases a real emotion developed, usually that of sorrow, with tears, sobs and sighings. This occurs, however, "only when the emotional predisposition of the patient is very marked," notably in hyperthyroid cases. In some instances Marañon found that this state supervened only when the adrenin was injected after a talk with the patients concerning their sick children or their dead parents. In short, only when an emotional mood already exists does adrenalin have a supporting effect.

From the evidence adduced by Marañon we may conclude that adrenin induces in human beings typical bodily changes which are reported as sensations, that in some cases these sensations are reminiscent of previous emotional experiences but do not renew or revive those experiences, that in exceptional cases of preparatory emotional sensitization the bodily changes may tip the scales towards a true affective disturbance. These last cases are exceptional, however, and are not the usual phenomena as James and Lange supposed. In normal conditions the bodily changes, though well marked, do not provoke emotion.

The numerous events occurring in the viscera in consequence of great excitement, as detailed in earlier chapters, have been interpreted as supporting the James-Lange theory. From the evidence just presented it should be clear that that interpretation is unwarranted. Since visceral processes are fortunately not a considerable source of sensation, since even extreme disturbances in them yield no noteworthy emotional experience, we can further understand now why these disturbances cannot serve as a means for discriminating between such pronounced emotions as fear and rage, why chilliness, asphyxia, hyperglycemia and fever, though attended by these disturbances, are not attended by emotion, and also why total exclusion of visceral factors from emotional expression makes no difference in emotional behavior. It is because the returns from the thoracic and abdominal "sounding-board," to use James's word, are very faint indeed, that they play such a minor rôle in the affective complex. The processes going on in the thoracic and abdominal organs in consequence of sympathetic activity are truly remarkable and various; their value to the organism, however, is not to add richness and flavor to experience, but rather to adapt the internal economy so that in spite of shifts of outer circumstance the even tenor of the inner life will not be profoundly disturbed.

John Dewey

(1859-1952)

INTRODUCTION

An outstanding American philosopher, John Dewey, like William
James, was associated with the pragmatist movement in philosophy.
And also like James, his interests included theoretical and applied
psychology. Beginning his career as a schoolteacher, Dewey continued his interest in education, formulating an enormously influential
theory of education, which stressed the importance of problem-solving situations in developing the child's intelligence. For ten years he
headed the Dewey School, where he tested his psychological and
educational theories.

Dewey obtained his degree in philosophy in 1884 and went on to
teach philosophy at the University of Michigan, the University of
Chicago, and Columbia University. Central to his philosophical
thought was the notion of experience, and two of his major works
are *Experience and Nature* (1925) and *Art as Experience* (1934).
Dewey discounted earlier accounts of human experience that
focused primarily on thinking and knowing. For Dewey, experience
was primarily an interaction with one's environment; and thus,
doing and feeling were also significant experiences. Dewey analyzed
experience in terms of conflict and harmony: we constantly confront
conflict, doubt, and indeterminateness, which we then resolve. This
is as true of the scientist who explains an indeterminate body of data
by means of a hypothesis as of the person who deliberates and
decides on a course of action when faced with a moral conflict. Also
central to his account of experience is a denial of any radical dis-

tinction between the subjective and the objective. A frightened person, for example, experiences his situation as frightening; this emotional quality is a real quality of the situation. This view of experience lies at the heart of Dewey's theory of emotion and his criticisms of Darwin and James. In "The Theory of Emotion," published in 1894 and reprinted here, Dewey attacks Darwin for thinking that behavior *expresses* emotions. The person who jumps when startled does not, in fact, experience his jumping as an expression of fear; to him, it is a purposeful movement of avoiding a threatening object. Had Darwin paid more attention to the experience of emotion itself, he would not have made this mistake. Dewey also sharply criticizes James's theory (which equates emotion with the perception of physiological disturbances) for not explaining why emotions are so significant in our lives. To account for this, Dewey argues that emotions are experiences of the world—they are directed toward things in the environment that possess such emotional qualities as frightening, cheering, and saddening. In spite of these objections, Dewey incorporates elements from James's and Darwin's theories into his own theory. He adds Darwin's emphasis on the survival value of emotional behavior and James's emphasis on physiological disturbances to his own emphasis on the role of problem-solving in our experience of the world. As a result, Dewey argues that the physiological disturbances and overt behaviors that characterize a particular emotion are necessary in our dealing purposefully with an emotional situation. Thus, for instance, holding the breath, straining the attention, and preparing for flight are all movements of judicious caution in dealing with a frightening situation.

Dewey offers a three-part definition of emotion. Emotions include (1) a "quale" or "feel" (the *feeling* of fear, joy, sadness, etc.), (2) purposeful behavior, and (3) an object that has an emotional quality. Although his explanation of these features is sometimes unclear, Dewey's theory of emotion is surprisingly sophisticated and complex and worthy of serious attention.

From The Theory of Emotion

1. EMOTIONAL ATTITUDES

In the following pages I propose, assuming Darwin's principles as to the explanation of emotional attitudes, and the James-Lange theory of the nature of emotion, to bring these two into some organic connection with each other, indicating the modifications of statement demanded by such connection. . . .

The necessity of bringing the two theories together may be seen from the fact that the very phrase "expression of emotion," as well as Darwin's method of stating the matter, begs the question of the relation of emotion to organic peripheral action, in that it assumes the former as prior and the latter as secondary.

1. Now this assumption, upon the basis of the discharge theory (as I shall call the James-Lange theory), is false. If one accept the latter theory, it is incumbent upon him to find the proper method of restating Darwin's principles, since there is no doubt of their substantial significance, however erroneous may be their underlying assumption as to the relation of emotion and peripheral disturbance.

2. One does not, however, need to be committed to James's theory to feel the need of a different way of stating the particular undoubted facts discovered by Darwin. Physiologists agree that there are no muscles intended primarily for purposes of expression. A psychological translation of this would be that there is no such thing (from the standpoint of the one having the experience) as expression. We call it expression when looking at it from the standpoint of an observer—whether a spectator or the person himself as scientifically reflecting upon his movements, or æsthetically enjoying them. The very word "expression" names the facts not as they are, but in their second intention. To an onlooker my angry movements are expressions—signs, indications; but surely not to me. To rate such movements as primarily expressive is to fall into the psychologist's fallacy: it is to confuse the standpoint of the observer and explainer with that of the fact observed. Movements *are,* as matter of fact, expressive, but they are also a great many other things. In

themselves they are movements, acts, and must be treated as such if psychology is to take hold of them right end up.

3. I shall attempt to show, hereafter, that this standpoint of expression of pre-existent emotion complicates and aborts the explanation of the relevant facts in the cases of "antithesis" and "direct nervous discharge." At this stage I wish to point out that in the case of "serviceable associated habits," the principle of explanation *actually* used, whatever the form of words employed, is that of survival, in the form of attitudes, of acts originally useful not *qua* expressing emotion, but *qua* acts—as serving life. In the discussion of movements in animals (*Expression*, pp. 42–48) the reference to emotion is not even nominal. It is a matter of "satisfaction of desire" and "relieving disagreeable sensations"—practical ends. The expressions of grief and of anxiety are explained, in their detail, whatever the general phraseology employed, by reference to acts useful in themselves. . . . *The reference to emotion in explaining the attitude is wholly irrelevant; the attitude of emotion is explained positively by reference to useful movements.*

An examination of one apparent exception may serve to clear up the principle. Of laughter, Mr. Darwin says, "We can see in a vague manner how the utterance of sounds of some sort would naturally become associated with a pleasurable state of mind" (*Expression*, p. 207). But Darwin does not use this idea, even in a "vague" way. With his inevitable candor he goes on, "But why the sounds which man utters when he is pleased have the peculiar reiterated character of laughter we do not know."

Now I am not so rash as to attempt to deal in detail with laughter and its concomitant features, but I think something at least a little less vague than Mr. Darwin's account may be given. I cannot see, even in the vaguest way, why pleasure *qua* feeling (emotion?) should express itself in uttering sounds. As matter of fact it does not, nor even in smiles; it is pleasure of a certain qualitative excitement or vivacity which breaks out in laughter, and what we can see, in a "vague way," is why excitement affecting the entire organism should discharge in the vocal apparatus.

Why should the excitation, admitting that it affects the vocal organs, manifest itself in this form? While I feel pretty sure of the following explanation, I cannot hope that it will convince many.

Though the result of considerable observation, it can be briefly summed up. The laugh is by no means to be viewed from the standpoint of humor; its connection with humor is secondary. It marks the ending (that is, the attainment of a unity) of a period of suspense, or expectation, an ending which is sharp and sudden. Rhythmical activities, as peek-a-boo, call out a laugh at every culmination of the transition, in an infant. A child of from one and a half to two years uses the laugh as a sign of assent; it is his emphatic "I do" or "yes" to any suggested idea to which he agrees or which suddenly meets his expectations.

A very moderate degree of observation of adults will convince one that a large amount of laughter is wholly irrelevant to any joke or witticism whatever. It is a constant and repeated "sign" of attaining suddenly to a point. Now all expectancy, waiting, suspended effort, etc., is accompanied, for obvious teleological reasons, with taking in and holding a full breath, and the maintenance of the whole muscular system in a state of considerable tension. It is a divided activity, part of the kinaesthetic images being fixed upon the immediately present conditions, part upon the expected end. Now let the end suddenly "break," "dawn," let one see the "point" and this energy discharges-the getting the point is the unity, the discharge. This sudden relaxation of strain, so far as occurring through the medium of the breathing and vocal apparatus, is laughter. Its rhythmical character seems to be simply a phase of the general teleological principle that all well-arranged or economical action is rhythmical.

[On this interpretation] the phenomena of matured grief become easily explainable. They are phenomena of *loss*. Reactions surge forth to some stimulus, or phase of a situation; the object appropriate to most of these, the factor necessary to co-ordinate all the rising discharges, is gone; and hence they interfere with one another—the expectation, or kinæsthetic image, is thrown back upon itself.

4. In dealing with grief we have unconsciously entered upon a new field. The point of our third head is that the principle which Darwin calls that of "movements useful in expressing an emotion" explains the relevant facts only when changed to read "useful as parts of an act which is useful as movement." In dealing with grief we have passed over into the phenomena of the breakdown of a given teleological coordination, and the performance of acts which,

therefore, objectively viewed, are not only useless but may be harmful. My proposition at this point is that the phenomena referred to the principle of direct nervous discharge (the response to an idiopathic* stimulus) are cases of the failure of habitual teleological machinery, through some disturbance in one or more of the adjusted members of the habit.

In order to avoid misconception, let me point out a great ambiguity in the use of the term idiopathic. In one sense even the "associated useful" movements are idiopathic, provided, that is, they originally were useful in reaching an end, and not simply in expressing an emotion. They are the reactions to their appropriate stimuli, and the sole difference between them and the liver changes, nausea, palpitation of heart, etc., usually classed as idiopathic, is that in them stimuli and reaction are more definitely limited to certain particular channels than in the latter cases; there is a defined, as against a vague and diffuse, direct nervous discharge.

Admitting, then, that all emotional attitudes whatever are idiopathic in the broad sense, the sole difference being in the definiteness or limitation of the stimulus and its response, what are we to do with the cases now disposed of as "idiopathic" in the narrower sense?—such phenomena as Mr. James briefly but excellently sums up (*Psychology,* Vol. II). My proposition, I repeat, is that all such idiopathic discharges, possessing emotional quality, are in reality disturbances, defects, or alienations of the *adjusted* movements. While not immediately teleological in the sense that they themselves are useful, they are teleologically conditioned. They are cases of the disintegration of associations (co-ordinations) which are serviceable, or are the use of means under circumstances in which they are totally inappropriate.

Idiopathic discharges which are not themselves adjusted movements or the disturbances of such adjusted movements do not appear to me to have any *emotional* quality at all. The trembling with cold or sheer fatigue is certainly qualitatively different from the tremble of rage or fear. . . . The change from mere cachinnation to mirthful emotion is a distinct change in psychical quality, and this change of

---

*Spontaneous, peculiar, cause(s) unknown.

quality does not seem to be adequately *accounted* for by mere addition of more discharges. . . .

This is but to say, from the psychological side, that all normal emotion of terror has an *object*, and involves an attitude *towards* that object; this attitude, under the given circumstances, perhaps not being useful, nay, being harmful, but yet the reproduction of an attitude or, rather, a mixture of attitudes which have been useful in the past. The uselessness of the attitude is due to the fact that some feature in the stimulus (the situation or object) awakens its appropriate reactions, but these do not co-ordinate with the reactions aroused by other features of the situation. The pathological emotion is, as Mr. James calls it, the *objectless* emotion, but its content is controlled by the active attitudes previously assumed towards objects, and, *from its own standpoint,* it is not objectless; it goes on at once to supply itself with an object, with a rational excuse for being. This immediate correlation of the emotion with an "object," and its immediate tendency to assume the "object" when it is not there, seem to me mere tautology for saying that the emotional attitude is normally rational in content (i.e., adjusted to some end), and, even in pathological cases, sufficiently teleological in form to subsume an object for itself.

Coming a little more to details, it is obvious that the teleological principle carries within itself a certain limitation. Normal and usual are identical; the habit is based upon the customary features of the situation. The very meaning of habit is limitation to a certain average range of fluctuation. Now if an entirely strange (forgive the contradiction in terms) stimulus occurs, there will be no disturbance of function, though the organism may be destroyed by the impact of the foreign force. But let some of the features of a situation habitually associated in the past with other features be present while these others fail, or let the ordinary proportion or relative strength of stimuli be changed, or let their mode of connection be reversed, and there is bound to be a disturbance and a resulting activity which, *objectively viewed,* is non-teleological. We thus get an *a priori* canon, as it were, for determining when, in a given emotion, we shall get symptoms falling under the "serviceable associated habit" principle and when under the idiopathic. Whenever the various factors of the act, muscular movement, nutritive, respiratory, and circulatory changes, are co-ordinated and reinforce each other, it is the former;

whenever they interfere (the "idiopathic"), the "feel" of this interference *is* (applying the general principle of James) the pathological
rage, or terror, or expectation.

Once more, we work in a wrong, a hopeless direction when we
start from the emotion and attempt to derive the movements as its
expression; while the situation clears itself up when we start from
the character of the movement, as a completed or disturbed co-ordination, and then derive the corresponding types of normal and pathological emotion. We can understand why the so-called idiopathic
principle comes into play in all cases of extreme emotion, the max-
imum limit seeming to be the passage into spasm when it assumes a
rigid type, of hysteria when it involves complete breakdown of co-
ordination.

The attitude of normal fear may be accounted for upon direct
teleological principles; the holding of breath marks the effort; the
opening of mouth, the act arrested half-ways; the opening of eyes,
the strained attention; the shiver, of retraction; the crouching down,
the beginning of escape; the rapid beating of heart, the working up
of energy for escape, etc. Now if these activities go on to complete
themselves, if, that is, they suggest the further reaction which will
co-ordinate into a definite response, we get judicious fear—that is,
caution. Now if these do not suggest a further movement which
completes the act, some or all of these factors begin to assert themselves in consciousness, isolatedly or in alternation—there is confusion. Moreover, each particular phase of the act which is normal in
co-ordination, as the more rapid beating of the heart, being now
uncontrolled by lack of its relevant motor associates, is exaggerated
and becomes more and more violent. The response to the normal
demand for more nutrition finds no regular outlet in supplying the
motor-energy for the useful act, and the disturbances of viscera and
associated organs propagate themselves. The trembling marks, so far
as I can see, simply this same discoordination on the side of the muscular system. It is the extreme of vacillating indecision; we start to
do this, and the other thing, but each act falls athwart its
predecessor.

The pathological emotion is, then, simply a case of morbid self-
consciousness. Those factors of the organism which relate most
immediately to the welfare of the organism, the vegetative func-

tions, absorb consciousness, instead of being, as they normally are, subsidiary to the direction of muscular activity with reference to the "object." This is equally true in extreme terror, and in being "beside one's self" with anger. The cases in which sanguine excitement and apprehension affect the bladder will be found, I believe, to be almost uniformly cases where it is not possible to do anything at once with the aroused activities; they cannot be controlled by being directed towards the putting forth of effort upon the "object," that being too remote or uncertain. . . .

All these facts taken cumulatively seem to me to render it fairly certain that the "idiopathic" cases, as a rule, are to be conceived of as the starting of activities formerly useful for a given end, but which now, for some reason, fail to function, and therefore stand out in consciousness apart from the needed end.

5. I come now to the principle of antithesis. According to Mr. Darwin, when certain movements have been habitually of service in connection with certain emotions, there is a tendency, when a directly opposite state of mind is induced, to the performance of movements of a directly opposite nature, *"though these have never been of any use"* (*Expression,* italics mine). Here we have a crucial case; if the antithesis of the emotion determines the antithesis of expression, James's theory is, in so far, overthrown; if, on the other hand, the antithesis of "expression" goes back to activities having their own ends, the ground is at least cleared for the discharge theory.

Beginning with animals, Mr. Darwin illustrates his principle of antithesis from the cat and dog. No one can read his account or examine the pictures without being convinced that the movements *are* antithetical. But there is something intolerable to the psychologist in the supposition that an opposite emotion can somehow select for itself channels of discharge not already used for some specific end, and those channels such as give rise to directly opposed movements. Antithesis is made a causal force. Such an idea is not conceivable without some presiding genius who opens valves and pulls strings. . . .

If, again, the matter be treated as a case of the connection of movements with reference to certain acts, the mystery vanishes. Mr. Darwin's cases are taken from domestic animals. Now wild animals have, speaking roughly, just two fundamental characteristic attitudes—those connected with getting food, including attack upon enemies, and those of defense, including flight, etc. A domestic animal, by the very fact that it is domestic, has another characteristic attitude, that of reception—the attitude of complete adaptation to something outside itself. This attitude is constituted, of course, by a certain co-ordination of movements; and these are antithetical to those movements involved in the contrary attitude, that of resistance or opposition. . . . The attitude of "humility" and "affection" consists, as Mr. Darwin well says, in continuous, flexuous movements. These movements are precisely those of response and adaptation. The centre of gravity is, as it were, in the master, and the lithe and sinuous movement is the solution of the problem of maintaining balance with respect to every change in this external centre of gravity. It is the attitude of receiving favor and food from another. The dependence is actual, not symbolic. . . .

Summing up, we may say that all so-called expressions of emotions are, in reality, the reduction of movements and stimulations originally useful into attitudes. But we note a difference in the form and nature of the reduction, and in the resulting attitudes, which explain the apparent diversity of the four principles of "serviceable associated habits," of "analogous stimuli," of "antithesis," and of "direct nervous discharge." A given movement or set of movements may be useful either as preparatory to, as leading up to, another set of acts, or in themselves as accomplished ends. Movements of effort, of bracing, of reaching, etc., evidently come under the former head. Here we have the case of useful associated movements in its strict sense. The culmination of all these preparatory adjustments is the attainment of food, or of the sexual embrace. In so far as we have attitudes which reflect these acts, satisfying in themselves, we get cases of so-called analogous stimuli. The antithetical attitudes of joy and grief, and all that is differentiated from them, mark the further development of actual attainment of an end (or failure to get it), occurring when the activity specially appropriate to the particular end reached (or missed) is reinforced and expanded by a wide range of contributory muscular and visceral changes. The cases of failure bring us to the breakdown of co-ordinations habitually useful, to their alienation, or to reciprocal disturbance of their various factors, and thus to the facts usually subsumed under the idiopathic principle. In this progression we have a continually changing ratio of the vegetative to the motor functions. In the preparatory adjustments the latter has the highest exponent, and the strictly emotional *quale* of feeling is at its minimum. In joy and grief, as in less degree with "sweetness," disgust, etc., the organic resonance is at its height, but strictly subservient to the motor performances. In the idiopathic these vegetative functions break loose and run away, and thus, instead of reinforcing the efficiency of behavior, interfere by their absorption of consciousness.

In the following article I shall take up the discharge theory of the nature of emotion, and discuss it in the light of the conclusions now reached.

II. THE SIGNIFICANCE OF EMOTIONS

In [the] preceding article I endeavored to show that all the so-called expressions of emotion are to be accounted for not by reference to emotion, but by reference to movements having some use, either as direct survivals or as disturbances of teleological co-ordinations. I tried to show that, upon this basis, the various principles for explaining emotional attitudes may be reduced to certain obvious and typical *differentiæ* within the teleological movements. In the present paper I wish to reconsider the James-Lange, or discharge, theory of the nature of emotion from the standpoint thus gained; for if all emotions (considered as "emotional seizures," *Affect* or "feel," as I may term it) are constituted by the reflexion of the teleological attitude, the motor and organic discharges, into consciousness, the same principle which explains the attitude must serve to analyze the emotion.

The fact, if it be a fact, that all "emotional expression" is a phase of movements teleologically determined, and not a result of pre-existent emotion, is itself a strong argument for the discharge theory. I had occasion to point out in my previous article that the facts brought under the head of "antithesis" and "analogous stimuli" are absolutely unaccountable upon the central theory, and are matters of course upon the James theory. But this statement may be further generalized. If every emotional attitude is referred to useful acts, and if the emotion is *not* the reflex of such an act, where does it come in, and what is its relation to the attitude? The first half of the hypothesis prevents its being the antecedent of the attitude; the latter half of the hypothesis precludes its being the consequent. . . . I think, then, that logic fairly demands either the surrender of the "central" theory of emotion or else a refutation of the argument of the preceding paper, and a proof that emotional attitudes are to be explained by reference to emotion, and not by reference to acts.

More positively, this reference to serviceable movement in explanation of emotional attitudes, taken in connection with the hypothesis that the emotional "feel" is always due to the return wave of this attitude, supplies a positive tool for the analysis of emotion in general and of particular emotions in especial. . . . The general conclusion indicated regarding the nature of emotion is that:

Emotion in its entirety is a mode of behavior which is purposive, or has an intellectual content, and which also reflects itself into feeling or Affects, as the subjective valuation of that which is objectively expressed in the idea or purpose.

This formula, however, is no more than a putting together of James's theory with the revision of Darwin's principles attempted in the last number. If an attitude (of emotion) is the recurrence, in modified form, of some teleological movement, and if the specific differentia of emotional consciousness is the resonance of such attitude, then emotional excitation is the felt process of realization of ideas. The chief interest lies in making this formula more specific.

In the first place, this mode of getting at it relieves Mr. James's statement of the admittedly paradoxical air which has surrounded it. . . . He expressly refers to his task as "subtracting certain *elements of feeling* from an emotional state supposed to exist *in its fulness*" (italics mine). And in his article, he definitely states that he is speaking of an *Affect*, or emotional seizure. By this I understand him to mean that he is not dealing with emotion as a concrete whole of experience, but with an abstraction from the actual emotion of that element which gives it its differentia—its feeling *quale*, its "feel." As I understand it, he did not conceive himself as dealing with that state which we term "being angry," but rather with the peculiar "feel" which any one has when he is angry, an element which may be intellectually abstracted, but certainly has no existence by itself, or as full-fledged emotion-experience. . . .

What the whole condition of *being* angry, or hopeful or sorry may be, Mr. James nowhere says, nor does he indicate why or how the "feel" of anger is related to them. Hence the inference either that he is considering the whole emotion-experience in an inadequate way, or else—as Mr. Irons took it—that he is denying the very existence of emotion, reducing it to mere consciousness of bodily change as such. Certainly, even when we have admitted that the emotional differentia, or "feel," is the reverberation of organic changes following upon the motor response to stimulus, we have still to *place* this "feel" with reference to the other phases of the concrete emotion-experience. . . .

If, preparatory to attempting such a placing, we put before us the whole concrete emotional experience, we find, I think, that it has two phases beside that of *Affect,* or seizure. (1) It is a disposition, a mode of conduct, a way of behaving. Indeed, it is this practical aspect of emotion which common speech mainly means to refer to in its emotional terms. When we say that John Smith is very resentful at the treatment he has received, or is hopeful of success in business, or regrets that he accepted a nomination for office, we do not simply, or even chiefly, mean that he has a certain "feel" occupying his consciousness. We mean he is in a certain practical attitude, has assumed a readiness to act in certain ways. I should not fear a man who had simply the "feel" of anger, nor should I sympathize with one having simply the "feel" of grief. Grief means *unwillingness* to resume the normal occupation, practical discouragement, breaking-up of the normal reactions, etc., etc. Just as anger means a tendency to explode in a sudden attack, not a mere state of feeling. We certainly do not deny nor overlook the "feel" phase, but in ordinary speech the behavior side of emotion is, I think, always uppermost in consciousness. The connotation of emotion is primarily ethical, only secondarily psychical. Hence our insulted feeling when told (as we hastily read it—our interpretation is "slap-dash" rather than the sentence itself) that we are not angry until we strike, for the sudden readiness to injure another is precisely what we mean by anger. Let the statement read that we do not have the emotional seizure, the "feel" of anger, till we strike, or clench our fist, or have our blood boil, etc., and the statement not only loses its insultingly paradoxical quality, but (unless my introspection meets a different scene from that of others) is verified by every passing emotion. (2) But the full emotional experience also always has its "object" or intellectual content. The emotion is always "about" or "toward" something; it is "at" or "on account of" something, and this prepositional reference is an integral phase of the single pulse of emotion; for emotion, as well as the idea, comes as a whole carrying its distinctions of value within it. The child who ceases to be angry *at* something—were it only the floor at last—but who keeps up his kicking and screaming, has passed over into sheer spasm. It is then no more an emotion of anger than it is one of æsthetic appreciation. Disgust, terror, gratitude, sulkiness, curiosity—take all the emotions seriatim and see what they would be without the intrinsic reference to idea or object. Even the pathological or objectless emotion is so only to the rational spectator. To the experiencer (if I may venture the term) it subsumes at once its own object as source or aim. This feeling of depression must have its reason; the world is dark and gloomy; no one understands me; I have a dread disease; I have committed the unpardonable sin. This feeling of buoyancy must have its ideal reference; I am a delightful person, or one of the elect or have had a million dollars left me.

It is perhaps at this point that the need of some reconstruction which will enable us to place the phases of an entire emotional experience becomes most urgent. In Mr. James's statement the experience is apparently (apparently, I say; I do not know how much is due to the exigency of discussion which necessitates a seeming isolation) split up into three separate parts: First comes the object or idea which operates only as stimulus; secondly, the mode of behavior taken as discharge of this stimulus; third, the *Affect*, or emotional excitation, as the repercussion of this discharge. No such seriality or separation attaches to the emotion as an experience. Nor does reflective analysis seem to establish this order as the best expression of the emotion as an object of psychological abstraction. We might almost infer from the way Mr. James leaves it that he is here a believer in that atomic or mosaic composition of consciousness which he has so effectively dealt with in the case of intellectual consciousness. However this may be, Mr. James certainly supplies us, in the underlying *motif* of this "chapter" on emotion, with an adequate instrument of reconstruction. This is the thought that the organic discharge is an *instinctive* reaction, not a response to an idea as such.

Following the lead of this idea, we are easily brought to the con-clusion that *the mode of behavior is the primary thing, and that the idea and the emotional excitation are constituted at one and the same time; that, indeed, they represent the tension of stimulus and response within the co-ordination which makes up the mode of behavior.*

It is sheer reflective interpretation to say that the activity in anger is set up by the object, if we by object mean something consciously apprehended as object. This interpretation, if we force it beyond a mere way of speaking into the facts themselves, becomes a case of the psychological fallacy. If my bodily changes of beating heart, trembling and running legs, sinking in stomach, looseness of bowels, etc., follow from and grow out of the conscious recognition, *qua conscious recognition,* of a bear, then I see no way for it but that the bear is already a bear of which we are afraid—our idea must be of the bear as a fearful object. But if (as Mr. James's fundamental idea would imply, however his language may read at times) this reaction is not to the bear as *object,* nor to the *idea* of bear, but simply expresses an instinctive co-ordination of two organic tendencies, then the case is quite different. It is not the idea of the bear, or the bear as object, but a certain *act of seeing,* which by habit, whether inherited or acquired, sets up other acts. It is the kind of *co-ordination of acts* which, brought to sensational consciousness, constitutes the bear a fearful or a laughable or an indifferent object. The fol-lowing sentence, for example, from James seems to involve a mix-ture of his own theory with the one which he is engaged in com-bating: "Whatever be our reaction on the situation, in the last resort it is an *instinctive reaction* on that one of its elements which strikes us for the time being *as most vitally important.*" The conception of an instinctive reaction is the relevant idea; that of reaction upon an element "which strikes us as important" the incongruous idea. Does it strike us, *prior* to the reaction, as important? Then, most certainly, it already has emotional worth; the situation is already delightful and to be perpetuated, or terrible and to be fled, or whatever. What does recognition of importance mean aside from the ascription of worth, value—that is, aside from the projection of emotional experience? But I do not think James's expression in this and other similar pas-sages is to be taken literally. The reaction is not made on the basis of the apprehension of some quality in the object; it is made on the basis of an organized habit, of an organized co-ordination of activities, one of which instinctively stimulates the other. The outcome of this co-ordination of activities constitutes, for the first time, the object with such and such an import—terrible, delightful, etc.—or constitutes an emotion referring to such and such an object. For, we must insist once more, the frightful object and the emotion of fear are two names for the same experience.

Here, then, is our point of departure in placing the "feel," the "idea," and the "mode of behavior" in relation to one another. The idea or object which precedes and stimulates the bodily discharge is in no sense the idea or object (the intellectual content, the "at" or "on account of") of the emotion itself. The particular idea, the specific quality or object to which the seizure attaches, is just as much due to the discharge as is the seizure itself. More accurately and definitely, the idea or the object is an abstraction from the activity just as much as is the "feel" or seizure. We have certain organic activities initiated, say in the eye, stimulating, through organized paths of association in the brain, certain activities of hands, legs, etc., and (through the co-ordination of these motor activities with the vegetative functions necessary to maintain them) of lungs, heart, vasomotor system, digestive organs, etc. The "bear" is, psychologically, just as much a discrimination of certain values, within this total pulse or co-ordination of action, as is the feeling of "fear." The "bear" is constituted by the excitations of eye and co-ordinated touch centres, just as the "terror" is by the disturbances of muscular and glandular systems. The reality, the co-ordination of these partial activities, is that whole activity which may be described equally well as "that terrible bear," or "Oh, how frightened I am." It is precisely and identically the same actual concrete experience; and the "bear," considered as one experience, and the "fright," considered as another, are distinctions introduced in reflection upon this experience, not separate experience. It is the psychological fallacy again if the differences which result from the reflection are carried over into the experience itself. If the fright comes, then the bear is not the bear of that particular experience, is not the object to which the feeling attaches, *except* as the fright comes. Any other supposition is to confuse the abstract bear of science with the concrete (*just this*) bear of experience.

If, then, I may paraphrase Mr. James's phraseology, the statement would read as follows: Our customary analysis, reading over into the experience itself what we find by interpreting it, says we have an idea of the bear as something to be escaped, and so run away. The hypothesis here propounded is that the factors of a co-ordination (whether due to inherited instinct or to individually acquired habit) begin to operate and we run away; running away, we get the idea of "running-away-from-bear," or of "bear-as-thing-to-be-run-from." I suppose every one would admit that the complete, mature idea came only in and through the act of running, but might hold that an embryonic suggestion of running came before the running. I cannot disprove this position, but everything seems to point the other way. It is more natural to suppose that as the full idea of running away comes in from the full execution, so the vague suggestion comes through the vague starting-up-of the system, mediated by discharge from the centres. . . .

We return, then, confirmed, to our belief that the mode of behavior, or co-ordination of activities, constitutes the ideal content of emotion just as much as it does the *Affect* or "feel," and that the distinction of these two is not given in the experience itself, but simply in reflection upon the experience. The mode of action constituted by the organic co-ordination of certain sensori-motor (or ideo-motor) activities, on one side, and of certain vegetative-motor activities on the other, is the reality, and this reality has a value, which, when interpreted, we call intellectual, and a value which, when interpreted we call Affect, or "feel." In the terms of our illustration, the mode of behavior carried with it the concept of the bear as a thing to be acted towards in a certain way, and of the "feel" of our reaction. It is brown and chained—a "beautiful" object to be looked at. It is soft and fluffy—an "æsthetic" object to be felt of. It is tame and clumsy—an "amusing" object to while away time with. It is hungry and angry—and is a "ferocious" object to be fled. The consciousness of our mode of behavior as affording data for other possible actions constitutes the bear an objective or ideal content. The consciousness of the mode of behavior as something in itself—the looking, petting, running, etc.—constitutes the emotional seizure. In all concrete experience of emotion these two phases are organically united in a single pulse of consciousness.

It follows from this that all emotion, as excitation, involves inhibition. This is not absolute inhibition; it is not suppression or displacement. It is incidental to the co-ordination. The two factors of the co-ordination, the "exciting stimulus" and the excited response, have to be adjusted, and the period of adjustment required to affect the co-ordination, marks the inhibition of each required to effect its reconstruction as an integral part of the whole act. Or, since we have recognized that the exciting stimulus does not exist as fact, or object, until constituted such by the co-ordination in the final act, let us say that the activities needing adjustment, and so partial inhibition, are the kinæsthetic (sensori-motor or ideo-motor) activities which translate themselves into the "object," and the vegetative-motor activities which constitute the "reaction" or "response" to the "object."

But here, again, in order to avoid getting on the wrong track it must be noted that this distinction of "object" and "response" is one of interpretation, or value, and not a plain matter of course difference in the experiencing. I have already tried to show that the "object" itself is an organic excitation on the sensori-motor, or, mediately, ideo-motor side, and that it is not *the* peculiar object *of* the emotion until the mode of behavior sets in, and the diffusive wave repercussates in consciousness. But it is equally necessary to recognize that the very distinction between exciting or stimulating sensori-motor activity and excited or responding vegetative-motor activity is teleological and not merely factual. It is because these two activities have to be co-ordinated in a single act, to accomplish a single end, and have therefore to be so adjusted as to co-operate with each other, that they present themselves as stimulus and response. . . .

In psychological terms, this tension is always between the activity which constitutes, when interpreted, the object as an intellectual content, and that which constitutes the response or mode of dealing with it. There is the one phase of organic activity which constitutes the bear as object; there is the other which would attack it, or run away from it, or stand one's ground before it. If these two co-ordinate *without friction,* or if one immediately displaces the other, there is no emotional seizure. If they co-exist, both pulling apart as complete in themselves and pulling together as parts of a new whole, there is great emotional excitement. It is this tension which makes it impossible to describe any emotion whatever without using dual terms—one for the *Affect* itself, the other for the object "at," "towards," or "on account of," which it is.

We may now connect this analysis with the result of the consideration of the emotional attitudes. The attitude is precisely that which was a complete activity once, but is no longer so. The activity of seizing prey or attacking an enemy, a movement having its meaning in itself, is now reduced or aborted; it is an attitude simply. As an instinctive reaction it is thoroughly ingrained in the system; it represents the actual co-ordinations of thousands and thousands of ancestors; it tends to start into action, therefore, whenever its associated stimulus occurs. . . . There is no reason to suppose that the original activity of attack or seizure was emotional, or had any *quale* attached to it such as we now term "anger." The animal of our ancestor so far as it was given up without restraint to the full activity undoubtedly had a feeling of activity; but just because the activity was undivided, it was not "emotion"; it was not "at," or "towards" an object held in tension against itself. This division could come in only when there was a need of co-ordinating the activity which corresponded to the perception and that which corresponded to the fighting, as means to an activity which was neither perceiving nor fighting. . . . Certainly, so far as I can trust my own introspection, whenever my anger or any strong emotion has gained complete possession of me, the peculiar *Affect quale* has disappeared. I remember well a youthful fight, with the emotions of irritation and anger before, and of partial fear and partial pride afterwards, but as to the intervening period of the fight nothing but a strangely vivid perception of the other boy's face as the hypnotizing focus of all my muscular activities. On the other side, my most intense and vengeful feelings of anger are associated with cases where my whole body was so sat on as to prevent the normal reaction. Every one knows how the smart and burn of the feeling of injustice increases with the feeling of impotency; it is, for example, when strikes are beginning to fail that violence from anger or revenge, as distinct from sheer criminality, sets in. It is a common-place that the busy philanthropist has no occasion to feel the extreme emotion of pathos which the spectator or reader of literature feels. Cases might be multiplied ad libitum.

It is then in the reduction of activities once performed for their own sake, to attitudes now useful simply as supplying a contributory, a reinforcing or checking factor, in some more comprehensive activity, that we have all the conditions for high emotional disturbance. The tendency to large diffusive waves of discharge is present, and the inhibition of this outgoing activity through some perception or idea is also present. The need of somehow reaching an adjustment of these two sides is urgent. The attitude stands for a recapitulation of thousands of acts formerly done, ends formerly reached; the perception or idea stands for multitudes of acts which may be done, ends which may be acted upon. But the immediate and present need is to get this attitude of anger which reflects the former act of seizing into some connection with the act of getting-even or of moral control, or whatever the idea may be. The conflict and competition, with incidental inhibition and deflection, is the disturbance of the emotional seizure.

Upon this basis, the apparent strangeness or absurdity in the fact that a mere organic repercussation should have such tremendous values in consciousness disappears. This organic return of the discharge wave stands for the entire effort of the organism to adjust its formed habits or co-ordinations of the past to present necessities as made known in perception or idea. The emotion is, *psychologically, the adjustment or tension of habit and ideal,* and the organic changes in the body are the literal working out, in concrete terms, of the struggle of adjustment. We may recall once more the three main phases presented in this adjustment as now giving us the basis of the classification of the emotions. There may be a failure to adjust the vegetative-motor function, the habit, to the sensori- (or ideo-) motor; there may be the effort, or there may be the success. The effort, moreover, also has a double form according as the attempt is in the main so to use the formed reactions as to avoid or exclude the idea or object, setting up another in its place, or to incorporate and assimilate it—e.g., terror and anger, dread and hope, regret and complacency, etc.

Stanley Schachter (1922-)
Jerome E. Singer (1934-)

INTRODUCTION

Schachter and Singer, two experimental psychologists, believe that James's theory should be supplemented by another, more "cognitive" theory of emotions. The emotion may be a bodily state of excitation, but there must also be other factors to account for the variety of our emotions and our ability to tell them apart. In particular, there is the simple act of "labeling" our emotions, naming them, whether correctly or incorrectly. Thus, it may be one and the same state of "arousal" that is anger, fear, or jealousy, but the label we give these emotions makes them distinct. How do we know which label to give an emotion? The physiological excitation experienced when greeting a man with a gun in an alley is fear, not love.

The Schachter-Singer theory of emotion has two elements—the Jamesian physiological component of arousal and a "cognitive" component that determines how emotions are labeled and discriminated among. (The theory is sometimes called "the two-component" theory of emotion.) The first component can be measured quite precisely, which was not the case in James's day. The second component, however, is complex and difficult to quantify. The Schachter-Singer experiments were designed primarily to distinguish between these two components and to identify the factors involved in the second, "cognitive" component of emotion.

In these experiments, subjects were injected with different amounts of epinephrine (adrenalin) or saline solution, for a placebo effect, and the circumstances were manipulated such that the subjects found themselves in certain defined situations in which one emotion label would be more "appropriate" than another, and also in ill-defined situations in which no particular emotion-label would be appropriate. It was hypothesized that emotions are a combination of physiological and cognitive factors; and it was concluded that a subject identifies physiological arousal states in terms of "the cognitions offered to him" and that a "completely satisfactory explanation" obviates the need to identify one's state in emotional terms. But Schachter and Singer also reiterate the basic Jamesian thesis, that "an individual will react emotionally only to the extent that he experiences a state of physiological arousal." The James-Lange theory is thus modified and amended, but not rejected in its most basic formulation.

From Cognitive, Social, and Physiological Determinants of Emotional State

The problem of which cues, internal or external, permit a person to label and identify his own emotional state has been with us since the days that James first tendered his doctrine that "the bodily changes follow directly the perception of the exciting fact, and that our feeling of the same changes as they occur *is* the emotion." Since we are aware of a variety of feeling and emotion states, it should follow from James' proposition that the various emotions will be accompanied by a variety of differentiable bodily states. Following James' pronouncement, a formidable number of studies were undertaken in search of the physiological differentiators of the emotions. The results, in these early days, were almost uniformly negative. All of the emotional states experimentally manipulated were characterized by a general pattern of excitation of the sympathetic nervous system but there appeared to be no clear-cut physiological discriminators of the various emotions. This pattern of results was so consistent from experiment to experiment that Cannon offered, as one of the crucial criticisms of the James-Lange theory, the fact that "the same visceral changes occur in very different emotional states and in non-emotional states."

More recent work, however, has given some indication that there may be differentiators. Ax and Schachter studied fear and anger. On a large number of indices both of those states were characterized by a similarly high level of autonomic activation but on several indices they did differ in the degree of activation. Wolf and Wolff studied a subject with a gastric fistula and were able to distinguish two patterns in the physiological responses of the stomach wall. It should be noted, though, that for many months they studied their subject during and following a great variety of moods and emotions and were able to distinguish only two patterns.

Whether or not there are physiological distinctions among the various emotional states must be considered an open question. Recent work might be taken to indicate that such differences are at best rather subtle and that the variety of emotion, mood, and feeling states are by no means matched by an equal variety of visceral patterns.

This rather ambiguous situation has led Ruckmick, Hunt, Cole, and Reis, Schachter and others to suggest that cognitive factors may be major determinants of emotional states. Granted a general pattern of sympathetic excitation as characteristic of emotional states, granted that there may be some differences in pattern from state to state, it is suggested that one labels, interprets, and identifies this stirred-up state in terms of the characteristics of the precipitating situation and one's apperceptive mass. This suggests, then, that an emotional state may be considered a function of a state of physiological arousal and of a cognition appropriate to this state of arousal. The cognition, in a sense, exerts a steering function. Cognitions arising from the immediate situation as interpreted by past experience provide the framework within which one understands and labels his feelings. It is the cognition which determines whether the state of physiological arousal will be labeled as "anger," "joy," "fear," or whatever.

In order to examine the implications of this formulation let us consider the fashion in which these two elements, a state of physiological arousal and cognitive factors, would interact in a variety of situations. In most emotion inducing situations, of course, the two factors are completely interrelated. Imagine a man walking alone down a dark alley, a figure with a gun suddenly appears. The perception-cognition "figure with a gun" in some fashion ~~initiates~~ a

initiates

state of physiological arousal; this state of arousal is interpreted in terms of knowledge about dark alleys and guns and the state of arousal is labeled "fear." Similarly a student who unexpectedly learns that he has made Phi Beta Kappa may experience a state of arousal which he will label "joy."

Let us now consider circumstances in which these two elements, the physiological and the cognitive, are, to some extent, independent. First, is the state of physiological arousal alone sufficient to induce an emotion? Best evidence indicates that it is not. Marañon, in a fascinating study . . . injected 210 of his patients with the sympathomimetic agent adrenalin and then simply asked them to introspect. Seventy-one percent of his subjects simply reported their physical symptoms with no emotional overtones; 29% of the subjects responded in an apparently emotional fashion. Of these the great majority described their feelings in a fashion that Marañon labeled "cold" or "as if" emotions, that is, they made statements such as "I feel *as if* I were afraid" or "*as if* I were awaiting a great happiness." This is a sort of emotional "déjà vu" experience; these subjects are neither happy nor afraid, they feel "as if" they were. Finally a very few cases apparently reported a genuine emotional experience. However, in order to produce this reaction in most of these few cases, Marañon points out:

> One must suggest a memory with strong affective force but not so strong as to produce an emotion in the normal state. For example, in several cases we spoke to our patients before the injection of their sick children or dead parents and they responded calmly to this topic. The same topic presented later, during the adrenal commotion, was sufficient to trigger emotion. This adrenal commotion places the subject in a situation of "affective imminence."

Apparently, then, to produce a genuinely emotional reaction to adrenalin, Marañon was forced to provide such subjects with an appropriate cognition.

Though Marañon is not explicit on his procedure, it is clear that his subjects knew that they were receiving an injection and in all likelihood knew that they were receiving adrenalin and probably had some order of familiarity with its effects. In short, though they underwent the pattern of sympathetic discharge common to strong emotional states, at the same time they had a completely appropriate cognition or explanation as to why they felt this way. This, we would suggest, is the reason so few of Marañon's subjects reported any emotional experience.

Consider now a person in a state of physiological arousal for which no immediately explanatory or appropriate cognitions are available. Such a state could result were one covertly to inject a subject with adrenalin or, unknown to him, feed the subject a sympathomimetic drug such as ephedrine. Under such conditions a subject would be aware of palpitations, tremor, face flushing, and most of the battery of symptoms associated with a discharge of the sympathetic nervous system. In contrast to Marañon's subjects he would, at the same time, be utterly unaware of why he felt this way. What would be the consequence of such a state?

Schachter has suggested that precisely such a state would lead to the arousal of "evaluative needs" (Festinger), that is, pressures would act on an individual in such a state to understand and label his bodily feelings. His bodily state grossly resembles the condition in which it has been at times of emotional excitement. How would he label his present feelings? It is suggested, of course, that he will label his feelings in terms of his knowledge of the immediate situation.[1] Should he at the time be with a beautiful woman he might decide that he was wildly in love or sexually excited. Should he be at a gay party, he might, by comparing himself to others, decide that he was extremely happy and euphoric. Should he be arguing with his wife, he might explode in fury and hatred. Or, should the situation be completely inappropriate he could decide that he was excited about something that had recently happened to him or, simply, that he was sick. In any case, it is our basic assumption that emotional states are a function of the interaction of such cognitive factors with a state of physiological arousal.

This line of thought, then, leads to the following propositions:

1. Given a state of physiological arousal for which an individual has no immediate explanation, he will "label" this state and describe

---

1. This suggestion is not new for several psychologists have suggested that situational factors should be considered the chief differentiators of the emotions. Hunt, Cole, and Reis probably make this point most explicitly in their study distinguishing among fear, anger, and sorrow in terms of situational characteristics.

his feelings in terms of the cognitions available to him. To the extent that cognitive factors are potent determiners of emotional states, it could be anticipated that precisely the same state of physiological arousal could be labeled "joy" or "fury" or "jealousy" or any of a great diversity of emotional labels depending on the cognitive aspects of the situation.

2. Given a state of physiological arousal for which an individual has a completely appropriate explanation (e.g., "I feel this way because I have just received an injection of adrenalin") no evaluative needs will arise and the individual is unlikely to label his feelings in terms of the alternative cognitions available.

Finally, consider a condition in which emotion inducing cognitions are present but there is no state of physiological arousal. For example, an individual might be completely aware that he is in great danger but for some reason (drug or surgical) remain in a state of physiological quiescence. Does he experience the emotion "fear"? Our formulation of emotion as a joint function of a state of physiological arousal and an appropriate cognition, would, of course, suggest that he does not, which leads to our final proposition.

3. Given the same cognitive circumstances, the individual will react emotionally or describe his feelings as emotions only to the extent that he experiences a state of physiological arousal.

PROCEDURE

The experimental test of these propositions requires (*a*) the experimental manipulation of a state of physiological arousal, (*b*) the manipulation of the extent to which the subject has an appropriate or proper explanation of his bodily state, and (*c*) the creation of situations from which explanatory cognitions may be derived.

In order to satisfy the first two experimental requirements, the experiment was cast in the framework of a study of the effects of vitamin supplements on vision. As soon as a subject arrived, he was taken to a private room and told by the experimenter:

> In this experiment we would like to make various tests of your vision. We are particularly interested in how certain vitamin compounds and vitamin supplements affect the visual skills. In particular, we want to find out how the vitamin compound called "Suproxin" affects your vision.

What we would like to do, then, if we can get your permission, is to give you a small injectionof Suproxin. The injection itself is mild and harmless; however, since some people do object to being injected we don't want to talk you into anything. Would you mind receiving a Suproxin injection?

If the subject agrees to the injection (and all but 1 of 185 subjects did) the experimenter continues with instructions we shall describe shortly, then leaves the room. In a few minutes a physician enters the room, briefly repeats the experimenter's instructions, takes the subject's pulse and then injects him with Suproxin.

Depending upon condition, the subject receives one of two forms of Suproxin—epinephrine or a placebo.

Epinephrine or adrenalin is a sympathomimetic drug whose effects, with minor exceptions, are almost a perfect mimicry of a discharge of the sympathetic nervous system. Shortly after injection systolic blood pressure increases markedly, heart rate increases somewhat, cutaneous blood flow decreases, while muscle and cerebral blood flow increase, blood sugar and lactic acid concentration increase, and respiration rate increases slightly. As far as the subject is concerned the major subjective symptoms are palpitation, tremor, and sometimes a feeling of flushing and accelerated breathing. With a subcutaneous injection (in the dosage administered to our subjects), such effects usually begin within 3–5 minutes of injection and last anywhere from 10 minutes to an hour. For most subjects these effects are dissipated within 15–20 minutes after injection.

Subjects receiving epinephrine received a subcutaneous injection of ½ cubic centimeter of a 1:1000 solution of Winthrop Laboratory's Suprarenin, a saline solution of epinephrine bitartrate.

Subjects in the placebo condition received a subcutaneous injection of ½ cubic centimeter of saline solution. This is, of course, completely neutral material with no side effects at all.

Manipulating an Appropriate Explanation

By "appropriate" we refer to the extent to which the subject has an authoritative, unequivocal explanation of his bodily condition. Thus, a subject who had been informed by the physician that as a direct consequence of the injection he would feel palpitations, tremor, etc. would be considered to have a completely appropriate explanation. A subject who had been informed only that the injection would have no side effects would have no appropriate explanation of his state. This dimension of appropriateness was manipulated in three experimental conditions which shall be called: Epinephrine Informed. (Epi Inf), Epinephrine Ignorant (Epi Ign), and Epinephrine Misinformed (Epi Mis).

Immediately after the subject had agreed to the injection and before the physician entered the room, the experimenter's spiel in each of these conditions went as follows:

Epinephrine Informed. I should also tell you that some of our subjects have experienced side effects from the Suproxin. These side effects are transitory, that is, they will only last for about 15 or 20 minutes. What will probably happen is that your hand will start to shake, your heart will start to pound, and your face may get warm and flushed. Again these are side effects lasting about 15 or 20 minutes.

While the physician was giving the injection, she told the subject that the injection was mild and harmless and repeated this description of the symptoms that the subject could expect as a consequence of the shot. In this condition, then, subjects have a completely appropriate explanation of their bodily state. They know precisely what they will feel and why.

Epinephrine Ignorant. In this condition, when the subject agreed to the injection, the experimenter said nothing more relevant to side effects and simply left the room. While the physician was giving the injections, she told the subject that the injection was mild and harmless and would have no side effects. In this condition, then, the subject has no experimentally provided explanation for his bodily state.

Epinephrine Misinformed. I should also tell you that some of our subjects have experienced side effects from the Suproxin. These side effects are transitory, that is, they will only last for about 15 or 20 minutes. What will probably happen is that your feet will feel numb, you will have an itching sensation over parts of your body, and you may get a slight headache. Again these are side effects lasting 15 or 20 minutes.

And again, the physician repeated these symptoms while injecting the subject.

None of these symtoms, of course, are consequences of an injection of epinephrine and, in effect, these instructions provide the subject with a completely inappropriate explanation of his bodily feelings. This condition was introduced as a control condition of sorts. It seemed possible that the description of side effects in the Epi Inf condition might turn the subject introspective, self-examining, possibly slightly troubled. Differences on the dependent variable between the Epi Inf and Epi Ign conditions might, then, be due to such factors rather than to differences in appropriateness. The false symptoms in the Epi Mis condition should similarly turn the subject introspective, etc., but the instructions in this condition do not provide an appropriate explanation of the subject's state.

Subjects in all of the above conditions were injected with epinephrine. Finally, there was a placebo condition in which subjects who were injected with saline solution, were given precisely the same treatment as subjects in the Epi Ign condition.

Producing an Emotion Inducing Cognition

Our initial hypothesis has suggested that given a state of physiological arousal for which the individual has no adequate explanation, cognitive factors can lead the individual to describe his feelings with any of a diversity of emotional labels. In order to test this hypothesis, it was decided to manipulate emotional states which can be considered quite different—euphoria and anger.

There are, of course, many ways to induce such states. In our own program of research, we have concentrated on social determinants of emotional states and have been able to demonstrate in other studies that people do evaluate their own feelings by comparing themselves with others around them (Schachter 1959; Wrightsman 1960). In this experiment we have attempted again to manipulate emotional state by social means. In one set of conditions, the subject is placed together with a stooge who has been trained to act euphorically. In a second set of conditions the subject is with a stooge trained to act in an angry fashion.

Measurement

Two types of measures of emotional state were obtained. Standardized observation through a one-way mirror was the technique used to assess the subject's behavior. To what extent did he act euphoric or angry? Such behavior can be considered in a way as a "semiprivate" index of mood for as far as the subject was concerned, his emotional behavior could be known only to the other person in the room—presumably another student. The second type of measure was self report in which, on a variety of scales, the subject indicated his mood of the moment. Such measures can be considered "public" indices of mood for they would, of course, be available to the experimenter and his associates.

Evaluation of the Experimental Design

The ideal test of our propositions would require circumstances which our experiment is far from realizing. First, the proposition that: "A state of physiological arousal for which an individual has no immediate explanation will lead him to label this state in terms of the cognitions available to him" obviously requires conditions under which the subject does not and cannot have a proper explanation of his bodily state. Though we toyed with such fantasies as ventilating the experimental room with vaporized adrenalin, reality forced us to rely on the disguised injection of Suproxin—a technique which was far from ideal for no matter what the experimenter told them, some subjects would inevitably attribute their feelings to the injection. To the extent that subjects did so, differences between the several appropriateness conditions should be attenuated.

Second, the proposition that: "Given the same cognitive circumstances the individual will react emotionally only to the extent that he experiences a state of physiological arousal" requires for its ideal test the manipulation of states of physiological arousal and of physiological quiescence. Though there is no question that epinephrine effectively produces a state of arousal, there is also no question that a placebo does not prevent physiological arousal. To the extent that the experimental situation effectively produces sympathetic stimulation in placebo subjects, the proposition is difficult to test, for such a factor would attenuate differences between epinephrine and placebo subjects.

Both of these factors, then, can be expected to interfere with the test of our several propositions. In presenting the results of this study, we shall first present condition by condition results and then evaluate the effect of these two factors on experimental differences.

[Results: the experiment did indeed confirm the hypothesis that epinephrine injections produce "symptoms of sympathetic discharge," and that, as expected, the subjects who were so affected were observed and more or less reported experiencing the emotion appropriate to their respective experimental situations, and in proportion to the epinephrine injection and the lack of any alternative explanation for the consequent experiences.]

DISCUSSION

Let us summarize the major findings of this experiment and examine the extent to which they support the propositions offered in the introduction of this paper. It has been suggested, first, that given a state of physiological arousal for which an individual has no explanation, he will label this state in terms of the cognitions available to him. This implies, of course, that by manipulating the cognitions of an individual in such a state we can manipulate his feelings in diverse directions. Experimental results support this proposition for following the injection of epinephrine, those subjects who had no explanation for the bodily state thus produced, gave behavioral and self-report indications that they had been readily manipulable into the disparate feeling states of euphoria and anger.

From this first proposition, it must follow that given a state of physiological arousal for which the individual has a completely satisfactory explanation, he will not label this state in terms of the alternative cognitions available. Experimental evidence strongly supports this expectation. In those conditions in which subjects were injected with epinephrine and told precisely what they would feel and why, they proved relatively immune to any effects of the manipulated cognitions. In the anger condition, such subjects did not report or show anger; in the euphoria condition, such subjects reported themselves as far less happy than subjects with an identical bodily state but no adequate knowledge of why they felt the way they did.

Finally, it has been suggested that given constant cognitive circumstances, an individual will react emotionally only to the extent that he experiences a state of physiological arousal. Without taking account of experimental artifacts, the evidence in support of this proposition is consistent but tentative. When the effects of "self-informing" tendencies in epinephrine subjects and of "self-arousing" tendencies in placebo subjects are partialed out, the evidence strongly supports the proposition.

Let us examine the implications of these findings and of this line of thought for problems in the general area of the physiology of the emotions. We have noted in the introduction that the numerous studies on physiological differentiators of emotional states have, viewed en masse, yielded quite inconclusive results. Most, though not all, of these studies have indicated no differences among the various emotional states. Since as human beings, rather than as scientists, we have no difficulty identifying, labeling, and distinguishing among our feelings, the results of these studies have long seemed rather puzzling and paradoxical. Perhaps because of this, there has been a persistent tendency to discount such results as due to ignorance or methodological inadequacy and to pay far more attention to the very few studies which demonstrate *some* sort of physiological differences among emotional states than to the very many studies which indicate no differences at all. It is conceivable, however, that these results should be taken at face value and that emotional states may, indeed, be generally characterized by a high level of sympathetic activation with few if any physiological distinguishers among the many emotional states. If this is correct, the findings of the present study may help to resolve the problem. Obviously this study does *not* rule out the possibility of physiological differences among the emotional states. It is the case, however, that given precisely the same state of epinephrine-induced sympathetic activation, we have, by means of cognitive manipulations, been able to produce in our subjects the very disparate states of euphoria and anger. It may indeed be the case that cognitive factors are major determiners of the emotional labels we apply to a common state of sympathetic arousal.

SUMMARY

It is suggested that emotional states may be considered a function of a state of physiological arousal and of a cognition appropriate to this state of arousal. From this follows these propositions:

1. Given a state of physiological arousal for which an individual has no immediate explanation, he will label this state and describe his feelings in terms of the cognitions available to him. To the extent that cognitive factors are potent determiners of emotional states, it should be anticipated that precisely the same state of physiological arousal could be labeled "joy" or "fury" or "jealousy" or any of a great diversity of emotional labels depending on the cognitive aspects of the situation.

2. Given a state of physiological arousal for which an individual has a completely appropriate explanation, no evaluative needs will arise and the individual is unlikely to label his feelings in terms of the alternative cognitions available.

3. Given the same cognitive circumstances, the individual will react emotionally or describe his feelings as emotions only to the extent that he experiences a state of physiological arousal.

An experiment is described which, together with the results of other studies, supports these propositions.

Sigmund Freud

(1856 – 1939)

INTRODUCTION

Freud did not develop a theory of emotion as such, but his psycho-analytical theories radically changed the whole idea of emotions and sorts of phenomena that theories of emotion are supposed to explain. With his concept of "the Unconscious," Freud recast our entire "topography" of the mind. Mental events, including emotions, were no longer assumed to be "in consciousness"; they could also undergo a variety of dynamically caused "vicissitudes," which sometimes prevented us from being aware of them. And yet, as Freud amply demonstrated in his meticulous case histories, an emotion, although unconscious, could still influence a person's behavior just as dramatically and in much the same way that it would if it were fully conscious. This, in turn, required a new way of thinking about emotions in general. For one thing, it meant that psychologists would pay less attention and give less credence to the conscious reports of a person; what was "going on" in his or her mind was not always a matter which he or she was most competent to discuss.

In all of Freud's theories of the mind, there were the same assumptions: the ultimate cause of the emotion is "psychic energy"; there are unconscious processes of which a person may not or cannot be aware; the mind is separated into different parts or "agencies," which come into conflict; and infantile experiences, especially those of a sexual nature, profoundly influence adult behavior and psychology. In the first part of his career, Freud divided the mind into three components, which he sometimes described as "chambers." There is the Conscious, a Preconscious, which can emerge into consciousness at any time, and the Unconscious, which cannot become conscious because of repression, which "censors" ideas and information too threatening or obscene or embarrassing. The first selection here, written in 1915, presents this system of thought. After 1923 Freud developed his better-known "agency" view of the mind, dividing it into the Id (the source of instincts), the Ego (the rational self), and the Superego (the internalization of the rules and restrictions learned from one's parents and other authorities). But in both theories, the notion of unconscious emotions played an important, but ambiguous role.

In fact, Freud never develops an adequate or consistent view of emotions and the Unconscious. He often referred to emotions as "affects," by which he usually meant a sensation, a "felt feeling" or "the conscious subjective aspect of an emotion"; as such, he denied that an emotion can be unconscious. But throughout his career, he referred without hesitation to such emotions as "unconscious guilt" and "repressed hostility." Thus, Freud ambiguously describes an emotion as just a "feeling-tone" or as a complex that includes not only a feeling (an affect), but also an *instinct* that motivates it and an *idea* that directs it towards an object. (Freud learned this terminology from Brentano, who was once his teacher. See Part III.)

It is possible to distinguish three different views of emotion in Freud's work, based on the three components instinct, idea, and affect:

1. An emotion is itself an instinct or an innate drive, which is essentially unconscious.
2. An emotion is an instinct plus an idea—a drive from within the unconscious, but aimed at a conscious object. In this analysis, an emotion becomes unconscious when the idea is separated from its instinct, so that one might experience it without knowing how or why.
3. An emotion is just an effect, just a feeling, or what William James called an "epiphenomenon," a by-product of the processes of the mind. In this analysis, an emotion cannot be unconscious, although its causes may be. The most common symptom in psychoanalytical studies, "free-floating

anxiety," is an affect that is no longer connected to any known cause or object.

Born in Freiburg, Freud lived in Vienna almost the whole of his life, until he was forced to flee the Nazis as an old man. He was always interested in philosophy, but entered a career in medicine, however, and became a clinical neurologist. In 1884, he collaborated with Joseph Breuer on studies of hysterical patients who had been cured by allowing them to express fears and feelings through hypnosis. In 1885, he continued these studies with Charcot in Paris, and in the next decade, he developed the theory of "free association" and analysis that would become "psychoanalysis." In 1900, he published his classic *Interpretation of Dreams,* and in 1905, his *Three Studies in Sexuality.* The two selections that follow are from his 1915 essay "The Unconscious" and his *General Lectures on Psychoanalysis* of the same period.

From The Unconscious

We have learnt from psycho-analysis that the essence of the process of repression lies, not in putting an end to, in annihilating, the idea which represents an instinct, but in preventing it from becoming conscious. When this happens we say of the idea that it is in a state of being "unconscious" and we can produce good evidence to show that even when it is unconscious it can produce effects, even including some which finally reach consciousness. Everything that is repressed must remain unconscious; but let us state at the very outset that the repressed does not cover everything that is unconscious. The unconscious has the wider compass: the repressed is a part of the unconscious.

How are we to arrive at a knowledge of the unconscious? It is of course only as something conscious that we know it, after it has undergone transformation or translation into something conscious. Psycho-analytic work shows us every day that translation of this kind is possible. In order that this should come about, the person under analysis must overcome certain resistances—the same resistances as those which, earlier, made the material concerned into something repressed by rejecting it from the conscious.

I. Justification for the Concept of the Unconscious

Our right to assume the existence of something mental that is unconscious and to employ that assumption for the purposes of scientific work is disputed in many quarters. To this we can reply that our assumption of the unconscious is *necessary* and *legitimate,* and that we possess numerous proofs of its existence.

It is *necessary* because the data of consciousness have a very large number of gaps in them; both in healthy and in sick people psychical acts often occur which can be explained only by presupposing other acts, of which, nevertheless, consciousness affords no evidence. These not only include parapraxes and dreams in healthy people, and everything described as a psychical symptom or an obsession in the sick; our most personal daily experience acquaints us with ideas that come into our head we do not know from where, and with intellectual conclusions arrived at we do not know how. All these conscious acts remain disconnected and unintelligible if we insist upon claiming that every mental act that occurs in us must also necessarily be experienced by us through consciousness; on the other hand, they fall into a demonstrable connection if we interpolate between them the unconscious acts which we have inferred. A gain in meaning is a perfectly justifiable ground for going beyond the limits of direct experience. When, in addition, it turns out that the assumption of there being an unconscious enables us to construct a successful procedure by which we can exert an effective influence upon the course of conscious processes, this success will have given us an incontrovertible proof of the existence of what we have assumed. This being so, we must adopt the position that to require that whatever goes on in the mind must also be known to consciousness is to make an untenable claim.

We can go further and argue, in support of there being an unconscious psychical state, that at any given moment consciousness includes only a small content, so that the greater part of what we call conscious knowledge must in any case be for very considerable periods of time in a state of latency, that is to say, of being psychically unconscious. When all our latent memories are taken into consideration it becomes totally incomprehensible how the existence of the unconscious can be denied. But here we encounter the objection that these latent recollections can no longer be described as psychical, but that they correspond to residues of somatic processes from which what is psychical can once more arise. The obvious answer to this is that a latent memory is, on the contrary, an unquestionable residuum of a *psychical* process. But it is more important to realize clearly that this objection is based on the equation—not, it is true, explicitly stated but taken as axiomatic—of what is conscious with what is mental. This equation is either a *petitio principii* which begs the question whether everything that is psychical is also necessarily conscious; or else it is a matter of convention, of nomenclature. In this latter case it is, of course, like any other convention, not open to refutation. The question remains, however, whether the convention is so expedient that we are bound to adopt it. To this we may reply that the conventional equation of the psychical with the conscious is totally inexpedient. It disrupts psychical continuities, plunges us into the insoluble difficulties of psycho-physical parallelism, is open to the reproach that for no obvious reason it overestimates the part played by consciousness, and that it forces us prematurely to abandon the field of psychological research without being able to offer us any compensation from other fields.

It is clear in any case that this question—whether the latent states of mental life, whose existence is undeniable, are to be conceived of as conscious mental states or as physical ones—threatens to resolve itself into a verbal dispute. We shall therefore be better advised to focus our attention on what we know with certainty of the nature of these debatable states. As far as their physical characteristics are concerned, they are totally inaccessible to us: no physiological concept or chemical process can give us any notion of their nature. On the other hand, we know for certain that they have abundant points of contact with conscious mental processes; with the help of a certain amount of work they can be transformed into, or replaced by, conscious mental processes, and all the categories which we employ to describe conscious mental acts, such as ideas, purposes, resolutions and so on, can be applied to them. Indeed, we are obliged to say of some of these latent states that the only respect in which they differ from conscious ones is precisely in the absence of consciousness.

Thus we shall not hesitate to treat them as objects of psychological research, and to deal with them in the most intimate connection with conscious mental acts.

The assumption of an unconscious is, moreover, a perfectly *legitimate* one, inasmuch as in postulating it we are not departing a single step from our customary and generally accepted mode of thinking. Consciousness makes each of us aware only of his own states of mind; that other people, too, possess a consciousness is an inference which we draw by analogy from their observable utterances and actions, in order to make this behaviour of theirs intelligible to us. (It would no doubt be psychologically more correct to put it in this way: that without any special reflection we attribute to everyone else our own constitution and therefore our consciousness as well, and that this identification is a *sine qua non* of our understanding.) This inference (or this identification) was formerly extended by the ego to other human beings, to animals, plants, inanimate objects and to the world at large, and proved serviceable so long as their similarity to the individual ego was overwhelmingly great; but it became more untrustworthy in proportion as the difference between the ego and these "others" widened. To-day, our critical judgement is already in doubt on the question of consciousness in animals; we refuse to admit it in plants and we regard the assumption of its existence in inanimate matter as mysticism. But even where the original inclination to identification has withstood criticism—that is, when the "others" are our fellow-men—the assumption of a consciousness in them rests upon an inference and cannot share the immediate certainty which we have of our own consciousness.

Psycho-analysis demands nothing more than that we should apply this process of inference to ourselves also—a proceeding to which, it is true, we are not constitutionally inclined. If we do this, we must say: all the acts and manifestations which I notice in myself and do not know how to link up with the rest of my mental life must be judged as if they belonged to someone else: they are to be explained by a mental life ascribed to this other person. Furthermore, experience shows that we understand very well how to interpret in other people (that is, how to fit into their chain of mental events) the same acts which we refuse to acknowledge as being mental in ourselves. Here some special hindrance evidently deflects our investigations from our own self and prevents our obtaining a true knowledge of it.

In psycho-analysis there is no choice for us but to assert that mental processes are in themselves unconscious, and to liken the perception of them by means of consciousness to the perception of the external world by means of the sense-organs. We can even hope to gain fresh knowledge from the comparison. The psycho-analytic assumption of unconscious mental activity appears to us, on the one hand, as a further expansion of the primitive animism which caused us to see copies of our own consciousness all around us, and, on the other hand, as an extension of the corrections undertaken by Kant of our views on external perception. Just as Kant warned us not to overlook the fact that our perceptions are subjectively conditioned and must not be regarded as identical with what is perceived though unknowable, so psycho-analysis warns us not to equate perceptions by means of consciousness with the unconscious mental processes which are their object. Like the physical, the psychical is not necessarily in reality what it appears to us to be. We shall be glad to learn, however, that the correction of internal perception will turn out not to offer such great difficulties as the correction of external perception—that internal objects are less unknowable than the external world.

III. Unconscious Emotions

We have limited the foregoing discussion to ideas; we may now raise a new question, the answer to which is bound to contribute to the elucidation of our theoretical views. We have said that there are conscious and unconscious ideas; but are there also unconscious instinctual impulses, emotions and feelings, or is it in this instance meaningless to form combinations of the kind?

I am in fact of the opinion that the antithesis of conscious and unconscious is not applicable to instincts. An instinct can never become an object of consciousness—only the idea that represents the instinct can. Even in the unconscious, moreover, an instinct cannot be represented otherwise than by an idea. If the instinct did not attach itself to an idea or manifest itself as an affective state, we could know nothing about it. When we nevertheless speak of an unconscious instinctual impulse or of a repressed instinctual impulse, the looseness of phraseology is a harmless one. We can only mean an instinctual impulse the ideational representative of which is unconscious, for nothing else comes into consideration. We should expect the answer to the question about unconscious feelings, emotions and affects to be just as easily given. It is surely of the essence of an emotion that we should be aware of it, i.e, that it should become known to consciousness. Thus the possibility of the attribute of unconsciousness would be completely excluded as far as emotions, feelings and affects are concerned. But in psycho-analytic practice we are accustomed to speak of unconscious love, hate, anger, etc., and find it impossible to avoid even the strange conjunction, "unconscious consciousness of guilt," or a paradoxical "unconscious anxiety." Is there more meaning in the use of these terms than there is in speaking of "unconscious instincts?"

The two cases are in fact not on all fours. In the first place, it may happen that an affective or emotional impulse is perceived, but misconstrued. Owing to the repression of its proper representative it has been forced to become connected with another idea, and is now regarded by consciousness as the manifestation of that idea. If we restore the true connection, we call the original affective impulse an "unconscious" one. Yet its affect was never unconscious; all that had happened was that its *idea* had undergone repression. In general, the use of the terms "unconscious affect" and "unconscious emotion" has reference to the vicissitudes undergone, in consequence of repression, by the quantitative factor in the instinctual impulse. We know that three such vicissitudes are possible: either the affect remains, wholly or in part, as it is; or it is transformed into a qualitatively different quota of affect, above all into anxiety; or it is suppressed, i.e. it is prevented from developing at all. (These possibilities may perhaps be studied even more easily in the dreamwork than in neuroses.) We know, too, that to suppress the development of affect is the true aim of repression and that its work is incomplete if this aim is not achieved. In every instance where repression has succeeded in inhibiting the development of affects, we term those affects (which we restore when we undo the work of repression) "unconscious." Thus it cannot be denied that the use of the terms in question is consistent; but in comparison with unconscious ideas there is the important difference that unconscious ideas continue to exist after repression as actual structures in the system *Ucs.*, whereas all that corresponds in that system to unconscious affects is a potential beginning which is prevented from developing. Strictly speaking, then, and although no fault can be found with the linguistic usage, there are no unconscious affects as there are unconscious ideas. But there may very well be in the system *Ucs.* affective structures which, like others, become conscious. The whole difference arises from the fact that ideas are cathexes—basically of memory-traces—whilst affects and emotions correspond to processes of discharge, the final manifestations of which are perceived as feelings. In the present state of our knowledge of affects and emotions we cannot express this difference more clearly.

It is of especial interest to us to have established the fact that repression can succeed in inhibiting an instinctual impulse from being turned into a manifestation of affect. This shows us that the system *Cs.* normally controls affectivity as well as access to motility; and it enhances the importance of repression, since it shows that repression results not only in withholding things from consciousness, but also in preventing the development of affect and the setting-off of muscular activity. Conversely, too, we may say that as long as the system *Cs.* controls affectivity and motility, the mental condition of the person in question is spoken of as normal. Nevertheless, there is an unmistakable difference in the relation of the controlling system to the two contiguous processes of discharge. Whereas the control by the *Cs.* over voluntary motility is firmly rooted, regularly withstands the onslaught of neurosis and only breaks down in psychosis, control by the *Cs.* over the development of affects is less secure. Even within the limits of normal life we can recognize that a constant struggle for primacy over affectivity goes on between the two systems *Cs.* and *Ucs.*, that certain spheres of influence are marked off from one another and that intermixtures between the operative forces occur.

The importance of the system *Cs.* (*Pcs.*) as regards access to the release of affect and to action enables us also to understand the part played by substitutive ideas in determining the form taken by illness. It is possible for the development of affect to proceed directly from the system *Ucs.*; in that case the affect always has the character of anxiety, for which all "repressed" affects are exchanged. Often, however, the instinctual impulse has to wait until it has found a substitutive idea in the system *Cs*. The development of affect can then proceed from this conscious substitute, and the nature of that substitute determines the qualitative character of the affect. We have asserted that in repression a severance takes place between the affect and the idea to which it belongs, and that each then undergoes its separate vicissitudes. Descriptively, this is incontrovertible; in actuality, however, the affect does not as a rule arise till the breakthrough to a new representation in the system *Cs.* has been successfully achieved.

ANXIETY

You will certainly have judged the information that I gave you about ordinary nervousness as the most fragmentary and most inadequate of all my accounts. I know that it was; and I expect that nothing surprised you more than that I made no mention of the "anxiety" which most nervous people complain of and themselves describe as their most terrible burden. Anxiety or dread can really develop tremendous intensity and in consequence be the cause of the maddest precautions. But in this matter at least I wished not to cut you short; on the contrary, I had determined to put the problem of nervous anxiety to you as clearly as possible and to discuss it at some length.

Anxiety (or *dread*) itself needs no description; everyone has personally experienced this sensation, or to speak more correctly this affective condition, at some time or other. But in my opinion not enough serious consideration has been given to the question why nervous persons in particular suffer from anxiety so much more intensely, and so much more altogether, than others. Perhaps it has been taken for granted that they should; indeed, the words "nervous" and "anxious" are used interchangeably, as if they meant the same thing. This is not justifiable, however; there are anxious people who are otherwise not in any way nervous and there are, besides, neurotics with numerous symptoms who exhibit no tendency to dread.

However this may be, one thing is certain, that the problem of anxiety is a nodal point, linking up all kinds of most important questions; a riddle, of which the solution must cast a flood of light upon our whole mental life. I do not claim that I can give you a complete solution; but you will certainly expect psycho-analysis to have attacked this problem too in a different manner from that adopted by academic medicine. Interest there centres upon the anatomical processes by which the anxiety condition comes about. We learn that the medulla oblongata is stimulated, and the patient is told that he is suffering from a neurosis in the vagal nerve. The medulla oblongata is a wondrous and beauteous object; I well remember how much time and labour I devoted to the study of it years ago. But to-day I must say I know of nothing less important for the psychological comprehension of anxiety than a knowledge of the nerve-paths by which the excitations travel.

One may consider anxiety for a long time without giving a thought to nervousness. You will understand me at once when I describe this form of anxiety as OBJECTIVE ANXIETY, in contrast to neurotic anxiety. Now *real* anxiety or dread appears to us a very natural and rational thing; we should call it a reaction to the perception of an external danger, of an injury which is expected and foreseen; it is bound up with the reflex of flight, and may be regarded as an expression of the instinct of self-preservation. The occasions of it, i.e., the objects and situations about which anxiety is felt, will obviously depend to a great extent upon the state of the person's knowledge and feeling of power regarding the outer world. It seems to us quite natural that a savage should be afraid of a cannon or of an eclipse of the sun, while a white man who can handle the weapon and foretell the phenomenon remains unafraid in the same situation. At other times it is knowledge itself which inspires fear, because it reveals the danger sooner; thus a savage will recoil with terror at the sight of a track in the jungle which conveys nothing to an ignorant white man, but means that some wild beast is near at hand; and an experienced sailor will perceive with dread a little cloud on the horizon because it means an approaching hurricane, while to a passenger it looks quite insignificant.

The view that objective anxiety is rational and expedient, however, will on deeper consideration be admitted to need thorough revision. In face of imminent danger the only expedient behaviour, actually, would be first a cool appraisement of the forces at disposal as compared with the magnitude of the danger at hand, and then a decision whether flight or defence, or possibly attack, offered the best prospect of a successful outcome. Dread, however, has no place in this scheme; everything to be done will be accomplished as well and probably better if dread does not develop. You will see too that when dread is excessive it becomes in the highest degree inexpedient; it paralyses every action, even that of flight. The reaction to danger usually consists in a combination of the two things, the fear-affect and the defensive action; the frightened animal is afraid *and* flees, but the expedient element in this is the "flight," not the "being afraid."

One is tempted therefore to assert that the development of anxiety is never expedient; perhaps a closer dissection of the situation in dread will give us a better insight into it. The first thing about it is the "readiness" for danger, which expresses itself in heightened sensorial perception and in motor tension. This expectant readiness is obviously advantageous; indeed, absence of it may be responsible for grave results. It is then followed on the one hand by a motor action, taking the form primarily of flight and, on a higher level, of defensive action; and on the other hand by the condition we call a sensation of "anxiety" or dread. The more the development of dread is limited to a flash, to a mere signal, the less does it hinder the transition from the state of anxious readiness to that of action, and the more expediently does the whole course of events proceed. The *anxious readiness* therefore seems to me the expedient element, and the *development* of anxiety the inexpedient element, in what we call anxiety or dread.

I shall not enter upon a discussion whether the words anxiety, fear, fright, mean the same or different things in common usage. In my opinion, *anxiety* relates to the condition and ignores the object, whereas in the word *fear* attention is directed to the object; *fright* does actually seem to possess a special meaning—namely, it relates specifically to the condition induced when danger is unexpectedly encountered without previous anxious readiness. It might be said then that anxiety is a protection against fright.

It will not have escaped you that a certain ambiguity and indefiniteness exists in the use of the word "anxiety." It is generally understood to mean the subjective condition arising upon the perception of what we have called "developed" anxiety; such a condition is called an affect. Now what is an affect, in a dynamic sense? It is certainly something very complex. An affect comprises first of all certain motor innervations or discharges; and, secondly, certain

sensations, which moreover are of two kinds—namely, the perceptions of the motor actions which have been performed, and the
directly pleasurable or painful sensations which give the affect what
we call its dominant note. But I do not think that this description
penetrates to the essence of an affect. With certain affects one seems
to be able to see deeper, and to recognize that the core of it, binding
the whole complex structure together, is of the nature of a *repetition*
of some particular very significant previous experience. This experience could only have been an exceedingly early impression of a
universal type, to be found in the previous history of the species
rather than of the individual. In order to be better understood I
might say that an affective state is constructed like an hysterical
attack, i.e. is the precipitate of a reminiscence. An hysterical attack
is therefore comparable to a newly formed individual affect, and the
normal affect to a universal hysteria which has become a heritage.

Do not imagine that what I am telling you now about affects is
the common property of normal psychology. On the contrary, these
conceptions have grown on the soil of psycho-analysis and are only
indigenous there. What psychology has to say about affects—the
James-Lange theory, for instance—is utterly incomprehensible to us
psycho-analysts and impossible for us to discuss. We do not however
regard what we know of affects as at all final; it is a first attempt to
take our bearings in this obscure region. To continue, then: we
believe we know what this early impression is which is reproduced
as a repetition in the anxiety affect. We think it is the experience of
birth—an experience which involves just such a concatenation of
painful feelings, of discharges of excitation, and of bodily sensations,
as to have become a prototype for all occasions on which life is
endangered, ever after to be reproduced again in us as the dread or
"anxiety" condition. The enormous increase in stimulation effected
by the interruption of the renewal of blood (the internal respiration)
was the cause of the anxiety experience at birth—the first anxiety
was therefore toxically induced. The name *Angst* (anxiety)—
angustiæ, Enge, a narrow place, a strait—accentuates the characteristic tightening in the breathing which was then the consequence of
a real situation and is subsequently repeated almost invariably with
an affect. It is very suggestive too that the first anxiety state arose on
the occasion of the separation from the mother. We naturally believe
that the disposition to reproduce this first anxiety condition has

become so deeply ingrained in the organism, through countless generations, that no single individual can escape the anxiety affect; even though, like the legendary Macduff, he "was from his mother's womb untimely ripped" and so did not himself experience the act of birth. What the prototype of the anxiety condition may be for other animals than mammals we cannot say; neither do we know what the complex of sensations in them is which is equivalent to fear in us.

It may perhaps interest you to know how it was possible to arrive at such an idea as this—that birth is the source and prototype of the anxiety affect. Speculation had least of all to do with it; on the contrary, I borrowed a thought from the naïve intuitive mind of the people. Many years ago a number of young house-physicians, including myself, were sitting round a dinner-table, and one of the assistants at the obstetrical clinic was telling us all the funny stories of the last midwives' examination. One of the candidates was asked what it meant when the meconium (child's excreta) was present in the waters at birth, and promptly replied: "That the child is frightened." She was ridiculed and failed. But I silently took her part and began to suspect that the poor unsophisticated woman's unerring perception had revealed a very important connection.

Now let us turn to neurotic anxiety; what are the special manifestations and conditions found in the anxiety of nervous persons? There is a great deal to be described here. First of all, we find a general apprehensiveness in them, a "free-floating" anxiety, as we call it, ready to attach itself to any thought which is at all appropriate, affecting judgements, inducing expectations, lying in wait for any opportunity to find a justification for itself. We call this condition *"expectant dread"* or "anxious expectation." People who are tormented with this kind of anxiety always anticipate the worst of all possible outcomes, interpret every chance happening as an evil omen, and exploit every uncertainty to mean the worst. The tendency to this kind of expectation of evil is found as a character-trait in many people who cannot be described as ill in any other way, and we call them "over-anxious" or pessimistic; but a marked degree of expectant dread is an invariable accompaniment of the nervous disorder which I have called anxiety-neurosis and include among the actual neuroses.

In contrast to this type of anxiety, a second form of it is found to be much more circumscribed in the mind, and attached to definite objects and situations. This is the anxiety of the extraordinarily various and often very peculiar phobias. Stanley Hall, the distinguished American psychologist, has recently taken the trouble to designate a whole series of these phobias by gorgeous Greek titles; they sound like the ten plagues of Egypt, except that there are far more than ten of them. Just listen to the things that can become the object or content of a phobia: darkness, open air, open spaces, cats, spiders, caterpillars, snakes, mice, thunder, sharp points, blood, enclosed places, crowds, loneliness, crossing bridges, travelling by land or sea, and so on. As a first attempt to take one's bearings in this chaos we may divide them into three groups. Many of the objects and situations feared are rather sinister, even to us normal people, they have some connection with danger; and these phobias are not entirely incomprehensible to us, although their intensity seems very much exaggerated. Most of us, for instance, have a feeling of repulsion upon encountering a snake. It may be said that the snake-phobia is universal in mankind. Charles Darwin has described most vividly how he could not control his dread of a snake that darted at him, although he knew that he was protected from it by a thick plate of glass. The second group consists of situations that still have some relation to danger, but to one that is usually belittled or not emphasized by us; most situation-phobias belong to this group. We know that there is more chance of meeting with a diaster in a railway train than at home—namely, a collision; we also know that a ship may sink, whereupon it is usual to be drowned; but we do not brood upon these dangers and we travel without anxiety by train and boat. Nor can it be denied that if a bridge were to break at the moment we were crossing it we should be hurled into the torrent, but that only happens so very occasionally that it is not a danger worth considering. Solitude too has its dangers, which in certain circumstances we avoid, but there is no question of never being able to endure it for a moment under any conditions. The same thing applies to crowds, enclosed spaces, thunderstorms, and so on. What is foreign to us in these phobias is not so much their content as their intensity. The anxiety accompanying a phobia is positively indescribable! And we sometimes get the impression that neurotics are not really at all fearful of those things which can, under certain conditions, arouse anxiety in us and which they call by the same names. There remains a third group which is entirely unintelligible to us. When a strong full-grown man is afraid to cross a street or square in his own so familiar town, or when a healthy well-developed woman becomes almost senseless with fear because a cat has brushed against her dress or a mouse has scurried through the room, how can we see the connection with danger which is obviously present to these people? With this kind of animal-phobia it is no question of an increased intensity of common human antipathies; to prove the contrary, there are numbers of people who, for instance, cannot pass a cat without attracting and petting it. A mouse is a thing that so many women are afraid of, and yet it is at the same time a very favourite pet name; many a girl who is delighted to be called so by her lover will scream with terror at the sight of the dainty little creature itself. The behaviour of the man who is afraid to cross streets and squares only suggests one thing to us—that he behaves like a little child. A child is directly taught that such situations are dangerous, and the man's anxiety too is allayed when he is led by someone across the open space.

The two forms of anxiety described, the "free-floating" expectant dread and that attached to phobias, are independent of each other. The one is not the other at a further stage; they are only rarely combined, and then as if fortuitously. The most intense general apprehensiveness does not necessarily lead to a phobia; people who have been hampered all their lives by agoraphobia may be quite free from pessimistic expectant dread. Many phobias, e.g. fear of open spaces, of railway travelling, are demonstrably acquired first in later life; others, such as fear of darkness, thunder, animals, seem to have existed from the beginning. The former signify serious illness, the latter are more of the nature of idiosyncrasies, peculiarities; anyone exhibiting one of these latter may be suspected of harbouring others similar to it. I must add that we group all these phobias under *anxiety-hysteria*, that is, we regard them as closely allied to the well-known disorder called conversion-hysteria.

The third form taken by neurotic anxiety brings us to an enigma; there is no visible connection at all between the anxiety and the danger dreaded. This anxiety occurs in hysteria, for instance, accompanying the hysterical symptoms; or under various conditions of excitement in which, it is true, we should expect some affect to be displayed, but least of all an anxiety-affect; or without reference to any conditions, incomprehensible both to us and to the patient, an unrelated anxiety-attack. We may look far and wide without discovering a danger or an occasion which could even be exaggerated to account for it.

Part Three
THE CONTINENTAL TRADITION

The study of the emotions in European philosophy continued with a fervor that had died out in Anglo-American philosophy. It was inspired by one of the most prominent European philosophers of modern times—Immanuel Kant. Kant's theory was hardly sympathetic to the emotions. Indeed, his whole "practical" philosophy focused on the powers of Reason, relegating emotions to the realm of the "pathological" (from *"pathos"* = feeling). But Kant himself had argued that the key to morality is a sense of respect, which looked dangerously like a feeling *(Gefühl)*, and his philosophical hero Rousseau had argued before him that ethics was largely a matter of "inner sentiment." Accordingly, it was not interest in emotions alone so much as the concern with ethics that lead many philosophers to a detailed study of the ethically relevant emotions, particularly love, hate, and sympathy.

A second major influence on the Continent, but again a philosopher who did not himself study the emotions, was the Czech-German "phenomenologist" Edmund Husserl. Husserl's method was greeted by many philosophers as a genuinely revolutionary insight into the nature and structures of knowledge and consciousness. Husserl was interested primarily in epistemology, but his most devoted followers carried his methods of "phenomenological description" into the "affective" realm, with intriguing results. Three of the philosophers represented here studied Husserl's work; two studied with Husserl; the fourth, Franz Brentano, was Husserl's teacher and anticipated several of his major insights. Max Scheler, a pupil of Husserl, did most of his work in ethics, spending much of his time attacking and revising Kant to give the emotions a more central place in morality. Martin Heidegger, also a student of Husserl, became mighty critical of his teacher and returned phenomenology to the service of metaphysics. He subsequently attacked the entire Western philosophical "tradition." Jean-Paul Sartre studied Husserl and Heidegger in France; their work was the greatest single influence in his early philosophical writings, including his studies in philosophical psychology, in the late 1930's, and *Being and Nothingness,* written in 1943.

Franz Brentano

(1838–1917)

INTRODUCTION

A German philosopher and psychologist, Franz Brentano entered the Roman Catholic priesthood in 1864 while a professor of philosophy at Würzburg. When it became clear, in 1873 that the doctrine of papal infallibility, which he could not accept, would not be overturned, Brentano left the priesthood and took a position at the University of Vienna, where he lectured on both philosophy and psychology until 1895. Among his students were Edmund Husserl, the father of the phenomenological movement and Max Scheler, a prominent phenomenologist with a special interest in emotions (see the following selection). Brentano's development of the notion of intentionality laid the groundwork for Husserl's phenomenological approach to philosophical issues; his writings on love and hate stimulated Scheler's work on the emotions and their role in moral knowledge.

Dissatisfied with the plurality of psychological systems existing in his day, Brentano set for himself the task of completely revising the field of psychology in the hope of unifying it into one system. To this end, he embarked on what he called "descriptive psychology"— a description and clarification of basic psychological concepts, as well as a categorization of psychological phenomena. Both his *Psychology from an Empirical Standpoint,* published in 1874, and *On the Classification of Psychical Phenomena,* published in 1911, deal with these issues.

In his descriptive psychology, Brentano distinguished mental phenomena from physical phenomena. Mental phenomena, he argues, "are uniquely characterized by the fact that they have an object, upon which . . . they are directed. Whoever thinks, thinks about something, whoever is angry is angry about something, and so on." His point is that no mental act, whether a thought or an emotion, is simply a mental act; rather, it always refers to something else, some object. Physical phenomena obviously lack this referential quality. Moreover, the objects of mental acts need not exist; when we think about unicorns, we are still thinking about something even though unicorns do not exist. This directedness toward, or reference to, an object is called "intentionality." In claiming that all mental phenomena, including emotions, are intentional, Brentano clearly rejects the traditional view of emotions, espoused by Descartes and Hume, which treats emotions as mere sensations. But Brentano's rejection of traditional views of emotion goes even farther; he argues that many emotions, specifically a special kind of loving and hating, are neither irrational nor subjective.

Brentano believed that we can be intentionally directed toward objects in three basic ways—by having something in mind (a representation or an idea), by accepting or rejecting it (a judgment), or by adopting an emotional pro or con attitude toward it (loving and hating). Love and hate (which have a technical meaning for Brentano) are carefully analyzed in both his psychological and ethical writings. Reprinted here is an excerpt from *On the Origin of Our Knowledge of Right and Wrong,* originally presented in lecture form and published in 1889. Carrying on the moral sentiment tradition begun by Hutcheson and Hume, Brentano argues that we experience the self-evident truth of value-judgments through loves and hates felt to be "correct." In defending this position, Brentano draws an analogy between judgment and emotion. Some of our judgments are mere opinions, which may be either true or false. Sometimes, however, as, for example, when we make mathematical and logical judgments (e.g., that a statement cannot be both true and false), we experience these judgments as being self-evidently true; there is no doubt about their truth. So too for lovings and hatings. Sometimes we love or hate things that do not necessarily deserve to be loved or hated; these feelings are like mere opinions. But sometimes we experience our love, e.g., our love of truth or honesty, as being a correct love. These sorts of emotions give us an insight into moral values. They are not subjective or irrational emotions.

Brentano distinguishes these "correct" lovings and hatings from those not giving us an insight into values, as well as from other emotions, such as fear, hope, and dread, which he says are "extraordinarily complex phenomena." Although writing little on these other emotions, Brentano outlines in the following passage the direction he thinks an investigation of these emotions should take, a direction, in fact, that many subsequent theorists did take: (1) an analysis of individual emotions, (2) an investigation of the use of emotion terms, and (3) an outline of the genetic relations among different emotions (e.g., by distinguishing the emotional type illustrated by love, infatuation and, affection from that illustrated by envy, jealousy, and resentment).

Subsequent theories of emotion, most of which argue for the intentionality of emotions, were profoundly affected by Brentano's theory of intentionality. Note, however, that moods do not seem to fit Brentano's model. When we are depressed or anxious we are not necessarily depressed or anxious about anything. Most subsequent theorists argue that moods, unlike other emotions, are not intentional.

From On the Origin of Our Knowledge of Right and Wrong

LOVING AND HATING

How are we to *know* that a thing is good? Should we say that whatever is loved or is capable of being loved is something that is worthy of love and therefore good? Obviously this would not be right, and it is almost impossible to comprehend how it could be that some have fallen in to such an error. One person loves what another hates. And, in accordance with a well-known psychological law already touched upon in this lecture, it often happens as a result of habit that what is at first desired merely as a means to something else comes to be desired for itself alone. Thus the miser is reduced to heaping up riches irrationally and even to sacrificing himself in order to acquire them. And so we may say that the fact that a thing is loved is no indication that it is worthy of being loved—just as we may say that the fact that something is affirmed or accepted is no indication that it is true.

Indeed, of these two statements, the former is the more obvious. It is hardly possible for a man to accept or affirm something and at the same time hold it to be false. But it may frequently happen that one loves something that one admits to be unworthy of such love. . . . How then, are we to know that a thing is good?

The matter may now seem very puzzling, but there is a simple solution.

To prepare the answer, let us consider once again the analogy that holds between the good and the true.

The fact that we affirm something does not mean that it is true, for we often judge quite blindly. Many of the prejudices that we acquired in our infancy may take on the appearance of indubitable principles. And all men have by nature an impulse to trust certain other judgments that are equally blind—for example, those judgements that are based upon so-called external perception and those that are based upon memories of the recent past. What is affirmed in this way may often be true, but it is just as likely to be false. For these judgements involve nothing that manifests correctness.

But they may be contrasted with certain other judgements which are "insightful" or "evident." The law of contradiction is one example. Other examples are provided by so-called inner perception, which tells me that I am now having such-and-such sound or colour sensations, or that I am now thinking or willing this or that.

What, then, is the essential distinction between these lower and higher forms of judgement? Is it a distinction with respect to degree of conviction or is it something else? It does not pertain to degree of conviction. Many of those blind, instinctive assumptions that arise out of habit are completely uninfected by doubt. Some of them are so firmly rooted that we cannot get rid of them even after we have seen that they have no logical justification. But they are formed under the influence of obscure impulses; they do not have the clarity that is characteristic of the higher form of judgement. If one were to ask, "Why do you really believe that?" it would be impossible to find any rational grounds. Now if one were to raise the same question in connection with a judgement that is immediately evident, here, too, it would be impossible to refer to any grounds. But in this case the clarity of the judgement is such as to enable us to see that the question has no point; indeed, the question would be completely ridiculous. Everyone experiences the difference between these two classes of judgement. As in the case of every other concept, the ultimate explication consists only in a reference to this experience.

In its essentials, all this is universally recognized. Only a few have contested it, and then with great inconsistency. Less notice has been taken of the analogous distinction between the higher and lower types of activity in the emotional sphere, in the sphere of inclination and disinclination.

The feelings of inclination and disinclination often resemble blind judgement in being only instinctive or habitual. This is so in the case of the pleasure the miser takes in hoarding money as well as in those powerful feelings of pleasure and displeasure that men and animals alike connect with the appearance of certain sensuous qualities. Moreover, different species and even different individuals are often affected in contrary ways; this is obvious, of course, in connection with matters of taste.

Many philosophers, and among them very significant thinkers, have taken into account only that mode of pleasure that is peculiar to the lower types of activity within the sphere of the emotions. They have entirely overlooked the fact that there is a higher mode of being pleased or displeased. . . . But the fact is undeniable. We may elucidate it by a few examples.

As I have said, it is natural for us to take pleasure in certain tastes and to feel an antipathy toward others. In both cases, our feelings are purely instinctive. But it is also natural for us to take pleasure in the clarity of insight and to feel displeased by error or ignorance. "All men," Aristotle says in the beautiful introductory words to the *Metaphysics*, "naturally desire knowledge." This desire is an example which will serve our purpose. It is a pleasure of the highest form; it is thus the analogue of something being evident in the sphere of judgement. It is a pleasure that is common to all the members of our species. Imagine now another species quite different from ourselves; not only do its members have preferences with respect to sense qualities which are quite different from ours; unlike us, they also despise insight and love error for its own sake. So far as the feelings about sense qualities are concerned, we might say that these things are a matter of taste, and *"De gustibus non est disputandum."* But this is not what we would say of the love of error and the hatred of insight. We would say that such love and hatred are basically perverse and that the members of the species in question hate what is indubitably and intrinsically good and love what is indubitably and intrinsically bad. Why do we answer differently in the two cases when the feeling of compulsion is equally strong? The answer is simple. In the former case the feeling of compulsion is merely instinctive. But in the latter case the natural feeling of pleasure is a higher love that is experienced as being correct. When we ourselves experience such a love we notice not only that its object is loved and capable of being loved, and that its privation or contrary hated and capable of being hated, but also that the one is worthy of love and the other worthy of hate, and therefore that the one is good and the other bad.

Our knowledge of what is truly and indubitably good arises from the type of experience we have been discussing, where a love is experienced as being correct—in all those cases where we are capable of such knowledge.[1]

We should note, however, that there is no guarantee that every good thing will arouse in us an emotion that is experienced as being

---

1. Love and hate may be directed upon entire classes as well as upon single individuals, as Aristotle had noted. We are angry, he said, only with the particular thief who has robbed us, or with the particular sycophant who has deceived us in our innocence, but we hate thieves and sycophants in general (*Rhetoric*, Book II, Chapter 4, 1382a). Acts of love and hate which are thus based upon some general concept are also frequently experienced as being correct. And then, along with the experience of the given act of love or hate, the goodness or badness of the entire class becomes obvious at a single stroke, so to speak, and without any induction from particular cases. This is the way, for example, that we attain to the general knowledge that insight as such is good. Since we have here the apprehension of a general truth without the induction from particular cases that is required to establish other empirical propositions, some philosophers have been tempted to look upon the universal judgement as a synthetic *a priori* form of immediate knowledge. The temptation is easy to understand. But it overlooks the fact that the apprehension of such a general truth is preceded by an emotion that is experienced as being correct. Herbart has a remarkable doctrine to the effect that one is suddenly elevated to a knowledge of general ethical principles; I suspect that he noticed something of this unique process but without becoming entirely clear about it.

correct. When this does not occur, our criterion fails, in which case the good is absent so far as our knowledge and practical purposes are concerned.

The phenomena of inner perception show us to be substances having psychical accidents. Examples of psychical accidents are: seeing, hearing, conceptual thinking of various kinds, judging, emotional activity, desiring, pleasure, anger, etc. Descartes grouped these together as being "thinking" in the broadest sense of the term. They are uniquely characterized by the fact that they have an object, upon which, as we might say, they are directed. Whoever thinks, thinks about something, whoever is angry is angry about something, and so on. The property of psychical accidents distinguishes every object of inner perception from any object of so-called outer perception. . . .

We may distinguish three basic types of reference to an object: (1) thinking, or having the object before the mind; (2) judging; and (3) loving or hating. Thinking may be ranked first, as being the basic and most general type of reference. We cannot form judgements about a thing—we cannot affirm or deny—unless we think about the thing. And we cannot feel love or hate toward a thing unless we think about the thing. Which are we to rank second—judging, or loving and hating? Here the answer may seem less clear. On the one hand, we can love a thing or desire it, without having made any judgement as to whether or not the thing exists. And on the other hand, we can judge about it, without desiring or detesting it. Some would rank judging second—after thinking and before the emotions—on the ground that judging is more like thinking than are the emotions. But actually there does not seem to be this great similarity. Some would rank the emotions before judging, and would defend themselves by saying that the will determines whether we believe or do not believe. In general, however, this is not the case. Willing requires judging; and evident inner perception is certainly knowledge which is independent of any willing.

The following points would seem to be the ones that are significant in deciding how to order these phenomena:

(1) Juding accompanies every act of inner perception; but it is possible to conceive of an act of inner perception which is not accompanied by any emotion.

(2) The emotions carry with them a much greater degree of complexity and diversity than does judging.

(3) Just as judging as such adds to the perfection of mere thinking, the emotions in turn appear to contribute a still greater degree of perfection, particularly by means of the feeling of happiness.

These three considerations warrant our saying that judging is the second of the three basic types of objective reference and loving and hating the third.

Let us turn, then, to the subspecies of this third type of reference. It is clear, first of all, that any differences in the thoughts or ideas which underlie our emotions will be carried over into the emotions themselves. . . .

Ideas themselves may be distinguished from several different points of view. (1) They may be distinguished by their objects. (2) And (what is connected in a certain way with the first point) they may be distinguished according to whether their objects are thought of in their individuality or only in general terms, and whether they are thought of absolutely or only relatively. (3) Ideas may be distinguished by reference to the temporal mode in which the object is thought. (4) They may be distinguished according to whether the object is thought of positively or negatively. . . . (5) We may distinguish between simple and compound ideas. Compound ideas, in turn, may have a greater or lesser degree of complication; for we can combine attributes in our thinking. Predication may be a matter of judging, as when we say "A tree is green"; but it may also be a matter just of thinking, or having ideas, as when we say "a green tree." And when we form the idea of numbers, such as 2, 3, 5, we compound ideas. We also think in a complex way when we distinguish the parts of a complex object and are able to say that we then have a clearer idea of the whole.

Each of these distinctions, so significant for the sphere of ideas, must correspond to a distinction within the sphere of *love and hate.*

(1) First of all, love, and also hate, may be distinguished according to its object.

(2) They may also be distinguished according to whether they are general or are directed upon some concrete particular, and so on.

(3) They may be distinguished according to the temporal mode with respect to which the object is loved or hatred. In this way, we distinguish the *regret* which pertains to the past, the *pain* or *sorrow* which is directed upon a present experience, and the *fear* of an evil to come.

(4) The emotional relations may be distinguished as positive or negative; it is this distinction which finds expression in the terms "love" and "hate."

(5) The distinction between simple and compound ideas, and of the ways of compounding ideas, should also have bearing upon the ways in which the emotions are directed upon their objects.

Distinctions with respect to jdugement, like those with respect to ideas, carry over into the sphere of the emotions. Thus my emotion will differ markedly depending upon whether some future happiness, which I may picture for myself, appears certain or uncertain, probable or improbable, attainable or unattainable. Again there may be something which is in itself indifferent to me, but which pleases me as being a *sign* of some other thing, or as being *instrumental* to some other thing; such an emotion is quite obviously influenced by judging. Indeed the simplest pleasures of the senses are characterized by the fact that they are experiences which we love and which we apprehend with evidence. We see the same thing in connection with willing and intending or undertaking. No one can will a thing he believes to be beyond his power, however much he may desire it. And no one can form the intention of doing something if he believes that he will never have the opportunity to do it. In such cases, the essential nature of the reference of our emotions is affected by the particular characteristics of the judgements underlying them. The nature of these emotions may perhaps be compared with the partic ular characteristics of the evident, in virtue of which we are able to distinguish judgements which are evident from judgements which are blind.

There are other distinctions which hold exclusively within the sphere of the emotions.

One is the distinction between *loving*, simply, and *preferring*. The latter act involves comparison. If I prefer one thing to another, then I love the one thing more and the other less. Similarly for hating; if I hate one thing more than another, then the one thing could be called, if the expression were permitted, the "preferred object of hate," and the other thing "the less preferred object of hate." In the sphere of judging, there is a true and a false, but of things that are true none of them is *more* true than another, and nothing is *held* to be more true than anything else. . . .

Moreover, there is, in the sphere of the emotions, a *correct* loving or hating and an *incorrect* loving or hating. This may seem to be the analogue of correct acceptance or affirmation and correct rejection or denial, but it is essentially different. . . .

There is another analogy between the emotions and judgement— but it is only an analogy. Sometimes we have an insight into the correctness of love or hate (either simple love or hate or preference) and sometimes we do not. If we have an indirect insight into such correctness, then this presupposes some other direct insight. The logical connection is to be understood in accordance with the usual rules of judgement. When we do have a direct insight into the correctness of an emotion, then the emotion is experienced as being correct. Sometimes, but by no means always, we have such an insight when we love or hate something in itself.

Closer study of these instances of correct emotion shows that they are not only similar to directly evident judgements in general; they bear a specific resemblance to those directly evident judgements in which the truth of the judgement is clear from the *concepts* which the judgement involves. Such judgements are made when contemplation of the object causes an evident rejection or denial, a rejection or denial that is seen to be correct. Thus if we attempt to imagine a round square, we are forced to deny or reject it, for we see that it is impossible. In much the same way, contemplation of knowledge causes a love that is experienced as being correct and contemplation of a painful experience—this being an experience which hates itself, so to speak—causes a feeling of hatred that is experienced as being correct. Consequently our knowledge of the correctness of such love or hatred is *apodictic;* we know that *only* love or hatred can be correct in these cases. Such love and hatred is similar to the apodictic judgement. For apodictic judgements, like these emotions, arise out of the contemplation of their objects.

What are we to say of such emotions as fear, hope, dread, anxiety, agitation, jealousy, envy, anger, terror, horror, uneasiness, lust, disgust—and so on and so forth? In almost every one of these cases we are dealing with an extraordinarily complex phenomenon. Many of the terms are difficult to define; we cannot fix their range of application with any degree of exactness. We come to learn them, not by means of definitions, but by using them in a variety of actual situations. Compare the concept of a high mountain. No one is able to define it so precisely that he could say, of a mountain that was not high, that it *would* be high if only one foot were added. The question of what it is for one person to be angry is similar.

Can one be angry with a non-living thing, such as a chair? Can one be angry with a man who lived many centuries in the past? Or can one be angry with someone who is depicted on the stage or in a novel? If one *can* be angry in these cases, must one have forgotten, for the moment, that the chair is not a living thing, that the historical person belongs to the distant past, and that the person depicted by the poet is only a thing of the imagination?

Such questions readily lead to disputes that are merely verbal. But a scientific treatment could accomplish this much: (a) it could contribute toward the analysis of particular, individual phenomena; (b) by appeal to philogy, it could set more or less definite limits to the use of certain ordinary expressions; and (c), what is of most importance for psychology, it could tell us what particular emotive phenomena, and what groups of such phenomena, are related genetically to each other. Since genetic laws are not exact, we would have to take into account the probability of various connections and relations. Psychological phenomena are connected genetically with physical phenomena, as well as with other psychological phenomena, and these connections can be indicated with some degree of probability for the complex cases we have mentioned. Thus it frequently happens that a frightened man becomes pale and trembles, whereas an angry man becomes both warm and red, "glowing" with anger. There may well be considerable doubt, therefore, about what essential mark of this class of cases really is.

Let us consider the angry man in more detail. It would seem that he wants to inflict evil upon a person toward whom he is hostile, a person who has interfered in some way with some of his own interests. But we cannot call him angry in virtue of this characteristic alone. He must also feel agitated and be seething with a rage which, like a kind of madness, is capable of overpowering him and carrying him away. He clenches his fist against the enemy, even though the enemy may be off in the distance entirely out of reach, and he grinds his teeth, as though he could tear the enemy into bits and then grind him into powder. Above all, the motive for his anger may disappear entirely from his memory, just as the danger to himself may go entirely unheeded; his wild excitement will continue to strengthen his hostile urge to inflict harm.

We know, of course, that animals are also capable of anger. The dog, for example, is easily made angry, because of his instincts, and his anger will quickly rise to a level of great vehemence. Anger in dogs is very much like fear in sheep; as soon as the sheep sees a wolf, he is instinctively overcome with fear. Similarly, other animals may be overcome by hunger, or by thirst, or during mating season by the sexual urge. The essential characteristic of the angry man is the overpowering urge to inflict harm, an urge which may have no clear motive and which is bound up with a great variety of passions and reflexes.

If one were able to excite all of these side-effects in a dog, then probably one could also create in him the urge to do harm, without his knowing what it is that he wishes to harm. Aristotle pointed out, similarly, that since fear makes one cold, people are often made fearful merely by becoming cold, without knowing what it is that they fear. If, therefore, the desire to inflict harm can induce a state of agitation and excitement, while, on the other hand, the state of agitation and excitement can create the desire to inflict harm, we may wonder whether the first or the second of these marks constitutes the essence of anger. We may do well in the meantime to regard the essence of anger as comprising, not only both of these things, but also a genetic relation to some prior experience which occasioned the whole hostile state. In the case of man, anger is commonly bound up with a desire for vengeance—a vengeance which is not merely a matter of receiving a just and proper compensation. The angry man would take out his vengeance on the enemy himself; he would cool off his anger by inflicting harm upon his enemy.

Max Scheler

(1874-1928)

INTRODUCTION

Max Scheler lived through the advent and rise of the philosophical movement known as "phenomenology," which was an attempt to get behind scientific and philosophical preconceptions to a description of the essences of things themselves, untainted by theoretical prejudices. Although the German philosopher Edmund Husserl is usually credited with fathering phenomenology, Scheler, who first met Husserl in 1901 and later corresponded with him claimed to have arrived independently at some of the crucial insights of the phenomenological method of doing philosophy. In his day, Scheler was regarded as one of its leading exponents. He was one of the four original co-editors of Husserl's *Jahrbuch,* which was devoted to phenomenological studies; his *Formalism in Ethics and Non-formal Ethics of Values* (excerpted here) first appeared in the *Jahrbuch.*

Like his contemporary, Martin Heidegger (excerpted in the following selection), who also falls within the phenomenlogical tradition, Max Scheler was preoccupied with the question "What is Man?" His work delves into the nature of man as an ethical, religious, cultural, historical, and natural being. For Scheler, the question can be answered only by investigating human emotional life. This is particularly clear in three major works, *Formalism, The Nature of Sympathy,* and *On the Eternal in Man. Formalism,* written in 1916, was Scheler's first major work. It is an ethical treatise on the nature of values and valuing. In it Scheler introduces and defends the idea that there is a *logique du coeur*—a ranked order of values, spanning from the lower values of the agreeable and disagreeable, through ethical values, to the highest value of the holy, which are "felt" or known through different emotional acts. The later *The Nature of Sympathy* (1931) and *On the Eternal in Man* develop ideas latent in *Formalism.* In *On the Eternal in Man,* Scheler attempts to work out the essence of the divine or holy, whereas in *The Nature of Sympathy,* he analyzes sympathy phenomenologically, as well as love, hatred, pity, and other emotions. In this latter work, Scheler argues that our knowledge and understanding of other minds is not inferential, based on our understanding of ourselves, but rather is the result of an immediate emotional contact with others.

Max Scheler has been described as a passionate man who not only pursued a wide range of philosophical and anthropological issues from ethics to the sociology of knowledge to the evolutionary development of the human psyche, but who also actively participated in current political and moral isues. During World War I, Scheler staunchly defended German involvement in the war in his *The Genius of War and the German War* and was sent on diplomatic missions by the German Foreign Office. (Toward the end of the war, however, Scheler made an about-face, defending pacifism on Christian grounds.) Throughout his life, Scheler wrestled with questions about the correct conception of religion and God. *On the Eternal in Man* is, in part, a defense of Christianity, particularly Catholicism. But only a year after its publication, Scheler left the Church, unable to reconcile his own views with Church dogmatism; and in *Formalism,* he claims he can no longer describe himself even as a theist.

Scheler held a number of academic positions. In 1901, he became a privatdozent at Jena; it was here that he first met Husserl. In 1907, he took a position at the University of Munich, where he met Brentano and a number of Husserl's students, resigning in 1910 to pursue philosophy on his own. And in 1919, Scheler received an academic appointment in philosophy and sociology at the University of Cologne.

The following selection is taken from Scheler's major work in moral philosophy, *Formalism in Ethics and Non-formal Ethics of Values.* Although heavily influenced by the ethical writings of Immanuel Kant, one of the great moral thinkers in the history of philosophy, Scheler repudiated the formality of Kant's ethics. For Kant, the moral value of any act resided solely in its conformity to a universal moral imperative, that is, in the fact that the act is the sort of act we could wish anyone to perform in similar circumstances. Thus, kindness, generosity, sincerity, and the like are not themselves moral values of actions. Rather, a kind act, for example, has value only insofar as it is one that can be universally commanded. This, Scheler thought, is an overly formal conception of value. By contrast, Scheler argued that such qualities as kindness, beauty, grace, nobility, and vitality are themselves value-qualities. In *Formalism*, Scheler works out a value system that contrasts sharply with Kant's; as part and parcel of this work, Scheler developed a distinctive theory about how we recognize values in persons, things, and acts (a theory, which, although novel, has its roots in the moral sentiment theories of philosophers like Francis Hutcheson and David Hume, as well as in Brentano's later work). He argues that we experience special feelings, which he calls "value-feelings" or "feeling-functions," through which we feel the grace, generosity, vitality, and so on of persons, things, and acts. Thus, our original awareness of valuable features in the world around us occurs in our emotional responses to them.

If any one statement could summarize Scheler's general position in the *Formalism*, it is Blaise Pascal's aphorism "the heart has its reasons, which reason does not know." In other words, Scheler's central project was to show that feeling is a form of cognition that allows us to "see" values in the surrounding world of facts ("the heart has its reasons") and that feeling is a form of cognition utterly distinct from and irreduceable to any rational or intellectual cognition ("which reason does not know"). It is crucial to Scheler that feeling be raised up from the level of "blind feeling." He argues vehemently against Cartesian analyses of emotion that reduce emotions to irrational affects that happen to us and that do not, except accidentally, contribute anything to our knowledge of the world. Scheler's own analysis of emotion is diametrically opposed to this and represents an attempt to overcome the traditional dichotomy between emotion and reason. For Scheler, at least some emotions stand on a par with reason, being a kind of "intuition" or "insight" into what is valuable or not valuable; such emotions provide our only access to the world of values. (His theory, in short, is that were we not emotional beings, our whole intellectual life would be confined to purely factual observations about the world, and we would never be able to evaluate these facts.)

Scheler's monumental reconstruction of our idea of emotion grew directly out of Franz Brentano's work. Both construct intentional theories of emotion; both wrestle with the relation between emotion and our knowledge of values; and both elevate emotion to a place of prominence in what might loosely be called the intellectual life. But two critical innovations especially distinguish Scheler's work from Brentano's. First, Brentano had not, in Scheler's opinion, adequately distinguished values from emotions. Brentano had not, in Scheler's terms, seen that values are autonomous "value-facts," independent of our cognitive apparatus. For Brentano, to say that a painting is beautiful *is* simply to say that it is correctly loved. Beauty is not an independent "value-fact" that we can then know or intuit through feelings of love or aesthetic delight. Rather, the beauty of a painting resides simply in the fact that it evokes a feeling of love, which we experience as being "correct" or appropriate. What this means is that, for Brentano, emotions are not cognitive mental acts in a strict sense—they do not inform us of independent features (namely, values) of the world. (A similar criticism could be made of moral sentiment theories like David Hume's theory.) By contrast, Scheler argues that emotions are cognitive in a strict sense. Through our emotions we "see" values in much the way that through our sense of sight we see colors and shapes. And thus our emotions are genuinely informative mental acts.

Second, whereas Brentano thought that all emotions are intentional mental acts involving a pro or con attitude toward things in the world, Scheler argues that only a select group of emotions, which he calls "value-feelings" or "feeling-functions," is intentional. Although it is not always clear in *Formalism* which emotions count as value-feelings, the distinction itself between value-feelings and what Scheler calls "feeling-states" is clear. Value-feelings are intentional, "presentational" (i.e., they make us aware of values) and play just as important a role in intellectual life as does reason. By contrast, feeling-states are nonintentional, they happen to us and last for a more or less determinate period of time, and they are explained in causal terms. Anger, for example, is, in Scheler's theory, a feeling-state; Scheler claims that we are not immediately aware of anything in anger, but rather must seek for the causal origin of our anger after the fact. These two very different accounts of emotion exist in uneasy tension in *Formalism.* At times, for example, he speaks of feelings of health or disease, disapproval and approval, bliss and despair as being feeling-states; at other times he calls them value-feelings. But even if he ultimately fails to explain why feeling-states and value feelings are both emotions, it is to Scheler's credit that he sees that there are two different, equally natural analyses of feeling—one of feelings as intentional cognitive acts and one of feelings as nonintentional and noncognitive phenomena caused by the appreciation of value.

From Formalism in Ethics and Non-Formal Ethics of Values

Feeling and Feeling-States

Until recent times philosophy was inclined to a prejudice that has its historical origin in antiquity. This prejudice consists in upholding the divison between "reason" and "sensibility," which is completely inadequate in terms of the structure of the spiritual. This division demands that we assign everything that is not rational—that is not order, law, and the like—to sensibility. Thus our *whole emotional life*—and, for most modern philosophers, our conative life as well, even love and hate—must be assigned to "sensibility." According to this division, *everything* in the mind which is alogical, e.g., intuition, feeling, striving, loving, hating, is dependent of man's *psychophysical organization.* The formation of the alogical becomes here a function of real changes in organization during the evolution of life and history, and dependent on the peculiarities of the environment and all their effects. Whether there are original as well as essential differentiations in rank among the essences of acts and functions at the base of the alogical of our spiritual life, that is, whether these acts and functions have an "originality" comparable to that of the acts in which we comprehend objects in pure logic—in other words, whether there is also a *pure intuiting and feeling, a pure loving and hating, a pure striving and willing,* which are *as* independent of the psychophysical organization of man as pure thought, and which at the same time possess their own original laws that cannot be reduced to laws of empirical psychic life—this question is not even asked by those who share this prejudice. Since no one asks this question, no one asks whether or not there are a priori interconnections and oppositions among the objects and qualities to which those alogical acts are directed, or whether or not there is an a priori lawfulness of these acts which corresponds to such interconnections and oppositions.

The consequence of this prejudice is that ethics has in the course of its history been constituted either as absolute and a priori, and therefore rational, or as relative, empirical, and emotional. That ethics can and must be both absolute *and* emotional has rarely even been considered.

Very few thinkers have tried to undermine this prejudice (and then nothing more than that, for none has managed to elaborate an opposing viewpoint). Two such thinkers are Augustine and Blaise Pascal. Throughout Pascal's works we find an idea which he calls *ordre du coeur* or *logique du coeur;* it runs through them like a golden thread. He says, "Le coeur a ses raisons." To him this means that there is an eternal and absolute lawfulness of feeling, loving, and hating which is as absolute as that of pure logic, but which is not reducible to intellectual lawfulness. . . .

It is strange to see how these remarks of Pascal have been misunderstood by so many of his interpreters! One of them thinks he means that "the heart, too, has its say when reason has spoken"! This is a well-known opinion, and it is held by philosophers, too. We are told, for example, that "philosophy's task is to furnish both reason and the heart with a satisfactory world view." That is, the word *reason (raisons)* is taken somewhat ironically. Supposedly Pascal does not mean to say that the heart *has* reasons or that there is anything which is *truly equivalent* to "reasons" in its rank and meaning, i.e., *"ses" raisons,* or its *own* reasons not borrowed from understanding: rather he means that one must not always seek "reasons" or their "equivalents," but must occasionally let the "heart" speak—blind feeling! But this is the exact *opposite* of what Pascal means. The stress of his proposition is on *ses* raisons and *ses* raisons. . . . [T]here is a type of experiencing whose "objects" are completely inaccesible to reason: reason is as blind to them as ears and hearing are blind to colors. It is a kind of experience that leads us to *genuinely* objective objects and the eternal order among them, i.e., to *values* and the order of ranks among them. And the order and laws contained in this experience are as exact and evident as those of logic and mathematics: that is, there are evident interconnections and oppositions among values and value-attitudes and among the acts of preferring, etc., which are built on them, and on the basis of these a genuine grounding of moral decisions and laws for such decisions is both possible and necessary.

We shall take up Pascal's idea at this point.

First, we must distinguish between the intentional *"feeling of something"* and mere *feeling-states.* This distinction in itself does not yet bear on the content given in intentional feelings, i.e., when we regard them as organs for comprehending values. *There is original* emotive intentionality. Perhaps this is most apparent when both a feeling and feeling it occur simultaneously, when a feeling is that toward which feeling is directed. Let us consider a feeling-state that is indubitably sensible, e.g., a sensible pain or state of pleasure, or a state of pleasure, or a state that corresponds to the agreeableness of a food, a scent, or a gentle touch, etc. Given such facts, such feeling-states, the kind and mode of feeling them is by no means yet determined. There are changing facts involved when I "suffer," "endure," "tolerate," or even "enjoy" "pain." What varies here in the functional quality of *feeling* it (which can also vary by degrees) is certainly not the *state of pain.* Nor is this variation to be found in general attention, with its levels of "noticing," "heeding," "noting," "observing," and "viewing." Pain observed is almost the opposite of pain suffered. In addition, all these kinds and levels of attention and interpretive viewings may freely vary to any extent within such qualities of feeling without any dissolution of the feeling itself. The limits of the feelable variations of the givenness of pain are quite different from those of a feeling-state in its relation to excitation and different also from the degrees of such a state. For this reason the ability to suffer or to enjoy has nothing to do with sensitivity to sensible pleasure and pain. An individual can suffer the same degree of pain more or less than another individual.

Hence feeling-states and feeling are totally different. The former belong to contents and appearances; the latter, to the functions of reception. This becomes clear when we heed the differences that are obviously present.

All specifically sensible feelings are, by their nature, states. They may be "connected" with objects through the simple contents of sensing, representing, or perceiving: or they may be more or less "objectless." Whenever there is such a connection, it is always *mediate*. The subsequent acts of relating which follow the givenness of a feeling connect feelings with objects. This is the case, for instance, when I ask myself: "Why am I in this or that mood today?" "What is it that *causes* my sadness or joy?" Indeed, the causal object and the feeling-state can enter perception or memory in terms of quite different acts. I relate the object and the feeling-state in such cases through "thinking." The feeling itself is not *originally* related to an object, e.g., when I "feel the beauty of snow-covered mountains in the light of the setting sun." In some cases a feeling is connected with an object through association or through a perception or representation of it. Surely there are feeling-states which at first appear to be without any relation to an object. I must then find the cause that produces the state. But in none of these cases is a feeling related *of itself* to an object. It does not "take" anything, nor is there anything that "moves" toward it, nor is there anything in it that "approaches me." There is no "signifying" in it, nor is there any immanent directedness in it. Finally, a feeling can, after it has frequently occurred in my lived body in connection with outer objects, situations, or changing experiences, become a *"token"* of these changes. This is the case, for example, when I recognize the beginning of an illness by the presence of specific pains because I have learned that these are connected with the onset of such an illness. In this case also, a symbolic relation is mediated only through experience and thinking.

However, the connection between *intentional feeling* and *what* is therein felt is entirely different from the above connection. This connection is present in all feeling *of* values.[1] There is here an orig-

---

1. Hence we distinguish: (1) The feeling of feelings in the sense of feeling-states and their modes, e.g., suffering, enjoying. I wish to add that apart from vacillations in the modes of an identical feeling-state, the feeling of the feeling-state itself can approximate a zero point. Very strong affectations of fright (e.g., on the occasion of an earthquake) often produce a virtually complete absence of feeling. (Jaspers' *All-*

inal relatedness, a directedness of feeling toward something objective, namely, *values*. This kind of feeling is not a dead state or a factual state of affairs that can enter into associative connections or be related to them; nor is such feeling a "token." This feeling is a goal-determined movement, although it is by no means an *activity* issuing forth from a center (nor is it a temporally extended movement). It is a punctual movement, whether objectively directed from the ego or coming toward the ego as a movement in which something *is* given to me and in which it comes to "appearance." This feeling therefore has the same relation to its value-correlate as "representing" has to its "object," namely, an intentional relation. It is not *externally brought together* with an object, whether immediately or thorugh a representation (which can be related to a feeling either mechanically and fortuitously or by mere thinking). On the contrary, feeling *originally* intends its *own* kind of objects, namely, *"values."* Feeling is therefore a meaningful occurrence that is capable of "fulfillment" and "non-fulfillment."[2] Consider an affect in contrast to this. An affect of anger "wells up within me" and then "takes its course in me." The connection of anger with the "about" of my anger is not intentional or original. A representation or a thought

---

gemeine Psychopathologie [Berlin: Springer, 1913], which I just received, gives some good descriptions of this.) In these cases sensitivity remains intact, and there is no reason to assume that the feeling-states are not *present.* What occurs in extreme cases is a marked increase in the *intensity* of the feeling; there is complete fulfilment by it, which makes us for a moment "feelingless" with respect to this feeling. We are put into a state of rigid and convulsive "indifference" toward it. In this case it is only when the feeling goes away, or when our complete fulfillment by it begins to disappear, that the feeling becomes an object of feeling proper. The rigid indifference begins to "dissolve," and we feel the feeling. In this sense the feeling of a feeling-state "relieves" and takes away the state of pressure. I have pointed out elsewhere that in a similar way true cofeeling with the suffering of another *frees* us from infection by this suffering. [See *Wesen und Formen der Sympathie*, pt. A, chap. 2, sec. 3 (toward the end).—*Ed.*] (2) The feeling of objective emotional characteristics of the atmosphere (restfulness of a river, serenity of the skies, sadness of a landscape), in which there are emotionally qualitative characteristics that can also be given as qualities of feeling, but never as "feelings," i.e., as experienced in relatedness to an ego. (3) The feeling of *values*, e.g., agreeable, beautiful, good. It is *here* that feeling gains a cognitive function in addition to its intentional nature, whereas it does not do so in the first two cases.

2. For this reason all "feeling of" is in principle "understandable," whereas pure feeling-states are subject only to observation and causal explanation.

or, better, the objects in these that I first "perceived," "represented," or "thought" are what "cause my anger." And it is later—even though in normal cases very quickly—that I relate this anger to these objects, and then always through a representation. Surely I do not "comprehend" anything in this anger. Certain *evils* must be "comprehended" beforehand in *feeling* if anger is to be aroused. It is quite different when I "rejoice in something," or when I "am sad about something" or when I "am merry" or "despondent." The use of the words *in* and *about* shows that in this rejoicing and sadness the objects "about" which I am glad, etc., are not first of all comprehended. They already stand *before* me in that they are not only perceived but also charged with the value-predicates which are given *in* feeling. The value-qualities in value-affair-complexes *demand* certain qualities in emotional "reactions of response" of the same type, and these reactions in a certain sense "reach their goal" in the value-qualities. They form complexes of understanding and meaning, complexes of their own kind which are not simply empirically contingent or dependent on the individual psychic causality of individuals. If value-demands appear to remain unfulfilled, we suffer as a result, e.g., we are sad because we cannot be happy about an event to the degree that its felt value deserves, or we cannot be as sad as the death of a beloved person "demands." Such peculiar "manners of conduct" (we do not call them acts or functions) have "direction" in common with intentional feeling; but they are *not* intentional in the strict sense of this term, if we understand *intentional* to indicate only those experiences that can *mean* an object and in whose execution an objective content can *appear*. This occurs only in emotional experiences, which, in a strict sense, constitute value-feeling. For here we do not feel "about something"; we immediately feel *something*, i.e., a specific value-quality. In this case, i.e., *in* the execution of feeling, we are not objectively conscious of feeling itself. Only a value-quality comes "upon" us from within or without. A new act of reflection is required if this "feeling of" is to become objective, thus enabling us to reflect subsequently on *what* we "feel" in the already objectively given value.

Let us call these feelings that receive values the class of *intentional functions of feeling*. It is not necessary for these functions to be connected with the objective sphere through the mediation of so-called objectifying acts of representation, judgment, etc. Such mediation is necessary *only* for feeling-states, *not* for geniuine intentional feeling. During the process of intentional feeling, the world of objects "comes to the fore" by itself, but only in terms of its *value-*aspect. The frequent lack of pictorial objects in intentional feeling shows that feeling is originally an "objectifying act" that does not require the mediation of representation. . . . Of course one overlooks these facts—indeed even the task of setting them forth—if he assigns the entire sphere of feeling to psychology *originaliter;* and then he can never see that part of *the world and the value-content of world* which *comes forth in* feeling, *in* preferring, *in* loving and *hating.* He sees only what we find in inner perception, i.e., in "representational" comportment, *if* we feel, *if* we prefer, *if* we love and hate, *if* we enjoy a work of art, *if* we pray to God.

It is necessary to distinguish emotional functions from the experiences that are based on *"preferring"* and *"placing after."* The latter constitute a *higher* stage in our emotional and intentional life, and *in* them we comprehend the ranks of values, their being higher and lower. "Preferring" and "placing after" are not conative activities like, say, "choosing," which is based on acts of preferring. Nor is preferring (or placing after) a purely feeling comportment. It constitutes a special class of emotional act-experiences. The proof is that we can "choose," strictly speaking, only between actions, whereas we can "prefer" one good to another, good weather to bad, one food to another, etc. Moreover, this "preferring" occurs immediately on the basis of the felt value-material and independent of its thing-bearers. It does not presuppose pictorial goal-contents or contents of purposes, whereas choosing does. On the contrary, the contents of goals in conation—contents that are not contents of purposes, which, as we saw, presuppose a reflection on preceding contents of goals and belong only to willing within conation—are *formed* with the cocondition of preferring. Therefore, preferring belongs to the sphere of *value-cognition, not* to the sphere of striving. This class of experiences, experiences of preferring, is in the strict sense intentional; these experiences are "directed" and sense-giving, but we classify them with loving and hating as "emotional acts," in contrast to intentional functions of feeling.

Finally, *loving* and *hating* constitute the highest level of our intentional emotive life. Here we are farthest from all states. The difference between them and reactive responses is marked even in language: we speak not of loving or hating "about something" or "in something," but loving or hating *something*. The fact that we frequently hear people assert that love and hate, like anger, rage, and spite, belong to the "affects," or that love and hate belong to feeling-states, can be explained only by the peculiar lack of learning in our age and the complete lack of phenomenological investigations of these matters. . . . In love and hate our spirit does much more than "respond" to already felt and perhaps preferred values. Love and hate are acts in which the value-realm accessible to the feeling of a being (the value-realm with which preferring is also connected) is either *extended* or *narrowed* (and this, of course, independent of the present world of *goods*, i.e., real valuable things, which are not presupposed in the plurality, fullness, and differentiation of felt values). In speaking of this "extension" or "narrowing" of the value-realm given to a being, I do not mean to imply in the least that values are created, made, or destroyed by love and hate. Values cannot be created or destroyed. They exist independent of the organization of all beings endowed with spirit. I do not mean to say that the nature of the act of love is such that it is directed in a "responding" fashion to a value *after* that value is felt or preferred; I mean, rather, that, strictly speaking, this act plays the *disclosing* role in our value-comprehensions, and that it is only this act which does so. This act is, as it were, a movement in whose execution ever *new* and *higher* values flash out, i.e., values that were wholly unknown to the being concerned. Thus this act does not *follow* value-feeling and preferring, but is ahead of them as a *pioneer* and a guide. And we must therefore attribute a *"creative"* role to this act to the extent that the range and nature of feelable and preferable values of a being, but not the existing values themselves, are concerned. Hence *all* of ethics would reach its completion in the discovery of the laws of love and hate, which, in regard to the degree of their absoluteness, apriority, and originality, go beyond the laws of preferring and those obtaining among their corresponding value-qualities.

Let us return to the discussion of intentional feeling. Allow me one historical observation. In my opinion there have been two major periods in the history of philosophy in which erroneous theories have been set forth on this point—though erroneous in very different ways. The first of these periods continued up to the nineteenth century. We find that the theory of intentional feeling was widely held until then. Spinoza, Descartes, and Leibniz shared this theory, though with modifications. None of these thinkers or their disciples identified the whole of the emotional life in its kind of giveness with, if I may use the expression, a pain in the stomach. If this is done, values of course cannot be found. It is likely that there never would have been an astronomy if the sun, the moon, and the stars that appear in the night skies had been regarded as statelike "complexes of sensations," i.e., as phenomena which are on the *same* level of givenness as a pain in the stomach, and which are "dependent" on the appearance of a pain in the stomach in different ways only to the extent that they differ from each other. Only in an age in which the confusion of hearts, the *désordre du coeur,* has reached the degree that it has in our own could the totality of our emotive life be considered a process of causally moved states which follow each other without meaning or ends, and only in such an age could our emotive life be denied "meaning" and intentional "contents." The error of these great thinkers was their assumption that feeling, loving, hating, etc., are nothing ultimate and original in spirit, and that values, on the other hand, are not ultimate and irreducible phenomena. Like Leibniz, they held that intentional feeling is simply "dark" and "confused" conceiving and thinking; the object of such confused and dark thought is constituted in evident and rational relations. According to Leibniz, for example, maternal love is a confused conception of the fact that it is good to love one's child. . . .

At the beginning of the nineteenth century (after Tetens and Kant) the *irreducibility* of the emotional life was gradually recognized. But since the intellectualistic attitude of the eighteenth century was maintained, *everything* emotional was degraded to *states.*

If we compare these two basic conceptions with what we said earlier, we can see that each contains something correct as well as something incorrect. The first contains insight that there is an *intentional* "feeling of," and that there are, in addition to feeling-states, emotional functions and acts in which something is given and which underlie autonomous laws of meaning and understanding. What is erroneous here . . . is the assumption that feeling can be reduced to "understanding," and that there is only a difference in degree between feeling and understanding. In the second theory the assumption that emotive being and life cannot be "reduced" to "understanding" is correct, but the implicit denial of intentional feeling and the abandonment of the entire emotional life to a descriptive psychology and its causal explanations is wrong. It hardly needs to be said that the concession of some modern psychologists that feelings (e.g., of different kinds of pain, of fatigue, appetite, fear, etc.) possess a *purposeful* character for life's activity and its guidance, and that these function as *signs* of certain present or future states to be further enhanced or avoided, has nothing to do with their *intentional* nature or their cognitive functions. Nothing is "given" in a mere signal. The modes of the feeling of life must therefore be reinvestigated on the basis of our basic thesis. And in this it will be shown that mere emotional states are, stricly speaking, only sensible feelings, but that vital feelings and pure psychic and spiritual feelings *can* always exhibit an intentional character, and that the purely spiritual ones exhibit it essentially.

Martin Heidegger

(1889-1976)

INTRODUCTION

Martin Heidegger is one of the most controversial—and difficult—philosophical authors of this century. His book *Being and Time,* published in 1927, was a major influence on the existentialist movement throughout Europe and, later on, in the Americas and even the Orient. The style of *Being and Time* is phenomenological, but with significant variations on the method Heidegger learned from his teacher, Edmund Husserl. Heidegger, unlike Husserl, was primarily interested in the woolier questions of metaphysics and the philosophical problems of life. Accordingly, where Husserl is concerned with questions about the foundations of knowledge and the nature of mathematics, *Being and Time* is filled with such concepts as "Being-unto-Death," "*Angst,*" and "Care." Heidegger's ambition in *Being and Time* is to develop an "ontology" (a theory of being) of human existence, which he calls "Dasein" (being-there). But instead of beginning with human consciousness and knowledge, as do most authors of the Western philosophical tradition (including his teacher Husserl), Heidegger insists that human existence (or Dasein) is first of all practical and concerned. Our way of existence (or Being-in-the-World) is not so much to *know* the world as it is to *care* about our place in the world.

Consequently, one of the key concerns of *Being and Time* is the phenomenon of *moods.* Heidegger talks only occasionally about specific emotions, but moods are, for him, the very basis of human awareness, not at all the occasional interruptions or "states" in which we are sometimes gloomy or joyful. But because moods are so fundamental to his philosophy, it is also difficult if not impossible to discuss Heidegger's theory of moods without also introducing the basic concepts of his very difficult system of philosophy. What Heidegger gives us is not just a new view of emotions and moods, but rather a new vision of ourselves and the world. It is the central importance of moods in Heidegger's philosophy, as much as any theory he holds about their nature, that has made his philosophy so influential and controversial.

Adding to the difficulty of the text is the impossibility of obtaining the right to reprint Heidegger's work. Accordingly, we have tried to resolve both difficulties by asking Heidegger-scholar Charles Guignon to write an essay especially for this book, in which he both summarizes the basic intentions of Heidegger's work and presents Heidegger's theory of moods.

Moods in Heidegger's *Being and Time*

Charles Guignon*

Heidegger's discussion of moods in *Being and Time* is part of his wider project of working out "the question of the meaning of Being": that is, the attempt to articulate our most fundamental sense of what it is to be. In order to pose this "question of Being" in an appropriate way, Heidegger suggests, we should first get clear about ourselves, the questioners. The assumption is that if we can clarify the structure of the entity that *understands* what it is to be, then we will have clarified the region in which the question of the *meaning* of Being can be posed. The published parts of *Being and Time*, therefore, deal solely with an analysis of being human—a phenomenon called *"Dasein"* or "being-there." If this investigation is to be truly fundamental, however, it cannot uncritically take over traditional assumptions about the nature of being human. For this rea-

*Charles Guignon is Assistant Professor of Philosophy at the University of Texas.

son, Heidegger says that the inquiry into the being of Dasein must be rooted in a "basic experience of the 'object' to be disclosed" (232).[1] This experience is pre-cognitive: it turns up not in thought, but rather in moods. Moods, according to Heidegger, are "a primordial kind of Being for Dasein, in which Dasein is disclosed to itself *prior to* all cognition and volition, and *beyond* their range of disclosure" (136). The account of moods in *Being and Time* therefore has a dual role: (1) it is part of the overall elucidation of the human condition, and (2) it paves the way towards securing a "phenomenal basis" for the characterization of Dasein and hence for the question of Being.

Heidegger believes that the prevailing ways of understanding the nature of being human are infected by deep-seated presuppositions that give us a distorted view of ourselves. There is a tendency to think of ourselves as "things" or "substances" of some sort. At a theoretical level, we are inclined to think of the self as a mind or "subject of experiences," as a physical organism in the natural world, or as an odd mixture of both. These alternatives, in Heidegger's view, involve uncritical ontological assumptions that need to be grounded in a deeper understanding of man. In a letter written to his teacher, Edmund Husserl, in 1927, Heidegger says that "the 'one-sided' reflections of somatology [i.e., physiology] and pure psychology are only possible on the basis of the concrete totality of man." In particular, the conception of the "mental" as definitive of human being "has originated at the outset from *epistemological* considerations" and therefore cannot provide us with a basis for an "ontology of man in totality."[2]

If the question of Being is to have a secure foundation, it must set aside all traditional interpretations of human existence and start from a fresh perspective. Heidegger attempts to capture the "concrete totality of man" as *agency* in everyday situations prior to any of the philosophical splits into mind versus body, subject versus object, or consciousness versus thing. To be human, as the term Das-

---

1. Numbers in parentheses refer to the German edition of *Sein und Zeit,* 12th edition (Tübingen: Niemeyer, 1972). The German pagination is found in the margins of the English edition of *Being and Time,* translated by Macquarrie and Robinson (New York: Harper & Row, 1962).

2. Letter to Husserl dated 22 October 1927, in E. Husserl, *Phänomenologische Psychologie,* ed. Walter Biemel, Husserliana, IX (The Hague: Nijhoff, 1962), p. 602.

ein suggests, is to be "there," caught up in the world, taking a stand on one's life, active and engaged in ordinary situations, with some overview of what is at stake in living. What characterizes human life in its most natural ways of being is not a relationship between mind and body but concrete "existing" in a world: "The *'substance'* of man is not spirit as a synthesis of soul and body," Heidegger says, "rather, it is *existence*" (117). Our most natural experience of ourselves is described as "Being-in-the-world," where "world" refers not to the universe studied by physics, but rather to a life-world in the sense in which we speak of "the academic world" or "the world of theater." To be "in" such a world is not like a pencil's being "in" a drawer; it is more like being engaged or involved in something, as is someone who is "into" astrology.

Dasein as existence in a world is far from being a "subject" or "center of experiences and actions" in any sense. One of the chief aims of *Being and Time* is to overcome the tradition of subjectivism that has dominated so much of philosophical anthropology. In Heidegger's view, the tendency to see man as a subject is a product of some highly sophisticated philosophical abstraction and does not give us a good clue to the basic nature of being human. For this reason he attempts to fully describe Dasein without bringing in mentalistic vocabulary, or by recasting our ordinary psychological words to bring out a non-mentalistic root meaning (e.g., the idea of "taking a stand" in "understanding"). This is not to *deny* the subjective and mental side of life: indeed, a "formal phenomenology of consciousness" would be an interesting undertaking (115). But it does deny that the subjective or psychological has any privileged position in comprehending what it is to be human. We know ourselves not by inward-turning and introspection, but by catching sight of ourselves as we are engaged and preoccupied in everyday practical contexts. Heidegger says that

> one's *own* Dasein becomes something that it can itself proximally "come across" only when it *looks away* from "experiences" and the "center of its actions," or does not yet "see" them at all. Dasein finds "itself" proximally in *what* it does, uses, expects, avoids—in those things environmentally on hand with which it is proximally *concerned.* (119)

True self-knowledge is reached not by "perceptually tracking down and inspecting a point called the 'self'" (146), but rather by catching a glimpse of ourselves when we are caught up in the flux and flow of living. Here the idea of a "mental" or "subjective" component of our lives simply has no role to play.

In order to bypass traditional objectifying views of the self, Heidegger characterizes Dasein as a "happening" or "event" of a life as a whole, "between birth and death" (233). According to this conception of Dasein as a happening, there are two aspects to human existence. On the one hand, we are "already-in" a world. Heidegger says that we are *delivered over to* ourselves: we are "thrown" into the task of living, and we find ourselves in a specific cultural and historical context, which provides us with a determinate range of possible roles and self-interpretations. In our world, for instance, we can be consumers and producers, but not vassals and seigneurs. The concrete context in which we find ourselves, together with the choices we have made at the crossroads of our lives, makes up our "facticity." But, on the other hand, we are also already "ahead of" ourselves in taking a stand on our lives. As engaged and active in the world, we take over concrete roles and self-interpretations that express our sense of what life is all about. Heidegger sees life as structured by goal-directedness and purposiveness: we are always under way towards the culmination or realization of life, our "Being-a-whole" or "Being-towards-death." This purposive thrust towards our completion, which is accomplished in taking up specific possibilities, is called "projection." Whether we realize it or not, each of our actions projects some sense of what our lives will add up to as a final configuration of meanings.

This "formal" temporal structure of Dasein's being as a thrown projection only achieves its concrete realization as Being-in-the-world. To be human is to be situated in a worldly context: a workshop, study, supermarket, garden, or office. In our normal, everyday situations, prior to philosophical reflection or scientific abstraction, we find ourselves caught up in the swim, handling equipment in order to realize particular aims and goals. There is a reciprocal relationship between our purposive agency and the practical contexts in which we find ourselves. Our goals, interests, and needs structure the ways in which things will *count* for us in the context. The wary shopper, for instance, encounters a supermarket where the bargains stand out and the over-priced junk recedes. But the context also determines the range of possible *self*-interpretations one can have: in a supermarket one can be a wise shopper or an impulse buyer, but not a mutineer. Our everyday Being-in-the-world forms a holistic field in which the means/ends relations of smoothly functioning equipment are tied into the goal-directedness of our being. Here there is no room for a Cartesian "I" or an epistemological subject distinct from a mere collection of objects. Heidegger opposes the modern tendency to displace meanings and values into the realm of the "subjective." What is originally "given" is a meaningful totality of worldhood, a seamless whole of Being-in-the-world.

To be human, then, is to be contextualized in a world. But that world is not "private" in any sense. Heidegger also emphasizes the fact that we are contextualized in a culture and in history. In our everyday lives, our routine tasks follow the norms and conventions that are laid out for us in the social world in which we live. We do things as "anyone" would do them in that context, so that Heidegger says that in "everydayness" we *are* the "Anyone" *(das Man)*. Who I am in my ordinary involvements is determined by the roles I take over from my historical culture. My self-interpretations are always a product of the social world I have grown into. In Heidegger's view, then, the "self" of everydayness is not so much an isolable unit as it is a crossing-point of cultural and historical forces that locate it in a communal context. For the most part, we are just place-holders in the social world.

The analysis of moods occurs in the context of Heidegger's attempt to identify the essential structures that make possible our everyday Being-in-the-world. There are three such structures: understanding, which opens a field of purposive activities in which equipment comes to appear in its functionality; discursiveness, which articulates our shared ways of encountering things; and situatedness *(Befindlichkeit)*, which discloses our mode of being contextualized at any given time.

Heidegger's neologism *Befindlichkeit*, which I have translated as "situatedness," is drawn from such ordinary German ways of speaking as *"Wie befinden Sie sich?"* meaning "How are you?" or "How are things going?" Literally, the question means "How do you find yourself?" Like our English "How is it going?" it asks not for a description of some inner psychic condition or frame of mind, but rather for a more general overview of how things stand with a person. It is therefore completely misleading to translate this term as "state-of-mind" (as is found in the English translation of *Being and Time*), for it is neither a "state" nor does it pertain to a "mind." Instead, the technical term is designed to capture the often inchoate background sense of "where we are at" or "where we find ourselves" that accompanies and pervades our involved agency in the world. The different modes of situatedness "make manifest 'how one is and how one is faring'" (134).

Situatedness is always manifested in some mood or other. The German word for "mood" *(Stimmung)* stems from the word for "tuning" (as in "tuning a piano"), and Heidegger frequently refers to moods as *"Gestimmtsein,"* which means "being attuned" or "attunement." A mood is a particular way we are "tuned in" to the world in our activities. For Heidegger, we are always in some mood or other: he discusses such examples as fear, boredom, hope, joy, enthusiasm, equanimity, indifference, gaiety, satiety, elation, sadness, melancholy, and desperation. But even the "pallid lack of mood which dominates 'grey everydayness'" (345)—the dreary blandness surrounding our humdrum activities—is a mood in this sense of the word:

> The pallid, evenly balanced lack of mood, which is often persistent and which is not to be mistaken for a bad mood, is far from nothing at all. Rather, it is in this that Dasein becomes satiated with itself. Being has become manifest as a burden. (134)

We can slip over from one mood into another, but we can never be free of moods altogether. As we will find in a moment, even the pure, "disinterested" theoretical attitude is a mood with its own way of disclosing the world.

How is the all-pervasiveness of moods consistent with Heidegger's goal of overcoming subjectivism? The answer to this question is found in the fact that, for Heidegger, moods are not "subjective" or "psychic" in any sense. Moods are not "fleeting experiences which 'color' one's whole 'mental attitude'" (340) in some fashion. They are not a "subjective coloring" that is cast over brute material "reality." Heidegger says that having a mood is not related to the psychical in the first place, and it is not itself an inner condition which then reaches forth in an enigmatical way and puts its mark on things and persons. (137)

Our situatedness cannot be discovered by inward-turning or introspection.

... Situatedness is far removed from anything like coming across a psychic condition. It has so little to do with a kind of apprehending that first turns around and turns back on itself, that only because the "there" has already been disclosed in situatedness can inward-turning reflection come across "experiences" at all. (136)

A mood is a quality of Being-in-the-world as a whole, and is therefore *prior to* any distinction of "inner" and "outer":

A mood assails us. It comes neither from "outside" nor from "inside," but arises out of Being-in-the-world, as a way of such Being. (136)

Moods arise out of and range over the holistic complex of Being-in-the-world. We saw that there is a reciprocal relation between our self-interpretations and the practical contexts we find ourselves in. To be human is to be contextualized in a meaningful situation: one that is awkward, dangerous, embarrassing, frightening, or just dull. Moods contribute to shaping the meaningfulness of these situations. Through my self-interpretations I constitute the meaning of the situation—as one that is "awkward," for instance, but not exactly "embarrassing." But the situation also constitutes my possible self-interpretations. I can only find out that the burning sensation I feel after doing something foolish is "shame" and not "guilt" because of my grasp of the situation and its significance in my culture. In Heidegger's conception of Dasein as Being-in-the-world, there is no way to demarcate the "subjective" side of things from the "objective" features of a context. Moods are discovered not by looking inward, but rather by getting a feel for the entire situation.

Heidegger claims that moods have a disclosing function that is both deeper than and prior to perception or cognition. Moods reveal our Being-in-the-world in three ways. First, they disclose to us the raw "givenness" of life—the fact that we *are* and that we have our being as a task that we must assume in some way or other.

In attunement, Dasein is always disclosed according to a mood as that entity to which it has been *delivered over* in its Being—as the Being to which it is delivered over and which, as existing, it has to be. (134; my italics)

Moods reveal "the pure 'that it is'" of Dasein's thrownness, its "naked 'that it is and has to be'" (134), which remains "veiled in its 'whence' and 'whither'" (135). This disclosure does not just bring us knowledge of the presence of a "thing." Instead, it brings us into a sense of the gravity and weightiness of the task of life that stands before us as our own. The biblical language of being "delivered over" to ourselves conveys the ominous undertone of a secularized banishment: in our moods we are disclosed as thrown onto ourselves, as forlorn in *"the facticity of being delivered over"* (135) to our own lives. Our existence "stares [us] in the face with the inexorability of an enigma" (136), as a burden that has to be taken up. Because our responsibility seems so burdensome, Heidegger says that our most common response to this disclosure is "evasiveness" and "fleeing" into the trivialities of commonplace affairs.

The second disclosing function of moods is to reveal the specific nature of our context as a totality.

The mood has already disclosed, in every case, Being-in-the-world as a whole, and makes it possible first of all to direct oneself towards anything. (137)

Our moods modulate and shape the totality of our Being-in-the-world, and they determine how things can count for us in our everyday concerns. Heidegger's point is that only when we have been "tuned in" to the world in a certain way can we be "turned on" to the things and people around us. Moods enable us to focus our attention and orient ourselves. Without this orientation, a human would be a bundle of raw capacities so diffuse and undifferentiated that it could never discover anything. What we *do* encounter in our attuned situatedness is not just worldhood, but rather a highly determinate cultural world. Through our moods we discover the range of possibilities laid out in our world. As Heidegger says, "In its way of attunement, Dasein 'sees' the possibilities out of which it proceeds" (148).

The third disclosing function of moods follows from the second. On the basis of our attuned ways of orienting ourselves in the world, entities can *matter* to us in specific ways. "The attunement of situatedness existentially constitutes the world-openness [*Weltoffenheit*] of Dasein" (137), and *through* this openness entities can come to *punctuate* our lives in some way or other. What we initially encounter in the world is not "sense data" or "bare particulars," but things that are useful, harmful, fascinating, dull, messy, appealing, or disgusting. The ability to come across things that are value-laden depends on our prior attunement to the world. If there were no attunement to the world—no pre-given "set" that gives us a template for approaching things—there would be no "experience" or "perception" either. Heidegger says that we could never be affected by anything "if situated Being-in-the-world had not already submitted itself to having entities in the world 'matter' to it in the ways which its moods have outlined in advance" (137).

As the world waxes and wanes with our shifting moods, things come to stand out as important or to recede into insignificance.

> To be affected by the unserviceable, resistant, or threatening character of what is ready-to-hand becomes ontologically possible only insofar as Being-in as such has been determined existentially beforehand in such a manner that what it encounters within the world can *matter to* it in this way. The fact that this sort of thing can matter to it is grounded in one's situatedness. . . . (137)

The all-pervasive background of mood guides and shapes our "sense of reality" and makes it possible for us to be agents in a familiar world.

It follows from this characterization of our situatedness that there can be no such thing as a pure, "disinterested" way of merely observing the world as it is "in itself." The Cartesian ideal of a purely comtemplative spectator or observer who simply registers "facts" is an illusion. Since interestedness is necessary for "seeing *as*"—that is, for focusing and orienting our perception—a pure "subject of experience" could never see anthing. For Heidegger, scientific disinterestedness is itself a form of interestedness. The attempt to see the world "objectively" as a collection of mere objects with properties requires a special adjustment that, far from leading to an absence of mood, creates a new and rather limiting sort of mood. The mood of pale "scientific objectivity" is governed by very specialized interests and therefore gives us no more privileged a view of "reality" than religious fervor or blinding rage.

> It is precisely when we see the "world" unsteadily and fitfully in accordance with our moods, that things in the world show themselves in their specific worldhood, which is never the same from day to day. By looking at the world theoretically, we have already dimmed it down to the uniformity of pure "objects," though admittedly this uniformity comprises a new wealth of things which can be discovered in pure determining and characterizing. (138)

Since there can be no moodless apprehending of things, even the purest *theoria* is a mood that governs how things will appear. There are no "facts" than can be discovered independent of all moods.

Although Heidegger says that moods "assail us" (136), he does not believe that we just passively suffer them. "Dasein can, should, and must, through knowledge and will, become master of its moods" (136). To think that we are merely buffeted about by uncontrollable moods would be a form of inauthenticity. But to say that we can control our moods "through knowledge and will" does not mean that we can get out of them altogether. "When we master a mood," Heidegger says, "we do so by way of a counter-mood; we are never free of moods" (136). I can only overcome my fearfulness, for instance, by fixing myself in a mood of equanimity or indifference.

It might seem that if we generally encounter the world "unsteadily and fitfully" through our shifting moods, Heidegger will have a hard time accounting for the obvious continuity, coherence, and harmony of our common ways of discovering the world. But it is important to realize that for Heidegger our moods are generally *public.* In everydayness, Dasein *is* the "Anyone," and that means that its attunement is always a *shared, communal* way of being tuned in to the world. As we grow up in the social world into which we are thrown, we also become masters of a determinate range of possible moods that are "accepted" in our world. According to Heidegger,

> Publicness, as the kind of Being that belongs to the Anyone, not only has in general its own way of having a mood, but needs moods and "makes" them for itself. (138)

Our moods are always regulated and generated by a shared attunement to public "forms of life" in our culture. Through this attunement (which Heidegger refers to as "finding a footing" in *The Essence of Reasons*[3]) we achieve something like what Wittgenstein calls the "agreement in judgments" *(Übereinstimmung)* that underlies and makes possible our regular, orderly practices.[4] What our attunement gives us is "not agreement in opinions but in form of life."[5]

To become a participant in an ongoing culture therefore always carries with it a process of attunement into the public background of situatedness, which lets things matter in determinate ways. What is given first is a "co-situatedness" that is made explicit in communicating with one another. Dasein is always a "we," a "co-Dasein" or "Dasein-with," and this "is already essentially manifest and public in a co-situatedness and a co-understanding" (162). In our everyday lives, we are generally "delivered over to" the public way of interpreting things, "which controls and distributes the possibilities of average understanding and of the situatedness belonging to it" (167–168). From this standpoint our moods are not "private" or "personal," but rather are essentially public, part of the "world" instead of something *in* the "self."

> The dominance of the public way in which things have been interpreted has already been decisive even for the possibilities of having a mood—that is, for the basic way in which Dasein lets the world "matter" to it. The Anyone prescribes one's situatedness and prescribes what and how one "sees." (169–170)

The unbounded optimism of the 1960's American "youth-culture" and the undercurrent of discouragement of the 1980's are examples of shared moods that give us a "set" through which we perceive things in common ways.

3. *The Essence of Reasons,* trans. Terrence Malick (Evanston: Northwestern, 1969), pp. 108–9.
4. Ludwig Wittgenstein, *Philosophical Investigations,* (New York: Macmillan, 1958), para. 242. Wittgenstein speaks of the need to "find our feet" with others on page 223.
5. *Ibid.,* para. 241.

Situatedness is directional or "intentionnal" (if that word is stripped of its usual mentalistic associations). Heidegger considers the "general structure of situatedness" (140) by examining the "inauthentic" mood of fear. Three components may be distinguished in fear. First, there is *that in the face of which* we fear: the frightening or fearsome, what threatens us. Second, there is *that about which* we fear: what we are fearful for, what is threatened. And, third, there is the *fearing as such:* the fearful mood that discloses the threatening as a threat. In the case of fear, what we are afraid *of* is always some definite entity within the world that is encountered as detrimental. What we are afraid *for* or *about* is always some definite possibilities for our lives: Heidegger says that "the target of this detrimentality is a definite range of what can be affected by it" (140). Finally, the fearing as such is the underlying mood that enables us to encounter things as threatening and lets them "matter" to us in a particular way. Fearfulness is "a slumbering possibility of situated Being-in-the-world" (141), which discloses the world and lets entities count for us as threatening.

It might be helpful to consider a concrete example. Suppose my marriage has been on the rocks for a while, and one night I storm out of the house and check into a motel. Returning the next morning I find the house empty and an ominous-looking letter addressed to me in my wife's hand on the kitchen table. My stomach tightens, my throat constricts: this is surely the end. I stare at it in horror, fumbling for a cigarette, glancing at the newspaper headlines without reading, humming a few bars of a TV jingle. My reaction is crippling fear. Heidegger says that fear "bewilders us and makes us 'lose our heads.'" (141). "One backs away in bewilderment" and "leaps from one thing to the next" (342). In this case, what is encountered as threatening—"that in the face of which" I fear—is a specific entity in the world: the letter and its full significance. What is threatened—"that about which" I fear—is a definite possibility of my existence: my understanding of myself as a husband and family man. I am fearful *for* myself in some of the roles I have taken over from the Anyone, roles that give me an identity and make me feel secure in the public world. Finally, what makes it possible for me to encounter the letter as threatening is the undertone of fearfulness that tunes me into the world. Only because I am attuned to the shared, public mood of fearfulness about the instability of marriages and the need for attachments can the letter stand out as frightening.

Heidegger's notorious analysis of what he calls the "basic situatedness" of anxiety or *Angst* presents an "objectless" mood similar to boredom or cheerfulness. But even anxiety has a directional structure and for this reason has a crucial disclosive role in revealing who we are. Unlike fear, anxiety is not anxious "in the face of" some specific entity in the world. "That in the face of which one has anxiety is not an entity in the world;" on the contrary, in anxiety the meaningful context of the practical world "collapses into itself; the world has the character of completely lacking significance" (186). The familiar world of objects, which had been a comfortable haven for our dispersal into everyday preoccupations and routines, suddenly begins to recede into utter meaninglessness:

> that in the face of which one has anxiety is not encountered as something definite with which one can concern oneself; the threatening does not come from [things in the world], but rather from the fact that none of these things "say" anything any longer. (343)

As entities recede into stark insignificance, "the world in its worldhood obtrudes itself" (187). What is threatening us in anxiety is not something *in* the world, but rather the world itself: *"That in the face of which one has anxiety is Being-in-the-world as such"* (186).

Whereas in fear one is afraid for oneself in particular roles, in anxiety *that about which* one is anxious is not a specific range of possibilities. Anxiety shatters our complacent confidence that the roles, status relations, and vocations we have taken over from the public world can ultimately define us and provide us with a meaning for our lives. What anxiety is anxious about is "naked Dasein" (343), stripped of its ordinary interpretations of itself as a place-holder in socially approved slots, and brought before itself as an "authentic ability-to-be-in-the-world" (187). The social roles and personae that we have drawn from the Anyone are seen for what they are—the property of the Anyone and therefore not really our own. In this way, "anxiety individualizes Dasein for its ownmost Being-in-the-world" (187). It reveals to us the fact that the task of living out our lives "to the end" is something uniquely our own—it cannot be shirked or delegated. Anxiety has a unique disclosive role because it reveals to us what it is to be human in the deepest sense. Whereas in everyday life we tend to be dissipated and distracted in an endless array of Anyone possibilities, in anxiety we are brought face to face with out ownmost responsibility for making something of our lives as a whole.

But the recognition of our uniqueness does not imply that we can exit from the social world to attain the status of a Nietzschean "Overman." Although anxiety may display our social life as a game that cannot ultimately define us, it is still the only game in town and we *have to* play it. Anxiety discloses our solitary obligation to make something of our lives as a whole, but it also reveals that this task can only be achieved *within* the context of Being-in-the-world. Heidegger says that "anxiety individualizes Dasein," but this individualization "brings Dasein face to face with its world as world, and thus brings it face to face with itself as Being-in-the-world" (188). Anxiety discloses being human as the "thrown projection" it is: a unique, undelegatable project of making something of a life that is inextricably caught up in a cultural context.

Jean-Paul Sartre

(1905–1980)

INTRODUCTION

A philosopher, novelist, playwright, and political activist, Jean-Paul Sartre continued to be one of the most controversial and lively figures in twentieth-century philosophy. His early plays, novels, and philosophical essays in "existentialism" (a label he adopted for his philosophy) are still considered among the most influential books of the century. In his longest and most famous work, *Being and Nothingness* (1943), he brought to fruition several years of study in both psychology and a new philosophical disciplines called "phenomenology," which he characterized as the study of the essential structures of human consciousness. But before he wrote *Being and Nothingness*, he had already completed a lengthy manuscript he proposed to call *The Psyche*. It was never published, and most of the manuscript (which we know about from Sartre's lifetime companion, Simone de Beauvoir) was lost. He did, however, publish two works based on this original manuscript—*The Psychology of Imagination* (1940) and *The Emotions: A Sketch of a Theory* (1939). In *The Emotions,* Sartre critized both the James-Lange theory of emotion as well as various psychoanalytic theories. He went on to sketch his own phenomenological theory of emotion, in which he focused on the way emotions alter our experience of the surrounding world. This theory is reprinted here.

At the core of Sartre's philosophy, from beginning to end, is the concept of freedom. His intention in *Being and Nothingness,* for example is to characterize human existence such that it is "without excuse." He argues relentlessly that we are responsible for everything we do and everything we are. And this includes our emotions. Thus Sartre could not disagree more with William James's theory, according to which emotions are largely instinctual, physiological reactions over which we have no control. Our emotions, Sartre says, are "magical transformations of the world," voluntary ways in which we alter our consciousness of events and things to give us a more pleasing view of the world. Typically, Sartre argues, these "transformations" are a form of "escape-behavior," ways of avoiding some crucial recognition about ourselves. Perhaps his most elegant and simple example is Aesop's fable about the fox and the grapes; the fox tries to reach the grapes on the vine, but cannot. He makes light of his failure by deciding "They are sour anyway." But, "it is not the chemistry of the grapes that has changed," Sartre says—it is the fox's attitude. He has come to look at the grapes as sour, to prove he didn't want them anyway. So too, he generalizes, our emotions are strategies we employ to avoid action, to avoid responsibility, to "flee from freedom," in the language of *Being and Nothingness.*

Although Sartre never developed a full-scale theory of the emotions, he nevertheless continued to use *The Emotions* in his later work, in particular, *Being and Nothingness.* There his view of emotions becomes even more voluntaristic; and some emotions, for example, anguish *(angoisse)* and shame, become the key to his overall interpretation of the "human condition" and the various ways we look at ourselves and others and come to make ourselves into the kind of creatures we are. His analysis in *The Emotions* of the way emotions are strategies for avoiding facing up to ourselves and our situation became the prototype for the notion of "bad faith," a central idea in *Being and Nothingness.*

From The Emotions: A Sketch of a Theory

A Sketch of a Phenomenological Theory

Perhaps what will help us in our investigation is a preliminary observation which may serve as a general criticism of all the theories of emotion which we have encountered.... For most psychologists everything takes place as if the consciousness *of* the emotion were first a reflective consciousness, that is, as if the first form of the emotion as a fact of consciousness were to appear to us as a modification of our psychic being or, to use everyday language, to be first perceived as a *state of consciousness*. And certainly it is always possible to take consciousness of emotion as the affective structure of consciousness, to say, "I'm angry, I'm afraid, etc." But fear is not originally consciousness *of* being afraid, any more than the perception of this book is consciousness *of* perceiving the book. Emotional consciousness is, at first, unreflective, and on this plane it can be conscious of itself only on the non-positional mode. Emotional consciousness is, at first, consciousness *of* the world. It is not even necessary to bring up the whole theory in order clearly to understand this principle. A few simple observations may suffice, and it is remarkable that the psychologists of emotion have never thought of making them. It is evident, in effect, that the man who is afraid is afraid *of* something. Even if it is a matter of one of those indefinite anxieties which one experiences in the dark, in a sinister and deserted passageway, etc., one is afraid *of* certain aspects of the night, of the world. And doubtless, all psychologists have noted that emotion is set in motion by a perception, a representation-signal, etc. But it seems that for them the emotion then withdraws from the object in order to be absorbed into itself. Not much reflection is needed to understand that, on the contrary, the emotion returns to the object at every moment and is fed there. For example, flight in a state of fear is described as if the object were not, before anything else, a flight *from* a certain object, as if the object fled did not remain present in the flight itself, as its theme, its reason for being, *that from which one flees*. And how can one talk about anger, in which one strikes, injures, and threatens, without mentioning the person who represents the objective unity of these insults, threats, and blows? In short, the affected subject and the affective object are bound in an indissoluble synthesis. Emotion is a certain way of apprehending the world. . . . The subject who seeks the solution of a practical problem is outside in the world; he perceives the world every moment through his acts. If he fails in his attempts, if he gets irritated, his very irritation is still a way in which the world appears to him. And, between the action which miscarries and the anger, it is not necessary for the subject to reflect back upon his behavior, to intercalate a reflexive consciousness. There can be a continuous passage from the unreflective consciousness "world-acted" (action) to the unreflective consciousness "world-hateful" (anger). The second is a transformation of the other.

At present, we can conceive of what an emotion is. It is a transformation of the world. When the paths traced out become too difficult, or when we see no path, we can no longer live in so urgent and difficult a world. All the ways are barred. However, we must act. So we try to change the world, that is, to live as if the connection between things and their potentialities were not ruled by deterministic processes, but by magic. Let it be clearly understood that this is not a game; we are driven against a wall, and we throw ourselves into this new attitude with all the strength we can muster. Let it also be understood that this attempt is not conscious of being such, for it would then be the object of a reflection. Before anything else, it is the seizure of new connections and new exigences.

But the emotive behavior is not on the same plane as the other behaviors; it is not *effective*. Its end is not really to act upon the object as such through the agency of particular means. It seeks by itself to confer upon the object, and without modifying it in its actual structure, another quality, a lesser existence, or a lesser presence (or a greater existence, etc.). In short, in emotion it is the body which, directed by consciousness, changes its relations with the world in order that the world may change its qualities. If emotion is a joke, it is a joke we believe in. A simple example will make this emotive structure clear: I extend my hand to take a bunch of grapes. I can't get it; it's beyond my reach. I shrug my shoulders, I let my hand drop, I mumble, "They're too green," and I move on. All these gestures, these words, this behavior are not seized upon for their own sake. We are dealing with a little comedy which I am playing *under* the bunch of grapes, through which I confer upon the grapes the characteristic of being "too green" which can serve as a substitute for the behavior which I am unable to keep up. At first, they presented themselves as "having to be picked." But this urgent quality very soon becomes unbearable because the potentiality cannot be realized. This unbearable tension becomes, in turn, a motive for foisting upon the grapes the new quality "too green," which will resolve the conflict and eliminate the tension. Only I cannot confer this quality on the grapes chemically. I cannot act upon the bunch in the ordinary ways. So I seize upon this sourness of the too green grapes by acting disgusted. I magically confer upon the grapes the quality I desire. Here the comedy is only half sincere. But let the situation be more urgent, let the incantatory behavior be carried out with seriousness; there we have emotion.

For example, take passive fear. I see a wild animal coming toward me. My legs give way, my heart beats more feebly, I turn pale, I fall and faint. Nothing seems less adapted than this behavior which hands me over defenseless to the danger. And yet it is a behavior of *escape*. Here the fainting is a refuge. Let it not be thought that this is a refuge *for me*, that I am trying to *save myself* in order not to *see* the wild animal *any more*. I did not leave the unreflective level, but, lacking power to avoid the danger by the normal methods and the deterministic links, I denied it. I wanted to annihilate it. The urgency of the danger served as motive for an annihilating intention which demanded magical behavior. And, by virtue of this fact, I did annihilate it as far as was in my power. These are the limits of my magical action upon the world; I can eliminate it as an object of consciousness, but I can do so only by eliminating consciousness itself. Let it not be thought that the physiological behavior of passive fear is pure disorder. It represents the abrupt realization of the bodily conditions which ordinarily accompany the transition from being awake to sleeping.

Passive sadness is characterized, as is well known, by a behavior of oppression; there is muscular resolution, pallor, coldness at the extremities; one turns toward a corner and remains seated, motionless, offering the least possible surface to the world. One prefers the shade to broad daylight, silence to noise, the solitude of a room to crowds in public places or the streets. "To be alone with one's sorrow," as they say. That is not the truth at all. It is a mark of good character to seem to meditate profoundly on one's grief. But the cases in which one really cherishes his sorrow are rather rare. The reason is quite otherwise: one of the ordinary conditions of our action having disappeared, the world requires that we act in it and on it *without that condition*. Most of the potentialities which throng it (tasks *to* do, people *to* see, acts of daily life *to* carry out) have remained the same. Only the means of realizing them, the ways which cut through our "hodological space" have changed. For example, if I have learned that I am ruined, I no longer have the same means at my disposal (private auto, etc.) to carry them out. I have to substitute new media for them (to take the bus, etc.); that is precisely what I do not want. Sadness aims at eliminating the obligation to seek new ways, to transform the structure of the world by a totally undifferentiated structure. In short, it is a question of making of the world an affectively neutral reality, a system in total affective equilibrium, of discharging the strong affective charge from objects, of reducing them all to affective zero, and, by the same token, of apprehending them as perfectly equivalent and interchangeable. In other words, lacking the power and will to accomplish the acts which we had been planning, we behave in such a way that the universe no longer requires anything of us. To bring that about we can only act upon our self, only "dim the light," and the noematical correlative of this attitude is what we call *Gloom;* the universe is gloomy, that is, undifferentiated in structure. At the same time, however, we naturally take the cowering position, we "withdraw into ourselves." The noematical correlative of this attitude is *Refuge.* All the universe is gloomy, but precisely because we want to protect ourselves from its frightening and limitless monotony, we constitute any place whatever as a "corner." It is the only differentiation in the total monotony of the world: a stretch of wall, a bit of darkness which hides its gloomy immensity from us.

We must first note that the few examples we have just cited are far from exhausting the variety of emotions. There can be many other kinds of fear, many other kinds of sadness. We merely state that they all are tantamount to setting up a magical world by using the body as a means of incantation.

True emotion is . . . accompanied by belief. The qualities conferred upon objects are taken as true qualities. Exactly what is meant by that? Roughly this: the emotion is undergone. One cannot abandon it at will; it exhausts itself, but we cannot stop it. Besides, the behavior which boils down to itself alone does nothing else than sketch upon the object the emotional quality which we confer upon it. A flight which would simply be a journey would not be enough to establish the object as being horrible. Or rather it would confer

upon it the formal quality of *horrible,* but not the matter of this quality. In order for us truly to grasp the horrible, it is not only necessary
to mimic it; we must be spell-bound, flooded by our own emotion;
the formal frame of the behavior must be filled with something
opaque and heavy which serves as matter. We understand in this
situation the role of purely physiological phenomena: they represent
the *seriousness* of the emotion; they are phenomena of belief. They
should certainly not be separated from behavior. At first, they present a certain analogy with it. The hyper-tension of fear or sadness,
the vaso-constrictions, the respiratory difficulties, symbolize quite
well a behavior which aims at denying the world or discharging it
of its affective potential by denying it. It is then impossible to draw
exactly a borderline between the pure difficulties and the behavior.
They finally enter with the behavior into a total synthetic form and
cannot be studied by themselves; to have considered them in isolation is precisely the error of the peripheric theory. And yet they are
not reducible to behavior; one can stop himself from fleeing, but not
from trembling. I can, by a violent effort, raise myself from my
chair, turn my thought from the disaster which is crushing me, and
get down to work; my hands will remain icy. Therefore, the emotion
must be considered not simply as being enacted; it is not a matter of
pure demeanor. It is the demeanor of a body which is in a certain
state; the state alone would not provoke the demeanor; the
demeanor without the state is comedy; but the emotion appears in a
highly disturbed body which retains a certain behavior. The disturbance can survive the behavior, but the behavior constitutes the
form and signification of the disturbance. On the other hand, without this disturbance, the behavior would be pure signification, an
affective scheme. We are really dealing with a synthetic form; *in
order to believe* in magical behavior it is necessary to be highly
disturbed.

   Thus the origin of emotion is a spontaneous and lived degrada-
tion of consciousness in the face of the world. What it cannot endure
in one way it tries to grasp in another by going to sleep, by approaching the consciousness of sleep, dream, and hysteria. And the disturbance of the body is nothing other than the lived belief of consciousness, insofar as it is seen from the outside.

Part Four
CONCEPTUAL ANALYSIS AND EMOTION

In the Anglo-American tradition, the analysis of emotions typically turns to emotion CONCEPTS and the language we use to ascribe and describe emotions. In fact, one of the primary questions raised in this tradition is whether emotion-words do, in fact, refer to any particular phenomenon, especially a "feeling" of the sort described by so many theorists. In the following selections, Gilbert Ryle raises this question about emotions as part of his overall campaign against "the myth of the ghost in the machine," the Cartesian idea that there is mind and there is body and emotion-words describe the former rather than the latter. Errol Bedford then raises more detailed questions about the idea that emotions are essentially "feelings," Anthony Kenny translates the Continental concern with "intentionality" into a more linguistic concern about the nature of certain kinds of "intensional" sentences in which emotions are described, and Irving Thalberg discusses the connection between emotion and belief. The last two essays summarize our own attempts to formulate a theory of emotion.

Gilbert Ryle

(1900 – 1978)

INTRODUCTION

Gilbert Ryle was appointed to the senior philosophical chair at
Oxford University when World War II ended in 1945. He began his
philosophical career as a phenomenologist, publishing his first
essays on Husserl and Heidegger, but by the 1930's, he had completely altered his approach to philosophical issues. This was largely
through the influence of the logical positivists (who argued that any
meaningful statement must be verifiable through experience, and,
thus, metaphysical, ethical, and religious claims are meaningless)
and Ludwig Wittgenstein (who emphasized the necessity of examining how concepts are used in ordinary discourse in order to understand their meaning). As a result, Ryle became instrumental in the
development of a common-sense movement in philosophy that has
since come to be called "ordinary language philosophy" or simply
"Oxford philosophy." Philosophy, Ryle argued, should discover the
"logical forms" of our ordinary language. That is, it should examine
how particular terms can and cannot be used. Thus, if we want to
know what anger is, we should not engage in metaphysical speculation about anger, but rather we should examine the conditions
under which it is ordinarily appropriate and meaningful to say
someone is angry. In taking this new approach, Ryle tried to eliminate those metaphysical mysteries that philosophers in the past created by using misleading expressions and abusing ordinary language.

Ryle's philosophy culminated in his important book, *The Concept
of Mind,* which he published in 1949. There he argues that earlier

theorists have presented us with a misleading and mistaken picture of the mind as a "ghost in a machine." They thought of the mind as something inside us, radically closed off from the view of other people. This picture of the mind, Ryle claims, resulted in the creation of numerous philosophical pseudo-problems, for example, the problem of determining whether other minds exist and of ever knowing what others are thinking or feeling. Ryle attempts, in *The Concept of Mind,* to eliminate this "ghost" entirely. He appeals to the way we use mental concepts, for example, emotion, thinking, and knowing, in ordinary language and then concludes that we do not use these terms to refer to private goings-on inside people. Rather, we use mental terms to indicate that people are disposed to behave in predictable ways. So, for example, when we say that John is angry, we do not mean that he is experiencing some private feeling we cannot see; rather we simply mean that John is disposed to shout, flush, hit people, break things, etc. What this means is that we are not in a better position to know what our feelings are than are others. For Ryle, an emotion is nothing but a disposition to behave in certain characteristic ways. And it is the same with thoughts, feelings, motives, desires, and all other mental occurrences.

"Nothing but" claims are always suspicious, and Ryle's claim that emotions are nothing but dispositions is no exception. Subsequently, philosophers have criticized Ryle's theory of emotion for being simplistic and for omitting, for example, cognitive features of emotion (see the selection from Bedford). Ryle's theory did, though, have the virtue of turning philosophers' attention to the importance of behavior in emotion. Although earlier behaviorist psychologists, such as Watson, had analyzed emotions in terms of behavior, such analyses went virtually unnoticed in philosophical circles. Not until Ryle's work was serious attention paid to the role of emotional behavior and to the importance of looking at the way we use emotion terms.

From The Concept of Mind

(1) Foreword

In this chapter I discuss certain of the concepts of emotions and feeling.

This scrutiny is necessary because adherents of the dogma of the ghost in the machine can adduce in support of it the consent of most philosophers and psychologists to the view that emotions are internal or private experiences. Emotions are described as turbulences in the stream of consciousness, the owner of which cannot help directly registering them; to external witnesses they are, in consequence, necessarily occult. They are occurrences which take place not in the public, physical world but in your or my secret, mental world.

I shall argue that the word "emotion" is used to designate at least three or four different kinds of things, which I shall call "inclinations" (or "motives"), "moods," "agitations" (or "commotions") and "feelings." Inclinations and moods, including agitations, are not occurrences and do not therefore take place either publicly or privately. They are propensities, not acts or states. They are, however, propensities of different kinds, and their differences are important. Feelings, on the other hand, are occurrences, but the place that mention of them should take in descriptions of human behaviour is very different from that which the standard theories accord to it. Moods or frames of mind are, unlike motives, but like maladies and states of the weather, temporary conditions which in a certain way *collect* occurrences, but they are not themselves extra occurrences.

(2) Feelings versus Inclinations

By "feelings" I refer to the sorts of things which people often describe as thrills, twinges, pangs, throbs, wrenches, itches, prickings, chills, glows, loads, qualms, hankerings, curdlings, sinkings, tensions, gnawings and shocks. Ordinarily, when people report the occurrence of a feeling, they do so in a phrase like "a throb of compassion," "a shock of surprise" or "a thrill of anticipation."

It is an important linguistic fact that these names for specific feelings, such as "itch," "qualm" and "pang" are also used as names of specific bodily sensations. If someone says that he has just felt a twinge, it is proper to ask whether it was a twinge of remorse or of rheumatism, though the word "twinge" is not necessarily being used in quite the same sense in the alternative contexts.

There are further respects in which the ways in which we speak of, say, qualms of apprehension are analogous to the ways in which we speak of, say, qualms of sea-sickness. We are ready to characterise either as acute or faint, sudden or lingering, intermittent or steady. A man may wince from a pricking of his conscience or from a pricking in his finger. Moreover, we are in some cases ready to locate, say, the sinking feeling of despair in the pit of the stomach or the tense feeling of anger in the muscles of the jaw and fist. Other feelings which we are not prepared to locate in any particular part of the body, like glows of pride, seem to pervade the whole body in much the same way as do glows of warmth.

James boldly identified feelings with bodily sensations, but for our purposes it is enough to show that we talk of feelings very much as we talk of bodily sensations, though it is possible that there is a tinge of metaphor in our talk of the former which is absent from our talk of the latter.

On the other hand, it is necessary to do justice to the crucial fact that we do report feelings in such idioms as "qualms of apprehension" and "glows of pride"; we do, that is, distinguish a glow of pride from a glow of warmth, and I shall have to try to bring out the force of such distinctions. I hope to show that though it is quite proper to describe someone as feeling a throb of compassion, his compassion is not to be equated with a throb or a series of throbs, any more than his fatigue is his gasps; so no disillusioning consequences would follow from acknowledging that throbs, twinges and other feelings are bodily sensations.

In one sense, then, of "emotion" the feelings are emotions. But there is quite another sense of "emotion" in which theorists classify as emotions the motives by which people's higher-level behaviour is explained. When a man is described as vain, considerate, avaricious, patriotic or indolent, an explanation is being given of why he conducts his actions, daydreams and thoughts in the way he does, and, according to the standard terminology, vanity, kindliness, avarice, patriotism and laziness rank as species of emotion; they come thence to be spoken of as feelings.

But there is a great verbal muddle here, associated with a great logical muddle. To begin with, when someone is described as a vain or indolent man, the words "vain" and "indolent" are used to signify more or less lasting traits in his character. In this use he might be said to have been vain since childhood, or indolent during his entire half-holiday. His vanity and indolence are dispositional properties, which could be unpacked in such expressions as "Whenever situations of certain sorts have arisen, he has always or usually tried to make himself prominent" or "Whenever he was faced by an option between doing something difficult and not doing it, he shirked doing the difficult thing." Sentences beginning with "Whenever" are not singular occurrence reports. Motive words used in this way signify tendencies or propensities and therefore cannot signify the occurrence of feelings. They are elliptical expressions of general hypothetical propositions of a certain sort, and cannot be construed as expressing categorical narratives of episodes.

It will however be objected that, besides this dispositional use of motive words, there must also be a corresponding active use of them. For a man to be punctual in the dispositonal sense of the adjective, he must tend to be punctual on particular occasions; and the sense in which he is said to be punctual for a particular rendezvous is not the dispositional but the active sense of "punctual." "He tends to be at his rendezvous on time" expresses a general hypothetical proposition, the truth of which requires that there should also be corresponding true categorical propositions of the pattern "he was at today's rendezvous in good time." So, it will be argued, for a man to be a vain or indolent man there must be particular exercises of vanity and indolence occurring at particular moments, and these will be actual emotions or feelings.

This argument certainly establishes something, but it does not establish the point desired. While it is true that to describe a man as vain is to say that he is subject to a specific tendency, it is not true that the particular exercises of this tendency consist in his registering particular thrills or twinges. On the contrary, on hearing that a man is vain we expect him, in the first instance, to behave in certain ways, namely to talk a lot about himself, to cleave to the society of the eminent, to reject criticisms, to seek the footlights and to disengage himself from conversations about the merits of others. We expect him also to indulge in roseate daydreams about his own successes, to avoid recalling past failures and to plan for his own advancement. To be vain is to tend to act in these and innumerable other kindred ways. Certainly we also expect the vain man to feel certain pangs and flutters in certain situations; we expect him to have an acute sinking feeling, when an eminent person forgets his name, and to feel buoyant of heart and light of toe on hearing of the misfortunes of his rivals. But feelings of pique and buoyancy are not more directly indicative of vanity than are public acts of boasting or private acts of daydreaming. Indeed they are less directly indicative, for reasons which will shortly appear.

Some theorists will object that to speak of an act of boasting as one of the direct exercises of vanity is to leave out the cardinal factor in the situation. When we explain why a man boasts by saying that it is because he is vain, we are forgetting that a disposition is not an event and so cannot be a cause. The cause of his boasting must be an event antecedent to his beginning to boast. He must be moved to boast by some actual "impulse," namely an impulse of vanity. So the immediate or direct actualisations of vanity are particular vanity impulses, and these are feelings. The vain man is a man who tends to register particular feelings of vanity; these cause or impel him to boast, or perhaps to will to boast, and to do all the other things which we say are done from vanity.

It should be noticed that this argument takes it for granted that to explain an act as done from a certain motive, in this case from vanity, is to give a causal explanation. This means that it assumes that a mind, in this case the boaster's mind, is a field of special causes; that is why a vanity feeling has been called in to be the inner cause of the overt boasting. I shall shortly argue that to explain an act as done from a certain motive is not analogous to saying that the glass broke, because a stone hit it, but to the quite different type of statement that the glass broke, when the stone hit it, because the glass was brittle. Just as there are no other momentary actualisations of brittleness than, for example, flying into fragments when struck, so no other momentary actualisations of chronic vanity need to be postulated than such things as boasting, daydreaming about triumphs and avoiding conversations about the merits of others.

But before expanding this argument I want to show how intrinsically unplausible the view is that, on each occasion that a vain man behaves vaingloriously, he experiences a particular palpitation or pricking of vanity. To put it quite dogmatically, the vain man never feels vain. Certainly, when thwarted, he feels acute dudgeon and when unexpectedly successful, he feels buoyant. But there is no special thrill or pang which we call a "feeling of vanity." Indeed, if there were such a recognisable specific feeling, and the vain man was constantly experiencing it, he would be the first instead of the last person to recognise how vain he was.

Take another example. A man is interested in Symbolic Logic. He regularly reads books and articles on the subject, discusses it, works out problems in it and neglects lectures on other subjects. According to the view which is here contested, he must therefore constantly experience impulses of a peculiar kind, namely feelings of interest in Symbolic Logic, and if his interest is very strong these feelings must be very acute and very frequent. He must therefore be able to tell us whether these feelings are sudden, like twinges, or lasting, like aches; whether they succeed one another several times a minute or only a few times an hour; and whether he feels them in the small of his back or in his forehead. But clearly his only reply to such specific questions would be that he catches himself experiencing no peculiar throbs or qualms while he is attending to his hobby. He may report a feeling of vexation, when his studies are interrupted, and the feeling of a load off his chest, when distraction are removed; but there are no peculiar feelings of interest in Symbolic Logic for him to report. While undisturbedly pursuing his hobby, he feels no perturbations at all.

Suppose, however, that there were such feelings cropping up, maybe, about every two or twenty minutes. We should still expect to find him discussing and studying the subject in the intervals between these occurrences, and we should correctly say that he was still discussing and studying the subject from interests in it. This point by itself establishes the conclusion that to do something from a motive is compatible with being free from any particular feelings while doing it.

Of course, the standard theories of motives do not speak so crudely of qualms, pangs and flutters. They speak more sedately of desires, impulses or promptings. Now there are feelings of wanting, namely those we call "hankerings," "cravings" and "itchings." So let us put our question in this way. Is being interested in Symbolic Logic equivalent to being liable or prone to feel certain special hankerings, gnawings or cravings? And does working at Symbolic Logic from interest in it involve feeling one such itching before each bit of the work is begun? If the affirmative answer is given, then there can be no answer to the question, "From what motive does the student work at the subject in the intervals between the itchings?" And if to say that his interest was strong meant that the supposed feelings were frequent and acute, the absurd consequence would follow that the more strongly a man was interested in a subject, the more his attention would be distracted from it. To call a feeling or sensation "acute" is to say that it is difficult not to attend to it, and to attend to a feeling is not the same thing as to attend to a problem in Symbolic Logic.

We must reject, then, the conclusion of the argument which tried to prove that motive words are the names of feelings or else of tendencies to have feelings. But what was wrong with the argument for this conclusion?

There are at least two quite different senses in which an occurrence is said to be "explained"; and there are correspondingly at least two quite different senses in which we ask "why" it occurred and two quite different senses in which we say that it happened "because" so and so was the case. The first sense is the causal sense. To ask why the glass broke is to ask what caused it to break, and we explain, in this sense, the fracture of the glass when we report that a stone hit it. The "because" clause in the explanation reports an event, namely the event which stood to the fracture of the glass as cause to effect.

But very frequently we look for and get explanations of occurrences in another sense of "explanation." We ask why the glass shivered when struck by the stone and we get the answer that it was because the glass was brittle. Now "brittle" is a dispositional adjective; that is to say, to describe the glass as brittle is to assert a general hypothetical proposition about the glass. So when we say that the glass broke when struck because it was brittle, the "because" clause does not report a happening or a cause; it states a law-like proposition. People commonly say of explanations of this second kind that they give the "reason" for the glass breaking when struck.

How does the law-like general hypothetical proposition work? It says, roughly, that the glass, *if* sharply struck or twisted, etc. *would* not dissolve or stretch or evaporate but fly into fragments. The mat-

ter of fact that the glass did at a particular moment fly into fragments, when struck by a particular stone, is explained, in this sense
of "explain," when the first happening, namely the impact of the
stone, satisfies the protasis of the general hypothetical proposition,
and when the second happening, namely the fragmentation of the
glass, satisfies its apodosis.

This can now be applied to the explanation of actions as issuing
from specified motives. When we ask "Why did someone act in a
certain way?" this question might, so far as its language goes, either
be an inquiry into the cause of his acting in that way, or be an
inquiry into the character of the agent which accounts for his having
acted in that way on that occasion. I suggest, what I shall now try to
prove, that explanations by motives are explanations of the second
type and not of the first type. It is perhaps more than a merely linguistic fact that a man who reports the motive from which something is done is, in common parlance, said to be giving the "reason"
for the action. It should be also noticed that there are lots of different kinds of such explanations of human actions. A twitch may
be explained by a reflex, the filling of a pipe by an inveterate habit;
the answering of a letter by a motive. Some of the differences
between reflexes, habits and motives will have to be described at a
later stage.

The present issue is this. The statement "he boasted from vanity"
ought, on one view, to be construed as saying that "he boasted and
the cause of his boasting was the occurrence in him of a particular
feeling or impulse of vanity." On the other view, it is to be construed
as saying "he boasted on meeting the stranger and his doing so
satisfies that law-like proposition that whenever he finds a chance of
securing the admiration and envy of others, he does whatever he
thinks will produce this admiration and envy."

My first argument in favour of the second way of construing such
statements is that no one could ever know or even, usually, reasonably conjecture that the cause of someone else's overt action was the
occurrence in him of a feeling. Even if the agent reported, what
people never do report, that he had experienced a vanity itch just
before he boasted, this would be very weak evidence that the itch
caused the action, since for all we know, the cause was any one of a
thousand other synchronous happenings. On this view the imputation of motives would be incapable of any direct testing and no rea-

sonable person would put any reliance on any such imputation. It would be like water-divining in places where well-sinking was forbidden.

In fact, however, we do discover the motives of other people. The process of discovering them is not immune from error, but nor are the errors incorrigible. It is or is like an inductive process, which results in the establishment of law-like propositions and the applications of them as the "reasons" for particular actions. What is established in each case is or includes a general hypothetical proposition of a certain sort. The imputation of a motive for a particular action is not a causal inference to an unwitnessed event but the subsumption of an episode proposition under a law-like proposition. It is therefore analogous to the explanation of reactions and actions by reflexes and habits, or to the explanation of the fracture of the glass by reference to its brittleness.

The way in which a person discovers his own long-term motives is the same as the way in which he discovers those of others. The quantity and quality of the information accessible to him differ in the two inquiries, but its items are in general of the same sort. He has, it is true, a fund of recollections of his own past deeds, thoughts, fancies and feelings; and he can perform the experiments of fancying himself confronted by tasks and opportunities which have not actually occurred. He can thus base his appreciations of his own lasting inclinations on data which he lacks for his appreciations of the inclinations of others. On the other side, his appreciations of his own inclinations are unlikely to be unbiased and he is not in a favourable position to compare his own actions and reactions with those of others. In general we think that an impartial and discerning spectator is a better judge of a person's prevailing motives, as well as of his habits, abilities and weaknesses, than is that person himself, a view which is directly contrary to the theory which holds that an agent possesses a Privileged Access to the so-called springs of his own actions and is, because of that access, able and bound to discover, without inference or research, from what motives he tends to act and from what motive he acted on a particular occasion.

We shall see later that a person who does or undergoes something, heeding what he is doing or undergoing, can, commonly, answer questions about the incident without inference or research. But what gives him those ready-made answers can and often does give his companions also those same ready-made answers. He does not have to be a detective, but nor do they.

Another argument supports this thesis. A person replying to an interrogation might say that he was delving into a ditch in order to find the larvæ of a certain species of insect; that he was looking for these larvæ in order to find out on what fauna or flora they were parasitic; that he was trying to find out on what they were parasitic in order to test a certain ecological hypothesis; and that he wanted to test this hypothesis in order to test a certain hypothesis about Natural Selection. At each stage he declares his motive or reason for pursuing certain investigations. And each successive reason that he gives is of a higher level of generality than its predecessor. He is subsuming one interest under another, somewhat as more special laws are subsumed under more general laws. He is not recording a chronological series of earlier and earlier stages, though of course he could do this if asked the quite different questions What first aroused your interest in this problem? and in that?

In the case of every action, taken by itself, for which it is natural to ask "From what motive was it done?" it is always possible that it was not done from a motive but from force of habit. Whatever I do or say, it is always conceivable, though nearly always false, that I did it, or said it, in complete absence of mind. The performance of an action from a motive is different from its performance out of habit; but the sorts of things which belong to the one class also belong to the other. Now to say that an action was done from force of habit is patently to say that a specific disposition explains the action. No one, I trust, thinks that "habit" is the name of a peculiar internal event or class of events. To ask whether an action was done from force of habit or from kindliness of heart is therefore to ask which of two specified dispositions is the explanation of the action.

Finally, we should consider by what tests we should try to decide a dispute about the motive from which a person had done something; did he, for example, throw up a well-paid post for a relatively humble Government job from patriotism or from a desire to be exempt from military service? We begin, perhaps, by asking him; but on this sort of matter his avowals, to us or to himself, would very likely not be frank. We next try, not necessarily unsuccessfully, to settle the dispute by considering whether his words, actions, embarrassments, etc., on this and other occasions square with the hypoth-

esis that he is physically timorous and averse from regimentation, or
whether they square with the hypothesis that he is relatively indifferent to money and would sacrifice anything to help win the war.
We try, that is, to settle by induction the relevant traits in his character. In applying, then, the results of our induction to his particular
decision, i.e. in explaining why he came to it, we do not press him
to recall the itches, pangs and throbs that he registered in making
it; nor, probably, do we trouble to infer to their occurrence. And
there is a special reason for not paying much heed to the feelings
had by a person whose motives are under investigation, namely that
we know that lively and frequent feelings are felt by sentimentalists
whose positive actions show quite clearly that their patriotism, e.g.
is a self-indulgent make-believe. Their hearts duly sink when they
hear that their country's plight is desperate, but their appetites are
unaffected and the routines of their lives are unmodified. Their bos-
oms swell at a march-past, but they avoid marching themselves.
They are rather like theatregoers and novel readers, who also feel
genuine pangs, glows, flutters and twinges of despair, indignation,
exhilaration and disgust, with the difference that the theatregoers
and novel readers realise that they are making-believe.

To say, then, that a certain motive is a trait in someone's character is to say that he is inclined to do certain sorts of things, make
certain sorts of plans, indulge in certain sorts of daydreams and also,
of course, in certain situations to feel certain sorts of feelings. To
say that he did something from that motive is to say that this action,
done in its particular circumstances, was just the sort of thing that
that was an inclination to do. It is to say "he *would* do that."

Errol Bedford

INTRODUCTION

Twentieth-century Anglo-American "analytic" philosophers did not pay nearly as much critical attention to the emotions as did their colleagues in Europe. In fact, the emotions were often explicitly dismissed from conceptual analysis precisely on the grounds that there was no logical structure to be analyzed, that emotions were strictly "non-cognitive" and the province of biology and psychology, not philosophy. In the 1940's, an ethical theory called "the emotive theory of ethics" gained considerable currency in both England and the United States (through such authors as A. J. Ayer and C. L. Stevenson, for example); according to this theory, entire domains of philosophy—ethics, aesthetics, and religion, in particular—were dismissed from further deliberation on the grounds that they were mere matters of "attitude" rather than belief or judgment.

In the 1950's, this began to change, and one of the primary reasons for the change was a widely influential article by Errol Bedford—"Emotions"—which was presented to and then published by the Aristotelean Society in London; in it emotions were given their philosophical due. Ryle's ideas are pervasive in Bedford's argument, but the attention to the details of emotional phenomena goes far beyond Ryle's general treatment in *The Concept of Mind.*

From Emotions

The concept of emotion gives rise to a number of philosophical problems. The most important of these, I think, concern the function of statements about emotions and the criteria for their validity. A solution to these problems is offered by what I shall call the traditional theory of the emotions, and I should like to begin by discussing some aspects of this. According to this view[1] an emotion is a feeling, or at least an experience of a special type which involves a feeling. Logically, this amounts to regarding emotion words as the names of feelings. It is assumed that to each word there corresponds a qualitatively distinct experience which may, although it need not, find "expression" in outward behaviour. If it does, this behaviour entitles us to infer the existence of the inner feeling, and therefore to assert, with some degree of probability, statements of the form "He is angry." Looked at in this way, emotions naturally come to be thought of as inner forces that move us, in combination with, or in opposition to other forces, to act as we do. Briefly, anger is a specific feeling which leads the angry man to show the signs of anger (e.g., striking someone) unless he is willing to, and able to, suppress them. It follows, I take it, that to explain behaviour by saying that a man acted as he did because he was angry, is to give a causal explanation, although, admittedly, a causal explanation of a special sort.

I am going to argue that this involves a fundamental mistake: the logical mistake of treating emotion words as names, which leads in

1. The details vary. For example, it is very commonly held that every emotion must have an object, and therefore that it is an experience involving a "cognitive" element, not a pure state of feeling. "We must hold," writes McTaggart, "that the cogitation of that to which the emotion is directed, and the emotion towards it, are the same mental state, which has both the quality of being a cogitation of it, and the quality of being an emotion directed towards it." (*The Nature of Existence*, Vol. 2, p. 146.) (I think it is important to ask what "directed towards" could mean here.) Russell claims that emotions also involve bodily movements. In *The Analysis of Mind* he says that "An emotion—rage, for example—(is) a certain kind of process . . . .. The inredients of an emotion are only sensations and images and bodily movements succeeding each other according to a certain pattern." (p. 284.) To discuss the details of these theories would complicate, without affecting, my argument, which is meant to show that an emotion is not any sort of experience or process.

turn to a misconception of their function. There might, all the same, be more to be said for this view if it were less inadequate at the psychological level, if it did not presuppose a richness and clarity in the "inner life" of feeling that it does not possess. What evidence is there for the existence of a multitude of feelings corresponding to the extensive and subtle linguistic differentiation of our vocabulary for discussing emotions? This assumption gains no support from experience. Indignation and annoyance are two different emotions; but, to judge from my own case, the feelings that accompany indignation appear to differ little, if at all, from those that accompany annoyance. I certainly find no feeling, or class of feelings, that marks off indignation from annoyance, and enables me to distinguish them from one another. The distinction is of a different *sort* from this . . ..

In any case, does the truth of such a statement as "He is afraid" logically require the existence of a specific feeling? I imagine that it would nowadays be generally conceded that emotion words are commonly used without any implication that the person they refer to is having a particular experience at any given time. But it may be said, granting this, that such expressions as "is afraid," "is angry," nevertheless gain their whole meaning from an indirect reference that they make to experiences, and can only be defined in terms of feelings. A man can feel angry as well as be angry; the expression "is angry" may not name an experience, but "feels angry" surely does, and all that can be meant by saying that someone is angry is that he is liable to, and sometimes does, feel angry. I do not think, however, that this argument can prove what it sets out to prove, i.e. that anger necessarily involves a specific feeling. In the first place, "feels angry" is often able to serve instead of "is angry." We can say, "I felt angry about it for days afterwards." A more important point is that one cannot understand what it is to feel angry without first understanding what it is to be angry. If we can assume the meaning of "is angry," or teach it (ostensively or by a descriptive account), we can go on to explain "feels angry" by saying that it is to feel as people often feel who are angry. But how could we explain the expression "feels angry" without presupposing that the person we are explaining it to understands "is angry?" The only possible method open to us would seem to be this: to make him angry, e.g., by insulting him, and then to say to him, "Well, feeling angry is feeling as you feel now." The difficulty is that, if the view I am criticising is correct, we cannot ensure in this way that we have taught him the meaning of the expression. We have to be certain that he has experienced a specific feeling. Yet it is logically possible that the insult (or other stimulus, and it is a crucial point that there is no *specific* stimulus) has failed in its object—it may have produced no feeling, or the wrong feeling, or so confused a mixture of feelings that he cannot discriminate the essential from the inessential (the matter is, if anything, even more difficult from his point of view). We cannot exclude this by arguing "He is angry, therefore he feels angry," for how are we to know that he is angry? *Ex hypothesi* his behaviour is not proof of this. And having as yet no guarantee that he has grasped what the question means, we obviously cannot ask him whether he feels angry. Nor can we discover that he has understood the meaning of the expression by observing that he uses it in the same way as we do, for, *ex hypothesi* again, this will not prove that he means the same by it. The conclusion to be drawn, if I am right, is that being angry is logically prior to feeling angry, and therefore that being angry does not entail feeling angry, and *a fortiori* does not entail having any other feeling.

Now it may seem that this does not accord with the confidence we have in our beliefs about our own and other people's emotions respectively. But is this really so? We do not first ascertain that a man feels angry, and then conclude that he is angry. On the contrary, we realise that he is angry, and assume (perhaps wrongly) that he feels angry. Behavioural evidence for a statement about emotions is evidence in its own right, so to speak, and not because it entitles us to infer to private experiences. For if we have good grounds for the assertion that a person is jealous, we do not withdraw this assertion on learning that he does not feel jealous, although we may accept this as true. It is, after all, notorious that we can be mistaken about our own emotions, and that in this matter a man is not the final court of appeal in his own case; those who are jealous are often the last, instead of the first, to recognise that they are. This is scarcely consistent with the view that the criterion for identifying an emotion is the recognition of the special qualities of an experience; it is intelligible if the criteria are different from, and more complex than this. I am going to discuss these criteria shortly. For the moment, I only want to suggest that the traditional answer to the question "How do we identify our own emotions?" namely, "By introspection," cannot be correct. It seems to me that there is every reason to believe that we learn about our own emotions essentially in the same way as other people learn about them. Admittedly, it is sometimes the case that we know our own emotions better than anyone else does, but there is no need to explain this as being due to the introspection of feelings. One reason for this is that it is hardly possible for a man to be completely ignorant, as others may be, of the context of his own behaviour. Again, thoughts may cross his mind that he does not make public. But the fact that he prefers to keep them to himself is incidental; and if they were known they would only be corroborative evidence, not indispensible evidence of a radically different sort from that which is available to other people. It is only in some respects, then, that each of us is in a better position to understand himself than anyone else is. Against this must be set the possibility of self-deception and a reluctance to admit that we are, for instance, vain or envious.

I must now meet what is, I think, the most serious objection that is likely to be made to this—the alleged impossibility of distinguishing, from an external observer's point of view, between real anger, say, and the pretence of it. It is sometimes claimed that although someone might behave as if he were angry, and give every appearance that he would persist in this behaviour, there would still be a sense in which he might be shamming. What then is the difference between being angry and merely pretending to be? It may be held that it can only lie in the fact that the man who is pretending is not in the appropriate state of inner feeling . . .. Let us contrast the cases of a man who is angry and another, behaving in a similar way, who is only pretending to be. Now it may well be true that the former feels angry, whereas the latter does not, but in any case it is not this that constitutes the difference between the fact that the other is only pretending to be. The objection rests on a misconception of what pretence is. There is necessarily involved in pretence, or shamming, the notion of a limit which must not be overstepped; pretence is always insulated, as it were, from reality. Admittedly, this limit may be vague, but it must exist. It is a not unimportant point that it is usually *obvious* when someone is pretending. If a man who is behaving as if he were angry goes so far as to smash the furniture or commit an assault, he has passed the limit; he is not *pretending,* and it is useless for him to protest afterwards that he did not feel angry. Far from his statement being *proof* that he was not angry, it would be discounted even if it were accepted as true. "He was angry, but he did not feel angry" is not self-contradictory, although it is no doubt normally false. If in a particular case it is difficult—as it may be—to settle the question, "Pretended or real?," that can only be because the relevant public evidence is inadequate to settle it. What we want is more evidence of the same kind, not a special piece of evidence of a different kind. . . .

II

Having, I hope, cleared the ground a little by putting some preliminary arguments against the traditional theory, I now want to consider whether an adequate alternative to it is provided by a dispositional theory of emotions, and to discuss the criteria for the use of emotion words. Can the concept of an emotion be fully elucidated without using non-behavioural, indeed non-psychological, concepts? I will try to justify the negative answer that I think should be given to this question.

To begin with, statements about emotions cannot be said to describe behaviour; they interpret it.[2] The situation seems to be that emotional behaviour, so to speak, is far from being homogeneous. The behavioural evidence for "He was angry" varies with the person and the occasion; in different cases it is not the same, and possibly it may not even be partially the same. Conversely, the same, or similar, behaviour, can be differently, and correctly, interpreted in different circumstances, for example as anger, indignation, annoyance, exasperation or resentment. Accordingly, categorical descriptive statements, e.g. (1) "He raised his voice and began to thump the table," and hypothetical descriptive statements, e.g. (2) "If I had gone on teasing him he would have thrown something at me," are evidence for such statements as (3) "He was very angry," but they

2. This is not to say that we do not also use the word "description" in such a way that (3) (immediately below) might form part of a description of some incident. When I say that (3) does not describe I am making what could be looked on as a technical distinction between description and interpretation, which is meant to indicate a difference of order between (3) and (1) or (2). Higher order statements explain and interpret what lower order statements describe.

are not part of what these statements mean. Clearly, on hearing (3), it would be proper to ask for details, and such details could be given in (1) and (2). (1) and (2) would therefore give additional information to that already given in (3). To put the matter another way, (1), (2) and (3) are independent of one another in respect of truth and falsity. (1) may be true when (3) is false (a man can thump the table and raise his voice—to emphasise a point—without being angry), and (3) may be true although (1) is false (for not all angry men thump tables). The same holds of the relationships of (2) and (3). The truth of (2) is perfectly compatible with joining in the fun; anger, on the other hand, is consistent with not being prepared to throw things. I think that this would still hold with other statements substituted for (1) and (2). It does not seem to be possible, therefore, to analyse (3) into a set, however, complex, of categorical and hypothetical statements that describe individual behaviour. (3) does not sum up, but goes beyond, the behavioural evidence for it, and it would always be logically possible to accept the evidence and deny the conclusion. Although when we say (3) we are in a sense talking about the behaviour on which its truth rests, anger is not merely a disposition, and cannot be reduced to a pattern of behaviour, actual or potential.[3] All that can be said about the logical relationships between (3) and such statements as (1) and (2) is that it is a necessary, but not a sufficient, condition for the truth of (3) that some statements such as (1) and (2) should be true, without it being possible to specify which . . ..

What I am suggesting is that people who share the same information and the same expectations about another person's behaviour may possibly place different emotional interpretations on that behaviour, if their knowledge is confined to descriptive statements about it. It may be urged that this difference of opinion can be eliminated as further evidence of the same type comes to light, and that it can only be eliminated in this way. The assumption underlying

---

3. Let me give an analogy. "Jones is responsible for this muddle" is a statement about the behaviour its truth is dependent on, although it is not shorthand for a set of statements describing that behaviour.

this—that the criteria for assertions about emotions are purely behavioural—is not, however, borne out by an examination of the way in
which we actually use emotion words. These words, when used
without qualification, carry implications, not merely about behaviour, but also about its social context. Consider the distinction
between two emotions that have a close similarity, shame and
embarrassment. The behaviour of an embarrassed man is often not
noticeably different from that of one who is ashamed; but there is
an important difference between the respective situations they are
in. In a newspaper article last year, Mr. Peter Davies, the publisher,
was said to be "to his mild embarrassment" the original of Peter Pan.
The embarrassment is understandable, and the epithet appropriate,
whether its application is correct or not. Yet we can say at once that
if the writer of the article had alleged that Mr. Davies was "to his
shame" the original of Peter Pan, this would have been incorrect; it
is scarcely conceivable that it could be true. The reason for this is
obvious, and it is logical, not psychological, since it has nothing to
do with Mr. Davies' behaviour, still less with his feelings. It is simply
that the fact that Barrie modelled Peter Pan on him is not his *fault*—
it was not due to an act of his, and there is nothing reprehensible
about it anyway. In general, it is only true to say of someone "He is
ashamed of so and so" if what is referred to is something that he can
be criticised for (the criticism is commonly, though not perhaps necessarily, moral). It is, in other words, a necessary condition for the
truth of the statement that he should be at fault. The word "embarrassed" is not connected in the same way with blame and responsibility; the claim that it makes is the vaguer and weaker one that the
situation is awkward or inconvenient and so on . . .. The connexion
between shame and responsibility is not, of course, ignored in the
traditional theory of emotions. It appears as the doctrine that every
emotion must have an appropriate object; that it is impossible (psychologically) to experience the feeling specific to shame unless you
recognise that you are open to criticism. But there are no limits to
what men may feel; we can only set limits to what they can say. This
is merely the misrepresentation of a logical point as a piece of
implausible *a priori* psychology.

The point of the example is to show that although knowledge of facts that is quite independent of knowledge of behaviour cannot by itself establish a given interpretation of that behaviour, it can be sufficient definitely to exclude it . . ..

Statements about emotions may also involve another, and somewhat different, type of commitment, which has an even closer bearing on the elucidation of their function. It can be illustrated in the contrast between hope and expectation, and I think this throws some light on the question why one is, and the other is not, usually counted as an emotion. The most apparent difference between them is that hoping for and expecting an event express different degrees of confidence that the event will happen. To expect something is to believe that it is more likely than not to happen. In the case of hope it is only necessary that it should not be an impossibility. This is, however, not the only, nor the most crucial, difference. Phrases which express a low degree of confidence, e.g. "I think it may . . .," "Perhaps it will . . ." cannot be substituted without loss for "I hope that. . . ." The expression "I hope that . . ." implies, in addition to a very vague estimate of probability, an *assessment* of whatever is referred to in the clause that follows. I think it is clear that one cannot hope for something, although one can expect something, without judging it favourably in some respect, or from some point of view. Compare (1) "I don't favour a higher purchase tax but I expect it will be raised," with (2) "I don't favour a higher purchase tax, but I hope it will be raised." (1) Creates no surprise; (2) demands further explanation. Does he think it bad for the country, but profitable to him personally because he has a large stock of goods on which he has already paid tax? Does he regard it as unsound fiscal policy in general, but advisable temporarily in an inflationary economy? Failing an answer to questions such as these (2) is surely a puzzling remark, and (3) "I don't favour a higher purchase tax in any respect, but I hope it will be raised" seems to me to be self-contradictory . . .. It is a psychological truism that men do not, with some exceptions, hope that their opponents will win; it is a truth of logic that they cannot hope that their opponents will win without approving of this in *some* respect. . . .

To generalize from this example: emotion words form part of the vocabulary of appraisal and criticism, and a number of them belong to the more specific language of moral criticism. Normally, the verbs in their first-person use imply the speaker's assessment of something, and in their third-person use they carry an implication about an assessment by the person they refer to. . . .[4]

So far I have discussed the conditions which appear to govern the truth and falsity of statements about emotions. While emotion concepts do not form an altogether homogeneous group, I believe that this is correct as a broad outline. But there is one respect in which it needs to be supplemented. This concerns the sense in which emotions (as opposed to statements about emotions) can be justified or unjustified, reasonable or unreasonable. It is fairly obvious, to begin with, that the behavioural criteria for the use of emotion words are not connected with the application of these predicates. The way in which a man behaves will determine whether he is or is not angry. But *if* he is angry, the behavioural evidence for this is not in itself relevant to the question whether his anger is justified or unjustified. On the other hand, if the claim that an emotion word makes about a situation is not satisfied, this is often indicated by saying that the emotion is unjustified or unreasonable. The attribution of the emotion, that is to say, is not withdrawn, but qualified. An example will make this clearer. Suppose that B does something that is to A's advantage, although A thinks that it is to his disadvantage [e.g. B, a solicitor administering A's affairs, sells some shares that A believes (wrongly) will appreciate]. Now it would be misleading to say simply, except to a fully informed audience, "A resents what B did"— this surely carries the incorrect implication that B has injured A. To guard against this it is necessary to add "but his resentment is quite unjustified," or some equivalent expression. A's belief that B has done something that affects him adversely is, however, a necessary condition if the word "resentment" is to be used at all. The distinction between what the situation is, and what it is believed to be, is normally unimportant, and for this reason emotion words make an objective claim unless special precautions are taken to exclude or cancel it [e.g. "He was afraid but no one else was" (there was no real

---

4. But the words "right," "unreasonable" etc., when used to qualify third person statements sometimes serve as endorsements of, or refusals to endorse, this assessment on the speaker's part. I discuss this point below.

danger), "Your surprise is quite unjustified" (it was only to be expected)].

How far can these distinctions be accounted for by theories in which emotion concepts are treated as psychological concepts? I am inclined to think that if an emotion were a feeling no sense could be made of them at all. It may be said that an emotion is unjustified when a feeling is inappropriate or unfitting to a situation. But I find this unintelligible. Feelings do not have a character that makes this relationship possible. In any case, the interpretation suggested is not what is meant by saying that e.g. a critic's contempt is unjustified. In general, I do not think it can be maintained that logical predicates apply either to feelings or to sensations. What reasons could be given for or against a feeling, or for or against its "inappropriateness" to a situation? If someone were to say "I felt a pang this afternoon," it would be meaningless to ask whether it was a reasonable or unreasonable pang. The matter is different if he says "pang of regret," but the phrase "of regret" does not *name* the feeling, as I have already argued, and the pang of regret is justified, if it is, not as a feeling, but because his regret is justified . . ..

A dispositional theory of emotions may be thought to be on stronger ground, since it can be argued that behaviour may be unreasonable or unjustified. To use a previous example again, to say that someone has an unjustified contempt for Bartok is to say, I take it, on this view, that certain categorical and hypothetical statements are true of him, and that these statements describe behaviour that is unjustified. In other words, the assertion that contempt for Bartok is unjustified means that a certain pattern of preferential behaviour is unjustified. But what is this pattern of behaviour? Presumably it will consist in doing (or being prepared to do) things of this sort: switching off when Bartok's music is announced on the Third Programme, wasting free tickets for a concert of his music, never buying records of Bartok, going for a walk when a neighbour plays his music on the violin, and so on; in short, choosing against this composer whenever a choice presents itself. Now let us suppose that contempt for Bartok is unjustified, as it undoubtedly is. Even so, this behaviour may be perfectly reasonable or justified, and therefore cannot constitute an unjustified contempt for Bartok. It is open to a different interpretation, that the person who behaves in this way is simply uninterested in this composer's music, or in modern music generally. Consistently to choose against something is not necessarily to condemn it, or to be contemptuous of it, because this choice is susceptible of rational explanation in other ways.

III

I must now amplify what I have said in passing about the functions performed by statements that refer to emotions. It is generally assumed that these functions are to report feelings, or to report, predict or explain behaviour. Now although some statements containing emotion words are used in these ways, and particularly as explanations, the force of the qualifications "unjustified" and "unreasonable" in itself suggests that this is much less common than might be thought, and my contention is that it would be a mistake to imagine that the primary function of these statements is to communicate psychological facts. Their principal functions are judicial, not informative, and when they are informative, it is often not merely psychological information that they give. Consider the following remarks, as they might be used in suitable contexts in everyday life:

(1) "They are very jealous of one another"
(2) "I envy Schnabel's technique"
(3) "I feel ashamed about it now"
(4) "I never feel the slightest pang of regret for what I did"
(5) "I am quite disgusted with the literary men" (Keats)
(6) "Well, I hope you are ashamed of yourself"
(7) "His pride in the Company's record is unjustified"
(8) "He is very disappointed in you"

Of these examples, the first is different from the rest, its point, I assume, being to inform the hearer that a certain relationship exists between the persons referred to, e.g. in a suitable context, that they are rivals in their profession. The other remarks have what I have termed, for want of a better word, a judicial function. (2) Praises Schnabel; it resembles, say, "Schnabel has a brilliant technique," although it is more tentative and personal, and implies more than this—it would only be said by another pianist. (3) is an admission of responsibility, or perhaps a plea in mitigation, and (4) is the justification of a choice. (5) and (6) imply highly unfavourable assessments. In (5) Keats condemns literary men, and he goes on (Letter of 8th October, 1817) to give part of his reasons for feeling disgusted by an anecdote about Leigh Hunt. The force of (6) seems to lie in its mixture of blame with imputation of responsibility—there are two general lines of reply to it, either (a) "No, I think I was quite right" or (b) "No, it wasn't my fault." (7) is either a way of saying that the person referred to is taking more credit than he deserves, or of saying that the Company's record is not as good as he believes. The normal conversational point of (8), I think would be to convey blame.

In general then, the affinities of (1) to (8) are not with descriptive statements about what people feel and do, but with a different type of statement altogether. . . .

IV

What kind of an explanation of behaviour are we giving when we account for it in terms of emotions? I should like, in conclusion, to sketch the general lines on which I think this question ought to be answered. As this is no more than a corollary of the preceding discussion I can put it very briefly.

The traditional theory gives the answer that emotion words explain behaviour by specifying its cause, i.e. a certain feeling or inner experience. But surely, when we ask what caused someone to do something, we usually neither expect nor receive an answer in terms of feelings. The answer takes the form of a reference to some external circumstance, if that is relevant, or to some thought, memory, observation, etc., that accounts for the action. If we refer to feelings at all, this appears to be a type of explanation that we fall back on as a last resort, because it is unilluminating and only one step removed from saying that the action is unaccountable. What seems to me to be wrong, then, on this score, with the traditional view is that it does not do justice to the explanatory power of emotion words. For the fact is that to know the feeling that may have preceded an action is not to understand it, or to understand it only very imperfectly. One can remember an action that one did many years ago, an action that one no longer understands, and the question "Why did I do it?" can remain in the face of the clearest recollection of what it felt like to do it. If emotion words merely named some inner experience that preceded or accompanied behaviour, to explain behaviour by using them would not give the insight that it does.

A quite different answer to this question is proposed by Professor Ryle in *The Concept of Mind*. Referring to what he calls "inclinations" or "motives," Professor Ryle writes, "The imputation of a motive for a particular action is not a causal inference to an unwitnessed event but the subsumption of an episode proposition under a law-like proposition" (p. 90). Again, "To explain an action as done from a certain motive is not to correlate it with an occult cause, but to subsume it under a propensity or behaviour-trend" (p. 110) . . . It does not seem to me that emotion words explain merely in the relatively superficial way that dispositional words explain, if "the glass broke because it was brittle" is to be taken as a model, however rough, of this kind of explanation. To refer to a man's laziness or fondness for gardening is to account for what he does on a particular occasion by removing the need for a *special* explanation of it; by showing that his conduct is not in any way surprising or unusual, but part of the regular pattern of things that he does or is likely to do. To assimilate emotion words closely to dispositional words is to give an incomplete account of their explanatory function; they explain behaviour more fully than could be done by saying, in effect, that it was only to be expected. ("To say that he did something from that motive is to say that this action, done in its particular circumstances, was just the sort of thing that that was an inclination to do. It is to say 'he *would* do that.'" *Ibid.* pp. 92–3.) I would suggest that emotion words go beyond this sort of explanation in two ways. First, by setting the action to be explained, not merely in the context of the rest of an individual's behaviour, but in a social context. "He was rude to you because he was jealous" resembles "I helped him because he was a friend" in accounting for his behaviour by the reference it makes to his relationship with other people. Secondly, emotion words explain by giving the reason for an action, in the sense of giving a justification for it. "He refused an interview because of his contempt for journalists" explains the refusal by connecting it with an assessment made by the person whose behaviour is referred to. In this respect it has some analogy with, for instance, "He reads Gibbon because he thinks highly of his style." Emotion concepts, I have argued, are not purely psychological: they presuppose concepts of social relationships and institutions, and concepts belonging to systems of judgement, moral, aesthetic and legal. In using emotion words we are able, therefore, to relate behaviour to the complex background in which it is enacted, and so to make human action intelligible.

Anthony Kenny

(1931-　)

INTRODUCTION

One of the key components of emotion, according to most Continental theorists, is the property of "intentionality." But however
central to the Continental philosophers this concept may have been,
it was treated with suspicion by many Anglo-American philosophers.
(See, for example, the quick dismissal of it in the first footnote of
Bedford's essay.) It was a matter of some significance, therefore,
when Anthony Kenny took on the topic of intentionality in his book,
Action, Emotion and Will, which was published in 1963. Kenny is
also a scholar of ancient and medieval philosophy and has written
extensively on Aristotle, Descartes, and the Scholastics. These influences are clearly represented in the following discussion of "intentional objects," in which he tries to make clear the nature of intentionality and the peculiar nature of the "objects" to which emotions
are "directed."

From Action, Emotion and Will

Objects

In the first part of this book I spoke frequently of the "object" of an emotion or desire, contrasting the object of such a mental attitude with its cause. In the last chapter I described the object of an action as being that which changes as a result of the action. It is clear that we have here two different senses of "object," or two different kinds of object. The objects of mental attitudes are sometimes called "intensional objects": let us call the object of an action which is not a mental act a "non-intensional object." We must now consider the relationships and the differences between intensional and non-intensional objects.

It will, I hope, have been clear to the reader throughout that when I speak of "the object of an action" I do not mean to refer to the point of an action, or the purpose or objective with which someone acts. I have also tried to avoid using the word "object" in such a way that it is equivalent to "thing" or "substance," as when people speak of finding a strange object in the cupboard, or philosophers talk of objects in the external world. The sense of "object" which I have hitherto employed and wish now to discuss is one which derives from the grammatical notion of the *object* of a transitive verb. The object of fear is *what* is feared, the object of love is *what* is loved, the object of cutting is *what* is cut, the object of heating is *what* is heated. In discussing the nature of objects we are simply discussing the logical role of the object-expressions which complete the sense of intensional and non-intensional verbs.[1]

There was a scholastic adage: *Obiectum specificat actum.* There are two ways in which objects specify acts. First, and obviously, one and the same verb may be used to report quite different actions if its sense is completed with different object-expressions. Smoking a pipe differs from smoking a cigar, and killing mice is not the same thing

---

1. If this is clearly understood, there seems to be little danger, and great convenience, in talking of "objects" rather than of "object-expressions." Geach criticizes this usage on the grounds that it leads to saying e.g. "some objects of mental acts do not exist." But this sentence is objectionable so long as it means only that some object-expressions lack reference.

as killing men. Verbs completed by object expressions describe species of the genus described by a verb alone: stealing silk handkerchiefs is one sort of stealing, and eating snails is one sort of eating. Some of these specific distinctions are more important than others; in different societies different distinctions play different roles. In most societies the difference between killing men and killing mice is clearly marked; in some eating pork is significantly different from eating lamb. Much of moral philosophy could be regarded as an attempt to discover or lay down which are the significant specific differences between human actions.[2]

Objects specify acts in another way, which was brought out by the scholastic distinction between material and formal objects. Anything which can be φd is a material object of φing. Beer, for example can be seen, and so beer is a material object of seeing; when the executioners burnt Joan of Arc, Joan was the material object of their burning. The formal object of φing is the object under that description which *must* apply to it if it is to be possible to φ it. If only what is P can be φd, then "thing which is P" gives the formal object of φing. Descriptions of formal objects can be formed trivially simply by modalising the relevant verbs: only what is edible can be eaten, only what is inflammable can be burnt, only what is tangible can be touched. But there are other descriptions of formal objects which are not trivial in this way. Only what is dirty can be cleaned, only what is wet can be dried, only what is coloured can be seen, only what is criminal can be committed, only what is difficult to obtain can be striven for, only other people's property can be stolen. "Other people's property" is a description of the formal object of *stealing,* just as "one's own spouse" is a description of the formal object of *divorcing.* Joan of Arc was the formal object of burning not *qua* saint, nor *qua* woman, but *qua* inflammable material.

To assign a formal object to an action is to place restrictions on what may occur as the direct object of a verb describing the action. The restrictions may be of various kinds. They may, for example, concern time: only what is past can be remembered or avenged, only what has not yet happened can be dreaded or awaited. Or they may

2. For the scholastic dictum cf. Aquinas, *Summa Theologica* Ia 77,3; and Ia IIae 18, 2; *actio habet speciem ex obiecto, sicut et motus ex termino.* The doctrine is based on passages in Aristotle, e.g. *De Anima* II 415 a 14ff, *N. Ethics,* 1774 b 5.

concern place: only what is present can be enjoyed, only what is absent can be missed. Or they may concern good and evil; only something thought to be good can be envied, only something thought to be evil can be regretted. There is no formal object of *thinking of,* because there are no restrictions on what may be thought of: any expression which can occur as an object-expression after any verb, can occur as an object-expression after the verb " . . . think of . . . ." So that if we are to say that there is a formal object of thought we must say that it is: anything whatever.[3]

A formal object should not be confused with an internal accusative, such as occurs in the expressions "to dream a dream," "to play a game." The dream is not anything over and above the dreaming, nor the game over and above the playing; but my neighbour's property can be identified as such quite independently of my stealing it, and my wife is not brought into existence by my divorcing her.

Formal objects specify actions in a manner different from that in which, as we saw above, all objects specify actions. Verbal nouns, like other nouns, may be ordered in accordance with the scheme of genus and species: murder is one sort of homicide, and homicide is one sort of killing; spying is one sort of treason, and treason is one sort of crime. One way in which a species of action may be differentiated from other species of the same genus is by a difference in its formal object.[4] Thus, if we take (voluntary) killing as a genus, homicide differs from other species in this genus as being the killing of *a human being;* if we take homicide as a genus, murder differs from other species in this genus as being the killing of an *innocent* human being. If we take making as a genus, then cobbling differs from tailoring because the formal object of the one is footwear and of the other clothes.

Now both intensional and non-intensional actions are specified by their formal objects: this, and not the mere grammatical similarity between such sentences as "Macbeth feared Banquo" and "Macbeth

---

3. This is the meaning of the scholastic expression *"obiectum intellectus est ens ut sic."* This dictum is sometimes quaintly interpreted by neo-Scholastics as meaning that the intellect is a faculty for the intuition of Pure Being.

4. There are other ways: roasting and boiling are species of cooking, but their formal objects are the same. So too one can *crawl to* anywhere that one can *walk to.* The difference between species in such cases is made by the manner, and not by the object, of the action (cf. Aristotle, *N. Ethics,* 1174 a 31).

killed Banquo," is the reason for treating intensional and non-intensional objects together before distinguishing between them. Emotional attitudes, like other mental attitudes, have formal objects; some of the philosophical errors about the emotions which we considered in the first part of this book might be described as mistakes about their formal objects. Descartes and Hume, with the philosophers and psychologists who followed them, treated the relationship between an emotion and its formal object, which is a logical one, as if it were a contingent matter of fact. If the emotions were internal impressions or behaviour patterns there would be no logical restrictions on the type of object which each emotion could have. It would be a mere matter of fact that people were not angered by being benefited, nor afraid of what they already know to have happened; just as it is a mere matter of fact that most people are nauseated by slugs crawling from beneath an upturned stone and sneeze on getting pepper in their nostrils. There would be no more reason why, once in a while, a man might not be grateful for being harmed, or be proud of a defect, than there is why, once in a while, a man may not feel a sinking in the stomach while being complimented, or weep on the receipt of good news.

In fact, each of the emotions is appropriate—logically, and not just morally appropriate—only to certain restricted objects. One cannot be afraid of just anything, nor happy about anything whatsoever. If a man says that he is afraid of winning £10,000 in the pools, we want to ask him more: does he believe that money corrupts, or does he expect to lose his friends, or to be annoyed by begging letters, or what? If we can elicit from him only descriptions of the good aspects of the situation, then we cannot understand why he reports his emotion as fear and not as hope. Again, if a man says that he feels remorse for the actions of someone quite unconnected with him, or is envious of his own vices, we are at a loss to understand him.

It is, of course, quite possible for someone to be grateful for a physical injury, if he regards it as having done him some good; as members of the House of Lords frequently tell us that they are grateful to those who caned them at school. It is also possible to be proud of a vice or a crime or a defect, if one can represent it to oneself as a virtue or an achievement or an advantage: as Don Juan may boast of his prowess with women, or Topcliffe brag of his skill as a torturer, or a beggar in a bazaar glory in the unsightliness of his sores. What is not possible is to be grateful for, or proud of, something which one regards as an evil unmixed with good. Again, it is possible to be envious of one's own fruit trees; but only if one mistakenly believes that the land on which they stand is part of one's neighbour's property; just as it is possible to feel remorse for the failure of the crops in Vietnam if one believes that it was due to the inadequacy of one's own prayers. What is not possible is to envy something which one believes to belong to oneself, or to feel remorse for something in which one believes one had no part.

The medieval schoolmen gave expression to restrictions such as those we have outlined by saying that the formal object of fear was a future evil, of envy another's good, or remorse one's own past sins. In this they were following Aristotle, who gives, in his *Rhetoric,* but without the terminology, a list of the formal objects of the emotions. It is not, of course, correct to say e.g. that the formal object of envy is another's good *tout court:* one must say that it is something *believed to* be good and *believed to* belong to another, as our example above shows. Thus Aristotle in defining anger says that it is a desire for *what appears to be* revenge for *what appears to be* an insult.[5] The description of the formal object of a mental attitude such as an emotion, unlike a description of the formal object of a non-intensional action, must contain reference to belief. Only what is wet in fact can be dried; but something which is merely believed to be an insult may provoke anger.

So far I have used "intensional action" and "intensional object" simply as equivalent to "mental act" and "object of a mental act or attitude" without giving any criterion for distinguishing intensional objects from non-intensional objects. We might define intensionality heuristically as "the formal property which is peculiar to the description of psychological events and states." The attempt, then, to give a proper definition of intensionality will consist in an attempt to find what formal property, if any, belongs always and only to descriptions of psychological phenomena. It was thus, historically, that the notion of intensionality was introduced, or reintroduced, into philosophy by Brentano.

Looking for a property which would mark off psychical phenomena from physical phenomena, Brentano first considered and

5. *Rhetoric,* 1378 a 30ff

rejected the suggestion that the peculiarity of psychical phenomena was that they lacked extension. He then proposed a different criterion of distinction:

> Every psychical phenomenon is characterized by what the medieval scholastics called the intensional (or mental) existence of an object, and what we, not quite unambiguously, would call "relation to a content" "object-directedness" or "immanent objectivity." ("Object" here does not mean reality.) Each such phenomenon contains in itself something as an object, though not each in the same manner. In imagination something is imagined, in judgement something is accepted or rejected, in love, something is loved, in hatred something is hated, in desire something is desired and so forth.
>
> This intensional existence is a property only of psychical phenomena; no physical phenomenon displays anything similar. And so we can define psychical phenomena by saying that they are those phenomena which contain an object intensionally (*Psychologie von Empirischen Standpunkt,* Book II, chapter 1, section 5).

In reading this passage we feel a certain difficulty. It is true that where there is love then *something* is loved, if there is to be hatred then *something* must be hated; but is it not also true that if heating takes place then *something* is heated and if cutting takes place then *something* is cut? "Heat" and "cut" are not psychological verbs: how then can Brentano say that object-directedness is peculiar to psychological phenomena? He appears to have taken a feature common to all grammatically transitive verbs as being a peculiarity of psychological verbs.[6]

The answer to this difficulty becomes clear only if we refer to the scholastics from whom Brentano borrowed the notion of intensionality. It will be remembered that in the last chapter we defined the object of an action as that which was changed as the result of an action. This definition applies only to nonpsychological actions; and the scholastics placed the intensionality of psychological actions precisely in the fact that they did not change their objects. If Peter has painted his house, then Peter's house must now be different from

---

6. Husserl, in a passage which reads like a commentary on Brentano's text, seems to accept the conclusion that *any* action which has an object is intensional.

what it was before he painted it; but if Peter has looked at his house, it may now be exactly the same as it was before he looked at it. To find out whether the doctor has cured his patient, we must examine the patient; to find out whether the doctor has fallen in love with his patient, we must ask or observe the doctor. Where a non-psychological action brings about a change, the change is in the object and not, save *per accidens,* in the subject; where a psychological action brings about a change, the change is in the subject and not, save *per accidens,* in the object.

Aquinas frequently makes this distinction between two different kinds of action: *actio manens in agente* and *actio transiens in obiectum.* Thus he writes:

> There are actions of two kinds: some actions, such as heating and cutting, pass over into external matter; others, such as understanding, perceiving, and wanting, remain in the agent. The difference between them is this: actions of the first kind bring about a state not of the agent which initiates the change, but of what is changed; whereas actions of the second kind bring about a state of the agent.[7]

This distinction solves the difficulty which we felt about Brentano's account of intensionality: but it presents difficulties of its own. The physician may heal himself, and the change thus brought about is in the agent; yet healing is not a psychological performance, since drugs can do it as well as men. This difficulty, though of venerable antiquity, is fairly trivial; a more serious one concerns local motion. When I climb the Matterhorn, the change brought about appears to be in me: I who was at the bottom of the mountain am now at the top. But "climb" is not, or not obviously, a psychological verb. In this case, the change brought about is a change in the *relation* between myself and the Matterhorn: the state which ensues upon

---

7. Aquinas goes on to explain how the sense of "change" differs when we talk of the agent as changing from when we talk of the object as changing. My translation of *"perfectio"* as *"bringing about* a state" may be questioned; it was suggested by the parallel passage in Ia 87, 3c where *aedificatio* (a performance and not a state in the sense defined in the previous (chapter) is called a *"perfectio."* Aquinas claims, perhaps without justification, to base his distinction on that made by Aristotle in *Metaphysics* Θ (1058 a 3–37).

my action is expressed by the relational proposition "I am on top of the Matterhorn." And we have all along admitted, in company with most logicians, that in a genuinely relational proposition both terms are on an equal footing. The result of the action has therefore no more claim to be regarded as a fact about the agent than as a fact about the object.

In our time, Brentano's thesis has been developed by Chisholm (*Perceiving*, Ch. XI). Chisholm gives three criteria for intensionality. The first is this:

> A simple declarative sentence is intensional if it uses a substantival expression—a name or a description—in such a way that neither the sentence nor its contradictory implies either that there is or that there isn't anything to which the substantival expression truly applies.

By this criterion, he observes, "Diogenes looked for an honest man" is intensional, whereas "Diogenes sat in his tub" is not.

Another criterion which Chisholm offers concerns what Quine calles "referential opacity." It may be summarized as follows. Let E be a sentence of the form "A = B" (where A and B are names). Then if P is a sentence containing A, and Q is a sentence like P except that it contains B wherever P contains A, P is intensional if P and E do not together imply Q. These are the criteria which Chisholm gives for diagnosing intensionality in sentences which do not contain propositional clauses.

An objection to these criteria is that by them many expressions containing psychological verbs are not intensional. "Know," for instance, is a psychological verb, but "Diogenes knows an honest man" implies that there is an honest man; and "Dr Jekyll = Mr Hyde" and "James knows Dr Jekyll" together imply "James knows Mr Hyde," though of course they do not imply "James knows that Dr Jekyll is Mr Hyde." So far as I can see these criteria as they stand are sufficient, but not necessary, conditions for intensionality. The scholastic criterion therefore seems preferable for diagnosing the intensionality of a verb which is followed by a direct object which is a substantival expression.

Psychological verbs occur not only in sentences of the simple sub-ject-verb-object form, but also, and most characteristically, in sentences containing *that*-clauses. Examples are "think," "say," "wish," "decide," and "regret." Such verbs, obviously, need not be followed by *that*-clauses in all their uses: many take an accusative and an infinitive, or simply an infinitive, where the accusative in question would be the same as the subject of the main verb. Other psychological verbs, such as "want," "intend," and "urge," show a marked preference for these latter forms. We can say that it is characteristic of many psychological verbs that they occur in sentences which, though not containing any truth-functional connectives, contain more than one verb. Thus Russell classed reports of beliefs, desires and so forth under the heading "propositions with more than one verb."[8] We might take the possibility of occurring as the main verb of such a sentence as a criterion of intensionality.

However, among sentences which contain more than one verb, we must distinguish between those in which one of the verbs is exponible and those where neither is exponible. "John began to smoke" differs from "John wanted to smoke" because the former sentence, unlike the latter, could be expanded into a compound sentence which contained no other verb but "smoke" and included expressions indicating times. Verbs such as "cease," "continue," "make a practice of," "repeat," "anticipate," though they all need to have their sense completed by the addition of a further verb, are all exponible no less than "begin." Thus, for example, when we say that Amundsen anticipated Scott in reaching the Pole we may mean no more than that Amundsen reached the Pole before Scott did. Such verbs, when so used, are not intensional verbs.

But besides psychological verbs and exponible verbs, there are other verbs which need completion by a second verb. Such are "help," "hinder," "imitate," "attempt," "avoid." One can help one's friends only by helping them to *do* something, and one can imitate one's boss only by imitating him *doing* something. There is no form of behaviour which is called "imitating" or "helping"; what counts as helping John or imitating James depends on what John is doing or on what James does. These verbs are not exponible: it is not sufficient for A to be helping B simply that the actions of A and B should between them produce a common result, nor is C imitating D merely because he is doing what D does. One raindrop does not

8. *Logic and Knowledge,* 216ff.

help another to wet the lawn, and waves following waves upon the
seashore are not imitating their predecessors.

However, these verbs do not form a separate class of intensional
verbs over and above the psychological verbs. If we ask what must
be true for John to be helping Mary to wash the dishes, besides the
fact that both John and Mary are washing the dishes, we shall find
ourselves having to mention such circumstances as that John *knows*
that Mary is washing the dishes. If we ask what must be true of
James to make it the case that he has avoided meeting Nigel, besides
his not having met Nigel, we shall have to say that he did not *want*
to meet Nigel. Verbs such as "assist" and "avoid" are non-exponible
only because of their psychological content.

The verb "to be able," however, is neither exponible nor psychological and yet it needs completion by another verb: modal propositions are members of the class of propositions with more than one
verb. Another non-exponible, non-psychological verb is "to bring it
about that." We cannot, therefore, use the two-verb criterion by
itself as a mark of intensionality.

Chisholm offers another criterion of intensionality which is of
assistance here. He says that any noncompound sentence Q which
contains a propositional clause P is intensional provided that neither
Q nor not-Q imply either P or not-P. By this criterion "it can be the
case that p" is not intensional, even though "it can be the case that
..." is not a truth-functional operator; for "it cannot be the case that
p" implies "not-p." But once again, Chisholm has given us a sufficient, but not a necessary, condition of intensionality. By this criterion "John knows that Queen Anne is dead" is not intensional,
since it implies "Queen Anne is dead."

Chisholm's earlier criterion, of referential opacity, though it was
inadequate as a diagnostic of intensionality in simple subject-verb-
object sentences, serves its purpose well here. If Tully = Cicero,
then if it is possible that Tully will rise from the dead, it is possible
that Cicero will rise from the dead; similarly, if the medium is bringing it about that Tully will attend the seance, she is bringing it about
that Cicero will attend the seance. So the criterion rules out "it can
be the case that" and "is bringing it about that" but does not, as the
other did, exclude "knows." For if John knows that Cicero was murdered it does not follow that he knows that Tully was murdered.

By these criteria of intensionality which we have borrowed from the scholastics and from Chisholm, reports of emotional states and acts of the will are intensional sentences. A consideration of the emotions and the will must therefore include an account of how such sentences containing intensional objects are to be analysed. . . .

Irving Thalberg

(1930-)

INTRODUCTION

As doubts multiplied about the adequacy of the Jamesian theory, attention shifted from physiological to "cognitive" factors in emotion. Schachter and Singer (Part II) represented such a shift in psychology, amending the James-Lange theory with a "two-components" analysis, in which "cognitive factors" in the environment and the appropriateness of certain "labels" became as critical to the identification of emotions as Jamesian bodily arousal. In philosophy, attention shifted to the logical relations between emotions and belief. It became clear that the connection between "being angry at Joe for his rudeness" and "believing Joe to have been rude" was not merely the linkage of cause and effect, but something more, such that the belief became a logical precondition for the having of the emotion. In the following article, Chicago philosopher Irving Thalberg investigates this critical connection.

From Emotion and Thought

Many emotions appear to be founded or based upon states of belief. If we hear that a cattleman is dismayed, anxious, or indignant about falling meat prices, have we any need to inquire whether the cattleman has thoughts concerning the price of beef? It seems perfectly obvious that he must not only imagine that the market value of beef is decreasing; he must be relatively sure of it, if that is what alarms, disquiets, or shocks him. Although it is so obvious that such emotions are founded upon some form of thought, it is not immediately clear what kind of dependency this is. And that is one reason I wish to examine the relation between a person's feelings, moods, inclinations or attitudes, and his convictions, doubts, or guesses. A more important reason for investigating this liaison between emotions and thought is that our pre-analytic view of it will neither accommodate nor show the impossibility of some baffling cases. Let me convey my perplexity by asking whether any of the following statements could be true of John, a dinner guest:

(a) John is embarrassed that he is late for dinner, but he doubts that he is (late for dinner);

(b) John is delighted that there will be champagne with dessert, but he merely conjectures that there will be;

(c) John resents the hostess for having gossiped about him, but he is not at all sure that she has done so.

There seems to be a discord, if not an inconsistency, between John's feelings and opinions. Is it possible to feel embarrassment over something which you believe not to have happened? Why rejoice about a future event when you have no assurance it will occur? Does it make sense to bear a grudge against a person when you are uncertain that the person has wronged you? . . .

These questions, as well as the standard replies to them, are peculiar. This suggests that we must begin with a brief inquiry into the concept of emotion. Then it will become clearer how, and why each sort of emotion—shame, anxiety, and so on—requires a particular cognitive consort. My analysis of emotion is not meant to be taxonomically exhaustive. Only those features of emotion will be discussed which seem important in determining the relation of feeling to thought.

I. OBJECTS OF EMOTION

For expository convenience I plan to stretch the label "emotion" to fit a heterogeneous assortment of reactions, moods, appetites, inclinations, aversions, desires, and attitudes, as well as emotions in the strict sense, like rage and disappointment. I mainly wish to exclude urges, impulses, decisions, intentions, resolutions, and similar dispositions to engage in some course of action. Consequently, to the extent that an emotion involves a proclivity to undertake overt action, as feeling vindictive includes a disposition to seek vengeance, I shall be silent about it. . . .

Now let me introduce some distinctions which will be crucial for an account of the relation between an emotion and the state of thought upon which the emotion is founded. All the emotions in my puzzling examples (a)–(c) share one feature which is not possessed by emotions like depression, euphoria, apathy, and the like: In each instance, John is worked up *about* something—his tardiness, the dessert wine, the hostess. . . .

We have, then, emotions which cannot take objects (depression, free-floating anxiety); emotions which must take objects (hope); and emotions which may be expected to have objects (embarrassment). Among the emotions which are always directed toward something, we may distinguish two sub-groups: Hate, aversion, love, admiration, appetite, and enjoyment must be focused on people, activities, events, things, or on groups of people, activities, events, or things. An infantryman cannot simply feel hate; he must, for instance, detest his sergeant or noncommissioned officers. A sybarite cannot simply feel aversion; he must dislike sports or physical exertion. I shall say that these emotions are directed toward *non-propositional* objects, to differentiate them from other "necessarily transitive" emotions whose objects may be characterized by means of complete declarative sentences. Hope exemplifies the other subclass. I may hope (that) I have been appointed ambassador to Bolivia, and I may hope for the appointment or the ambassadorship. Of the emotions which *may* take objects, we seem to have a choice, in all cases, between propositional and non-propositional descriptions of their objects. Consider a unionist's feelings about the forthcoming strike. It is clearer to use the propositional idiom, and say, "He is glad (afraid, sorry, angry, dismayed) (that) there will be a strike"; but it is never incorrect to say "He is pleased (worried, etc.) about the impending strike. . . ."[1]

1. Professor R. M. Chisholm makes use of the term "propositional object" in *perceiving* (Ithaca, 1957), p. 142. It has been suggested to me (by Professor Mary Moth-

I have not discovered any philosophical significance in the grammatical fact, noted above, that emotions like hate and enjoyment are always given non-propositional objects. Nevertheless it is a fact that we cannot specify a propositional object for the infantryman's loathing. Suppose, for example, that the sergeant has assigned our hero to Kitchen Police. We can say, "The soldier is furious (pleased, astonished) that the sergeant put him on K.P.," but not; "The soldier detests that the sergeant put him on K.P." And if we declare, "The soldier detests the sergeant because the sergeant put him on K.P.," we have not specified a propositional object of his loathing; rather, we have mentioned the fellow's grounds or reason for despising his sergeant.

II. GROUNDS FOR EMOTION

The last distinction, between the objects of and the grounds for an emotion, demands some comment. . . .

For this purpose, consider a government security agent who learns that Brown, a candidate for the diplomatic service, receives a number of Marxist periodicals. The investigator begins to suspect that Brown has subversive tendencies, because Brown subscribes to Marxist periodicals. However, the sleuth is not at all convinced that

---

ersill) that the objects of many emotions are best construed as possible or probable states of affairs. As I understand this view, it would have us say, of a prudent lathe-operator who buys accident-insurance, "He fears a possible (probable) injury," rather than "He fears an injury." In the *patois* of propositional objects, we should say, "He fears that he *might* be mutilated," or "He fears that he will probably be mutilated (that his chances of mutilation are such-and-such)," instead of "He fears that he will be mutilated." Is there any reason to adopt this analysis for fear and other anticipatory emotions? I think not. How can the object of the machinist's fear be a possible—or even a likely—injury? An *actual* mutilation will hurt; it will require hospital care; it will prevent the machinist from working; it will leave scars. If he suffers an actual mutilation, the additional fact that it was possible, or likely, will not make it any more painful, costly, time-consuming, or disfiguring. Further, imagine that the machinist retires without having suffered any actual injuries, although it was possible, or probable, that he would be injured. In other words, imagine that his injuries were merely possible or probable. Could he have feared these possible or probable, but nonactual injuries? Did his possible or probable injuries hurt? Did they need medication? Did they keep him from working? Did they spoil his looks? If not, then probable or possible injuries were not what he feared when he bought insurance.

Brown is disloyal. Now plainly the security man does *not suspect* that Brown reads Marxist periodicals; his misgivings are directed toward Brown's loyalty, not Brown's reading habits; presumably the investigator is sure of Brown's reading habits, if that is why he suspects Brown of disloyalty. In this example, then, we must distinguish the object from the grounds. . . .

How are a man's thoughts connected with the object of, and the grounds for, his emotions? Let us start with a normal fellow, our cattle-breeder who believes that meat prices are falling, and who is indignant about it. From this description of him, it sounds as if the object of his indignation is his belief that meat prices are falling. But plainly this analysis of the object of his indignation will not work: For it is false to say, "He is indignant about his belief that meat prices are falling" or "He is indignant that he believes that meat prices are falling." His outrage is not directed toward himself or his own belief! He is furious about prices.

What is the connection between his belief and the object of his emotion? His belief is directed toward the same object as his outrage; he believes that livestock prices are falling and he is indignant that they are. . . .

I shall not be able to dodge some other metaphysical questions, but let me postpone them in order to describe the relation between the grounds for an emotion and the thoughts (convictions, doubts, conjectures) upon which an emotion is founded. I shall use the cattleman again, and suppose that the *reason* he is indignant about falling beef-prices is that the Secretary of Agriculture had assured livestock owners that meat prices would be high this year. The cattleman believes that the Secretary made this claim. Under the circumstances it is correct to say, "The cattleman is outraged that meat prices are dropping, because he believes that the Secretary of Agriculture assured. . . ." It would be pedantic to drive a logical wedge between the cattleman's belief and the grounds for his outrage. His belief is his reason for being angry. However, the belief upon which his emotion is *grounded* is not the belief upon which his emotion is *founded:* His indignation that prices are falling is *founded* on his belief that prices are falling; his indignation that prices are falling is *grounded* on his belief that the Secretary gave assurances to livestock owners. Is this distinction between "grounded" and "founded" a pedantic one? No! For it enables us to talk of groundless hopes, suspicions, and resentments, without implying that such emotions are unaccompanied by assumptions, surmises, or convictions. Suppose that our investigator, mentioned above, has no reason to suspect that Brown is unpatriotic. It would be true to say, "His suspicion is not grounded on any belief, conjecture, or assumption," but this does not mean: "The investigator neither believes, supposes, takes it for granted, conjectures, or doubts that Brown is unpatriotic!"

III. ARE OBJECTS OF EMOTION CAUSES OF EMOTION?

My metaphysical worries would be over if I could identify objects of emotion with causes of emotion. In fact many of the things we like, fear, long for, and so on, are causes of our enjoyment, our fright, and our longing. If a rhinoceros is bearing down on me, and I fly in terror of it, the rhinoceros is both the object and the cause of my fear of it; you could use the same declarative sentence to describe the propositional object of my fear and the state of affairs which makes me frightened: "The rhinoceros is chasing him." (To say that the approaching rhinoceros causes my fear is not to deny that other circumstances—the condition of my nervous system, previous experiences with wild animals, etc.—contribute to my terror.)

Is it always possible to rank the object of emotion as a cause of emotion? Unfortunately for our metaphysics, no. For suppose that I am in a state of terror as I cross New York's Central Park, and when sympathetic passersby ask me what is bothering me, I declare: "I am terrified that I shall be chased by a rhinoceros during my stroll." Call my fear unmanly, ridiculous, or peculiar; the fact remains that the propositional object of my fear is correctly described by the sentence, "I shall be chased by a rhinoceros during my stroll." Does this sentence describe the cause of my fear? Well, perhaps a rhinoceros is in the offing—one escaped from the zoo and made its way to Central Park. In these circumstances it is true to say that I shall be chased by a rhinoceros. Even so, how could the future chase produce my current fear? In this case it is, to say the least, implausible to maintain that the object of my fear also causes my fear. And the assimilation of object to cause fails utterly when Central Park is free of rhinoceri. The sentence, "I shall be chased by a rhinoceros," still describes the propositional object of my fear, but does not, *ex hypothesi,* describe a cause of my fear. I assume that only actual events, states of affairs, and things can cause other events, states of affairs, and things. No rhinoceros is in the cards. Therefore it is false to say that my fear is caused by a rhinoceros attack. So the object of my emotion (a rhinoceros attack) is not a cause of my emotion.

Let me generalize from this odd example: Whenever an emotion is directed toward a future event or state of affairs, or something yet to be born, and whenever an emotion is concerned with something that did not, does not, or will not occur or exist, the object of emotion is not a cause of emotion. If very strict nominalists grumble—heroically—that a person *cannot really* fear what does not exist, my reply is this. Such a method of controlling the population of superfluous entities has the consequence that nobody has ever really feared ghosts, goblins, demons, or other imaginary powers. I doubt that superstitious fears will be destroyed by this sort of verbal magic.

IV. ARE THOUGHTS CAUSES OF EMOTION?

Our initial problem was to explain how emotions are based on thoughts (beliefs, assumptions, speculations). The main requirement we set was that the analysis of the relation should show whether it is possible, e.g., for a man to be embarrassed that he is late for dinner, but doubt that he is late for dinner. Enough distinctions have been established to consider one hypothesis: An emotion is founded upon a thought if and only if the thought is a cause of the emotion. "Cause" must mean "empirically necessary condition" rather than "empirically sufficient condition." Even if my conviction that the milkman beats his horse sometimes makes me angry with the milkman, I may at times be too distracted with my own cares to work up any emotion about the milkman's cruelty, despite my belief that he is mean to his animal.

According to this hypothesis, the puzzling cases (a)–(c) (on the first page of this essay) would be at most causally impossible. I find some merit to the conclusion, but the analysis from which it follows is seriously defective.

If a man's thoughts are only causal conditions of his emotions, then it is conceivable that, for any emotion he has, he might have had precisely that emotion without the concurrence of any thoughts at all. On the causal analysis, people just happen to be fairly sure that some event will occur when they rejoice that it will occur. If their makeup or conditioning were different, they might be in the same affective state, although they neither believe, doubt, nor imagine the event will occur.

Why do I resist this view? I admitted, in Section I, that moods like depression, euphoria, and total apathy may be caused by the subject's beliefs, doubts, or conjectures. Why not say the same of embarrassment and other emotions? Because the latter group of emotions may have objects, whereas depression, euphoria, total apathy, and free-floating anxiety—as its title indicates—are not about anything.

Let me explain why this fact invalidates the hypothesis that emotions with objects are effects of the convictions, doubts, or conjectures upon which these emotions are founded. Take the annoyance of a balletomane who thinks that no seats are left for this evening's dance recital. It is irrelevant for the time being, to specify whether he simply takes it for granted that seats are unavailable, whether he is convinced of it, whether he merely conjectures that seats are unavailable, or whether he doubts it. Whatever the nature of his thought, could it be the cause of his annoyance that no seats are left? In so far as his annoyance is a form of agitation, including physiological disturbances and behavioral changes like fidgeting and inability to concentrate, his annoyance resembles objectless emotions. So his agitation might be a result of his thought that seats are unavailable. However, will any examination of his pulse rate, blood pressure, galvanic responses, salivation, or his bodily motions disclose that he is annoyed over the lack of seats for tonight's performance? If not, then a study of his agitation will leave out an essential feature of his annoyance, It will not yield an answer to the question, always germane in such cases: "What is he annoyed about?"

Of course we shall get a quick answer if we interrogate him. His reply, "I'm annoyed that no tickets are left," indicates the propositional object of his chagrin. But his words also reveal that he has thoughts regarding the tickets. How does this prove that his thought cannot be a cause of his annoyance that tickets are gone? It seems to me that any time you claim one event or condition is a cause of another event or condition, you must be able to gather evidence of the effect which is logically independent of your evidence of its putative cause. According to this principle, you may claim, "There was a short circuit in the warehouse, which caused a fire in the warehouse," but not: "There were flames in the warehouse, which caused a fire in the warehouse." Evidence of a conflagration is not always evidence of a short circuit, but it is always evidence of flames. How does this principle apply to the particular hypothesis concerning the ballet enthusiast, "His thought that tickets are gone caused his annoyance that tickets are gone"? Well, it appears that if we prove he is vexed that tickets are gone, we also prove that he thinks (believes, conjectures, doubts) that tickets are gone; therefore we cannot claim that his emotion is the effect of his thought. . . .

I conclude that the relation between thought and emotions which have objects is not a causal relation.[2]

2. The causal theory is not entirely made of straw; it is Hume's doctrine in the *Treatise.* See pages 368, 386, 415–426, 439–446, Selby-Bigge edition (Oxford, 1955). His kind of analysis of the relation between feeling and thought has been under intermittent attack, but I find the most current objections fairly weak. It is said that my belief that I inherited somebody's fortune cannot be a cause of my pleasure that I did, because: (i) I cannot be mistaken when I relate my pleasure to my belief; however, one can, in principle, be mistaken regarding the causes of any phenomenon; (ii) I never need to observe the concomitance of my belief and my pleasure, nor do I make use of inductive evidence of similar effective-cognitive couples in my past experience; but one always needs this sort of evidence when claiming that something is the cause of another thing; (iii) thoughts and many emotions are not processes, but causes and their effects are events having earlier and later spatiotemporal phases. Of course I accept the conclusion of these arguments, but I think that (i) confuses two distinct notions: a person's *de facto* or (perhaps) *de jure* incorrigibility when he makes some first-person psychological statements, and the logical status of assertions (by anyone) regarding someone's psychological condition; (ii) seems to me to embody a similar confusion, between the plausible claim that one does not utilize observational procedures in making some first-person psychological statements, and the dubious claim that inductive evidence is irrelevant to other people's assessment of the truth or falsity of one's first-person statements; (iii) seems to me to depend on a very restrictive notion of "cause and effect." For extremely persuasive developments of (i), (ii), (iii), and other arguments against the casual view, consult: B. A. O. Williams, "Pleasure and Belief," *Proceedings of the Aristotelian Society Supplementary Volume* 33 (1959), pp. 57–59; and J. Teichmann, "Mental Cause and Effect," *Mind,* vol. 70 (1961), January number.

V. TWO ALTERNATIVES

What have we proved thus far? Only that emotions which have objects are logically tied to *some* form of thought about the same object. So there are two methods of resolving the odd cases I listed at the beginning of this paper:

(1) We can declare that each sort of emotion which has an object is based (founded) upon a particular kind of thought, in the sense that the latter is a logically necessary condition of the former;[3]

(2) We can hold that each sort of emotion is based upon some form of thought or other, i.e., thought is a logically necessary condition of every emotion which has an object, but it happens that people have some kinds of emotion when they doubt, and other kinds when they conjecture. With regard to example

(a) John is embarrassed that he is late for dinner, but he doubts that he is (late for dinner),

a champion of the first analysis would assert that my imaginary situation is logically impossible: My description of John's mental state is self-contradictory. According to the second view, the situation is unusual though possible; my description of John is unlikely to be true, but it might be. Analysis (1) commits us to the view that the sentential function, "—— is embarrassed that . . ." means, *inter alia,* "—— believes that . . ."; "—— is worried that . . ." means, *inter alia,* "—— believes or conjectures or doubts that . . ."; and so on for each item in our emotion-vocabulary. Analysis (2) requires, for its intelligibility, some hint of an explanation for the observed concomitance of types of emotion and types of thought, if this correlation is not due to the meaning of emotion-words.

A number of considerations favor analysis (1). The argument I used against the hypotheses that there is only a causal relation between emotion and thought applies here with equal force. Any proof that John is embarrassed that he is late for dinner seems to prove that John is convinced he is late, and thus to falsify the con-

---

3. This is Bedford's view in "Emotions." Discussing the statement, "*A* resents what *B* did," Bedford writes: "*A*'s belief that *B* has done something that affects him adversely is . . . a necessary condition if the word 'resentment' is to be used at all" (p. 295); elsewhere he says, "The expression 'I hope that . . .' implies . . . a very vague estimate of probability . . ." (p. 293).

junction, "John is embarrassed that he is late for dinner, but doubts that he is late for dinner." If John makes a sincere avowal, "I'm embarrassed that I'm late for dinner," has he not expressed his conviction that he is late? Plainly he has not manifested disbelief! Add to this evidence various forms of non-linguistic behavior: his manner, his gestures and carriage, his sheepish grin, his blushes. Isn't this the picture of a man who believes he is late?

Now what if all this confirms the seemingly redundant hypothesis, "John is embarrassed that he is late, and he believes he is late?" Have we thereby refuted the claim, "John is embarrassed that he is late, but he doubts he is late?" To save space, I wish to use shorthand names for the statements under examination:

  E for the statement "John is embarrassed that he is late"
  D for "John doubts he is late"
  B for "John believes he is late"
  B' for "John believes he is not late"
  not-B for "It is not the case that John believes he is late"

If we use "&" as a name of the conjunction operator, then example (a) will read: E & D. My problem is this: I admit that any proof of E will count in favor of B. Therefore I must admit that nothing would ever prove that E & D is true.

I think the argument is faulty. It does not matter whether E entails B, or whether the truth of E makes B very probable. It is not obvious to me that the truth of B entails the falsity of D. I assume that D is equivalent to B' rather than not-B. If that is so, then the truth of E & B does not entail the falsity of E & B' (E & D), although E & B does entail the falsity of E & not-B. In other words, E, B and B' might all be true. That is, John might believe he is late and believe he is not late.

Is such a thing logically possible? I admit the following points: (i) John's belief that he is late is inconsistent with his belief that he is not late; (ii) consequently, to assert "John believes he is late and John believes he is not late" (B & B') is to assert that John has inconsistent beliefs. Notice, however, that (i) and (ii) do not show that statement B & B' is an inconsistent statement. . . .

The upshot is that analysis (1) will exclude the imaginary situations (a)–(c) only if we take it for granted that nobody can (logically) hold inconsistent beliefs. It is not my purpose here either to vindicate or to give a counter-example to that difficult assumption. However, I should like to show that analysis (2) will take care of the odd cases without the disputed assumption. Let me explain this alternative analysis by reference to,

    (b) John is delighted that there will be champagne with dessert, but he merely conjectures that there will be.

Why does this statement bother us, although its counterpart,

    (b′) John hopes that there will be champagne with dessert, but he merely conjectures that there will be,

sounds quite plausible?

A follower of the second view would explain that in (b), John's emotion is somehow inappropriate to his state of thought; there is an incongruity between his conjecture and his delight. (b′), on the other hand, ascribes an emotion to John which somehow fits his cognitive outlook. I suggest two interpretations of the claim that a conjecture is an inappropriate foundation for anticipatory pleasure, but an appropriate basis for hope. The verdict, "His emotion is inappropriate," may mean:

(I) It is normal for people to feel pleasure about a future event when they merely conjecture that it will occur. People do not, as a rule, feel that sort of emotion, or that degree of it, when they are only guessing; so on statistical grounds alone we wonder: "Perhaps John is secretly convinced that champagne will be served? Or if he is just guessing, then he is probably in a state of hope rather than anticipatory delight." Statistics will entitle us to assume that John's thoughts are consistent, i.e., that he does not believe or doubt that champagne is forthcoming at the same time that he conjectures that champagne is forthcoming. We can go on to account for the concomitant variation we observe in John's community between people's emotions and their states of thought, as well as their tendency to alter their beliefs when they notice inconsistencies among their opinions. I assume that the account would show the observed regularities to be the effect of brain processes, social conditioning, and so forth. If we have an adequate explanation of the regularities, it would also indicate how odd cases like (b) might result from cerebral lesions, childhood traumas, or insufficient training. There is no need to add the following: We might find quite different correlations between types of emotion and types of thought, when we compare groups which have diverse hereditary proclivities or dissimilar social institutions.

(II) A man's emotions may be inappropriate—in kind or degree—to his state of thought in another respect. We might judge that John is unreasonable to feel anticipatory pleasure when he merely conjectures that there will be champagne. Is it reasonable for him to hope? At least it is not unreasonable. The notion that our feelings can be reasonable or unreasonable, vis-à-vis our cognitive state, depends upon their similarity to many of our habitual and instinctive actions. It is reasonable for a pugilist to duck or to raise his guard when he believes his opponent is throwing an uppercut, and it is unwise of him to stiffen before the other man's punch. To be sure, the boxer does not decide to move out of range or to hold his position; but his movements are reasonable or unreasonable in the sense that they are effective means for him to achieve victory and to avoid a pummeling. Now compare emotions like anticipatory pleasure to the boxer's defensive activity. Emotions of this sort are also forms of readiness. In example (b), John is prepared for champagne. Perhaps he is *set to drink* champagne as well, but we are not considering the conative aspects of emotion. How then may emotions, as states of readiness, acquire the labels "reasonable" and "unreasonable"? A man's emotions are reasonable when, in view of the man's beliefs, doubts, or conjectures, the form of readiness they involve is likely to be effective and necessary. When they involve inadequate or superfluous preparations, his feelings are unreasonable. In example (b), John only guesses there will be champagne; consequently he must think that his delight is probably an otiose form of preparation. He is like a boxer who engages in elaborate dodging and protective maneuvers when he believes his challenger is staggering on the ropes. . . .

My thesis in this final section was that two analyses of the rapport between feelings and thought will do justice to the important distinctions made in the preliminary discussion of objects, grounds, and causes of emotion. In section IV we had to discard the view that a person's beliefs, doubts, and speculations are nothing but causes of his emotions; we rejected it, ultimately, because it was epistemologically vacuous, for we could discover no way to specify the object of someone's emotion without assuming that he had thoughts about the object. The remaining views may be reformulated quite simply:

(1) A particular type of thought is a logically necessary condition of each type of emotion which has an object;

(2) Some type of thought is a logically necessary condition of each type of emotion which has an object, and each type of emotion is appropriate to particular types of thought, inappropriate to others.

If we take (1) as an explication of phrases like "resignation is founded on certainty, pleasure is founded on belief," the relation between emotions and their cognitive cohorts is entirely logical. However, we can exclude the difficult cases (a)–(c) only by appealing to a disputable maxim, "A person cannot (logically) hold inconsistent beliefs." (2) makes the relation between emotion and thought partly logical, partly causal, and—if we say that "appropriate" means "reasonable" as well as "statistically normal"—partly normative. Analysis (2) seems more in keeping with a flexible, empirically oriented psychological theory of emotion. (1) would present us with fixed *a priori* relations between various forms of emotion and thought. Explication (2) of what it is for an emotion to be founded upon an appropriate type of thought does appeal to some obscure normative considerations. But this is not a compelling reason to discard (2). In fact, it may be illuminating to investigate further the similarities, (i) between admiring, disliking, resenting, or fearing something, and appraising or evaluating it; (ii) between moral justification or censure of someone's emotion, and the kind of assessment that is involved in judging someone's emotion appropriate or inappropriate to his beliefs, doubts, or conjectures.

Robert C. Solomon

(1942-   )

INTRODUCTION

Robert C. Solomon is the author of *The Passions* (1976) and a number of essays on the nature of emotion. He is Professor of Philosophy at the University of Texas at Austin. In this essay, he defends a "cognitive" theory of emotions in which *judgments* play an essential role.

Emotions and Choice

Do we choose our emotions? Can we be held responsible for our anger? for feeling jealousy? for falling in love or succumbing to resentment or hatred? The suggestion sounds odd because emotions are typically considered occurrences that happen to (or "in") us; emotions are taken to be the hallmark of the irrational and the disruptive. Controlling one's emotion is supposed to be like the caging and taming of a wild beast, the suppression and sublimation of a Freudian "it."

Traditionally, emotions have been taken to be feelings or sensations. More recently, but also traditionally, emotions have been taken to be physiological disturbances. Accordingly, much of this century's literature on emotions is dedicated to mapping out the relationship between sensations and correlative occurrences. William James, for example, takes consciousness of emotions to be consciousness of physiological occurrences. Other philosophers and psychologists, for one reason or another, have tried to reduce the emotion to a physiological occurrence, or, alternatively, have focused on the feeling of emotion and denied any conceptual role to the physiological occurrence. But these traditional worries should be quite irrelevant to any analysis of the emotions, for an emotion is neither a sensation nor a physiological occurrence, nor an occurrence of any other kind. "Struck by jealousy," "driven by anger," "plagued by remorse," "paralyzed by fear," "felled by shame," like "the prick of Cupid's arrow," are all symptomatic metaphors betraying a faulty philosophical analysis. Emotions are not occurrences and do not happen to us. I would like to suggest that emotions are rational and purposive rather than irrational and disruptive, are very much like actions, and that we choose an emotion much as we choose a course of action.[1]

Emotions are intentional; that is, emotions are "about" something. "I am angry *at John for stealing my car.*" It is not necessary to press the claim that *all* emotions are "about" something. Kierkegaard's dread may be an emotion which is not "about" anything, or, conversely, may be "about" everything. Similarly, *moods,* which are much like emotions, do not have a specific object. Euphoria, melancholy, and depression are not "about" anything in particular, though they may be caused by some particular incident. We might wish to say that such emotions and moods are "about" the world rather than anything in particular. In fact, Heidegger has suggested that *all* emotions are ultimately "about" the world and never simply "about" something particular. But we will avoid debating these issues by simply focusing our attention on emotions that clearly seem to be "about" something specifiable.

"I am angry at John for stealing my car." It is true that I am angry. And it is also true that John stole my car. Thus we are tempted to distinguish two components of my being angry; my feeling of anger and what I am angry about. But this is doubly a mistake.

---

1. Perhaps we should distinguish getting into an emotional state and being in one (e.g., getting angry vs. being angry). But nothing turns on this, for being in a state as well as getting into a state, like God's maintenance of the Universe as well as his creation of it, requires devoted activity. Accordingly, I shall be arguing both that we choose an emotion and that we continuously choose our emotions. There is no need to separate these arguments.

It requires that a feeling (of anger) be (contingently) directed at something (at John's having stolen my car). But feelings are occurrences and cannot have a "direction." They can be caused, but to say that I am angry "about" John's having stolen my car is very different from saying his stealing my car caused me to be angry. John's act might cause me to be angry "about" something else, e.g., my failure to renew my insurance. It might be false that John stole my car, though I believe that he did. Then it is false that John's stealing my car caused me to be angry, but still true that what I am angry "about" is John's stealing my car. One might suggest that it is not the alleged *fact* of John's stealing my car that is in question, but rather my *belief* that he did. But what I am angry "about" is clearly not that I believe that John stole my car, but rather *that John stole my car.*

Feelings do not have "directions."[2] But I am angry "about" something. The relationship between my being angry and what I am angry about is not the contingent relation between a feeling and an object. (Though it is surely contingent that I am angry at John for stealing my car.) An emotion cannot be identified apart from its object; "I am angry" is incomplete—not only in the weak sense that there is more information which may be available ("Are you angry about something?") but "I am angry" requires that there *must* be more information available ("*What* are you angry about?") But feelings have no such requirements. Anger is not a feeling; neither is anger a feeling plus anything else (e.g., what it is "about").

Neither can "what I am angry about" be separated from my being angry. Of course, it makes sense to say that John's having stolen my car is something different from my being angry at him for doing so. But it is not simply the *fact* that John stole my car that is what I am angry about; nor is it, as I said above, my *belief* that John stole my car about which I am angry. I am angry about the intentional object "that John stole my car." Unlike the *fact* that John stole my car, this intentional object is opaque; I am not angry that John stole a vehicle

---

2. I take this to be definitive of the difference between "emotion" and "feeling" as I am using those terms here. Emotions are intentional; feelings are not. I do not deny that the everyday use of "feeling" is broader than this and includes both of these concepts. I find this ambiguity less objectionable than others surrounding "sensation" and like terms.

assembled in Youngstown, Ohio, with 287 h.p., though that is a true description of the fact that John stole my car. I am not angry that someone 5'7" tall got his fingerprints on my steering column, yet that is a true description of the fact that John stole my car. Sartre attempts to point out this feature of what emotions are "about" by saying that their object is "transformed"; D. F. Pears points to the same feature by noting that it is always an "aspect" of the object that is the object of an emotion. What emotions are "about," as in beliefs, can only be identified under certain descriptions, and those descriptions are determined by the emotion itself. This does not mean that what emotions are about are beliefs—only that emotions share an important conceptual property of beliefs. "Being angry about . . ." is very much like "believing that. . . ." To be angry is to be angry "about" a peculiar sort of object, one that is distinguished by the fact that it is what I am angry "about." Husserl describes this peculiarity of mental acts in general by insisting that an intentional act and an intentional object are "*essentially* correlated." For our purposes, the point to be seen is that emotions cannot be discussed in terms of "components," by distinguishing feeling angry and what I am angry about. (Pears, e.g., begins by making this distinction.) In Heideggerian phrase, I am never simply angry, but there is always "my-being-angry-about-. . . ."

If there is no legitimate distinction between feeling angry and what I am angry "about," or, to put it in a different way, if the connection between my being angry and what I am angry "about" is a conceptual and not causal connection, then it is easy to explain a feature of emotions that has been pointed out by many analysts. A change in what I am angry "about" demands a change in my anger; if I no longer feel wronged by John, who only bought a car that looks like mine, I cannot be angry at John (for stealing my car) any longer. One cannot be angry if he is not angry "about" having been wronged. Similarly, one cannot be ashamed if he does not accept some responsibility for an awkward situation, nor can he be embarrassed if he does not find the situation awkward. If emotions were feelings, it would be a peculiar coincidence that the feelings were so faithful to our views of our situation, that they did not hold onto us with a momentum of their own after opinions had passed, that they were not so "irrational" as to pay no attention to our opinions at all. But emotions are not feelings, nor feelings plus what they are "about"; the format of an emotion is " . . . -about-. . . ." And so it is no surprise that emotions change with our opinions, and so are "rational" in a very important sense.

Emotions typically involve feelings. Perhaps they essentially involve felings. But feelings are never sufficient to differentiate and identify emotions, and an emotion is never simply a feeling, not even a feeling plus anything. Moreover, it is clear that one can have an emotion without feeling anything. One can be angry without feeling angry: one can be angry for three days or five years and not feel anything identifiable as a feeling of anger continuously through that prolonged period. One might add that one must have a disposition to feel angry, and to this, there is no objection, so long as being angry is not thought to *mean* "having a disposition to feel angry." I do not know whether it makes sense to suppose that one can be angry without ever feeling angry. But I do know that it does not even make sense to say that one feels angry if one is not angry. This might seem mysterious, if we accept the traditional view that anger has an identifiable feeling attached to it (for then why could one not have the feeling without whatever else is involved in anger?). And this might seem obvious on the traditional view that anger *is* a feeling (for then being angry is nothing but having the feeling of anger). But on our account, anger is not a feeling, nor does it involve any identifiable feeling (which is not to deny that one does feel angry—that is, flushed, excited, etc., when he is angry). One can identify his feeling as feeling angry only if he is angry. It is true that I often feel something when I become angry. It is also true that I feel something after I cease to be angry. I am angry at John for stealing my car. Then I discover that John did not steal my car: I cease (immediately) to be angry. Yet the feeling remains: it is the same feeling I had while I was angry (flushing, etc.). The feeling subsides more slowly than the anger. But the feeling, even if it is the same feeling that I had while I was angry, is not a feeling of anger. Now it is just a feeling. Sometimes one claims to feel angry but not be angry. But here, I would argue that the correct description is rather that one does not know exactly what one is angry "about" (though one is surely angry "about" something); or perhaps one is angry but does not believe he ought to be. One cannot feel angry without being angry.

A familiar move in the analysis of emotions subsequent to the discovery that emotions are not feelings or occurrences is the thesis that emotions are conceptually tied to behavior; that is, the ascription of an emotion to a person is the ascription to him of various sorts of behavior. Thus, to be angry is necessarily to "anger-behave." Of course, it is evident that one can *pretend* to be angry, that is, anger-behave without being angry, and so pretending has become a major topic in the analysis of emotions. (More on this in Section II.) What is generally agreed is that a single piece of behavior is never conceptually sufficient to identify an emotion, or to distinguish emotions from pretense. E. Bedford, for example, suggests that what is always needed is at least "more of the same." Since Ryle's *Concept of Mind,* this "more of the same" is provided by the suggestion that ascribing an emotion to a person is not to simply describe one or more episodes of behavior but rather to ascribe to him a disposition to behave. But there is considerable confusion about the nature of such disposition-ascriptions, and the suggestion is clearly unsatisfactory as an analysis of *my* having an emotion. The behavioral analysis does maintain one important feature of emotions, their intentionality, though authors (e.g., Ryle, Armstrong) who favor this analysis are often intent to reject "intentionality" as well. But for our purposes, we can remain uninvolved in these issues that have become virtually definitive of "philosophy of mind." We can agree that it is undeniably true that if a person is angry he has a disposition to anger-behave and leave it entirely open whether this connection between emotions and behavior is conceptual, or causal, or something else. The purpose of this essay is to show that emotions are very much like actions, and if it should turn out that emotions are actions in any such straightforward sense, this can only make our task easier. And so, we can simply say of the behavioral analysis: insofar as it is true, it supports our thesis.

"Emotions are caused." The idea that emotions are occurrences naturally gave rise to the idea that emotions are caused. Many philosophers would argue that, if emotions are occurrences, then they must be caused, and conversely, that if emotions are caused they must be occurrences. But if, as I am arguing, emotions are not occurrences, then they cannot be caused.

But surely this is wrong. We do speak of the cause of anger, the cause for sadness, a cause for fear. And surely emotions, as intentional, are typically if not necessarily *reactions* to something that happens to us. Sometimes this cause is manifest in what the emotion is "about"; for example, I am angry about your hitting me; your hitting me is the event which caused me to become angry. But sometimes the cause for an emotion is *not* what the emotion is "about." The cause of my anger might be too litttle sleep and too much coffee. The cause of my love might be sexual deprivation. But I am not angry "about" lack of sleep and hyperstimulation, and I am not in love with my sexual deprivation (nor is my love "about" a cure for my sexual deprivation).

The cause of an emotion is a function in a certain kind of explanation. The cause must in every case be distinguished from what my emotion is "about" (its "object"). The cause is always an actual event (or state-of-affairs, etc.). The object of my emotion is always an intentional object. The cause is subject to certain lawlike generalizations in a way that objects of emotions are not. If I claim to be angry because of a harsh review of my book, pointing out that I have not become angry at previous harsh reviews of my book is sufficient to show that the cause of my becoming angry is not (my reading of) the review of my book, but it is not sufficient to show that I am not angry "about" the harsh review. I am not in any special position to know the cause of my emotion (though only I know, as a matter of fact, that I did not sleep last night, that I had had four cups of coffee); I am always in a privileged position to identify the intentional object of my emotion. This is *not* to say that my knowledge of the object of my emotion is "immediate" or "direct," nor is it to claim that my identification of the object of my emotion is "incorrigible." It is possible and not unusual that I should misidentify—sometimes in a gross way—what I am angry about, or whom I love, or why I am sad. I may identify the object of my anger as John's having stolen my car, but I am really angry at John for writing a harsh review of my book. I may think that I love Mary, when I really love my mother. And I may think that I love Mary when I am really angry about the harsh review of my book. The problem of "unconscious emotions" would take us far beyond our current argument. For now, it should suffice for us to insist that the difference between identification of the cause of an emotion and its object is not a difference between direct and indirect knowledge—as traditionally conceived—or a difference between corrigible and incorrigible identification.

The cause of an emotion is an occurrence (state-of-affairs, etc.) of a type that stands in a lawlike connection with emotions of that type. The object of an emotion is simply "what the emotion is about," whether or not it is also the cause, whether or not it is even the case, and whether or not the subject himself knows it to be the object of his emotion.[3]

We have noted that emotions are interestingly similar to beliefs. We can now explain this similarity by claiming that emotions are judgments—normative and often moral judgments. "I am angry at John for taking ("stealing" begs the question) my car" *entails* that I believe that John has somehow wronged me. (This must be true even if, *all things considered,* I also believe that John was justified in taking my car.) The (moral) judgment entailed by my anger is not a judgment *about* my anger (although someone else might make such judgments to the effect that my anger is justified or unjustified, rational, prudent, foolish, self-indulgent, therapeutic, beneficial, unfortunate, pathological, or amusing). My anger *is* that judgment. If I do not believe that I have somehow been wronged, I cannot be angry (though I might be upset, or sad). Similarly, if I cannot praise my lover, I cannot be in love (though I might want her or need her, which, traditional wisdom aside, is entirely different). If I do not find my situation awkward, I cannot be ashamed or embarrassed. If I do not judge that I have suffered a loss, I cannot be sad or jealous. I am not sure whether all emotions entail such judgments; moods (depression and euphoria) surely present special problems. But emotions in general do appear to require this feature: to have an emotion is to hold a normative judgment about one's situation.

The idea that an emotion is a normative judgment, perhaps even a moral judgment, wreaks havoc with several long cherished philosophical theses. Against those romantics and contemporary bour-

3. There is nothing in our analysis which is not compatible with an all-embracing causal theory. We might agree with writers like A. I. Goldman, who argues that intentional characterizations of actions (in terms of "reasons") also function in causal explanations of a Hempelian variety. I do not wish to argue a similar thesis regarding emotions here, but I want to be careful not to preclude any such theory. Similarly, nothing I have said here bears on the so-called "free will problem"; I want to show that emotions should be viewed in the same categories as actions, whether or not there are further arguments that might lead us to conclude that not even actions are chosen freely.

geois therapists who would argue that emotions simply *are* and must be accepted without judgment, it appears that emotions themselves are already judgments. And against several generations of moral philosophers who would distinguish between morality based upon principle and morality based upon emotion or "sentiment," it appears that every "sentiment," every emotion is already a matter of judgment, often moral judgment. An ethics of sentiment differs from ethics of principle only in the fact that its judgments are allowed to go unchallenged: it is an ethics of prejudice while the latter is typically an ethics of dogma.

We can now see why "what an emotion is about" is not simply a fact; nor is it even a fact under certain descriptions. The object of an emotion is itself "affective" or normative. It is not an object *about* which one makes a judgment but is rather defined, in part, by the normative judgment. The peculiar emotional object, *that John stole my car,* can only be fully characterized as the object of my anger. "That John stole my car" is also the name of the object of my belief, of course, and perhaps of any number of other propositional attitudes I hold. But the object of my anger, that John stole my car, is an inseparable piece of my being angry. This sounds strange, no doubt, if the intentional object of the emotion is thought to be a fact or a proposition. But my anger-at-John-for-stealing-my-car is inseparable from my judgment that John in so doing wronged me, while it is clear that the *fact* that John stole my car is very different from my anger or my judgment. My anger *is* my judgment that John has wronged me.

It has always been recognized that there is some difference between our ascriptions of emotions to ourselves and our ascriptions of emotions to others. I know that I am angry and what I am angry about very differently than I know that John is angry and what he is angry about. (This first person privilege remains the presupposition of, and is not undermined by, either the Freudian concept of "unconscious emotions" or by recent philosophical attacks on "incorrigibility.") On the traditional view in which emotions are feelings, this difference has been explained by appeal to the peculiar "privacy" of sensationlike occurrences. But emotions are not feelings and not occurrences, we have argued, but rather judgments. Yet the difference between first- and other-person cases can still be made out, and in a far more convincing way than on the feeling-analysis of emotions. *You* can say of me, "he is angry because he thinks John stole his car, which he did not." *You* can say of me, "he is angry about the review, which actually was favorable, but only because of his lack of sleep and his having drunk too much coffee." *You* can say of me, "he doesn't really love Mary, but rather a mother-surrogate." But *I* cannot say these things of *myself*. "I am angry at John because I think that he stole my car, which he didn't" is nonsense. If emotions are judgments, then the sorts of "pragmatic" paradoxes that have long been celebrated regarding judgments in general will apply to emotions also. "I am angry about x, but not x" raises the same problems as "P, but I do not believe P." No feeling-account of emotions can account for such paradoxes. But, if emotions are intentional, emotions must partake in conceptual relationships in a way that mere occurrences, feelings, or facts do not. If I am angry about John's stealing my car, there are certain beliefs which I logically cannot hold, for example, the belief that John did not steal my car.

The difference between first- and other-person ascriptions of emotions lies in the realm of the "pragmatic paradoxes." Given that I have certain emotion, there are certain beliefs which you can have (including beliefs about me) but which *I* cannot have. The most interesting set of beliefs in this regard are those which pertain to the *cause* of an emotion. Earlier, we argued that the cause of an emotion is a fact (state of affairs, etc.) which can be variously ("transparently") described and occupies a role in lawlike generalizations. The *object* of an emotion, however, is limited by certain judgments (is "opaque") which are determined in the subject's having that emotion. But this distinction, we can now add, breaks down in the first-person case. If I am angry *about* John's stealing my car (the object of my anger), then I cannot believe that the sufficient *cause* of my anger is anything other than John's stealing my car. *You* can attribute my unjust anger to my lack of sleep. *I* cannot. If I attribute my anger to lack of sleep, I cannot be angry at all. And this is not simply to say that my anger is "not reasonable." (I cannot say that of myself either, except perhaps in extremely peculiar circumstances, for example, following extensive psychoanalytic treatment, which here, as elsewhere, confuses all distinctions as well as the patient regarding first- vs. other-person ascriptions of emotions, motives, intentions, etc.) I can only be angry so long as I believe that what has caused me to be angry is what I am angry about. Where the cause is different from what I am angry about, I cannot know that it is.

One can argue that the person who is angry (or in love, or sad) is in the worst position to pick out the cause for his anger (or love or sadness) *as opposed to* its object.[4] We can only add that this thesis marks out a conceptual necessity. We earlier pointed out the familiar phenomenon that our emotions change with our opinions and argued that this was not a causal matter and not a coincidence, but a consequence of the thesis that emotions are themselves judgments. We can now add that our emotions change with our knowledge of the causes of those emotions. If I can discover the sufficient cause of my anger, in those cases in which the cause and the object are different (and in which the newly discovered cause is not itself a new object for anger, as often happens), I can undermine and abandon my anger. It is here that Freud's often debated notion that emotions are "defused" by bringing them to consciousness contains an important conceptual truth too often and too easily dismissed by philosophers. Once one becomes aware of the cause of his emotions as opposed to its intended object, he can indeed "defuse" his emotion. And in those familiar Freudian cases in which one mistakenly identifies the object of his emotion (he thinks he is angry at his teacher: he is "really" angry at his father), correcting this identification can, in those cases where the correctly identified object is also the cause of the emotion, also "defuse" it. Where Freud opened himself to unnecessary criticism, I believe, was in his construing this as a *causal* relationship, a "catharsis" of repressed emotional air bubbles in the mental digestive system. But it is not as if my recognition

4. Freud has a curious way of defending this thesis, which is surely central to much of his theory. Because he attempted to maintain a thesis of the intentionality of the "affects" within a strictly causal model, he obscured the distinction between object and cause. Without crucifying Freud on this point, as Peters, MacIntyre, and others have attempted to do, it is important to see that Freud typically confuses first person and third person accounts, and the concept of the "unconscious" as an "assumption" (e.g., see the essay "The Unconscious," *Collected Papers,* Vol. VI) often depends upon the failure of the subject to be capable of applying third person ascriptions—notably, ascriptions of the cause as opposed to the object of an emotion—to himself. Without in the least detracting from Freud's overall conception of the unconscious, we must insist that the subject is never logically privileged with respect to the causes of his emotions, but that he does have some such authority (without infallible authority) with respect to what he is "affected about."

of the true cause of my anger *causes* the easing of my emotion. Rather, my recognition of the true cause of my emotion amounts to a denial of the judgment which is my lack of sleep and overdose of coffee, I thereby abandon my anger. Of course, the flushing, pulsing, irritable *feelings* of anger may thus be *caused* to diminish by the disappearance of my anger, but these are, as we have argued, in no case my anger.

If emotions are judgments and can be "defused" (and also instigated) by considerations of other judgments, it is clear how our emotions are in a sense *our doing,* and how we are responsible for them. Normative judgments can themselves be criticized, argued against, and refuted. Now if *you* criticize my anger at John by maintaining that he has not wronged me, you may conclude that my anger is unreasonable, unfair, and perhaps unbecoming. But if you should convince *me* that John has not wronged me, I do not simply conclude that my anger is unreasonable, unfair, or unbecoming, I *cease to be angry.* Similarly, I can make myself angry at John by allowing myself to be convinced that he has wronged me. I can dwell on minor behavioral misdemeanors on John's part, building them into a pattern of overall deceit and abuse, and then become angry at any one or any number of these incidents.

Since normative judgments can be changed through influence, argument, and evidence, and since I can go about on my own seeking influence, provoking argument, and looking for evidence, I am as responsible for my emotions as I am for the judgments I make. My emotions *are* judgments I make. Now one might argue that all we have shown is that one can take steps to *cause* changes in his emotions, such as one can take steps to diminish a pain by pulling out a splinter or take steps to prevent being hit by a bus by crossing only on the proper signals. And it is true, of course, that one cannot *simply* choose to be angry or not to be angry, but can make himself angry or cease being angry only by performing other activities. But this is true of judgments in general: I cannot simply choose to judge a situation fortunate, awkward, or dangerous.[5] It is worth noting that I cannot *simply* perform most actions either: I cannot simply assassinate a dictator. I must do something else (pull the trigger of a rifle, let slip the string of the bow, push the button activating the deto-

---

5. Though perhaps I can simply *express* such a judgment.

nator). Yet, although it is also true that I cause the death of the dictator (I do not cause the killing of him), I kill the dictator. Similarly, making judgments is something I *do,* not something that happens to me and not something I simply cause, even though I cannot *simply* make a judgment in many cases. (Legal judgments by an appropriately empowered judge or judiciary should *not* be taken as paradigm cases here.)

I must be in appropriate circumstances to pass judgment, have some evidence, know something of what the judgment is about. Of course, one can make judgments rashly, with minimal evidence and with superficial knowledge of what the judgment is about. Emotions, we can now see, are rash judgments, something I do, but in haste. Accordingly, the evidence upon which I become emotional is typically (but not necessarily) incomplete, and my knowledge of what I am emotional about is often (but again not necessarily) superficial. I can take any number of positive steps to change what I believe and what judgments I hold and tend to make. By forcing myself to be scrupulous in the search for evidence and knowledge of circumstances, and by training myself in self-understanding regarding my prejudices and influences, and by placing myself in appropriate circumstances, I can determine the kinds of judgments I will tend to make. I can do the same for my emotions.

II

Against the near-platitude "emotions are irrational," we want to argue that emotions are rational. This is not only to say that they fit into one's overall behavior in a significant way, that they follow a regular pattern (one's "personality"), that they can be explained in terms of a coherent set of causes. No doubt this is all true. But emotions, we have argued, are judgments, and so emotions can be rational in the same sense in which judgments can be rational. (Of course, judgments can be irrational, but only within the context of a rational activity.) Judgments are actions. Like all actions, they are aimed at changing the world. But, although the expression of a judgment may actually produce such a change, the judgment itself is more like the winding of the mainspring of an intention to change the world rather than the overt activity which will do so. But if emotions are judgments, and judgments are actions, though covert, emotions too are actions, aimed at changing the world (whether or not their expression actually does succeed in changing the world). In other words, emotions are purposive, serve the ends of the subject, and consequently can be explained by *reasons* or "in-order-to" explanations.

Because emotions are usually thought to be occurrences that we suffer, the idea that emotions are purposive actions has not been given sufficient attention. But consider the following very familiar sort of case:

Joanie wants to go to a party: her husband does not. She begins to act bored and frustrated; he watches television. She resigns herself to reading, sighing occasionally. He asks if she has picked up some shirts from the laundry: she says "no." He flies into a rage. He needs shirts (he has hundreds). He needs one of *those* (they are all the same). She is negligent (she was busy). She takes advantage of him (she stays with him). Naturally, she rebels, but she is upset, with mixed guilt and anger. She thinks him unreasonable, impossible, and slightly neurotic. Their encounter is short-lived. She goes off to read; he settles back before the television. The party is out of the question.

What are we to say of this familiar sort of case? It appears to be given that the husband's anger is inappropriate to the incident. His being angry about his wife's failure to pick up his shirts seems unreasonable; and the *intensity* of his anger is most surely unwarranted. To this, the standard response, since well before Freud, has been to suppose that the husband is really angry about something else; perhaps he is redirecting anger from his day at his office—anger which could not be expressed as safely toward his superiors as it could to his wife. Or perhaps the anger is accumulated anger from weeks or months of minor marital frictions. Or perhaps, it might be suggested, the anger is caused by the fact that the husband is tired.

But, in this case—and many other cases—there is an alternative sort of explanation that is available and persuasive. The anger can be explained, not in terms of what it is "about" or what causes it, but in terms of its *purpose*. The husband, in this case, has *used* his anger to manipulate his wife. He has become angry "about" the shirts *in order to* get his wife's mind off the party and in order to stop her irritating reminders. His anger is not a disruption of his activities (watching television, refusing to go to the party) but a part of it, its winning strategy. The best explanation of his anger is not that it was caused by anything (although that is not precluded) and not that it was "about" anything in particular (although that is surely true), but that he got angry at his wife *in order* to continue watching television and in order to ensure that his refusal to go to the party would be successful.

But if emotions are rational and purposive, why is it that emotions are so often counterproductive and embarrassing to us, detours away from our aspirations and obstacles blocking our ambitions? Why do emotions so often appear as disruptions in our lives, threats to our successes, aberrations in our rational behavior? We can outline three distinct accounts of the apparent "irrationality" of emotions.

First, it is the situation in which one becomes emotional that is disruptive, a detour, an obstacle, a threat, and not the emotional response. Emotions are urgent judgments; emotional responses are emergency behavior. An emotional response occurs in a situation in which usual intentions are perverted or frustrated; an unusual response is necessary. The normative judgments involved in having an emotion are inseparable from the overall network of our motives, beliefs, and intentions. The fact that emotions typically lead to apparently "pointless" behavior is not a consequence of emotions being irrational, but rather a natural consequence of the fact that emotions are responses to unusual situations in which usual behavior patterns seem inappropriate. The intentions of an emotional reaction are not infrequently impossible. The angry or sad man may wish to undo the past; the lover may want to possess, and be possessed by, his loved one. This is why Sarte calls the emotions "magical transformations of the world." One can always reduce the range of his emotional behavior by developing stereotyped responses, by avoiding all unusual situations, or by treating every situation as "usual." These are common but perhaps pathological ways of choosing our emotions. But such common "control" is not the avoidance or the suppression of a wild psychic beast; it is simply the avoidance of situations (or recognition of situations) where one's behavior patterns will not suffice. Emotions are rational responses to unusual situations. They differ from "cool" judgments and normal rational deliberate action in that they are prompted in urgency and in contexts in which one's usual repetoire of actions and considered judgments will not suffice. An emotion is a necessarily hasty judgment in response to a difficult situation.

It must be added that the "hastiness" of a judgment does not entail that it is made quickly. For example, one can make a hasty judgment after weeks of halfhearted deliberation. Similarly, although emotions are typically urgent and immediate responses, one can become increasingly angry over a period of time, or one finds that an emotion that is formed in urgency is then maintained in full force for weeks or even years. But what distinguishes emotions from ordinary judgments is their lack of "cool," their seeming urgency, even after weeks of simmering and stewing. There are no cold emotions, no cool anger, no deliberate love. Emotions are always urgent, even desperate, responses to situations in which one finds oneself unprepared, helpless, frustrated, impotent, "caught." It is the situation, not the emotion, which is disruptive and "irrational."

Second, and consequently, emotions are short-term responses. Emotions are rational in that they fit into a person's overall purposive behavior. But this is not to say that a person's various purposes are always consistent or coherent. Short-term purposes are often in conflict with rather than a means toward the fulfillment of long-term purposes. My desire to drink at the reception may tend toward disaster regarding my meeting of the celebrity who is my reason for going to the reception. My desire to visit Peking may undermine my ambition to become an FBI agent. Similarly, emotions often serve short-term purposes that are in conflict with longer-term purposes. I may be angry with John because I feel I have been wronged, but this may be inconsistent with my desire to keep a close, unblemished friendship with John. I may love Mary, but this might be totally inconsistent with my intention to preserve my marriage, to remain celibate, or to concentrate on my writing. Thus, the husband in our example might succeed in staying home from the party by becoming angry, but break up his marriage in so doing. It is in this sense that emotions are "blind"; more accurately, they are *myopic*. Emotions serve purposes and are rational; but because the purposes emotions serve are often short-sighted, they appear to be nonpurposive and irrational on a larger view. For the sake of a passion, we destroy careers, marriages, lives. Emotions are not irrational; people are irrational.

Third, there is an anthropological response to the idea that emotions are irrational. In a society that places taboos on emotional behavior—condemns it in men and belittles it in women—it is only to be expected that emotions will be counter to ambitions. A society that applauds "cool" behavior will naturally require strategies that are similarly "cool." In such a society, emotional behavior appears as "irrational" because it is bad strategy, not because it is not purposive. Perhaps it is not at all difficult to envision a society in which *only* emotional behavior would appear rational—where only short-term emotional responses had any meaning at all. But it is surely not Anglo-American society in which "reason is and ought to be the slave of the passions."

Against our view that emotions, as actions, are purposive and that a person chooses his emotions rather than being victimized by them, there is a uniquely powerful objection. A person cannot identify at the time the purpose of his emotion. The husband who uses his anger to manipulate his wife cannot identify the purpose as opposed to the object-cause of his anger. If he were to identify the manipulative function of his anger, the effect would be the destruction of his anger. One cannot be angry and know that his anger has a purpose.

This is much more, of course, than a mere pragmatic claim. It is certainly true that the husband cannot tell his wife that his anger is purposive, for the very purpose of the anger is to distract his wife from that purpose. But the claim here is that the husband cannot even think to himself, "I am being angry in order to. . . ." If the husband is unusually self-aware, he may know that he, in general, uses his anger to manipulate people; but he still cannot entertain that thought at the time of his anger and remain angry. If he does, he ceases to be angry and continues, at most, only to act angry—to feign anger.

One's inability to see the purpose of his emotion is a conceptual matter, just as before we pointed out that one cannot (conceptually) make certain judgments, such as the judgment that what he is angry about is not the case, or that the cause of his anger, where this is different from the object of his anger, is a sufficient explanation of his anger. We can now add to this list of conceptual inabilities the inability of one to suspect the *purpose* of his emotion. Now many philosophers would argue that, regarding intentional actions in general, one cannot fail to be aware of his motives and intentions at the time of acting. It would take us too far astray to argue against this view here, but notice that this inability to notice one's *purpose* is not limited to emotions. Consider, for example, Nietzsche's account of belief in God as a belief whose function is to serve certain purposes (achievement of salvation; a basis for "slave-morality" and self-righteousness; to seek power). Yet, even if a purposive analysis of belief in God is true, this neither denies that people do in fact believe in God nor need it suggest that believers could state these purposes. To the contrary, we can add, if they were to think seriously that their belief was held to serve a purpose rather than because it was true, we would have to conclude that they did not believe at all. (A conclusion that Nietzsche too easily comes to on the basis of an argument from the third person to the first person case.) To believe is not to believe for a purpose; yet beliefs can still be purposive.

Judgments in general, not only emotions, can be purposive but cannot be recognized (by the person who makes them at the time that he makes them) as purposive. If I judge, calmly and deliberately, without a hint of that urgency and intensity that characterizes anger, that John has wronged me by stealing my car again (he does it all the time), I may be rationalizing an opportunity to take out John's wife. In fact, I may even say to myself, "since he has wronged me so, I feel justified in taking out his wife." But I cannot believe that my judgment that John has wronged me has been made for this purpose. I can at most believe that since he has wronged me, I am justified. . . . Similarly, I may judge, calmly and deliberately, that Mary is a magnificent woman, attractive and intelligent, strongwilled and sensitive, but without the slightest hint of that urgency and intensity that characterizes love. But, knowing that Mary is John's wife, I may be so judging as a way of rationalizing an opportunity to run off with John's mistress. Now I may openly judge that John does not need his mistress, since his wife is so magnificent, and so I can feel justified in running off with his mistress. But I cannot believe that my judging that Mary is magnificent is made for this purpose. In other words, judgments, no matter how calm and deliberate, when they are made for some purpose (leaving open the question whether all are so made), cannot be recognized as having been made for a purpose. In this sense, all judgments are "blind." To recognize the purpose for which a judgment is made is to undermine the judgment. One cannot judge that he has been wronged and at the same time recognize that he has judged that he has been wronged only in order to. . . .

One must also consider apparently "unintentional" actions, to which emotions bear a striking resemblance. Some act-types allow for only intentional acts, for example, murder, fishing. Others allow for only unintentional acts, for example, forgetting, slipping, stumbling, tripping, losing, in short, most of those actions that make up the subject matter of what Freud calls the "psychopathology of everyday life." Yet Freud demonstrated that such "unintentional" actions function in a remarkable accordance with a subject's overall purposes and intentions. Freud surely does not want to say that these simply *appear* to be intentional (as some authors have argued, e.g., R. S. Peters, A. MacIntyre), but rather that they truly are intentional, the difference being, in his terms, the "inaccessibility" of the intention to the subject. The status of such actions remains a matter of controversy, but we feel reasonably confident that most philosophers and most everybody else would agree that such "actions" are indeed actions and can be demonstrated in at least some cases to be done for a purpose; yet the subject cannot state their purpose. And once again, the "cannot" is a *logical* "cannot," since a man who knows that he is losing his wedding ring in order to show his opinion of his marriage is making a gesture, not losing his ring. And a man who knows he is forgetting to call his office in order to avoid extra work is not forgetting but refusing to call his office. Thus, we can see in what senses such actions may appear to be both intentional and "unintentional." They are intentional insofar as they clearly fit into the purposes and intentions of the subject; they appear to be unintentional insofar as they cannot be stated as purposive or intentional by the subject. Similarly, anger is purposive and intentional insofar as it can be clearly shown to fit into the structure of the subject's purposes and intentions; it appears to be "unintentional" and thus differs from many straightforward actions, in that these purposes and intentions cannot be known by the subject at the time. Emotions, when they are purposive and intentional, are essentially devious.

Can one feign anger? One might think, "Of course, act angry when you are not angry." But what is it that constitutes the anger apart from acting angry? The traditional answer to this is simple enough: a feeling. To feign anger is to act angry but not feel angry. To feign love is to act lovingly but not feel love. To feign an emotion would be, in general, to pretend one has a feeling which one does not have, as a child pretends—usually badly—to have a cramp in order to stay away from school. But we have seen that an emotion is not a feeling. This traditional analysis does lend support to our contention that to have an emotion in order to . . . is not to have that emotion. But, on our account, the difference is not due to the presence or lack of a feeling. Rather, to have an emotion is to make certain judgments; to feign an emotion, then, is to pretend that one holds certain judgments which one does not hold.

But this makes the notion of feigning emotion much more difficult than has been supposed on the simple "feeling" analysis. André Gide has written that feigned emotion and "vital" emotion are indistinguishable, and in this there is an often unseen giant of a truth, one that would appear absurd on the thesis that emotions are feelings. Miss Anscombe, replying to J. L. Austin, has distinguished between mock performances and real pretenses. The most obvious differences between the two is that one is intended to mislead others, the other not. Accordingly, the one should be more cautiously consistent and prolonged than the other: a successful mock performance may be announced as lasting only 35 seconds, a real pretense must go on as long as it must go on. But the most important difference between mock performances and real pretenses is the *context* (what we have been calling "the situation"). A mock performance may be performed on a stage, in any context in which it can be announced or in which it is evident that this is a *mere* pretense. A real pretense, however, requires that the context of performance be appropriate; anger can only be feigned in real pretense if the situation is one in which anger is appropriate. One can only pretend to be in love with someone whom it is plausible that he should love. But the appropriateness of the situation is not a causal determinant of a feeling of love or anger. Rather it is the context in which judgments of the requisite kinds make sense and are plausible. But if to feign anger is to act angry in a context in which the anger-related judgments are plausible, it is easy to see how one could, upon prolonged pretense, come to accept those very judgments. If, over a protracted period of time, I pretend to love a woman whom I have married for her father's wealth, it is more than likely that I shall grow to love her (if I do not first come to openly despise her). And if I pretend to be angry about a political issue in order to be accepted by my friends, it is not at all unlikely that I shall come to be really angry about the same issue. Perhaps there is no better way to choose to have an emotion than to decide to pretend that one has it. As Sartre has said, the best way to fall asleep is to pretend that you are asleep. And here, I think we may say that Gide's theory has a plausibility which cannot be explained on the idea that what one pretends to have is a feeling.

Emotions are intentional and rational, not disruptive and "irrational." Emotions are judgments and actions, not occurrences or happenings that we suffer. Accordingly, I want to say that emotions are choices and our responsibility. Yet I am never aware of making such a choice. Emotions, we argued, are hasty and typically dogmatic judgments. Accordingly, they cannot be made together with the recognition that they are dogmatic and not absolutely correct. What distinguishes emotions from other judgments is the fact that the former can never be deliberate and carefully considered. Emotions are essentially nondeliberate choices. Emotions, in this sense, are indeed "blind" as well as myopic; an emotion cannot see itself. Few things are more disconcerting than suddenly watching one's angry reflection in the mirror, or reflecting on one's anger to see its absurdity *in media res.*

If emotions are judgments or actions, we can be held responsible for them. We cannot simply have an emotion or stop having an emotion, but we can open ourselves to argument, persuasion and evidence. We can force ourselves to be self-reflective, to make just those judgments regarding the causes and purposes of our emotions, and also to make the judgment that we are all the while *choosing* our emotions, which will "defuse" our emotions. This is not to opt for a life without emotions: it is to argue for a conception of emotions which well make clear that emotions are our choice. In a sense, our thesis here is self-confirming: to think of our emotions as chosen is to *make* them our choices. Emotional control is not learning to employ rational techniques to force into submission a brutal "it" which has victimized us but rather the willingness to become self-aware, to search out, and challenge the normative judgments embedded in every emotional response. To come to believe that one has this power *is* to have this power.

In response to our argument, one might conclude that we have only argued that one can choose and is responsible for his *interpretation* of his situation and his emotions. But then I simply want to end by once again drawing Nietzsche to my side and quipping, with regard to emotions, "there are only interpretations. . . ."

Cheshire Calhoun

(1954-)

INTRODUCTION

Cheshire Calhoun has written extensively on "moral sentiment" theories of emotion and their impact in ethics. She teaches philosophy at the College of Charleston. In this essay, written especially for this volume, she reconsiders the "cognitive" theory of emotion and raises a number of serious objections to it.

Cognitive Emotions?

Tess and Carl have been married two years. Tess works to support them, since Carl is in graduate school. Tess' parents (who never liked Carl) constantly warn her that Carl may just be using her to get through school, but Tess denies this. Recently, though, Tess has found herself feeling resentful. She now notices how often she gets stuck with doing the housework, shopping for groceries, and feeding the dog. Carl finds time to read novels and visit friends; Tess doesn't. She notices the luxuries she denies herself so that she can pay for their joint entertainment. She also notices how Carl spends his rare monetary windfalls on himself. Tess feels helpless and trapped in her marriage even though she still denies that Carl is using her.

This paper was written with the support of the National Endowment for the Humanities Summer Seminar Program.

Beliefs dominate this tale of resentment. Doubts raised by her parents may have sparked Tess' resentment. Once sparked, her resentment unfolds in beliefs about unfair burdens she has to shoulder in her marriage which seem to add up to the unhappy belief about Carl that Tess denies.

Although main characters in stories of emotion, do beliefs actually constitute emotions? Are Tess' thoughts about Carl at least part of her resentment? Most cognitive theorists say, Yes. They usually arrive at this answer after rejecting what they see as the only possible alternative—a causal theory that beliefs cause emotions and emotions, in turn, cause other beliefs. (Carl's excusing himself from housework makes Tess resentful. Her resentment, in turn, causes her to remember other occasions when Carl got out of his fair share of drudgery.) But if beliefs are only causes and effects of emotion, what, asks the cognitivist, is the emotion? A *feeling?* Not all emotions, particularly not dispositional ones, have a "feel." Even when emotional episodes involve "feels," identifying the emotion and marking it off from its emotional cousins seem to require our knowing something about the person's beliefs. Anger and resentment or jealousy and envy differ little, if a whit, in their "feel." Their cognitive consorts set them apart. That we appeal to beliefs in identifying emotions suggests that emotion is not merely contingently, causally connected to belief. (For emotions to be so connected, we would have to be able to identify the belief and the emotion independently.[1])

Suppose we agree. Strictly causal accounts of belief and emotion will not do. Even so, other worries may beset the cognitivist's making beliefs constitutive of emotion. We may simply be leaping from the frying pan of causality into the fire of cognitive emotion.

The cognitivist is prey to the incredulous query "What! Emotions are *beliefs?* Isn't that a contradiction in terms?" This is, as I shall presently argue, a perfectly defensible skepticism. Unfortunately,

---

1. Even if emotions are beliefs, causal stories may have their place and use. Not all the constituents of emotion (beliefs, behavior, "feels," desires, and so on) are contemporaneous. Causal tales help us trace the different stages of emotion; and one might speak quite properly, for example, of certain beliefs causing emotional behaviors or physiological disturbances. But her causal stories are not employed to elucidate the causes and effects *of an emotion,* but rather to explain the relations between the *constituent stages* of emotion.

most cognitive theories are explicated in such a way that they fail to elicit this response (when they should). To see the conceptual obstacles to "cognitive emotion" and how they become masked, we might compare two basic sorts of cognitive theory, which I will call "patchwork" and "unity" accounts.

In both accounts, emotions, though most importantly beliefs, are also many other things—patterns of behavior, the "feel" of physiological changes, desires, etc. Patchwork accounts group essentially nonemotional phenomena (nonemotional because they may also occur outside emotion) and treat emotion as a collage of beliefs and other psychological, behavioral, and physiological phenomena. Such patchwork accounts are either logico-linguistic or ontological. For the logico-linguistic philosopher, when we say that emotions are in part beliefs (or behaviors or desires), we eliptically point out that ascriptions of emotions entail ascriptions of certain sorts of beliefs (or behaviors or desires).[2] The claim "*P* feels *E*," if true, logically entails that *P* holds a belief of sort *B*. Ontologists, not confining themselves to emotion language's logic, boldly assert that beliefs (or behaviors or desires) *are* ingredients of emotion.[3]

Significantly, patchwork accounts deny that emotional beliefs *qua* beliefs differ in nature from nonemotional beliefs. Emotional beliefs are just garden-variety beliefs (although they may have typical contents, e.g., a reference to values). My belief that Mr. Dehaney is a boor is, in all respects, exactly the same whether it forms part of my disgust with Mr. Dehaney or whether it is a cool, disinterested judgment. If anything, features *external* to the belief itself distinguish emotional from nonemotional beliefs. (When I am disgusted, my belief occurs *in the context* of behavioral dispositions, desires, "feels"—a context lacking in nonemotional beliefs.)

Not so in a unity account, which does not reconstruct emotion out of nonemotional phenomena and does not use "emotion" simply as an umbrella term for unique concatenations of these phenomena. If behavior, the "feel" of physiological changes, and most impor-

2. Representative logico-linguistic philosophers of emotion are Anthony Kenny (*Action, Emotion and Will*), Errol Bedford ("Emotion"), George Pitcher ("Emotion"), and Gilbert Ryle (*The Concept of Mind*).

3. Ontological versions are advocated, for example, by Frithjof Bergmann ("A Monologue on the Emotions") and Robert Solomon (*The Passions*).

tantly, beliefs constitute emotion, they do so only by taking on uniquely emotional qualities. Sartre, for example, claims that "purely physiological phenomena represent the *seriousness* of the emotion; they are phenomena of belief."[4] In a similar vein, Dewey argues that only in abstraction can we separate emotional belief from behavioral and physiological phenomena; in reality, behavioral and physiological phenomena actually make up emotional belief.[5] Obviously, "belief" has undergone an extensive transformation. How can a physiological disturbance *be* a belief? Are not these, logically and ontologically, distinct categories?

In engendering such skeptical queries, unity accounts show us what is misleading about patchwork accounts and also what is paradoxical about all cognitive theories. "Emotions are beliefs" does, or at least should, strike as discordant a note as "Physiological disturbances are beliefs." A cognitive emotion is a paradox because the conceptual terrain where "belief" finds its home differs vastly from that of "emotion." On a conceptual map, "belief" lies near "responsibility" (we are culpable for our beliefs and, hence, there could plausibly be an ethics of belief), "activity" (belief is something we do not suffer), "rationality" (even if some beliefs are irrational, the activities of acquiring and holding beliefs occur within our rational, intellectual life), and "judgment" (beliefs have their native home in fully conceptualized and articulated judgments). "Emotion," on the other hand, has a different set of conceptual consorts. Although often tied to (causal or constitutive) cognitions, emotion nevertheless is paradigmatically passive (it happens to us), involuntary (we are not culpable), and a- or ir-rational (it is part of our animal-physical nature and often interferes in our rational-intellectual life).[6] This

4. Jean-Paul Sartre, *The Emotions: Outline of a Theory.* New York: Philosophical Library, 1948, p. 74.

5. John Dewey, "The Theory of Emotion." In *John Dewey: The Early Works,* Vol. 2, Carbondale, Il.: Southern Illinois University Press, 1967.

6. One might, of course, deny that "emotion" and "belief" are as disparate concepts as they traditionally have been made out to be. E. M. Curley ("Descartes, Spinoza and the Ethics of Belief"), for instance, has critically attacked the notion that beliefs are voluntary acts for which we are always culpable. He suggests instead that "coming to believe is something much more like falling in love then like raising one's arm" (but note Curley's presumption of involuntarily suffered emotions). On the other side of the fence, Robert Solomon has defended the voluntariness of emotional experience and our responsibility for our emotions on the ground that emotions are

conceptual gulf between "emotion" and "belief" bodes ill for patchwork cognitive theories, which do not reevaluate the nature of emotional belief. Logico-linguistic versions, particularly, fall prey to the charge of sidestepping legitimate questions about the intelligibility of the cognitivist thesis, and the demands for a remapping of "belief" and "emotion" so that they do not, as it were, occupy different conceptual countries. (This because entailment language is not as strong as ontological language. As long as we focus on the logical relation between emotion and belief ascriptions, we never directly confront the dissonance between "emotion" and "belief," as we do when the talk shifts to emotions' *being* beliefs.)

Even supposing the cognitivist could bridge the conceptual gulf between "emotion" and "belief," she still is not out of the woods. The cognitivist banks on convincing us that fear always goes hand in hand with acknowledged beliefs about danger, resentment with acknowledged beliefs about unfair treatment, and so on. Although this may be true in most of our emotional experience, it is not *always* true. Sometimes emotion is in conflict with our avowed beliefs. (That is, given our emotions we ought to believe something other than we do.) Tess, for instance, claims that Carl does not exploit her, yet she is resentful. Tess' emotions conflict with her avowed beliefs in other areas too:

> Tess has a spider phobia. Spiders make her skin crawl and she jerks out of their way, pleading for someone else to kill them. Yet Tess believes spiders are harmless and knows enough spider biology to back up this belief.
>
> Raised in a conservative household, Tess acquired, among other beliefs, the belief that homosexuality is unnatural and immoral. But in college, both friends and professors challenged this. After extensive discussion and reflection, Tess came to believe that homosexuality is neither unnatural nor immoral. But several years later, she suddenly discovered that a good friend is a lesbian and she experienced feelings of shock and revulsion.

Sometimes such emotion-belief conflicts only *appear* to be conflicts. As it turns out, the person's avowed beliefs are mere pretenses

beliefs (and, of course, beliefs are voluntary acts). But the fact that both Curley and Solomon feel compelled to challenge standard accounts by *likening* belief to emotion or emotion to belief only underscores the conceptual gulf between the two.

or products of self-deception; the emotion actually fits the *real*, una-vowed beliefs. Were all emotion-belief conflicts like this, the cog-nitivist would have no problem. But Tess does not fit this model. The evidence favors her *really* believing what she claims to believe. Why? First, she claims them as her beliefs. And although ultimately we may discredit a person's belief-avowals, we nevertheless give *prima facie* credence to them. (People are innocent of self-deception or pretense until proven guilty.) Second, Tess can justify her beliefs. If she is minimally rational, she ought to and will believe claims for which she can adduce adequate supporting evidence and against which she is unable to provide adequate evidence. Finally, let us suppose she consistently upholds her avowed beliefs over time. Her beliefs here are not mere transients in her doxic life, but fixed ten-ants. In short, lacking additional strong evidence to the contrary, we cannot justifiably discredit as mere pretense or self-deception Tess' self-consciously held, reasoned convictions.[7]

So unless she purchases the cognitivist position at the price of making it, *a priori,* unchallengable, the cognitivist must seriously entertain the apparent possibility of there being emotions that do not entail having the emotion-relevant beliefs. In doing so, she has two options, She might concede the existence of some noncognitive emotions. Or she might try to find a nonquestion-begging way of preserving the tie between emotion and belief in cases of emotion-belief conflict.

With the first option, the cognitivist makes a serious concession. Allowing that there are some noncognitive emotions amounts to denying the centrality of belief and to abandoning the initial project of analyzing emotion in general *via* beliefs, in favor of piecemeal accounts of different sorts of emotions for which only some accounts will invoke beliefs. This might not be so bad. Emotions may lack the homogeneity necessary for a theory of emotion *in general.* But beware of this move. After all, beliefs obtained a central place largely because identifying emotions independently of their cogni-tive consorts presented such overwhelming difficulties.

Although avoiding this drawback, the second option is a difficult project.

7. Her having a strong psychological motive for holding beliefs other than the ones she avows might, for instance, lead us to doubt her belief-avowals.

BRUTE EMOTIONS AND THE COGNITIVIST

The cognitivist would like to deny brute emotions that lack an intelligible wellspring in belief. Fear minus a belief in danger is not fear.[8] She might seek refuge from Tess' seemingly brute resentment, fear, and revulsion (which persist in the face of unresentful, fearless, and unrevolted beliefs) in either the "inertia hypothesis" or the "conflicting belief hypothesis."

The emotional inertia hypothesis. Emotional habits persist through doxic vicissitudes. In her early years, Tess unquestioningly adopted her parents' belief in the immorality of homosexuality and found this life-style revolting. The deep roots of belief in Tess' childhood socialization make her acquisition of emotional habits connected with homosexuality unsurprising. But now, her emotional responses have failed to keep pace with her revised beliefs. Thus, although unintelligible, given her present beliefs, Tess' revulsion is perfectly intelligible given her former beliefs.

The cognitivist thus preserves the universal applicability of her thesis—emotions must have emotion-relevant beliefs—by introducing one qualification. The emotion-relevant belief need not be presently held. This salvaging technique, though, has its price. In emotion-belief conflicts, belief and emotion become fairly radically detached from one another. At these points, one's doxic life and one's emotional life part company. Thus, although Tess' present beliefs about homosexuality occur alongside peculiar (irrational) emotional habits, her beliefs are no worse off for this. Her beliefs would be no better (no sounder) did she feel an appropriate emotion such as indifference or even approval. Intuitively, though, this does not seem right. We use "feeling" and "believing" interchangeably, as though feeling were a way of believing. If Tess really believes in the moral neutrality of homosexuality, she should not only *think* that it is morally neutral, but also *feel* that it is. Her inability to do so signals a defect in her belief; her belief would be better (sounder)

8. The cognitivist turns James's questions upside down. James asked us to imagine what would happen to fear if we subtracted from the belief in danger the physiological underpinnings of fear. We would, he thought, have only a cool intellectual recognition of danger devoid of affective tone. The cognitivist asks what would happen to fear if we subtracted from its noncognitive underpinnings the belief of danger. We would have only physiological disturbance devoid of affective tone.

if she felt the right emotions. And partly for this reason, she may regret feeling revolted and want to alter her emotions. (I will return to this crucial notion of defective belief.)

More crucially, one might (and the cognitivist would) question why emotion should have more inertia than belief. Surely if Tess' original beliefs were deeply rooted in her early upbringing, her beliefs themselves, not just her emotions, should have a kind of inertia. In fact, the assumption that beliefs change while emotions continue invariably the same depends on their being a conceptual gulf between belief (activity/voluntariness) and emotion (passivity/involuntariness)—a conceptual gulf that makes the cognitivist position all the more difficult.

The conflicting belief hypothesis. In avoiding the pitfalls of emotional inertia, the cognitivist might deny that people always live up to our ideal of rationality by holding a unified, consistent belief system. People may hold inconsistent beliefs at different levels. Emotionally, Tess has real qualms about a homosexual life-style; but from a critical, reflective viewpoint, she believes it is acceptable. Neither counts as her only real belief. Thus, an unresolved tension pervades her belief system.

To its credit, this resolution explains why we should take our emotions seriously. Emotions are not merely recalcitrant habits that persist long after their appropriate belief consorts have passed. They are symptoms of a doxic ailment that needs to be remedied. Also to its credit, this resolution requires a complex portrait of doxic life. We may never entirely shed beliefs acquired in early childhood. They simply become overshadowed by ones acquired in mature life, losing their affective force as motives as well as their centrality in our belief matrix.

Positing conflicting beliefs to avoid brute emotions has its own dangers. Tess' seemingly surd emotions are neither atypical nor pathological. They are ordinary emotions in an ordinary emotional life. So what must we suppose about our doxic life?—inconsistent beliefs are ordinary occurrences. Surely we are not *this* irrational, even though we may never attain our proud ideal of complete rationality.

Worse yet, the conflicting belief hypothesis violates the language of belief. Linguistically, we *are* entitled to take Tess' avowed beliefs as her (only) real beliefs. We are *not* entitled to accuse her of pretense, self-deception, or what is equally uncharitable, inconsistent beliefs without evidence. The evidence is lacking. Typically, inconsistent beliefs show up simultaneously in *both* emotions and belief-avowals. We could reasonably charge Tess with inconsistent beliefs if she vacillated between accusing Carl of exploiting her (and feeling resentment towards him) and defending the distribution of burdens as equitable (and not feeling resentment). But Tess vacillates neither in her belief-avowals nor in her emotional responses. Here, her inappropriate emotions constitute the sole evidence for conflicting beliefs. Taking this as sufficient evidence begs the question. Do all emotions entail corresponding appropriate beliefs?

In sum, the emotional inertia and conflicting belief hypothesis lead to dead ends. But these dead ends suggest some tentative conclusions. First, we have to concede to critics of cognitive theories that people *can* experience emotions without holding the emotion-relevant belief. Tess can fear spiders without believing they are dangerous. Second, I am strongly inclined to agree with the cognitivist's intuition that there is something defective about beliefs accompanied by inappropriate emotions. Tess' belief that spiders are harmless would be more acceptable were she unafraid of spiders. (The cognitivist errs when she explains this intuition by discrediting Tess' avowed belief entirely or by postulating conflicting beliefs.) Finally, we seem to need to build *some* cognitive element into emotion (although not a belief) to explain how we distinguish between closely related emotions *and* to explain why beliefs accompanied by inappropriate emotions are defective. In short, cases of emotion-belief conflicts doom cognitive theories that make *belief* a constituent of emotion. They do not, however, doom *any* cognitive theory.

DEFECTIVE BELIEFS

Tess' fear of spiders indicates that something is missing from her belief that spiders are harmless. What? We might take our clue from an analysis of belief and defective belief in general. In the end, I want to suggest that the same belief can be held "intellectually" or "evidentially"; and defective belief occurs when we hold a belief only intellectually under conditions that ordinarily would permit its being held evidentially.

Believing evidentially. Sometimes our beliefs are borne out by our own experience. I hold this belief: Main Street is heavily trafficked. When I survey, from my front porch, the stream of traffic down Main Street, this perceptual awareness bears out my belief. (The content of my belief is immediately experienced.) At such times, I hold my belief evidentially.

Sometimes, though, our beliefs are products of inferences, I tell my friend, who has never seen Main Street, about its heavy traffic. He now shares my belief, but only intellectually, by drawing the simple inference from "She says . . ." to "It is. . . ." Another person may have seen Main Street on a map, noted that it was a major thoroughfare, and concluded that it must carry a lot of traffic. Neither individual believes this on the basis of his or her own experience, but rather on the basis of other beliefs from which the character of Main Street can be inferred. They hold the same belief I do, but intellectually, not evidentially.

Neither way of holding a belief is intrinsically superior. Intellectually held beliefs can be poorly grounded (e.g., believing on another's doubtful authority); so can evidentially held beliefs (e.g., believing on the basis of what is in fact an optical illusion). Both ways can be well grounded. They differ only in this: In evidential believings, the belief's content seems to be given in the believer's experience; experience confirms belief. In intellectual believings, the belief's content could have, but has not, been experienced; other beliefs confirm it. (Of course, one might believe both evidentially and intellectually by having the appropriate experiences and the inferential reasons.)

The sorts of experience requisite for evidential belief vary with the sort of belief. Empirical beliefs will naturally be held evidentially in perceptual experiences. Beliefs in abstract claims like logical truths will be held evidentially in experiences that might aptly be called insights. Evaluative beliefs are typically brought to evidence in emotion. A student believes evidentially in the validity of modus ponens when he stops merely accepting his logic text's word and *sees* that (Aha!) modus ponens is valid. A child believes evidentially in the obligatoriness of truth-telling when she stops being merely obedient to parental authority and feels the imperative force of this obligation.

Many beliefs cannot be held evidentially in virtue of their content—beliefs about long-past historical events, about other galaxies, about four-dimensional space, or about what it is like to belong to another culture. These beliefs are not defective. Defect enters in when a belief *could* be held evidentially, but we *fail* to hold it so under just those circumstances when a person ordinarily would. Here, believing merely intellectually *is* a defective way of believing. The hopeless logic student, who cannot for the world see modus ponen's validity, but nevertheless believes intellectually that it is valid, holds a defective belief. So too with the aesthetically insensitive person who fails to delight in artistic excellence, but intellectually holds many aesthetic beliefs (either by adopting the good judge's beliefs or by using mechanical rules for judging excellence). These failures the person himself may regret; and we can criticize him for failing (although without implying willful failure).

Defective beliefs can differ in etiology. The logic student fails simply because he lacks an intellectual ability others have. In some cases, habitual patterns of attention (ways of interpreting the world) actually work *against* evidential belief:

Carl was raised to believe that women belong in the home and are incapable of rivaling men in intellectual achievement. As an adult, he came to reject these beliefs. To his mind, he has good reasons for thinking that men and women are equally capable of intellectual achievement. In spite of this, he finds himself preferring male to female colleagues, more inclined to accept the opinions of male interlocutors, and more critical of woman teachers.

In short, although Carl believes intellectually that men and women are equally capable, he *experiences* women as less capable. He has deep-rooted associations between intellectual ability and a masculine deportment (deep voice, masculine clothes and mannerisms, etc.). These associations work against his holding his beliefs evidentially. Moreover, they are also the source of just those experiences that would enable him to believe evidentially in women's intellectual inferiority.

Because this example directly parallels what I take to be happening in emotion-belief conflicts, let me tarry over its salient features.

1. Not only does Carl *lack* the experience requisite for evidential believing (as our logic student did), but he also *has* experiences that

conflict with what he believes intellectually. He resembles a person viewing a mirage; he plainly sees water on the highway ahead and yet knows intellectually there is none. He must now distinguish appearance from reality, constructing reality intellectually rather than being guided by his experience. But like the sufferer from optical illusion, Carl does not waver in the sincerity or firmness of his convictions. His way of experiencing women does not fool him, just as the mirage does not fool us. He may have to remind himself that men and women are equally capable, just as we may have to remind ourselves that the "water" is only a mirage. But the need to remind ourselves springs from the force of the illusion, not the weakness of the belief.

2. Carl's failure to hold his beliefs evidentially is not, as it was for the logic student, radical and inexplicable. It is due to a complex cognitive set (or interpretive scheme) that permeates his experience. The illusion of women's inferiority, *unlike* an optical illusion, has its origin in a set of associations and patterns of attention at a prereflective level, which he *brings* to his experience.

3. This cognitive set (including his association of intellectual ability with masculine deportment) *need not form part of his belief system.* His belief system comprises a set of reflectively held, articulable judgments. His cognitive set, by contrast, is a prereflectively held, originally unarticulated system. He may or may not attain reflective, articulate awareness of this cognitive set. Were he to, he might well deny any belief in masculine deportment as an index of intellectual ability (even though this part of his cognitive set is operative in his experience of women).

In short, our cognitive life is not limited to clear, fully conceptualized, articulated beliefs. Instead, beliefs constitute only a small illuminated portion of that life. The greater portion is rather a dark, cognitive set, an unarticulated framework for interpreting our world, which, if articulated, would be an enormous network of claims not all of which would be accepted by the individual as his beliefs.[9]

9. Recent work on artificial intelligence seems to confirm this suggestion. In constructing a computer that can use natural language, the complexity of the cognitive structure underlying even the most simple-minded conversation has become increasingly evident. To construe this complex cognitive structure as a *belief* matrix would surely do violence to ordinary conceptions of "belief"; we would then have to impute

4. Cognitive sets may be largely passively acquired. Carl acquired his cognitive set concerning women during his early childhood. Because it depends on many variables, including how intimately connected it is with other parts of his overall cognitive set, Carl may never be able to experience women other than he does now. If not deeply rooted, a cognitive set may change with a change of belief. But if it is deeply rooted, Carl's cognitive set may impede his holding his beliefs about women evidentially until he openly rejects his cognitive set from his belief system.

COGNITIVE EMOTIONS

How does this bear on emotion? Suppose that although beliefs are not constituents of emotion, a certain kind of experience is—a "seeing the world as. . . ." To have an emotion is, in part, for the world to seem to be a certain way. And it seems just *that* way that would enable a person to hold evidentially those beliefs that most cognitive theorists want to tie conceptually with emotions. When Tess regards her lesbian friend with revulsion, her friend looks to Tess like a freak of nature. Through the eyes of her resentment, Carl's actions are those of the mainpulative exploiter. If she believed that homosexuality is unnatural or that Carl exploits her, Tess would find in these experiences the substance for evidential believings. Yet like the mirage-seer, Tess need not believe in her emotional world-view. Just as we deny the mirage by calling on beliefs about conditions for optical illusions, so Tess invokes beliefs she holds about herself and Carl to arm herself against the illusion of resentment. She remembers his unfeignable professions of love and his customary, if not indefatigable sensitivity to her needs.

---

to persons much vaster belief systems than the ordinary individual would acknowledge having.

This thesis (that dark cognitive sets comprise a large portion of our cognitive life) suggests that striving for the ideal of rationality may be largely a matter of bringing to light and articulating our cognitive set. The unreflective, intellectually inactive person may have just as complex a cognitive set as the reflective, intellectually active individual; but they differ in the number of beliefs they hold, the former holding very few in the sense of "belief" I have been urging, the latter sustaining an extensive belief system.

In each instance, the world presents a face to Tess that, intellectually, she denies. In each, she distinguishes what appears emotionally from what she believes is so. Thus, when emotion and belief are in conflict, something like, although not identical with, a conflict of belief transpires. Had she taken her emotionally seen world at face value, she *would* have believed evidentially something that conflicts with what she in fact believes. But she does not take it at face value. Because of her beliefs, Carl's seeming to exploit her is deflected before it can burgeon into an inconsistent belief.

Nevertheless, Tess' beliefs about Carl's character, about the harmlessness of spiders, and the moral neutrality of homosexuality are defective. She *should not* feel resentment, fear, or revulsion; she should not be caught up in these illusions, but instead she should be able to see the world differently and thus hold her beliefs evidentially. The feared spiders are not like a mirage. We are not at fault for seeing a mirage (nothing about us as individuals precludes our seeing dry road), and we cannot intelligibly rebuke ourselves for seeing water as Tess can rebuke herself for fearing spiders.

Tess' feared spiders resemble Carl's inferior women. Carl brings to his encounters with women a cognitive set that tailors women to the size of his interpretive mold. Similarly, Tess' emotions channel her cognitive life down well-worn streams, sometimes catching it up in whirlpools of obsessive thoughts and images. Emotions are themselves cognitive sets, interpretive frameworks, patterns of attention. A host of cognitive presuppositions constitute Tess' resentful experience of Carl. She regards herself as a captive in her relationship to him, not free to refuse the demands of that relationship (she *has* to support him, she *has* to do the housework). The salient foci of attention are how benefits and burdens are distributed and, especially, how they are distributed to her disadvantage (*he* has time to read novels, *she* does not). The concepts of fairness, entitlements, desert, and property make up her interpretive framework (that is *his* laundry, so she *shouldn't* have to do it; she shares her money with him, so she is *entitled* to a share of his). The relationship is an ego-centered (and thus potentially adversary) one between two self-interested parties (he gets what he wants, she does not get what she wants). Her resentful cognitive set rivets her attention on everything that fits its framework and forgetfully winks at all else. ("See! There he goes refusing to do laundry again.") In a fairly literal sense, Tess does not see Carl's generosity and solicitousness toward her needs because they do not fit the exploitive frame. (If seen at all, they are twisted: "He vacuumed. He must want something from me.") She must remind herself intellectually that his actions *are* generous.[10]

No part of this resentful cognitive set need emerge in her belief system. Tess need not believe that she is trapped with Carl, nor that a just distribution of benefits and burdens is the cornerstone of a good relationship. Nor need she be reflectively aware of her cognitive set. Emotions provide enormously fertile ground for psychological explorations precisely because their cognitive sets are submersed; and emotional "seeings of the world as . . ." resist alteration largely because we lack a clear view of the cognitive set operative in these "seeings as. . . ."

Emotional cognitive sets may be passively acquired. Tess' resentment creeps up on her. Her present circumstances may be solely responsible for generating an emotional cognitive set (a few unhappy bouts with Carl about the laundry). But sometimes emotional cognitive sets grow out of nonemotional (or other emotional) ones. Tess may already be predisposed to moralize, to think in terms of rights and fairness, and to regard others from a self-interested perspective. She may also be acutely attuned to dominance relations.

CONCLUSION

Cognitive theorists have been misled by thinking that the cognitive element of emotion must be a belief or a judgment. The results of so thinking are a conceptual dissonance within those theories (reverberating in the conceptual gap between "emotion" and "belief"), an inability to handle plausibly instances of emotion-belief conflict, and sometimes a grossly simple-minded analysis of the cognitive element

10. The evidential character of emotion may explain the enormous difficulty of loosening oneself from bondage to any particular emotion (of "talking oneself out of" an emotion). The stronger the evidentiality of the emotion (one might say, the stronger the *emotion*), the less foothold our real beliefs have in commanding our attention. Overcoming an emotion that conflicts with one's beliefs would, on this account, be largely a matter of avoiding situations that reinforce the cognitive presuppositions of the emotion and of constructing or seeking out situations that are most likely to enable the person to make his beliefs evidential.

in terms of one or a few beliefs (rather than, if anything an elaborate system of beliefs). But our cognitive life involves more than clear, fully conceptualized, articulated beliefs. Interpretive "seeings as . . ." and their background cognitive sets constitute a large portion of our cognitive life. These latter, not beliefs, make up emotion.

Reading cognitive emotions this way pays off. Not only can we explain emotion-belief conflicts, but we can also explain the passivity and involuntariness of emotion as contrasted with belief. Reason and emotion can fall out of step, and emotions can resist change even when beliefs change. Moreover, this reading provides the machinery with which to account for both the tunnel vision of emotional cognition and its dark richness.

What can we infer from a person's emotions? We can legitimately infer that the world must *appear* to them a certain way. To the acrophobic, heights appear dizzyingly treacherous. To the jealous, the beloved appears to have betrayed his love. But can we infer that the person must *believe* that the world is as it appears? No. The world often is not what it appears to be. And although we cannot prevent it from appearing the way it does, we can refrain from giving credence to the appearance. We can deny the real treacherousness of heights. We can deny the real betrayal of love *in spite of* appearances. As inferences about beliefs go, it is best to assume that a person believes or would believe (if she reflected on her experience and cognitive set) in the reality of the world she sees. But this is only a likely wager because sometimes people have what seem to them good reasons for rejecting appearances.

Thus, although the view of emotion I have presented denies the cognitivist claim that beliefs are constituents of emotion or that emotion ascriptions entail belief ascriptions, it is nevertheless a view that sees a grain of truth in these cognitive theories. Ordinarily, emotions do go hand in hand with typical beliefs. But this is not because emotions *are* beliefs. It is because ordinarily we believe that things are as they seem.

Bibliography

HISTORICAL LITERATURE

Agonito, Rosemary. "The Paradox of Pleasure and Pain: A Study of the Concept of Pain in Aristotle." *Personalist* 57(1976): 105–112.

Ardal, Pall S. *Passion and Value in Hume's Treatise.* Edinburgh: Edinburgh University Press, 1966.

Aristotle. *De Anima; Nicomachean Ethics; Rhetoric.*

Arnold, Magda B. "Historical Development of the Concept of Emotion." *Phil Stud* (Ire.) 22(1974): 147–157. [Part of a symposium on emotion in this issue. See Arnold's other works listed under *Psychological Literature.*]

Brett, G. S. "Historical Development of the Theory of the Emotions." In *Feelings and Emotions,* The Wittenberg Symposium, edited by M. L. Reymert. Worcester, Mass.: Clark University Press, 1928.

Bricke, John. "Emotion and Thought in Hume's *Treatise.*" *Can J Phil Supp* 1(1974): 53–71.

Broad, C. D. "Emotion and Sentiment." *J Aesth Art Crit* 13(1954): 203–214.

Browning, Robert W. "Broad's Theory of Emotion." In *The Philosophy of C. D. Broad,* edited by Paul Arthur Schilpp. New York: Tudor, 1959.

Calhoun, Cheshire. "The Humean Moral Sentiment: A Unique Feeling." *Sw J Phil* 11(1980): 69–78.

Cicero: *On Friendship.*

Davidson, Donald. "Hume's Cognitive Theory of Pride." *J Phil* 73(1976): 744–756.

Dewey, John. *Art as Experience.* New York: G. P. Putnam's Sons, 1958.

———. "Feeling." In *John Dewey: The Early Works, 1882–1898,* vol. 2. Carbondale, Ill.: Southern Illinois University Press, 1967.

Epictetus. *The Discourses of Epictetus.* Translated by P. E. Matheson. New York: Heritage Press, 1968.

Fortenbaugh, William W. "Aristotle's Rhetoric on Emotions." *Archiv für Geschichte der Philosophie* 52(1970): 40–70.

Gardiner, P. L. "Hume's Theory of the Passions." In *David Hume: A Symposium,* edited by D. F. Pears. London: Macmillan, 1963.

Gordy, Michael. "Kant's Moral Incentive." *Phil Forum* (Boston) 4(1974): 323–339.

Gosling, J. "More Aristotelian Pleasures." *Proc Aris Soc* 74(1973–74): 15–34.

Green, O. H. "Wittgenstein and the Possibility of a Philosophical Theory of Emotion." *Metaphilosophy* 10(1979): 256–264.

Hearn, Thomas K. "General Rules and the Moral Sentiments in Hume's *Treatise.*" *Rev Metaph* 30(1976): 57–72.

Hegel, G. W. F. *The Phenomenology of Mind.* 2nd ed. Translated by J. B. Baillie. New York: Macmillan, 1967.

Hobbes, Thomas. *Leviathan.* Edited by Michael Oakeshott. Oxford: B. Blackwell, 1946. [See especially Pt. 1, Ch. 6.]

Hume, David. *An Inquiry Concerning the Principles of Morals.* Edited by Charles W. Hendel. New York: Library of Liberal Arts, 1957.

Hutcheson, Francis. *A System of Moral Philosophy.* Collected Works of Francis Hutcheson. Hildesheim: Georg Olms Verlagsbuchhandlung, 1969.

——. *An Essay on the Nature and Conduct of the Passions and Affections with Illustrations on the Moral Sense.* Gainesville, Fla.: Scholars' Facsimiles and Reprints, 1969.

Kant, Immanuel. *Critique of Practical Reason.* Translated by Lewis White Beck. New York: Bobbs-Merrill, 1956.

——. *Anthropology From a Pragmatic Point of View.* Translated by Mary J. Gregor. The Hague: Martinus Nijhoff, 1974.

——. *Critique of Judgment.* Translated by J. H. Bernard. New York: Hafner Publishing Company, 1972.

Locke, John. *An Essay Concerning Human Understanding.* Edited by Peter H. Nidditch. Oxford: Clarendon Press, 1975. [See especially Bk. 2, Ch. 20.]

MacBeath, A. Murray. "Kant on Moral Feeling." *Kantstudien* 64(1973): 283–314.

Malebranche, Nicolas. "Des Passions." In *Recherche de la Verité.* Oevres de Malebranche, edited by Genevieve Rodis-Lewis, vol. 2. Paris: Librairie Philosophique J. Vrin, 1963.

Marcus Aurelius. *The Meditations.*

Neu, Jerome. *Emotion, Thought and Therapy.* Berkeley: University of California Press, 1977. [Contains chapters on Hume and Spinoza.]

Norton, David Fate. "Hutcheson's Moral Sense Theory Reconsidered." *Dialogue* (Canada) 13(1974): 3–23.

Pascal, Blaise. *Pensées.* Translated by W. F. Trotter. New York: E. P. Dutton, 1958.

Pears, D. F. "Aristotle's Analysis of Courage." *Midwest Stud Phil* 3(1978): 273–285.

Plato. *Phaedrus; Philebus; Symposium.*

Rabel, Robert J. "The Stoic Doctrine of Generic and Specific Pathē." *Apeiron* 11(1977): 40–42.

Raphael, D. Daiches. *The Moral Sense.* Oxford: Oxford University Press, 1947.

Rice, Lee C. "Emotion, Appetition, and Conatus in Spinoza." *Rev Int Phil* 31(1977): 101–116.

Senault, J. *The Use of the Passions.* London, 1649.

Seneca. *De Ira.*

Smith, Adam. *Theory of Moral Sentiments.* Oxford: Oxford University Press, 1976.

Solmsen F. "Aristotle and Cicero on the Orator's Playing upon the Feelings." *Classical Philol* 33(1938): 393–394.

Stendhal. *De l'amour.* Edited by Henri Martineau. Paris: Éditions Garnier Frères, 1966.

Sutherland, Stewart R. "Hume on Morality and the Emotions," *Phil Quart* 26(1976): 14–23.

Vlasto, Gregory. "The Individual as an Object of Love in Plato." In *Platonic Studies.* Princeton: Princeton University Press, 1973.

Vygotskii, L. S. "Spinoza's Theory of the Emotions in Light of Contemporary Psycho-Neurology." *Soviet Stud Phil* 10(1972): 362–382.

Whitehouse, P. G. "The Meaning of 'Emotion' in Dewey's *Art as Experience.*" *J Aesth Art Crit* 37(1978): 149–156.

Wittgenstein, Ludwig. Philosophical Investigations. Translated by G. E. M. Anscombe. Oxford: Oxford University Press, 1956.

———. *Zettel.* Translated by G. E. M. Anscombe. Berkeley: University of California Press, 1967.

PSYCHOLOGICAL AND BIOLOGICAL LITERATURE

Since the early 1900's, psychologists have written a great deal on emotion, and much of this work draws on biological and anthropological studies. Because the psychological literature is so vast, the following bibliography focuses on recent psychological and some biological and anthropological works as well as some of the heavily referenced older ones. Also included are some philosophical critiques of psychological theories of emotion.

Angell, J. "A Reconsideration of James' Theory of Emotion." *Psych Rev* 23(1916): 251–261.

Angier, Roswell Parker. "The Conflict Theory of Emotion." *Amer J Psychol* 39(1927): 390–401.

Arnold, Magda B. "Physiological Differentiation of Emotional States." *Psych Rev* 52(1945): 35–48.

———. "The Status of Emotion in Contemporary Psychology." In *Present-Day Psychology,* edited by A. Roback. New York: Philosophical Library, 1955.

———. *Emotion and Personality.* 2 vols. New York: Columbia University Press, 1960.

———. "Human Emotion and Action." In *Human Action,* edited by Theodore Mischel. New York: Academic Press, 1969.

———, ed. *Feelings and Emotions.* New York: Academic Press, 1970.

———, ed. *The Nature of Emotion.* Baltimore: Penguin, 1971.

———, ed. *Loyola Symposium on Feelings and Emotions.* New York: Academic Press, 1972.

Averill, James R. "Grief: Its Nature and Significance." *Psych Bull* 70(1968): 721–748.

———. "An Analysis of Psychophysiological Symbolism and Its Influence on Theories of Emotions." *J Theor Soc Behav* 4(1974): 147–190. [Includes a commentary on the theories of Plato, Aristotle, Plotinus, Aquinas, and Descartes.]

———. "The Emotions." In *Personality: Basic Issues and Current Research,* edited by E. Staub. Englewood Cliffs, N.J.: Prentice-Hall, 1978.

Bain, Alexander. *The Emotions and the Will.* New York: Appleton, 1859.

Beck, Aaron. *Depression.* Pittsburgh: University of Pennsylvania Press, 1972.

Beebe-Center, J. "Feeling and Emotion." In *Theoretical Foundations of Psychology,* edited by H. Helson. New York: Van Nostrand, 1951.

Black, Perry, ed. *Physiological Correlates of Emotions.* New York: Academic Press, 1970.

Brenner, Charles. "On the Nature and Development of Affects: A Unified Theory." *Psychoanal Quart* 43(1974): 532–556.

Bridges, K. "A Genetic Theory of the Emotions." *J Genet Psychol* 37(1930): 514–527.

Bryant, Sophie. "Prof. James on Emotions." *Proc Aris Soc* 3(1896): 52–64.

Bull, Nina. "The Attitude Theory of Emotion." *Nervous and Mental Disease Monographs,* No. 81. New York: 1951.

Cannon, Walter B. "Recent Studies of Bodily Effects of Fear, Rage, and Pain." *J Phil* 11(1914): 162–165.

——. *Bodily Changes in Pain, Hunger, Fear and Rage.* 2nd ed. New York: Appleton, 1929.

——. "The James-Lange Theory of Emotions: A Critical Examination and an Alternative Theory." In *The Nature of Emotion,* edited by Magda B. Arnold. Baltimore: Penguin, 1971.

Del Carril, Mario, "Freud on Unconscious Emotion." *Dialogos* 14(1979): 109–124.

Delgado, Jose. "Emotional Behavior in Animals and Humans." *Psychiat Res Rep* 12(1960): 259–271.

——. *Emotions.* Dubuque, Iowa: W. C. Brown, 1966.

Dembo, T. "The Dynamics of Anger." In *Field Theory as Human-Science,* edited by Joseph de Rivera. New York: Gardner Press, 1976.

de Rivera, Joseph. *A Structural Theory of the Emotions.* Psychological Issues, Monograph No. 40. New York: International Universities Press, 1977. [An original theory plus critiques of McDougall, James, Paulhan, Rapaport, Arnold, Sartre, Pribram, Hillman, and others.]

Duggy, Elizabeth. "An Explanation of 'Emotional' Phenomena Without the Use of the Concept 'Emotion.'" *J Gen Psychol* 25(1941): 283–293.

——. "Leeper's Motivational Theory of Emotion." *Psych Rev* 55(1948): 324–328.

Dunlap, K., ed. *The Emotions.* Baltimore: Williams & Wilkens, 1922.

Ekman, Paul, Sorenson, E. Richard, and Friesen, Wallace V. "Pan-Cultural Elements in Facial Displays of Emotion." *Science* 164(1969): 86–88.

——. Friesen, Wallace V.; and Ellsworth, Phoebe. *Emotion in the Human Face.* New York: Pergamon Press, 1972.

——, ed. *Darwin and Facial Expression: A Century of Research in Review.* New York: Academic Press, 1973.

Ellis, Albert. *Reason and Emotion in Psychotherapy.* New York: Lyle Stuart, 1962.

Fehr, Fred S., and Stern, John A. "Peripheral Physiological Variables and Emotion: The James-Lange Theory Revisited." *Psych Bull* 74(1970): 411–424.

Feinstein, Howard. "William James on the Emotions." *J Hist Ideas* 31(1970): 133–142.

Fox, Michael. "Unconscious Emotions: A Reply to Professor Mullane's 'Unconscious and Disguised Emotions.'" *Phil Phenomenol Res* 36(1976): 412–414.

Freud, Sigmund. *The Standard Edition of the Complete Psychological Works of Sigmund Freud.* Translated and edited by J. Strachey. London: Hogarth Press, 1966–1974.

Gardiner, Harry, Metcalf, R., and Beebe-Center, J. *Feeling and Emotion: A History of Theories.* New York: American Book Co., 1937.

Gellhorn, Ernest, "Prolegamena to a Theory of the Emotions." *Perspect Biol Med* 4(1961): 403–436.

———, and Loofbourrow, G. *Emotions and Emotional Disorders: A Neurophysiological Study.* New York: Harper & Row, 1963.

———. *Biological Foundations of Emotion.* Glenview, Ill.: Scott, Foresman, 1968.

Glass, D. *Neurophysiology and Emotion.* New York: Rockefeller University Press, 1967.

Goldstein, Melvin L. "Physiological Theories of Emotion: A Critical Historical Review from the Standpoint of Behavior Theory." *Psych Bull* 69(1968): 23–40.

Gordon, Robert M. "Emotion Labelling and Cognition." *J Theor Soc Behav* 8(1978): 125–135. [A critique of Schacter and Singer's study.]

Hebb, D. O. "On the Nature of Fear." *Psychol Rev* 53(1946): 259–276.

———. "Emotion in Man and Animal: An Analysis of the Intuitive Processes of Recognition." *Psychol Rev* 53(1946): 88–106.

———. *Organization of Behavior.* New York: Wiley, 1949.

Hillman, James. *Emotion, a Comprehensive Phenomenology of Theories and Their Meanings for Therapy.* Evanston, Ill.: Northwestern University Press, 1961.

Irons, J. "Prof. James' Theory of Emotion." *Mind* 3(N.S.)(1894): 77–97.

Izard, Carroll. *The Face of Emotion.* New York: Appleton-Century-Crofts, 1971.

———. *Patterns of Emotions: A New Analysis of Anxiety and Depression.* New York: Academic Press, 1972.

———. *Human Emotions.* New York: Plenum Press, 1977.

Jacobsen, E. *Biology of Emotions.* Springfield, Ill.: Charles Thomas, 1967.

James, William. "The Emotions." In *Principles of Psychology,* Vol. 2. New York: Dover Publications, 1950. [Originally published 1890.]

———, and Lange, C., *The Emotions.* Baltimore: Williams & Wilkins, 1922. [Originally published 1885.]

Janet, P. *De l'angoisse á l'ecstase, Études sur les croyances et les sentiments,* 2 vols. Paris: 1926, 1928.

———. "Fear of Action as an Essential Element in the Sentiment of Melancholia." In *Feelings and Emotions.* Wittenburg Symposium, edited by M. Reymert. Worchester, Mass: Clark University Press, 1928.

———. *L'amour et la haine.* Edited by M. Epstein. Paris: 1932.

Johnston, C. "Ribot's Theory of the Passions." *J Phil* 5(1908): 197–207.

Knapp, P. H., ed. *Expression of the Emotions in Man.* New York: International Universities Press, 1963.

Laird, James D. "Self-Attribution of Emotion: The Effects of Expressive Behavior on the Quality of Emotional Experience." *J Pers Soc Psychol* 29(1974): 475–486.

Lazarus, Richard S. *Psychological Stress and the Coping Process.* New York: McGraw-Hill, 1966.

——, Averill, J. R., and Opton, E. "Cross-Cultural Studies of Psychophysiological Responses During Stress and Emotion." *Int J Psychol* 4(1969): 83–102.

——: Averill, J. R., and Opton, E. "Towards a Cognitive Theory of Emotion." In *Feelings and Emotions,* edited by Magda B. Arnold. New York: Academic Press, 1970.

——, and Averill, J. R. "Emotion and Cognition: With Special Reference to Anxiety." In *Anxiety,* edited by C. D. Spielberger. New York: Academic Press, 1972.

——. "The Self-Regulation of Emotion." *Phil Stud* (Ire.) 22(1974): 168–179. [Part of a symposium on emotion.]

Leeper, Robert Ward. "A Motivational Theory of Emotion to Replace 'Emotion as Disorganized Response.'" *Psych Rev* 55(1948): 5–21.

Lewin, Kurt. *A Dynamic Theory of Personality.* Translated by Donald K. Adams and Karl E. Zener. New York: McGraw-Hill, 1935.

Mandler, G. "Emotion." In *New Directions in Psychology,* edited by R. Brown et al., Vol. 1. New York: Holt, Rinehart and Winston, 1962.

——. *Mind and Emotions.* New York: Wiley, 1975.

McDougall, William. *An Introduction to Social Psychology.* London: Methuen, 1960. [Originally published 1908.]

——, Shand, A, and Stout, G. "Symposium: Instinct and Emotion." *Proc Aris Soc* (N.S.) 15(1914–1915): 22–100

——. "Emotions and Feeling Distinguished." In *Feelings and Emotions.* The Wittenberg Symposium, edited by M. Reymert. Worchester, Mass.: Clark University Press, 1928.

McGill, V. J., and Welch, Livingston. "A Behaviorist Analysis of Emotions." *Phil Sci* 13(1946): 100–122.

Mullane, Harvey. "Unconscious Emotion." *Theoria* 31(1965): 181–190.

——. "Unconscious and Disguised Emotions." *Phil Phenomenol Res* 36(1976): 403–411

Myers, Gerald. "William James' Theory of Emotion." *Trans Charles S. Peierce Soc* 5(1969): 67–89.

Osgood, C. E., May, W. H., and Miron, M. S. *Cross Cultural Universals of Affective Meaning.* Urbana, Ill.: University of Illinois Press, 1975.

Paulhan, F. *The Laws of Feeling.* Translated by C. K. Ogden. New York: Harcourt Brace, 1930. [Originally published 1884.]

Peters, Richard. "Emotions, Passivity and the Place of Freud's Theory in Psychology." In *Scientific Psychology*, edited by B. Wolman and E. Nagel. New York: Basic Books, 1965.

Plutchik, Robert. "Some Problems for a Theory of Emotion." *Psychosomatic Med* 17(1955): 306–310.

———. "The Multi-Factor-Analytic Theory of Emotion." *J Psychol* 50(1960): 153–171.

———. *The Emotions: Facts, Theories and a New Model.* New York: Random House, 1962.

———, and Ax, Albert F. "A Critique of *Determinants of Emotional State* by Schacter and Singer." *Psychophysiology* 4(1967): 79–82.

Pribram, Karl. "The New Neurology and Biology of Emotion." *Amer Psychologist* 22(1967): 830–838.

———, and Melges, F. T. "Psychophysiological Basis of Emotion." In *Handbook of Clinical Neurology*, edited by P. J. Vinken and G. W. Brunyan. Amsterdam: North-Holland, 1969.

Pritchard, Michael S. "On Taking Emotions Seriously: A Critique of B. F. Skinner." *J Theor Soc Behav* 5(1976): 211–232.

Rapaport, David. "On the Psycho-analytical Theory of Affects." In *Psychoanalytic Psychiatry and Psychology*, edited by R. P. Knight and C. R. Friedman. New York: International Universities Press, 1954.

———. *Emotions and Memory.* New York: International Universities Press, 1959.

Reymert, M., ed. *Feelings and Emotions.* The Wittenberg Symposium. Worchester, Mass.: Clark University Press, 1928. [Contains articles by Adler, Buhler, Janet, and others.]

———, ed. *Feelings and Emotions.* The Mooseheart Symposium. New York: McGraw-Hill, 1950. [Contains articles by Arnold, Mead, and many others.]

Robot, Theodule. *The Psychology of the Emotions.* London: 1897.

Rosensohn, William. "A Logical Method for Making a Classification of Emotions, Using Wielhelm Wundt's Theory of Emotion Formation." *J Psychol* 55(L963): 175–182.

Sachs, David. "On Freud's Doctrine of Emotion." In *Freud: A Collection of Critical Essays*, edited by Richard Wollheim. New York: Anchor Books, 1974.

Schacter, Stanley. "The Interaction of Cognitive and Physiological Determinants of Emotional State." *Psych Rev* 69(1962): 379–399.

———. *Emotion, Obesity and Crime.* New York: Academic Press, 1971.

Schafer, Roy. "A Psychoanalytic View of Emotion." *Phil Stud* (Ire.) 22(1974): 157–167.

Shand, Alexander. "M. Ribot's Theory of the Passions." *Mind* (N.S.) 16(1907): 477–505.

———. "Of Impulse, Emotion and Instinct." *Proc Aris Soc* 20(1919–1920): 208–236.

Skinner, B. F. *Science and Human Behavior.* New York: Macmillan, 1953.

Spencer, Herbert. "Emotion in the Primitive Man." *Popular Science Monthly* 6(1875): 331–339.

Stumpf, Carl. "Über Gefühlsempfindungen." *Zetschr f.d. Psych u. Physiol der Sinnesorgane* 44(1907).

Titchener, Edward. *Lectures on the Elementary Psychology of Feeling and Attention.* New York: Macmillan, 1909.

Tolman, Edward Chase. "A Behaviorist Account of the Emotions." *Psych Rev* 30(1923): 217–227.

Tomkins, S. *Affect, Imagery, Consciousness.* 2 vols. New York: Springer, 1962. [See especially Vol. 1, *The Positive Affects.*]

Vallins, Stuart. "Cognitive Effects of False Heart-Rate Feedback." *J Personal Soc Psych* 4(1966): 400–408. [A study similar to Schacter and Singer's.]

Watson, John B. *Psychology from the Standpoint of a Behaviorist.* Philadelphia: J. B. Lippincott, 1919. [See especially "Unlearned Behavior: 'Emotions.'"]

———. *Behaviorism.* Chicago: University of Chicago Press, 1930. [See especially Chapter 7 and 8.]

———, and R. Raynor. "Conditioned Emotional Reactions." *J Exper Psychol* 3(1920).

Weber, Alden, and Rapaport, David. "Teleology and the Emotions." *Phil Sci* 8(1941): 69–82.

Wundt, Willhelm. *Outlines of Psychology.* Translated by C. Judd. Leipzig: W. Engelman, 1897.

Young, Paul T. "By What Criteria Can Emotion be Defined?" *Psych Bull* 38(1941): 713.

———. "Emotion as Disorganized Response—A Reply to Prof. Leeper." *Psych Rev* 56(1949): 184–191.

———. *Emotion in Man and Animal,* rev. ed. New York: R. Krieger, 1973.

CONTINENTAL LITERATURE

Bergson, Henri. *The Two Sources of Morality and Religion.* Translated by R. Ashley Audra and Cloudesly Brereton. New York: Doubleday, 1954.

Brentano, Franz. *Psychology From the Empirical Standpoint.* Translated by D. B. Terrell. London: Routledge and Kegan Paul, 1971.

———. *Von der Klassifikation der psychischen Phänomene.* Leipzig, 1911.

Buber, Martin. "Guilt and Guilt Feelings." In *The Knowledge of Man: Selected Essays of Martin Buber.* Edited by Maurice Friedman. Translated by Maurice Friedman and Ronald Gregor Smith. New York: Harper & Row, 1965.

———. *I and Thou.* 2nd ed. Translated by Ronald Gregor Smith. New York: Scribner, 1958.

Buytendijk, F. J. J. "The Phenomenological Approach to the Problem of Feelings and Emotions." In *Feelings and Emotions,* the Mooseheart Symposium, edited by Martin L. Reymert. New York: McGraw-Hill, 1950.

Chisholm, Roderick M. "Brentano's Theory of Correct and Incorrect Emotion." *Rev Int Phil* 20(1966): 395–415.

Fell, Joseph P. *Emotion in the Thought of Sartre.* New York: Columbia University Press, 1965.

Findlay, J. N. *Meinong's Theory of Objects and Values.* 2nd ed. Oxford: Oxford University Press, 1963.

Frings, Manfred S. *Max Scheler: A Concise Intoduction into the World of a Great Thinker.* Pittsburgh: Duquesne University Press, 1965.

———. "Insight-Logos-Love (Lonergan-Heidegger-Scheler)." *Phil Today* 14(1970): 106–115.

Hamlyn, D. W. "The Phenomenon of Love and Hate." *Philosophy* 53(1978): 5–20. [Includes a discussion of Brentano's theory of love and hate.]

Hanly, Charles. "Emotion, Anatomy and the Synthetic A Priori." *Dialogue* (Canada) 14(1975): 101–118. [A critique of Sartre's theory of emotion.]

Hartmann, Nicholai. *Ethics.* 2 vols. Translated by Stanton Coit. New York: Macmillan, 1932.

Heidegger, Martin. *Being and Time.* Translated by John Macquarrie and Edward Robinson. New York: Harper & Row, 1962.

Husserl, Edmund. *Ideas: General Introduction to Pure Phenomenology.* Translated by W. R. Boyce Gibson. New York: Humanities Press, 1931. [See, for examples, sections 117, 127, 147.]

Jaspers, Karl. *Philosophy.* 3 vols. Translated by E. B. Ashton. Chicago: University of Chicago Press, 1963.

Kierkegaard, Søren. *The Concept of Dread.* Translated by Walter Lowrie. Princeton: Princeton University Press, 1957.

———. *The Sickness Unto Death.* Translated by Walter Lowrie. Princeton: Princeton University Press, 1941.

———. *Works of Love.* Translated by D. F. Swenson. Princeton: Princeton University Press, 1946.

Luther, Arthur. "Hocking and Scheler on Feeling." *Phil Today* 12(1968): 93–99.

Marcel, Gabriel. "Feeling as a Mode of Participation." In *The Mystery of Being,* translated by G. S. Fraser and Rene Hague. London: Harvill Press, 1950.

Meinong, Alexius. *On Emotional Presentation.* Translated by Marie-Luise Kalsi. Evanston, Ill.: Northwestern University Press, 1972.

Nietzsche, Friedrich. *Twilight of the Idols.* In *The Portable Nietzsche,* edited and translated by Walter Kaufmann. New York: Viking Press, 1971.

———. *On the Genealogy of Morals.* Translated by Walter Kaufmann and R. J. Hollingdale. New York: Vintage Books, 1969.

———. *The Will to Power.* Translated by Walter Kaufmann and R. J. Hollingdale. New York: Vintage Books, 1967. [See, for example, paragraphs 383, 387, and passim.]

Ortega y Gasset, Jose. *On Love.* Translated by Tony Talbot. London: Victor Gollancz, 1959.

Pfänder, Alexander. "Zur Psychologie die Gessinungen." *Jahrbuch für Philosophie und phänomenologische Forschung* 1(1913): 325; 3(1916): 1.

———. *Phenomenology of Willing and Motivation.* Translated by Herbert Spiegelberg. Evanston, Ill.: Northwestern University Press, 1967.

Pleydell-Pearce, A. G. "Freedom, Emotion and Choice in the Philosophy of Jean-Paul Sartre." *J Brit Soc Phenomenol* 1(1970): 35–46.

Ricoeur, Paul. "Intentionality and Inwardness of Feeling." In *Fallible Man,* translated by Charles Kelbley. Chicago: Regnery, 1965.

———. "Emotion and Habit." In *Freedom and Nature: The Voluntary and the Involuntary,* translated by Erazim V. Kohak. Evanston, Ill.: Northwestern University Press, 1966.

Rodie, C. Christopher. "Emotion, Reflection and Action in Sartre's Ontology." *Man World* 7(1974): 379–393.

Sartre, Jean-Paul. "Affectivity." In *The Psychology of the Imagination,* translated by Bernard Frechtman. New York: Washington Square Press, 1948.

———. *Being and Nothingness.* Translated by Hazel E. Barnes. New York: Philosophical Library, 1956. [See especially "The Look" and "Concrete Relations with Others."]

Scheler, Max. *Ressentiment.* Translated by W. W. Holdheim. New York: Free Press, 1961.

———. *The Nature of Sympathy.* Translated by Peter Heath. New York: Archon Books, 1970.

———. "Repentence and Rebirth." In *On the Eternal in Man,* translated by Bernard Noble. New York: Harper, 1960.

Schneider, Carl D. "The Reddened Cheek'–Nietzsche on Shame." *Phil Today* 21(1977): 21–31.

Smith, Quinton. "Husserl and the Inner Structure of Feeling-Acts." *Res Phenomenol* 6(1976): 84–108.

———. "Scheler's Stratification of the Emotional Life and Strawson's Person." *Phil Stud* (Ire.) 25(1977): 103–127.

———. "Sartre and the Phenomenon of Emotion." *S J Phil* 17(1979): 397–412.

Solomon, Robert C. "Paul Ricoeur on Passion and Emotion." In *Studies in the Philosophy of Paul Ricoeur,* edited by Charles Reagan. Athens: Ohio University Press, 1979.

Strasser, Stephan. *Phenomenology of Feeling.* Translated by Robert E. Wood. Pittsburgh: Duquesne University Press, 1977.

CONTEMPORARY ANALYTIC LITERATURE

Within the past two decades the number of philosophical publications on emotion has increased dramatically. The following bibliography lists a good portion of that recent work. Other contemporary philosophical writings on historical, psychological, and continental theories of emotion may be found under those three heads; and those works often contain noteworthy contributions to the general discussion of emotion.

Ahumada, Rodolfo. "Emotion, Knowledge and Belief." *Personalist* 50(1969): 371–382.

Alston, William P. "Emotion and Feeling." In *The Encyclopedia of Philosophy,* edited by Paul Edwards, Vol. 2. New York: Macmillan, 1967.

Aquila, Richard E. "Emotions, Objects, and Causal Relations." *Phil Stud* 26(1974): 279–285. [Includes a critique of J. R. Wilson's *Emotion and Object.*]

———. "Causes and Constituents of Occurrent Emotion." *Phil Quart* 25(1975): 346–359. [A criticism of Irving Thalberg's views.]

Arnstine, Donald. "Shaping the Emotions, the Sources of Standards for Aesthetic Education." *J Aesth Educ* 1(1966): 45–69.

Audi, Robert. "The Rational Assessment of Emotions." *Sw J Phil* 8(1977): 115–119. [A critique of Robert C. Solomon's "The Rationality of the Emotions."]

Aufhauser, Marcia Cavell. "Guilt and Guilt Feelings: Power and the Limits of Power." *Ethics* 85(1975): 288–297.

Aune, Bruce. "Feelings, Goods and Introspection." *Mind* 72(1963): 187–208.

Bergmann, Frithjof, "Monologue on the Emotions." *Understanding Human Emotions* (Bowling Green, 1980).

Bertocci, Peter A. "Susanne K. Langer's Theory of Feeling and Mind." *Rev Metaph* 23(1970): 527–551.

Browning, Douglas. "The Privacy of Feelings." In *Persons, Privacy and Feeling,* edited by D. Van de Vate. Memphis: Memphis State University Press, 1970.

Cassin Chrystine. "Emotions and Evaluations." *Personalist* 49(1968): 563–571. [Includes a discussion of articles by Bedford, Gosling, and Pitcher.]

De Sousa, Ronald. "Self-deceptive Emotions." *J Phil* 75(1978): 684–697.

———. "The Rationality of Emotions." *Dialogue* (Canada) 18(1979): 41–63.

Donnellan, Keith S. "Causes, Objects, and Producers of the Emotions." [Abstr.] *J Phil* 69(1970) 947–950.

Earle, William James. "Do Feelings Cause Actions?" *Phil Phenomenol Res* 35(1975): 540–548.

Ewing, A. C. "The Justification of Emotions." *Proc Aris Soc Suppl* 31(1957): 59–74. [See Mary Warnock's companion piece in the same issue.]

Fingarette, Herbert. "Feeling Guilty." *Amer Phil Quart* 16(1979): 159–164.

Fisher, Mark, "Reason, Emotion and Love." *Inquiry* 20(1977): 189–203.

Gean, William D. "Emotion, Emotional Feeling and Passive Body Change." *J Theor Soc Behav* 9(1979): 39–51.

Gordon, Robert. "Emotions and Knowledge." *J Phil* 66(1969): 408–413.

———. "Judgmental Emotions." *Analysis* 34(1973): 40–48.

———. "The Aboutness of Emotions." *Amer Phil Quart* 11(1974): 27–36.

Gosling, J. C. "Mental Causes and Fear." *Mind* 71(1962): 289–306.

———. "Emotion and Object." *Phil Rev* 74(1965): 486–593.

———. *Pleasure and Desire.* Oxford: Oxford University Press, 1969.

Green, O. H. "The Expression of Emotion." *Mind* 79(1970): 551–568.

———. "Emotions and Belief." *Amer Phil Quart* 6(1972): 24–40.

———. "Obligations Regarding Passions." *Personalist* 60(1979): 134–138.

Hampshire, Stuart. "Feeling and Expression." In *Freedom of Mind and Other Essays.* Princeton: Princeton University Press, 1972.

Henle, Mary. "In Search of the Structure of Emotion." *Phil Stud* (Ire.) 22(1974): 190–197.

Hoffman, W. Michael. "The Structure and Origins of Religious Passions." *Int J Phil Relig* 8(1977): 36–50.

Howarth, J. M. "On Thinking of What One Fears." *Proc Aris Soc* 76(1975–76): 53–74.

Isenberg, Arnold. "Natural Pride and Natural Shame." *Phil Phenomenol Res* 10(1949): 1–25.

Kelly, Jack. "Reason and Emotion." *S J Phil* 10(1972): 379–382.

Kenny, Anthony. *Action, Emotion and Will.* New York: Humanities Press, 1964.

Lackey, Douglas P. "Mental Terms and Negative Privacy." *J Crit Anal* 6(1976): 40–47.

Langer, Susanne K. *Feeling and Form: A Theory of Art.* New York: Charles Scribner's Sons, 1953.

Lemos, Ramon M. "Emotion, Feeling and Behavior." *Critica Rev Hisp Amer Filos* 4(1970): 97–117.

Lyons, William. "A Note on Emotion Statements." *Ratio* 15(1973): 132–135.

———. "Physiological Changes and Emotions." *Can J Phil* 3(1974): 603–617.

———. "Emotions and Motives." *Can J Phil* 6(1976): 501–516.

———. "Emotions and Feelings." *Ratio* 19(1977): 1–12.

———. "Emotions and Behavior." *Phil Phenomenol Res* 38(1978): 410–418.

———. *Emotion.* Cambridge: Cambridge University Press, 1980.

MacIntyre, Alasdair. "Emotion, Behavior and Belief." In *Against the Self-Images of the Age.* London: Duckworth, 1971.

MacMurray, John. *Reason and Emotion.* London: Faber and Faber, 1962.

Melden, A. I. "Anger: The Conceptual Dimensions of Emotions." In *Human Action: Conceptual and Empirical Issues,* edited by T. Mischel. New York: Academic Press, 1969.

Neblett, William. "Indignation: A Case Study of the Role of Feelings in Morals." *Metaphilosophy* 10(1979): 256–264.

Neu, Jerome. *Emotion, Thought and Therapy.* Berkeley: University of California Press, 1977.

Oaklander, Nathan L., and Gull, Richard. "The Emotions." *Phil Res Arch* 4, No. 1272, 1978.

Pears, D. F. "Causes and Objects of Some Feelings and Psychological Reactions." In *Philosophy of Mind,* edited by Stuart Hampshire. New York: Harper & Row, 1966.

Perkins, Moreland. "Emotion and Feeling." *Phil Rev* 75(1966): 139–160. [A criticism of Bedford's "Emotions."]

———. "Emotion and the Concept of Behavior." *Amer Phil Quart* 3(1966): 291–298.

Peters, R. S., and Mace, C. A. "Emotions and the Category of Passivity." *Proc Aris Soc* 62(1961–62): 117–142.

Pitcher, George. "Emotion." *Mind* 74(1965): 326–346.

Pleydell-Pearce, A. G. "Feelings, Values and Judgments." *J Brit Soc Phenomenol* 9(1978): 158–166.

Quinn, Michael Sean. "Emotions, Actions and Self-Esteem." *Sw J Phil* 8(1977): 121–127.

Rorty, Amelie Oksenberg. "Explaining Emotions." *J Phil* 75(1978): 139–161.

——, ed. *Explaining Emotions.* Berkeley: University of California Press, 1980. [A collection of philosophical and some psychological articles on emotion, including many not published elsewhere.]

Ryle, Gilbert. *The Concept of Mind.* New York: Barnes & Noble, 1949.

——. "Feelings." *Phil Quart* 1(1951): 193–205.

Sankowski, Edward. "The Sense of Responsibility and the Justifiability of Emotions." *S J Phil* 13(1975): 215–233.

——. "Emotion and the Appreciation of Art." *J Aesth Educ* 10(1976): 45–67.

——. "Responsibility of Persons for Their Emotions." *Can J Phil* 7(1977): 829–840.

Schrag, Francis. "Learning What One Feels and Enlarging the Range of One's Feelings." *Educ Theory* 22(1972): 382–394.

——. "Learning and the Expression of Emotion." *Stud Phil Educ* 8(1973): 30–50.

Sharpe, Robert A. "Seven Reasons Why Amusement is an Emotion." *J Val Inq* 9(1975): 201–203.

Shibles, Warren. *Emotion.* Whiteware, Wis.: The Language Press, University of Wisconsin, 1974. [A comprehensive survey of philosophical and psychological theories of emotion with an extensive bibliography.]

Shiner, Roger A. "Classifying Objects of Acts and Emotions." *Dialogue* 10(1971): 751–767.

——. "Wilson on Emotion, Object, and Cause." *Metaphilosophy* 6(1975): 72–96. [A critique of J. R. Wilson's *Emotion and Object.*]

Solomon, Robert C. "Emotions and Choice." *Rev Metaph* 27(1973): 20–41.

——. "Emotions and Anthropology: The Logic of Emotional World Views." *Inquiry* 21(1978): 181–199.

——. "The Logic of Emotion." *Nous* 11(1977): 41–49.

——. "The Rationality of the Emotions." *Sw J Phil* 8(1977): 105–114.

——. *The Passions.* New York: Doubleday-Anchor Books, 1977; Notre Dame: University of Notre Dame Press, 1983.

Staude, Mitchell. "Irving Thalberg's Component Analysis of Emotion and Action." *Phil Quart* 24(1974): 150–155.

Sterling, Marvin C. "The Cognitive Theory of Emotions." *Sw J Phil* 10(1979): 165–176. [A critique of Solomon's *The Passions.*]

Tanner, Michael. "Sentimentality." *Proc Aris Soc* 77(1976–77); 127–147.

Taylor, Gabriele. "Justifying the Emotions." *Mind* 84(1975): 390–402.

——. "Love." *Proc Aris Soc* 76(1975–76): 147–164.

Thalberg, Irving. "Natural Expressions of Emotion." *Phil Phenomenol Res* 22(1962): 387–392.

———. "Remorse." *Mind* 72(1963): 545–555.

———. "Constituents and Causes of Emotion and Action." *Phil Quart* 23(1973): 1–13.

———. *Perception, Emotion and Action.* New Haven: Yale University Press, 1977.

———. "Could Affects be Effects?" *Austl J Phil* 56(1978): 143–154.

Tietz, John. "Emotional Objects and Criteria." *Can J Phil* 3(1973): 211–224.

———. "Knowledge Requiring Emotions." *Sw J Phil* 6(1975): 155–158. [A critique of Gordon's "Emotion and Knowledge."]

Trigg, Roger. *Pain and Emotion.* Oxford: Oxford University Press, 1970.

Van den Berg, J. H. "The Intentionality of Feelings." *Humanitas* 4(1968): 101–106.

Walter, Edward. "The Logic of Emotions." *S J Phil* 10(1972): 71–78.

Warnock, Mary. "The Justification of Emotions." *Proc Aris Soc Supp* 31(1957): 43–58. [See A. C. Ewing's companion piece in the same issue.]

Whitely, C. H. "Love, Hate and Emotion." *Philosophy* 54(1979): 235.

Williams, B. A. O. "Pleasure and Belief." In *Philosophy of Mind,* edited by Stuart Hampshire. New York: Harper & Row, 1966.

———. "Morality and the Emotions." In *Problems of the Self.* Cambridge: Cambridge University Press, 1973.

Wilson, J. R. S. *Emotion and Object.* Cambridge: Cambridge University Press, 1972.

Wolheim, Richard. "Thought and Passion." *Proc Aris Soc* 68(1967–68): 1–24.

DATE DUE